The CRUISING LIFE

The CRUISING LIFE

A Commonsense Guide for the Would-Be Voyager

Jim Trefethen

Camden, Maine • New York • San Francisco • Washington, D.C.
Auckland • Bogotá • Caracas • Lisbon • London • Madrid
Mexico City • Milan • Montreal • New Delhi
San Juan • Singapore • Sydney • Tokyo • Toronto

International Marine
A Division of The *McGraw-Hill* Companies

10 9 8 7 6 5 4

Copyright © 1999 International Marine

Printed in the United States of America

Library of Congress Cataloging-in-Publication Data
Trefethen, Jim. 1942–
    The cruising life: a commonsense guide for the would-be voyager/
JimTrefethen
        p.   cm.
    Includes bibliographical reference (p.   ) and index.
    ISBN 0-07-065360-7 (alk. paper)
    1. Boat living. 2. Boats and boating. I. Title.
GV777.7.T74 1999
797.1—dc21   98-40755

Questions regarding the content of this book should be addressed to:

International Marine
P.O. Box 220
Camden, ME 04843
Visit us at www.internationalmarine.com

Questions regarding the ordering of this book should be addressed to:

The McGraw-Hill Companies
Customer Service Department
P.O. Box 547
Blacklick, OH 43004
Retail customers: 1-800-262-4729
Bookstores: 1-800-233-4726

This book is printed on acid-free paper.

Printed by R. R. Donnelley, Crawfordsville
Design by Chris McLarty, Silverline Studios
Project management by Janet Robbins
Page layout by Shannon Thomas
Edited by Jonathan Eaton; Amanda Williams; Nancy Hauswald

Dedication
To Sarah, my tropic bird

CONTENTS

Preface 9

Acknowledgments 10

Introduction 11

Chapter 1: So You Want to Go Cruising 15
Fantasy versus Reality 16
Eschew Delusion through Enlightenment 18
Cruising Mythologies 19
The Boat Isn't as Important as You Might Think 21

Chapter 2: Profiles of the Cruising Community 24
Looking for Brian Lecur 24
Types of Cruisers 27
Common Traits of Successful Cruisers 32

Chapter 3: Should You Go Cruising? 35
Start Now to Develop Your Plan for Departure 35
Who Is Going with You? 36
And Why Are You Going? 38
The Nays 45
And the Nay Nays 47

Chapter 4: The Decision to Go 49
Two Paths Up the Same Mountain 49
Epiphany 56
Don't Commit Yourself until You Have to Commit Yourself 57

Chapter 5: Cruising without a Boat: Meet the Cruising Kitty 59
Getting Gone 59
You're on Your Way 61
The Cruising Kitty 62
Richard and the Warm Cervezas 62
The Size of the Kitty 64
Three Types of Cruising Kitties 64

Chapter 6: Feeding the Kitty 68
Start Saving Now 68
Minimalism—The Key to the Cruising Life 69
Meet Your New Minimalist Lifestyle 70
Credit: The Most Frivolous of All Frivolities 77
Work to Live 81
Put Your Money to Work 83
The All-Service Discount Brokerage 84
Grooming Your Kitty 85
Risk Management 85
Investment Vehicles 88
Dividend Reinvestment Options 91

Worry-Free Kitties 91
Don't Cry, Diversify 91
How Not to Buy Stocks 92
Planning for What Comes Next 93

Chapter 7: Planning Departure 94
Uncle Freddy and the Pompadour Kid 94
Learning to Sail 95
Learning about Cruising 100
You're Almost Ready 101
Susan and the Wonder Cruise 101
Destinations—The Long-Range Plan 103
Charts and Guidebooks 106
The First-Year Plan 108
Don't Become a Liveaboard 110

Chapter 8: Life Aboard 112
An Incident at Aitutaki 112
Cruising Skills 115
Noncruising Cruising Skills 119
Skills You'll Need Ashore 123
Skills to Sell to Other Cruisers 126
Skills to Sell Ashore 129

Chapter 9: OK, Let's Buy a Boat 131
Delphus and the Doofus 131
Looking at Boats 133
A Liability, Not an Asset 138
Pay Cash 139
Insurance 140
A Few Things to Look for in Your Cruising Boat 141
New Boats versus Old Boats 143
Let the Search Begin 144
The Hull 147
The Engine 148
What's Your Price Range? 152
Some Favorite Boats 155
Making an Offer 166
Get a Survey 166
Building Your Own Boat 167

Chapter 10: Commence Cruising 169
Let's Get Going 169
The Rigging 171
The Electrical System 173
Batteries and Charging Systems 181
The Engine 186
Sea Trials 190

Chapter 11: Food and the Cruising Galley 198
The Most Important Part of the Boat 198
Galley Layout and Hardware 205

The Kitchen Sink 209
Storage 209
Pots and Pans 211
Galley Gadgets 213
Sharing the Chores 214
A Few Fantastic Recipes from *Sultana*'s Galley 215

Chapter 12: The Electronics Revolution **222**
Electronic Marvels 222
Electronic Navigation 223
Radar 228
Communications 231
The Internet 232
Personal Computers 236
Water, Water, Everywhere 238
Safety at Sea 240

Appendix **245**

Recommended Reading **247**

Index **250**

PREFACE

What little I know about the yarn-spinning trade I learned from my maternal grandpappy, Sam, who taught me that the first responsibility of a writer was to entertain the reader, and if the writer could impart a bit of useful information in the process, so much the better. Old Grandpap always approached the truth like a tanner approaches a fresh hide—the hide is useless in its raw state, so it is first stretched to fit a frame, then it's worked over with tools and chemicals to make it flexible and pliable. Only then is it ready to be fashioned into something useful or beautiful or, in the best of circumstances, both. Thus, all of the material in this manuscript is true or at least based on the truth. If you notice a few stretch marks here and there, you can attribute them to the way I was raised and the free exercise of my artistic license, valid in Canada, the U.S. (with the possible exception of California), and the District of Columbia.

However, in what may prove to be a futile effort to preserve the few friendships I will have left after publication of this book, to disguise the identity of guilty parties, and to protect myself from the litigious nature of certain humorless individuals, many of the names and settings I have used herein are changed ever so slightly. Please forgive these trifling detours from the straight and narrow path of literal honesty; they are a sign of the times rather than any attempt by your humble and fanatically factual author to deceive. Read with an open mind and a generous temper. And above all, and in the spirit of my ancient and respected ancestor, enjoy.

ACKNOWLEDGMENTS

The list of people who helped write this book is a long one, and my first and most difficult task is to apologize to those who should be in it but aren't—people like Hugh and Cathie Marriott on *Tacit;* Murrie Cullen on *Goatlocker;* Bob "The Mad Pom" Schofield on *Mistress Margaret;* Captain Dick Bunker on *Sans Souci;* Sussane Huber and Lucky on *Glory;* and Mike "Maori Mike" Gladding of Aitutaki. All of these wonderful people and dozens more like them taught us how to live the cruising life while providing enough material to last an ardent storyteller a lifetime.

A special thanks goes to my wife, Susan, and to our children, Sarah and Phillip, for their patience and forbearance, without which none of this would have happened and without whom life itself wouldn't be worth living. The entire editorial team at International Marine, especially Kate Mallien and Amanda Williams, gets a big pat on the back for putting up with missed deadlines and the foibles and follies of an enthusiastic but unskilled author. A big "ta" to my Kiwi mate, Susan Harper (who doesn't know a boat from an apple box), for her skill and persistence in organizing and reviewing material and for providing encouragement and a large measure of that rarest of all commodities, common sense.

Fellow cruising author Beth Leonard (*The Voyager's Handbook*), who also happens to be an internationally acclaimed financial consultant, revised and rewrote large parts of chapter 6. Much of the material on finance, and all of the lucid bits on finance, are hers. Marine communications consultant, Don Melcher of HF Radio on Board, did the same with the communications section in chapter 12. Any remaining oddities in either section are mine, not theirs.

Most of all, I want to thank all the cruisers of the world, on and off boats, just for being cruisers.

INTRODUCTION

Somewhere on the south side of Nuku Hiva in the Marquesas, high on the western wall of the deep valley that runs north from Daniel's Bay, there is a ledge where two white tropic birds make their nest. The valley is as old as time and filled with the ghosts and relics of a civilization long gone and forgotten by the relentless march of the centuries. And we four—myself; my wife, Susan; and our two children, Sarah and Phillip—were there in search of the mighty waterfall that spectacularly defined the head of the valley. The view, we had been told, was worth a day's march through the jungle.

Tropic birds are remarkable creatures—white as angels and just as stunning. They sport a pair of tail feathers that grow to a meter or more in length and stream behind like the tails of kites as the birds fly. As Susan and I watched through the ship's binoculars from our perch on a rock high above a forest of coconut palms, our tropic birds swooped and swerved in giant arcs and circles, first spiraling down to the valley floor, then zooming high to the peaks above. The black face of the cliffs made the movements of the stark white birds easy to follow, and the 100-meter-high waterfall plunging from the top of the cliffs in the distant background made for a most lovely vista.

We had left *Sultana* anchored in the bay and rowed ashore in the dinghy at dawn. Then we hiked for hours through the steaming jungle and the ruins of the houses of the ancient Polynesians who lived there long ago. Now Susan and I sat watching the birds while Sarah and Phillip searched for a few not-too-ripe coconuts to accompany the sandwiches Susan had made for our lunch.

"I wonder why they're doing that," Susan whispered.

"Because we need a drink with lunch," I whispered back.

"Not the kids, silly, the birds. I wonder why they fly in circles like that. They're so beautiful I could cry."

"Well," I began. But Susan rolled her eyes as if to say, "Oh no . . . not another lecture on instinct and the nature of birds . . . not here."

"Well, they do it for the same reason that you cruise—it's what they must do—and when we're cruising, you're every bit as beautiful as they are when they're flying."

Susan giggled and jabbed me in the ribs with a finger the way she does when I lay it on a little too thick, but then she relaxed and rested her chin on my shoulder. I knew I had said the right thing, however corny it may have been, and that my secret campaign for a dinner of Susan's special lasagna was showing promise. Now, several worlds and thousands of miles later, I think often of those two tropic birds soaring among the cliffs and peaks of that ancient faraway valley. I wonder if I'll ever see them again, all the while knowing that I won't—not like that, not like then, anyway. And I ponder the similarities between cruisers and birds.

Thus, I'm writing this book for all the tropic birds of the world, for all the vagabond people who are testing their wings and who will do what they do because that's what they must do. I'm writing for those who would sail in the wind, swooping low and soaring high on the breezes and currents that carry them off to wherever they're going next. More specifically, this book is for those tropic birds who yearn to soar but who lack material wealth and don't want to wait for retirement to pursue their dream.

Perhaps you're one of these tropic birds. Perhaps you, too, dream of sailing off in a boat to visit places most people only read about in books or watch on TV travel shows. Perhaps you'd like to sail among the islands of paradise or cruise the coast of Shangri-La and stop to eat of the red bananas and drink of the green coconuts. Or perhaps you'd choose to stay closer to home and explore the mossy reaches of the Tombigbee or the quiet coves of Georgian Bay. Perhaps you'd like to join the annual migration to the sun and beaches of the Bahamas.

Perhaps you think you'd like to do these things, but you don't because . . . because why? Let's take a quick look at just a few possible reasons.

- You don't have enough money.
- You don't want to leave your family, friends, cat, neighborhood, Saturday bridge game, etc.
- Your career is just getting off the ground.
- You aren't eligible for parole until 2052.
- You don't know what to do with all your belongings.
- You've just gotten your garden looking the way you want it.
- You've too many commitments, responsibilities, obligations, etc.
- You're still making payments on your Porsche.
- You don't want to lose your welfare check.
- No one will water your fuschia.

The list goes on and on. But except for the first, these are all valid reasons for not going cruising. If you enjoy your Saturday bridge game so much that you are loathe to leave, or if that Porsche is the most important thing in your life, that's great. We all have choices to make. (If I had to choose between a Porsche and the cruising life, the choice would be easy—I wouldn't own a Porsche if you gave me one. No, that's not true. I'd love for you to give me a Porsche, but I'd sell it and put the money straight into *Sultana*'s cruising kitty.) That's the most wonderful thing about this wonderful life we live—the choices we have about how we want to live it. The tragedy is that many of us labor away at jobs we don't like in places we don't want to be with people we fear and envy, never realizing that there's an alternative. Most of us live in democracies that allow us to go where we want, do what we want, and be what we want, but millions of us, through conditioning, fear, or blind ignorance, never realize our potential.

No, I'm not one of those razzle-dazzle podium-thumping self-realization gurus who insists that if you want something badly enough and work hard enough for it, you'll get it, no matter what it is. The truth is, we all encounter limits, but those limits are far less restrictive than most of us ever realize. If you want to go cruising you can go cruising, but for all those reasons I just listed (except the first), and thousands more, you can also choose to lead a full and rewarding life right at home.

So, you say you don't have enough money to go cruising? Sure you do. Here's how to get it. Let's make another list.

- Take half your monthly rent or mortgage payment and make that the first item on your list.
- Now take your car payment (that's right, the whole thing) and make that the second item.
- Now add on your cable TV bill.
- Add up all the money you are paying out every month for credit cards. Take principal, interest, and fees, and if it varies a lot from month to month, take an average, and add that to the list.
- Next, put in the amount you pay each month for lottery tickets. Come on, tell the truth. (Most people fudge on this one.)
- Now add all of the dues and fees you pay to clubs and organizations— yacht clubs, country clubs, motorcycle gangs, health clubs, quilting bees, etc. Throw in the amount you pay for magazine subscriptions, divide the total by 12, and add this number to the list.
- Do you smoke, drink, gamble, do drugs, or hang around at Scientology rallies? If so, multiply the money you spend on these activities by four (the real cost of this sort of thing is at least four times your out-of-pocket cost). Add that number to the list.

Add all these numbers and multiply the total by 60 (the number of months in five years). With a red felt-tipped pen, write your total on a piece of stiff paper, underline it, and stick it on the refrigerator door right next to your granny's recipe for ginger cake.

Of course, I have no way of knowing what your number is, but if you are an average citizen of an industrialized nation, or even close to average, I'll guarantee it's enough to buy a cruising sailboat—maybe not a fancy one, but a good one that will do the job.

If your monthly total was $500 (for many people, that won't even cover the car payment), you'll have $30,000 pasted on the refrigerator door, and that's before we multiply it using the investment approach discussed in chapter 6.

So what does this prove? Well, nothing really, but it does show that most of you reading this book already make enough money to be cruising in five years, even if you couldn't make any more (which you can, as we'll discover in Chapter 6). All you need to do is stop spending what money you have on frivolous nonsense and put that money to work building a new life.

Susan and I have been cruising full-time for the past four years while watching our kids change from children into young adults. Susan is really the adventurer in the family. She and Sarah love cruising, while Phillip and I sort of follow along because . . . well, because we love Susan and Sarah. We've learned a lot in our travels though—a little of when to do what and a lot of when not to do what else— but we don't call it wisdom. Buddhists say that wisdom is the knowledge that you don't really know anything. (Which, I suspect, is the very reason that you seldom see Buddhists in cruising sailboats.) So lest we seem unwise in our wisdom, we'll use the terms "tips and tricks" in this book and dispense them, as best we can, with humor and profundity.

Much of the material in this book deals with the way we live (or should live) our lives.more than with the specifics of cruising and sailing. Most cruising books gloss over the crucial art of living on a boat while dwelling on such trivialities as the shape of your anchors and the range of your radar. Thus, this is a lifestyle book more than a cruising book. True, I write about a few of the life skills we have learned to use on *Sultana,* our 35-year-old wooden ketch, and there is plenty of good, solid boat lore scattered around, but much of what follows would apply to living on a farm in the country, in a condo in Malibu, or in a hut in the forest. To cruise well, you must first learn to live well. And once you learn to live well—*really* well—cruising, or any other way you choose to live, becomes incidental.

I think often of those two tropic birds on that island far away, and I would, indeed, like to return to see them once again. But there are other birds on other islands also far away, and I'd like to see them first. You can come along if you like—if you really want to. (And by the way, the lasagna was delicious.)

1

SO YOU WANT TO GO CRUISING

"And we are the dreamers of dreams,

Wandering by lone sea breakers."

—Arthur William Edgar O'Shaungnessy

There are those among us who would be cruisers and those who would be dreamers of cruising. There are those who will go cruising on a whim, with hardly a second thought or backward look or even a clear idea of what they are doing or where they are going—they are going cruising and that is enough. And there are others, lots of others, who plan and save and dream and scheme most of their lives about the glorious day when they are finally ready to leave on that trip around the world or across the lake to the other shore—but they never leave because ready never comes. Still others amass huge fortunes in banks and on balance sheets against the day when they will throw off the fetters of toil, stress, and worry to sail away to freedom and adventure, only to find that the very fortunes that were to buy their freedom have become their shackles. Others sail the oceans of their dreams without a dime in their pocket—with naught but a grip on the tiller and an eye on the horizon. And there are the few among us who plan carefully and act cautiously. But act they do and cruising they go, while others watch from shore.

And this is as it should be because ocean voyaging isn't for everyone. Those who stay ashore are also lucky, because that is where they belong, as surely as the ones who go belong in a small boat upon the sea. Those who stay ashore envy the adventure and excitement of sailors' lives at sea; those who sail envy the stability and predictability of those who stay ashore. Whether our dreams are lucid plans or ridiculous fantasies depends not on the nature of the dreams but on the nature of the dreamer.

Which sort of dreamer are you? A little honest introspection and a few hundred pages of reading should yield the answer, so let's go take a look. We'll cover the fantasy first and save the hard parts for later.

Fantasy versus Reality

It is amazing how many people think they want to go sailing on the oceans of the world on a small boat. You are one of them or you wouldn't be reading this book. Go ahead and admit it. The desire to go cruising is nothing to be ashamed of, and it might help you to know that you are in good company. Later, I will tell you about ordinary people for whom the dream of cruising in a sailboat—whether for a few months, for a few years, or for a lifetime—has become a reality. I will also tell you that it is an amazingly easy thing to do, once you make up your mind to really do it, that is. And I will tell you that nearly everyone who makes up their mind to do it, can. First, though, I will ask you to think a bit, to ponder the ramifications of a major change in your life and to consider all the effects that change will have on you and on those whom you care about the most.

Sure you'd like to quit your job, sell your possessions, buy a boat (an old fishing schooner or a retired Baltic trader will do), and sail away from the rat race with all its pretensions and injustices and demands that you live your life in a way that you would, perhaps, rather not be living. You can envision a land where the breezes blow warm, where the sky is always blue, where people are judged by the kind of people they are rather than by the size of their bank accounts, and where the only clothing you'll need is a T-shirt, shorts, and a pair of shower clogs for those rare days when you want to dress up.

To pay for it all you can . . . well, let's see . . . you can write that novel you've been thinking about for the past 10 years and live off the royalties and the residuals from the sale of the movie rights, or maybe you can win the lottery, or perhaps some unknown relative will expire and endow you with more wealth than you can spend in one lifetime.

Lots of people have done it before you. Old Joshua Slocum did it all by himself (and he didn't even have a GPS). Sir Francis Chichester did it. Eric Hiscock did it. Lin and Larry Pardey did it (and they didn't even have an engine in their boat). Robin Lee Graham and Tania Aebi did it when they were only kids, for Pete's sake. The list goes on and on. Even the likes of your humble but intrepid author did it, and God only knows that if he can do it, anyone who can eat soup with a spoon can do it.

Ocean voyaging, or what I prefer to call the cruising life, is within reach of anyone who really wants to do it. The idea of selling everything we own, buying a boat, and sailing off into the sunset is one of the world's most popular fantasies. In fact, as fantasies go, (or at least those we can discuss in a family-oriented book), the cruising fantasy is among the "Big Three"—right up there with writing the great American novel and becoming a rock/movie/sports star.

Not everyone who wants to be a rock/movie/sports star can do it, of course, and only a tiny percentage of the great American novels that are written are ever published, with an even smaller percentage of them making it to the best-seller lists. The cruising fantasy, however, is achievable—it simply needs to be tempered with a dose of reality.

Images of the cruising life are universal: white sand beaches, sunsets, and piña coladas under the stars. We envision days on end of bounding through gentle seas with a billowing main and flying jib pulling us to lands of adventure and romance. We don't see the loneliness of separation from friends and family, the terror of experiencing a storm at sea, the humiliation of being ignored by an arrogant port captain, or the drudgery of rowing out a kedge at 3 A.M. while the rain is falling and the wind is rising.

We read the sailing magazines and see the glossy photos of sleek yachts lying at anchor; of cookouts under the stars; and of smiling cruisers shopping in exotic markets. We see what the magazines want us to see or, perhaps, what we want to see. When we look at the cruising life in this light, it isn't surprising that so many people adopt it; what's surprising is that so many don't.

I never fail to be amazed at how many people say to me, "I've always wanted to cruise but Mabel doesn't like boats," or "Sidney gets seasick" (where Sidney is the dog), or "That's just what I'm going to do after the kids leave home and I can divorce George," or my personal favorite, "I was going to do just what you're doing, but then I got lumbago (or a trick knee, married, or promoted)."

Everyone wants to go

No one knows for sure just how many cruisers are out there plying the world's oceans in sailboats (and this slightly disreputable anonymity is one of the things about the cruising life that appeals to many of us), but the consensus seems to be that the world's population of active cruisers has stabilized at about 25,000 people. (Note: Any competent mathematician will call the following figures "backdoor statistics" and tell you that the numbers and any conclusions drawn from them are hopelessly invalid, but what the hell, we'll use them anyway.) For the sake of my argument, let's say that for every 1,000 people who dream of the cruising life, only one ever buys a boat. And for every 100 people who buy a boat in which to pursue their dream, only one ever does it. That means that with a little creative extrapolation we can deduce that about 2,500,000 people worldwide have bought boats in which to go cruising, but for one reason or another haven't gone, and a whopping 250,000,000 people (that's more than four percent of the population of the world) wanted to buy a boat in which to go cruising but didn't.

More reality

Bluewater cruising is a difficult lifestyle that involves hard work, sacrifice, risk, and yes, even danger on a scale that most rational people aren't willing to accept. Those white sandy beaches often turn out to be black slimy mud banks or insect-infested swamps. Our dreams of billowing sails and gentle seas disappear as we wallow in leftover swells while the empty sails slat and slap in the airless heat. Even those cookouts on the beach get rained on once in a while. Life on a cruising boat is hard work—much harder than most noncruisers can imagine. In fact, Susan and I never worked as hard in our lives as we did during our first year on *Sultana*. People often ask if we get bored on the long passages, and the answer is always the same: never. There is always more work to do than there is time to do it. And when we finally do reach safe harbor, there is a week or so of toil and labor, much of it dirty and unpleasant, that needs to be done before we can begin to relax and enjoy ourselves.

The physical and psychological comforts that a cruiser forfeits when shoving off to sea are many, but the financial sacrifice of leaving a steady job and the emotional sacrifice of leaving friends, family, and a comfortable home are the hardest for most people to bear and often the reasons that, as the fantasy starts to become a reality, it also begins to lose some of its luster and appeal. A lot of wannabe cruisers plan to take off after they retire, when money won't be a problem, and many do indeed go cruising then. Others, though, find that when they retire they've aged a bit and the idea of adventure on the high seas is less attractive than a country house with an easy chair and a view of the lake.

A lot of people are used to owning a lot of insurance. Upon learning that most active cruising boats are uninsurable and that most owners of insurable boats can't afford the premium, would-be cruisers are troubled. The thought of loading all their worldly possessions onto a frail craft and sailing off into dangerous waters quails many otherwise stout hearts.

What about those who do decide to sell up and sail out? Do their stories usually have happy endings? And do they usually find the paradise of their dreams? The answer to these questions, at least most of the time, is a reserved "yes." Reserved because few find the life they expected to find, but "yes" because those who try it usually find that cruising is one of the healthiest and most rewarding ways to live.

Eschew Delusion through Enlightenment

Cruisers and would-be cruisers tend to be optimistic folks. (I can recall meeting only one man living on a cruising yacht whom I would consider a full-time pessimist.) Optimists are doughty souls who remain sanguine in the face of adversity and blasé in the shadow of misfortune. They are prone to hear and see only what they want to hear and see, and this predisposition to self-delusion, along with lack of preparation for a major change in lifestyle, are the two major reasons that the dream of the cruising life sometimes turns sour. Many people who sacrifice everything to go cruising without preparing properly find they have made a very costly mistake and return home disappointed.

One of the first steps anyone can take toward making the cruising fantasy become reality is to read everything there is to read on the subject. But danger lies there, too. Books on the cruising life are, for the most part, a celebration of cruising. Good cruising books—from Joshua Slocum's *Sailing Alone around the World* to David and Daniel Hays' *My Old Man and the Sea*—are written by good cruisers. Except for liferaft sagas, which always seem to find a ready audience, few readers are interested in gloomy stories about failed or disastrous voyages, and few publishers are interested in printing them. Thus, inexperienced and impressionable readers with optimistic bents might get the idea from the world-cruising literature that the cruising life is all a bed of roses. And that just ain't so.

Cruising isn't what it used to be

A yacht should expect the unexpected while cruising in developing countries. Politics and finances can change rapidly, leaving cruising guides outdated as soon as they are printed. For example, all of our guidebooks on French Polynesia said that the moorings at the Bora Bora Yacht Club were free to visiting cruisers. When we arrived there and picked one up, we found that there was a substantial nightly charge. And when Mexico devalued its currency, the Yucatan almost immediately became an inexpensive place to visit—except for those cruisers who were already there with pocketfuls of pesos. They watched the value of their cash cut in half, and they weren't the least bit happy about it.

In all but the most remote islands, cruising boats are no longer unusual, and many new cruisers are astonished when no one even looks up as they drop anchor in a harbor where Slocum, Chichester, and Hiscock each received royal welcomes. Some cruising books tell of chiefs on small islands who welcome boats with open arms and a pig roast, but today you are much more likely to be greeted with an open palm and a roasting for anchoring too close to the chief's black-pearl farm. Of course, you can still partake of a welcoming feast when you arrive at many popular Pacific islands—the only difference is that now it's a commercial venture, and you'll pay 50 bucks a head for the privilege. (But it's not to be missed at twice that price.) The one we attended in the Vava'u Island Group of Tonga was complete with the kava ceremony, native dancing, and a roast pig with all the trimmings.

No, cruising isn't what it used to be—it's better. And in many ways, it's much better.

Cruising Mythologies

Many books about cruising are responsible for fostering cruising mythologies. My favorite myth is the almost universal belief among cruisers that Joy dishwashing detergent possesses some magical properties that make it the sole detergent capable of cutting grease or producing suds in salt water. Actually salt water is terrible for washing anything (except teak decks), and it doesn't make a prune pit's worth of difference what kind of soap you use. Detergent suds are produced by phosphates and, although manufacturers might have used unlimited amounts of phosphates 20 years ago, they are now strictly regulated. Thus, most detergents made in the U.S. and Canada produce about the same amount of suds. I don't have anything against Joy, but the idea that it is dramatically different from any other detergents is silly. If you really want suds, wait until you get to South America, then buy some Axion dishwashing detergent. It's sold in sticks, like dynamite, and without FDA regulations you'll see plenty of suds.

By the way, the cruising myth that shampoo makes a fine dishwashing detergent isn't a myth at all. Liquid dishwashing detergents and shampoos are essentially the same thing—only their colorings and fragrances are different. The next time you run out of dish soap, a little shampoo will make a fine substitute, and if you need a truly exotic shampoo, try some of that Joy. (Don't use Axion as a shampoo, though. That stuff will dissolve anything organic, including your scalp.)

As another example of how cruising literature has influenced our actions, take those silly little wooden plugs that nearly every cruising boat has safety wired to all its seacocks. These plugs have an interesting history that goes all the way back to the very first through-hull fittings that were used to direct cooling water to the first internal-combustion engines used in small boats. Often, these fittings didn't have seacocks, and the plugs were insurance against the fairly common failure of the early hoses. Today, though, they have no practical purpose. Even so, nearly every cruising book that has been written in the past 30 years says that these plugs are a necessary safety item, and many racing rules require them, but no one says how to use them. The most common cause of leaks at seacocks is hose failure—which often results from an overly enthusiastic application of hose clamps, in which case closing the seacock stops the leak. (Another bit of cruising lore that is often false is the necessity of having two hose clamps on seacock fittings.) In the unlikely event that a seacock is ripped from the hull, the hole would be far too big to be stoppered by a plug, and if a seacock were to snap off at the flange (another astronomically unlikely event), an old sock or piece of T-shirt stuffed into the opening would make a far better stopper than a wooden plug. In nearly 50 years of messing around in boats, I have never used one of these plugs to stop a leak, nor have I ever heard of anyone else using one. (Well, that's not quite true. Beth Leonard tells me that she had to use a wood plug to stopper a faulty seacock during sea trials of her new boat. That makes once in 50 years.)

Let me shoot down one more cruising myth. Forget about turning over your eggs every few days while you're cruising. That practice is even less necessary on a boat than it is at home because, except in California, houses seldom jump around the way boats are inclined to do in a seaway. (We'll revisit this one in chapter 11.)

Cruising can be economical, but it isn't cheap

A lot of cruising literature also fosters the idea that cruising is a cheap way to live. Once upon a time it was possible to live on a boat and spend very little money, but today, living on a boat is becoming more costly all the time, and world cruising is a rather expensive undertaking for most people.

Annie Hill, in her delightful book *Voyaging on a Small Income*, champions a cruising lifestyle that costs the author and her husband only a few thousand pounds a year. It's an austere life that reminds me of the back-to-nature movement of the 1960s. I knew three families then who bought separate plots of land in New Hampshire and planned to return to nature and the good life, chopping their own firewood, and eating their own organically grown vegetables. Unfortunately, they failed to consider the rigors of New England winters and the fact that woodchucks and deer also like organically grown vegetables. Two of the families quit halfway through the first winter, and the third lasted about two years. Of course, it is possible to live in the woods and eat nuts and berries. Our ancestors did it, and were happy for the chance to do so, but today most of us demand at least the minimum of modern comforts, and the appeal of a life without them wears thin with the first hunger pangs.

The ascetic cruising life described by Hill is certainly within the grasp of anyone willing to make the sacrifices to live it; *Sultana* has met several boats with crews who were living on pasta and spunk. But cruising seems to lose some of its objectives when you are forced to avoid attractive destinations because of expensive clearance fees (for the privilege of entering a country), or you can't afford to rent a car for a country tour, or you can't eat at a local restaurant.

Yes, there are still many countries that charge low fees (although the number is shrinking rapidly), and yes, the very best way to see many countries and meet local people is by riding the local bus, and yes, indeed, the tastiest food most often comes from the smallest shops and sidewalk vendors. But even riding buses and eating local food require money. People in Third World countries who once viewed yachts as curiosities now see them as a source of revenue and are charging accordingly. The total clearance fees (customs, immigration, and the like) for *Sultana*'s international stops, excluding bribes that are unavoidable in some places, came to a little less than $200 in each country we visited. On a three-year, 50-country cruise then, which is a healthy world tour, required fees alone will run about $10,000 U.S.—or more than half of Annie Hill's entire cruising budget.

The costs continue to climb

Boat maintenance, labor, moorings, provisions, and entertainment are more expensive today than they were yesterday no matter where you go. Even if you do most of the work on your boat yourself, the cost of materials seems to continue on an upward spiral. However, a dramatic increase in the availability of goods and services in places that were once remote and isolated means that supplies and services are available, often at reasonable prices, where there were none before.

A good example of this transformation from wilderness to economic center is the Rio Dulce in eastern Guatemala. Most guidebooks still refer to this lovely area as a primitive jungle wilderness. In reality, it is rapidly becoming the hub of cruising activity for the western Caribbean with new boatyards, marinas, shops, restaurants, and communications facilities opening all the time. True, there are still a few rough edges, and "primitive" is still an appropriate adjective for many of the services there, but the trend is toward more development. The irony is that, as these sorely needed services become available, the attractiveness of the Rio as a haven for budget cruisers correspondingly diminishes. The cost of staying there is rising, and the region's natural beauty is increasingly marred by development that should have been better controlled and directed.

It costs a lot more to equip a boat now than it did just a few years ago. Not only do individual items cost more, but advances in technology mean that there are a lot more things to buy. Some cruisers still choose to sail without a single-sideband radio or a good liferaft because of their substantial costs, but radar is rapidly becoming a must-have item, only fools venture offshore without a GPS, and most of us wouldn't go without a 406 MHz EPIRB.

If you think you would like to try a cruise on the cheap, be forewarned that truly economical cruising is much more difficult now than it used to be, and as the global economy warms up, that trend will continue. Overly optimistic expectations of cost—which is often followed by disillusionment—comprise one of the major problems faced by new cruisers.

The Boat Isn't as Important as You Might Think

What's the most important element in the successful cruising equation? "The boat, of course," is the obvious and most resounding answer. But it's also wrong—dead wrong. Successful cruisers are out there in the most incredible assortment of boats that can be imagined. There are new boats and old boats, fat boats and skinny boats, big boats and little boats, fast boats and slow boats. In any popular cruising port you will see custom-designed and -built floating palaces costing millions of dollars moored next to cement-and-chicken-wire tubs that some lubber has thrown together in a backyard. In Bora Bora we were anchored between a brand-new ocean-racing catamaran and a lovely old Dutch sailing barge from the Zuider Zee. The proud crew of the catamaran claimed that, on a reach, it could sail 25 percent faster than the wind, and I suspect the Dutch barge would sail downwind about 25 percent faster than a log would float. Yet in spite of their differences, they were both lovely boats and good sturdy sea vessels in which their respective owners took a great deal of justifiable pride.

A study in contrast

In Panama we met a couple from Russia who were sailing around the world with a baby in an engineless 25-foot sloop. In Rangiroa in the South Pacific, we met a couple from the United States with two kids on a custom-designed 60-foot Deerfoot ketch with every electronic gizmo and gadget known to man, including a commercial satellite link and electronic sail furling and reefing. They, too, were sailing around the world. You could, I suppose, make an argument that the family from the United States was learning more and having more fun than the couple from Russia, but if that were true it was hard to tell. The American captain was furious because his satellite link was down (again), and he spent three days in an expensive resort hotel faxing his displeasure to the equipment manufacturer.

The obvious difference between the two families, except for the size of their boats and the ages of their kids, was the amount of money they were spending. If dispensing cash makes a person happy, then the Deerfoot crew were ecstatic. These two boats represent the extremes in family cruising. The only quality that successful bluewater cruising boats have in common is that they are sturdy and seaworthy—beyond that, anything goes.

A logical conclusion

Although I know I risk the ire of boat lovers and lifelong cruisers by saying so, the type of boat you go cruising in doesn't matter anywhere near as much as most people would like to believe. The cruising boat is a means to an end—the freedom of the cruising life—and as such, it's one of the last things you need to worry about. True, we have seen several long-planned voyages come to grief because the inexperienced and ill-advised sailors bought the wrong craft, but Susan and I have seen far more cruises ruined because the right boat ended up with the wrong cruisers. Thus, the most important element in the cruising equation is you. Boats can sink and burn and disappear in the night, but a captain and crew with a positive attitude go on forever.

Don't buy a boat until you have to

Buying a boat too early in the planning process is one of the most common mistakes made by potential cruisers. Unless you have a lot of experience with bluewater craft and many years of coastal cruising, it is unlikely that you know just what you will want or need in a cruising boat. When Susan decided that the cruising life was the life for us, we were convinced we wanted a catamaran. We had a growing family and catamarans have lots of room, they are safe and easy to sail, and their shoal draft promised access to the small harbors and out-of-the-way anchorages we have always favored. But after looking at every catamaran on the East Coast that was for sale in our price range, we changed our mind. Cats were a lot more expensive to buy than monohulls; the best are built to flimsy scantlings that make them sensitive to weight (and we were never very good at traveling light); and they are cumbersome and awkward at anchor—which is where cruising boats spend most of their time. If we had bought one of the first few boats we looked at, we would have been stuck with the wrong boat. Of course, it would have worked out because there are lots of happy cruisers living on catamarans and, as I've said, the boat isn't that important, but by waiting a few years we got just the right boat for us and we saved a pot full of money in the process.

Buying a boat early in your planning means you have to pay for and care for the thing while you are getting ready to leave and, although this sounds like a logical thing to do, it's often a serious mistake. Boats, especially boats sturdy enough for ocean cruising, are expensive to buy and maintain, and the newer ones depreciate faster than fish rot. If you own one during the years you are preparing to leave, you will be spending a huge amount of money on the boat that would be better off going into your cruising kitty (the cruiserly equivalent of a bank account), and you will be spending a lot of time sailing and working on the boat that is better spent working for cash that will further fatten that kitty.

You say that your boat is paid for and stored behind the house, so it isn't costing you anything? Take a closer look. For one thing, dry storage can cause more wear and tear on a boat and gear than heavy use. Two, there is always what the accountants like to call the opportunity cost—i.e., the money you would make if you had invested in something more profitable than a boat. For example, if your boat is worth $100,000 (after sales commissions and taxes) and you sold it and put the money into a good stock fund paying 10 percent total annual return, you would not only save the maintenance, depreciation, insurance, and all the other costs associated with owning a boat, but in two years with compounding interest you would accumulate more than an additional $20,000 in capital gains and dividends to put into savings. The total addition to your cruising kitty from selling your $100,000 boat would be well over $30,000, which is more than enough to keep the crew of *Sultana* cruising in style for a year or more.

I know that a lot of would-be cruisers justify the purchase of a boat early in the planning stage by saying they need the time to get the boat ready to go and to learn to sail it well, but this sort of reasoning is rationalization, and all it will get you is broke. Unless you've done it before, no matter how much you try to get everything sorted out on your boat before you leave, you are going to find dozens of changes you want to make once you've been underway for a year or so simply because you have no way of knowing what will work for you until you try it. Of course there are some advantages to owning the boat before you try cruising in it— a lot of them in fact—but none of them is worth the time and money that boat ownership will detract from your cruising kitty. Concentrating on the boat while ignoring the critical tasks of living and accumulating cash is the big reason so many people who buy cruising boats never go.

If you have a boat that you are convinced is just what you want to start your cruising life in and your departure is imminent—say within the next two years— sure, hold on to it. But if you won't be leaving for at least two or three years or if you own a mortgaged boat, selling the boat now and buying another when you are ready to go might make sense.

Dreams make the impossible possible, dedication makes the possible probable, and work makes the probable happen. Modern cruising is a difficult way to live. It requires hard work and sacrifices, but for many who crave personal freedom and a simple life, it's worth it. The trick is to realize what you're getting yourself into before you cast off the lines and head out to sea.

2

PROFILES OF THE CRUISING COMMUNITY

"The sea speaks a language

polite people never repeat."

–Carl Sandburg

Looking for Brian Lecur

A long time ago, as I sat at my desk in a Boston office building, a singular event occurred that would pound my complacent rock of a life into sand. It was a frigid day in January, and the Montreal Express was howling down Congress Street piling the snow in drifts everywhere, when I looked up to see a man approaching. He had long brown hair tied in a knot at the back of his head and a friendly smile on his bearded face. He appeared to be about 40 years old or a little more, and he said his name was Brian Lecur.

He plopped a substantial toolbox on the floor next to my chair and asked in a polite, soft-spoken voice if he could stand on my desk while he made some adjustments in the electrical apparatus that resided behind a panel in the suspended ceiling over my head. It's not every day that a large hairy person asks to stand on your desk so, lacking any reason why he shouldn't and welcoming the diversion, I agreed.

The electrician and I hit it off right away, and at the end of an hour or so we were chatting away like old buddies. As he worked I handed him tools, and he told me his tale.

Brian, as it turned out, was an adventurer. He had spent his life on the road living where he felt like living, going where he wanted to go, doing what he felt like doing with whomever he wanted to do it. He had lived in Australia and Terra del Fuego and Afghanistan. He met his Bavarian wife, Greta, while hiking in the Sierra Leone, and for three years they lived in a cabin they built from logs on the sunny side of the Brooks Range in Alaska. They shot moose for meat and trapped animals in the winter for fur. They moved south to Idaho when she became pregnant, and he worked on a dude ranch teaching schoolteachers and accountants how to ride horses and guiding hunters from the city after elk. They moved to Berkeley when his daughter, Sally, was born, and with his masters degree from MIT, he got a job teaching high school science and math. Sally, now nine, was being homeschooled by Greta, who was also debugging software for the local computer industry. Brian spoke five languages and was now working as an electrician in Boston because it paid better than teaching and involved "fewer hassles." They were saving all the money they could and in the spring would head to California, where they had an old Westsail 32 waiting for them at Marina del Rey. They were going to move aboard and set sail for the South Pacific. Their first stop would be Hawaii.

"It's time to settle down," Brian said, "I can't live this crazy footloose life any more—too hard on my little girl."

"You call sailing the South Pacific in a 32-foot boat 'settling down'?" I asked without expecting an answer.

That noontime we shared sandwiches from his ample lunch pail. "Why Hawaii?" I asked, unable to drop the subject.

"Because we wanted to start the little girl off on an easy one," he answered.

Brian's work in the ceiling over my head ended up taking most of two days, partly because the job turned out to be more complicated than it first appeared and partly because we spent most of the time talking about such things as hunting wild pigs in Australia, hiking through Greece, and trout fishing in Argentina. As bits of wire and scraps of insulation rained down from above, I bombarded Brian with questions. Some were rather blunt.

"Do you ever think of getting a regular job?"

"Sure," answered Brian. "I worked at teaching four years straight after my girl was born."

"Why'd you quit?"

"Well, a friend owned a shrimp boat down in Louisiana and needed some help, so we went down to give him a hand. Besides, I needed some air. I worked there for two years."

"Why'd you leave that?"

"Boat sank."

"Oh, but what about your daughter? Isn't it tough on her traveling around and never going to school?"

"Nope. Greta's a good teacher, and Sally's the smartest nine-year-old there is; smarter than any kid in regular school."

"But isn't it hard on her not having any friends?"

"Sally has plenty of friends. She's real popular with her church group, and there are plenty of kids her age where we live now."

"Church? You go to church?"

"Sure, every week. Wouldn't miss it. You meet great folks at church."

"What kind of church?"

"Small ones."

"But what denomination?"

"Doesn't matter. Whatever's handy. We're going to a Baptist Church now. Went to a synagogue in Berkeley."

"Isn't that kind of cynical?"

"Naw. My parents were Jewish and Greta was born a Catholic. Same God. He doesn't care."

"You know that for sure?"

"Yep."

"But what about health insurance? Don't you get a little nervous not having any insurance?"

"Nope. Don't get sick."

"But what if you broke a leg or something?"

"Don't do that either."

"What about money? Doesn't it get tough not having any money?"

"We've got plenty of money. We always keep enough in the bank to live for a year just in case."

"How much is that?"

"Oh, probably about what you make in two months."

"OK, but what about major expenses? What do you do when you need a new car or television?"

"Well, we never pay more than $500 for a car, and I haven't owned a television set since the bastards took Perry Como off the air."

And so it went. Sitting at my desk in my business suit, I initially felt superior to Brian in his overalls and carrying his toolbox, but once I got over that feeling, I was a bit shaken. Brian put away his tools and left when the job was done. I never saw him again, but I never forgot him either. I ended up sitting at that desk or one just like it for eight more years, and as I sat I would often think of Brian and wonder what trails he was hiking or which ocean he was sailing. I compared his lifestyle to mine and, with time, a clear picture of two simple but divergent philosophies emerged.

Brian lived a life that was dictated by his interests and he did whatever he had to do to support those interests. Of course, many people would call him an irresponsible bum, but he always voted at election time and always paid his taxes. Some people might call him selfish, but he was devoted to his family and I doubted if he would ever want to do anything they couldn't do together. He owned neither a new car like I did nor a spacious house in the suburbs like mine, and while he didn't seem to begrudge me these things, he didn't seem to want them either. Brian wasn't irresponsible or selfish—he just refused to play the game the rest of us were playing, and I somehow found that unsettling.

When I compared my life with Brian's, the contrast was remarkable even though this was in the freethinking 1960s. There was no way I could wear my hair long and tied in a knot the way he did. I dressed the way the company wanted me to dress, lived in a house I knew they would approve of, and drove a car that looked like the cars driven by every other young management employee where I worked. I attended all of the company parties and other social functions that I felt would further my career. My life was driven by my job—and it wasn't even a great job. It was a dull and boring job that I was good at, and it paid well. I consoled myself with the knowledge that I was soon due for a promotion, but then I realized that my boss's job was even more dull than mine and his boss's job was even worse. And I also realized that, although Brian had not made any attempt to denigrate the way I lived or to convince me that his lifestyle was better than mine in any way—he lived the way he wanted to live and I was free to do the same—it was the freedom to choose how we live that was the most unsettling. I was living the way my parents and my company and the local authorities and IRS and the advertisers of the products I consumed wanted me to live. I was a paragon of the young urban wage earner and fortune was smiling on my efforts even though I was not. I realized that my role model was no longer some high-level executive in the marketing department, it was a bearded guy in overalls who had spent two days getting footprints and wire scraps all over my desk.

After our children, Sarah and Phillip, were born, the image of Brian Lecur worked itself into my psyche and eventually, with a major push from Susan, it prevailed. In 1993, Susan quit her job and I closed my small-but-profitable yacht-repair business. We rented (and eventually sold) our house in the trendy Boston suburb of Marblehead, rescued a broken-down sailing yacht from under a pile of plastic tarps and pigeon guano from a barn in Maine, moved aboard, and sailed away. Slowly but surely the pervasive arguments of an itinerant electrician who, 25 years earlier, had stood with his feet on my desk and his head in the clouds prevailed. Brian taught me that it was OK to be a dreamer and that it was possible to render dreams into reality once you learn to trust your instincts and ignore the sheepdogs of convention that are determined to keep humanity running together as a flock. Now when anyone asks me why it is we are doing what we are doing, I answer that we are looking for Brian Lecur.

Types of Cruisers

Brian Lecur has come to represent, for me, the paragon of the cruising sailor. The freedom for which he worked so hard allowed him to make his own rules yet thrive in the face of a society that was determined to force ever more of its own rules upon him. He lived his life in a way that many, perhaps most, would scorn as being irresponsible and indifferent—yet there remains a vestige of begrudging admiration in all of us for the few among us with the courage to jump the track and head off in a new direction. The rugged individualism of the American pioneer is the stuff of folklore and legend. It is elevated to ever higher plateaus with each telling of stories that are so embellished that we can't possibly know which actually happened and which were invented by our collective imagination. But Brian is real and he is now, and there is nothing that he has done that the rest of us couldn't do if we wanted. Who cares if the track we follow has been worn broad and deep by all the Brians that have gone before us, and that the appellations of "pioneer" and "adventurer" have been replaced by "proselyte" and "disciple"? The cruising life is there for those of us who want it.

But the cruising life doesn't appeal to everyone. It's not that the cruising community is exclusive or that ocean voyaging is overly difficult, it's just that when the actual cost of cruising in dollars, personal sacrifice, and hard work are considered, the majority of us bow out and find some less disruptive activity closer to home. Others find that their personal commitments, relationships, and fondness for the shoreside life won't allow them to chuck it all and sail away.

This is fine and as it should be. There are, after all, many advantages to a conventional shoreside life that can't be denied: your house is unlikely to drag anchor in the middle of the night; if your basement fills with water through some misadventure of the plumbing system, you will at least be spared the agony of watching your home slide beneath the waves; and even if your house were to sink, the local emergency services (fire, police, ambulance and such) wouldn't need to home in on an ELT beacon just to find you. The cruising life isn't necessarily better than the shoreside life, but it is different—a lot different. One reason why I'm writing this book is to help you decide, rationally and systematically, if the cruising life is for you. Remember that it's OK to have your head in the clouds as long as you keep your feet on the ground, and I'll try to show you how you can do just that.

For now, let's assume that you are one of those fortunate few to whom the cruising life, after close scrutiny, retains its exotic allure. Although cruisers as a whole are maddeningly hard to categorize, what follows is a rough grouping of the types of people for whom this lifestyle is often most appropriate.

Retired cruisers

The cruising life has undeniable and natural appeal to people who have worked a full and rewarding life, who are looking for more than shuffleboard tournaments and mall prowling, and who shudder at the prospect of living in a retirement community in Florida or Arizona. Retirees with a moderate pension supplemented by social security can live quite well on a boat. But please note: Just because you have retirement income doesn't mean you don't have to tend to your cruising kitty. In chapter 4 I'll discuss a few principles that can help you stretch a meager retirement income.

Many retirees keep going well into their seventies, and I've even encountered the occasional oceangoing octogenarian. In fact, if there is a problem with retired cruisers it is that a few of them don't know when to quit—and I say that with fond admiration for their perseverance. The vigorous and healthy cruising life seems to keep older people going longer.

Age, however, is a reality that we must all deal with sooner or later, and as with most things, it is better and easier to deal with it earlier. If you intend to cruise well into your retirement years, be aware that your cruising skills and abilities will change with your advancing years and plan accordingly.

Middle-aged retirees

The rash of forced early retirements and corporate layoffs in the 1980s and early 1990s resulted in a flood of retirees in their forties and fifties with a steady income and nothing to do. Many of them bought sailboats and tried cruising. In addition, there are more and more cruisers in their early fifties who have decided to step out of harness with less retirement income just so they can start cruising while they have the health and stamina to enjoy it. For them the financial sacrifice of not working an extra 10 years until the common retirement age of 65 is worth it many times over. This observation is reinforced by the most prevalent comment we hear from cruisers who didn't get started until after age 65: "If I'd only known how wonderful it is, I would have quit the job and started earlier."

We have also met retired people who are even younger, a fortunate few of whom are in their thirties. Most of these folks have family money to draw on, have sold a business, invented something profitable, or otherwise accumulated enough cash to allow them to relax and enjoy life at an early age. We have yet to meet a cruiser who was able to sail away because of a killing in the stock market or a winning number in the lottery, which leads me to believe that while there are sure to be notable exceptions, stock-market killings and lottery winnings are probably not reliable ways to finance the cruising life.

Before we leave the subject of retired cruisers, I can't resist the temptation to mention another social phenomenon that has slightly tragicomic overtones—tragic if it happens to you, comic if it happens to someone else. That is, the current trend of adult children returning to the nest, often with grandkids in tow. We have several shoreside friends to whom this very thing has happened. I met a guy in Florida who was building his own boat and making all the bunks 5 feet 8 inches long because his son-in-law, a strapping lad who had just moved with his bride back into dad-in-law's house, was 6 feet tall. I'm not sure if cruising is a good way to avoid this sort of thing (assuming it's something you want to avoid), but I do think that a small boat in a big ocean might have less appeal to clingy offspring than the posh family homestead.

Sabbatical cruisers

Susan and I have met a lot of cruisers who have interesting and rewarding careers ashore that they have no intention of abandoning or even neglecting long enough to do anything as frivolous as casting off on a sailboat for the rest of their lives. But they do have a powerful urge to experience the romance and adventure of a high-seas voyage. They want something more than a few weeks or months in the tropics, but they don't want to devote their lives to living on a boat. Most of these temporary cruisers are in the fortunate position of being able to take off for a few years while they sail around the world, do the Intracoastal Waterway or the Inland Passage, or just sail away from the world of cell phones and traffic jams long enough for the steam to evaporate from their pressure-cooker lives. Tenured professors are naturals for this type of cruising, of course, but we have also met successful physicians, stockbrokers, and business consultants. The typical cruisers in this category have a lot of money and influential positions where they can dictate their own terms and return to a life pretty much as they left it. While we may admire or even envy these cruisers, most of us cannot emulate them, so we'll give them a friendly wave as they blast by in their Deerfoots and their Hinckleys, then return to our task of forging an interesting life on a somewhat smaller anvil.

The ultrarich cruiser

The next rung up on the socioeconomic cruising ladder takes us to the truly absurd level of the ultrarich cruiser. Typically, these cruisers own huge boats manned by professional crew who sail the boat to whatever port the owner dictates, then the owner flies in to do some "cruising."

The ultrarich owner is often a celebrity, like William F. Buckley, or the head of a large corporation. Fans of Buckley know him as an avid sailor and have read *Airborne,* his account of his circumnavigation on his schooner *Cyrano.* That he was able to complete the trip without interrupting his busy TV and editorial schedule is quite remarkable, but I doubt if he could have done it without his crew.

We have met a surprising number of ultrarich cruisers in the course of our travels. I recall a large motor yacht with a full-time husband-and-wife crew anchored in Honduras awaiting the arrival of an owner who had invented a popular type of charcoal grill, and a huge catamaran that we first met in the Marquesas belonging to the owner of a large restaurant chain. One of the biggest and loveliest private yachts that we've encountered was a 160-foot three-master that belonged to the owner of a huge running-shoe company (no, not *that* running-shoe company—the other one) and manned by a full-time crew of four young Kiwis.

Working cruisers

What about those of us who don't want to wait until we retire to go cruising, are unencumbered by a business or family fortune, or haven't invented a computer chip or heart valve that will produce enough royalties to pay the way? In other words, what about most of us? Well, the working cruise is an attractive option for a lot of people, so let's take a look at it.

The working cruise is best defined as a work-as-you-go cruise where the cruisers sail into an attractive port, make semipermanent liveaboard arrangements for the boat, then seek employment ashore. This sort of arrangement is often the best option for younger people who don't have children, who don't have a good start on a large kitty, and who don't want to wait around long enough to accumulate one. It also appeals to highly trained professionals with high-demand skills that are easily marketed in diverse locations. Most of the people we met in this category had engineering backgrounds (civil, structural, electrical, and even agricultural), but we also met diesel mechanics, welders, computer programmers, teachers, and, in Pago Pago, we met a young cruiser who was working as an airline pilot.

Short-term cruisers

Many people, of course, yearn to cruise but don't want to or can't make it a lifetime commitment, and lack the resources of sabbatical cruisers. For these cruisers, working for 5 to 10 years to accumulate a kitty is not an attractive option. They want to do more than coastal cruising on weekends and holidays and can save or borrow enough for a one- or two-year cruise. We have met many cruisers who are doing just that. Quite a few of these people just quit their jobs, went sailing, and then went job hunting when the kitty ran dry. This tactic works particularly well for professionals such as computer programmers and engineers; for people between jobs; and for self-employed individuals—particularly those in the building trades.

Borrowing money, often as a mortgage on the family home, seems to be the most popular option among short-term cruisers. Then, after the money is gone, they go back to work to pay for the cruise. Although many people get to go cruising quickly by borrowing money, I constantly argue against doing so. Borrowing money to finance a cruise is financial lunacy and a good way to wreck your life. I'll talk more about this later, but for now keep foremost in your mind that, if you want to go cruising, work first, cruise later.

Unemployed cruisers

I wouldn't bother to mention these cruisers except that we have met several who were collecting unemployment benefits while cruising. On the Okeechobee River adjacent to the Everglades we met a young man on a 27-foot sloop who claimed to be cruising the East Coast and entirely financing his trip with an emotional disability benefit from social security. He was a bit emaciated and the boat was a long way from being a nautical showplace, but otherwise he seemed to be doing fine.

On the island of Aitutaki in the Cook Islands, we met another young man who had lost his accounting job in Paris and was sailing around the world in his beautifully built 32-foot steel cutter on the two years of full unemployment compensation offered by his government. To top that, the unemployment agency deposited his monthly check directly into his bank for him. Now that's what I call benefits.

Noncruising cruisers

A lot of people are cruising through life, living a low-impact existence, getting by the best they can on what they have without credit cards or fancy cars, with naught but a kind word for their fellow travelers and a helping hand for the less fortunate souls they meet. These are people who embody all of the very best attributes found in cruisers but don't know the first thing about boats, and have no interest in learning about them. Perhaps you are lucky enough to know a few of these lifestyle cruisers. I'm lucky enough to know several—in fact, there are a few in my family and they are among the most valuable of my friends.

My good pal Jerry has lived his entire life as an educator without regard to material gain or self-aggrandizement, and in 30-odd years has never failed me when I needed a helping hand or a kind word. A list of Jerry's friends would be longer than the phone book for many cities.

Another cruiser without a boat is my brother-in-law, Eddy. Many years ago, Eddy gave up the life of a union machinist to live in the woods and cut trees for a living just because he likes living in the woods and cutting trees. He lives year-round in a trailer far back in the Maine woods where moose nibble the vegetables in his garden and bears regularly feast from his garbage pit. But Eddy is not your average logger; he owns no giant log skidder of the kind that most loggers use to harvest thousands of board feet of lumber in a single day. He cuts his trees one at a time and transports the logs to the road in an old jeep. Most logging areas look like war zones once they are completely cut; when Eddy finishes a job in a forest, the deer and the squirrels hardly notice he was there. Eddy doesn't make a lot of money, but he makes enough to do what he wants to do the way he wants to do it.

The third member of my rogues' gallery is a hermit who lives with his parrots and dogs in a hollow log in the woods and eats nothing but Fruit Loops and chili. He is none other than my brother Clint, the most cruiserly cruiser of all the cruisers I know, on or off the water. He lives life wholly by his own standards, uninfluenced by the demands of a materialistic society. He doesn't really live in a hollow log—I just made that up—but he would be just as happy if he did.

Cruisers like you and me

One of the best ways to participate in the cruising life, and the one championed in this book, is to work your butt off while limiting your expenses over a long period of time so you can accumulate a cash reserve (the kitty) that you will invest in a judicious and profitable manner so that the return on the investment (and not the investment itself) will pay all or a substantial part of your cruising expenses. I'll talk much more about the care and feeding of the cruising kitty in chapter 6, but for now all that is required is a willingness to work hard, a few major and a lot of minor changes in your lifestyle, a slight shift in your value system, and time.

How long it will take to get you cruising depends on your earning power, your willingness to cut out frills, and your cruising requirements, but 5 to 10 years is a good average. Although this may seem like a long time, most successful cruisers I have talked to have spent about 10 years in the planning and preparation process. Naturally, this assumes that you will be young enough to enjoy the cruise once you accumulate your kitty. However, we did meet a man in South Carolina who was in his eighties when he started building his cruising boat. As I've said before: cruisers are optimists.

Common Traits of Successful Cruisers

The international cruising society is made up of a diverse and disparate group of colorful and stimulating people from all walks of life, from many countries, and from all social and economic strata—but we share several traits. Cruisers are

- optimists who view life as a stroll from the shade into the sun
- rainbow chasers and magic-bean buyers who often have unrealistic expectations of the worlds that are about to be conquered and the dragons that are about to be slain
- idealists who believe that life should be a little better than it is, and work to make it so
- fatalists who accept life as it comes, know that there are a few jokers in every deck, and realize that fate doesn't always deal a winning hand
- realists who know that someday the sun will set on the final anchorage and who can sail on to whatever comes next without regrets, remorse, or a glance at the wake
- loners who thrive on solitude and understand when another boat just wants to be left alone
- gregarious and friendly to a fault and always ready to dinghy for miles through a swamp on a rainy night to attend a potluck supper or to come to the aid of a fellow cruiser
- inclined to gossip like fishwives at every cruiser gathering (cruisers call it the coconut telegraph, and it is one of the most efficient grapevine communications systems on earth)
- suckers for a good sea story or yarn, and always ready to sail off in search of some rumored perfect harbor or pristine anchorage
- able to find the material for great stories in ordinary circumstances
- independent and self-reliant to a fault
- free-spirited (sometimes to the point of capriciousness)

Not all of these traits are positive, of course, but they are as much a part of cruising as rusty anchors and sunsets, and they combine to make life afloat a little more simple and basic than life ashore, to make it easier to accept the bad things that happen while emphasizing the good things, and to carry on into the storm when noncruisers come about and head for harbor. The fact that you are reading this book is evidence that you already have a few of these traits.

Cruising—the simple and basic life

There are vast differences between life ashore and life on a small boat. Life is simpler on a boat in that you are free from shoreside stresses, anxieties, and pressures wrought by the largely artificial environment we have constructed for ourselves above the tide line. Few cruisers worry about getting to work on time, almost none give a thought to the color of their power tie or fret about the stylishness of their new business suit, and it's been years since I have been caught in a traffic jam. The social and economic stratification endemic to most shoreside neighborhoods disappears when you move aboard and sail away, and those who live on actual boats are all in the same metaphorical boat regardless of wealth and position.

More subtle differences also exist. People on boats tend to be more friendly and open then when they are ashore. Often, they even allow themselves to be more vulnerable to disappointment and rejection. I have no way of knowing if cruising changes a person's personality or if it simply appeals to those with a certain disposition, but I suspect it is, like a good confection, a subtle blend of many ingredients that makes boat people more aware of their surroundings and more sensitive to the feelings of others than when they were house people. If these differences are small—tiny, really—then so be it. By its simplicity, life in the cruising community can be a bit closer to fundamental and real than any other way we can live; thus, it is just slightly closer to being human. And if that isn't a step in the right direction, then what is?

But, as in all things, you get what you pay for, and if the rewards of the cruising life are high then so too can be the price. Our nannie society provides cops, ambulances, hospitals, marriage counselors, and teachers for our children. We have grown to expect and even demand these things, and to expect our society to take care of us when we are ill or old or poor or crazy. But when we sail away we sail into a life where a kidney stone or a slip on the deck can be fatal, where exotic diseases and ignorance proliferate and where there are few schools or hospitals to correct or cure them. If we become ill or old or poor or crazy we are left to look after ourselves.

The shift to the cruising life can be traumatic. Ashore we live our lives according to schedules. We have schedules for our education, our career advancement, servicing the family car, and getting our hair cut. Afloat we live by the winds, the tides, and the seasons, and any attempt to schedule anything is frustrated. Ashore we have rules, regulations, laws, and nosy neighbors to monitor our behavior and keep us from doing things we ought not to do. But afloat, and especially in Third World countries where corruption, thievery, and chicanery are a part of everyday life, there are few laws and regulations, and our behavior is guided by our moral turpitude and our character. Ashore, when we want something we go to the store, whip out our credit card, and buy it. Afloat we agonize over every item that comes aboard: Do we really need it? Can we afford it? Will it do the job? Do we really need it? Is there room for it in the forepeak? Will it stand up to salt water? Do we really need it? Do we really . . . ?

Most of us are used to a pretty easy life—no, let's be realistic, most of us are as soft as wet bread. But the cruising life is a rigorous physical life with no Sunday football marathons and no daytime talk shows to fill the empty hours of sedentary days. Afloat, your feet are almost always your sole means of shoreside transportation. Cruisers walk a lot—to post offices, grocery stores, chandleries, boatyards, and laundromats. Recreation often means a game of volleyball on a beach, a brisk row around a harbor, or diving for dinner. Exercise and fresh air prevail in the cruising life, and obese cruisers are rare.

The constant physical activity and the reduction of stress and anxiety are important reasons why cruising is a healthy way to live, but there are other conditions intrinsic to the lifestyle that make it a healthy way to live. For one thing, cruisers tend to eat well. In most popular cruising locales fresh vegetables and fruits are readily available and cheap, and they are nearly always organic because the native farmers usually can't afford expensive fertilizers and pesticides. At the same time, beef, pork, and other red meat is scarce, expensive, and of poor quality; chicken or other fowl not killed and dressed on the spot is always suspect. Thus, a cruiser's diet usually drifts away from meat and shifts almost automatically to the more beneficial fruits and vegetables—a move that health professionals have been begging us to adopt for years. Many cruisers even become de facto vegetarians, not by intent but by default, as their diet gradually shifts from fat and sugar-laden foods to a healthier and more practical diet of natural foods.

If you think you would like to adopt the cruising life, you should start now to alter the way you think and live, to start becoming simple and basic in all things, and to learn to depend on no one but yourself and your family. I'll show you how you can alter a few of your basic beliefs and routines by making small and periodic adjustments in your lifestyle and attitude so you can avoid drastic and unsettling changes. The shift from the shoreside life to the cruising life can be a gradual but steady movement away from the objective world of material goods and status you will be leaving toward the more subjective world you will be entering. The transition is a lot easier than you think, and even if you never do go cruising, it will be one of the most rewarding things you have ever done.

The cruising life isn't for everyone. If you try it and don't like it, you are likely to not like it a lot. It's much better to be sitting at home wishing you were cruising than to be cruising wishing you were sitting at home, so before you head out on your adventure make sure that you are really a candidate for the cruising life and haven't just been listening to too many Jimmy Buffett records.

3

SHOULD YOU GO CRUISING?

"The sea is mother-death and she is a mighty female,

the one who wins, the one who sucks us all up."

–Anne Sexton

I f you try to think of the cruising life as a simple and basic way of living on the fringe of normal society rather than as an escape or departure from society, you'll be on the right track. If you realize from the beginning that cruising is a lot of work, that it is often scary and sometimes terrifying, but nearly always rewarding, you won't go too far wrong.

Start Now to Develop Your Plan for Departure

Schedules don't work in the cruising life, but you should establish a rough plan for your departure. After all, if you've read this far, you're serious about it. First, determine what type of cruiser (retired, working, short-term, or combination as described in chapter 2) you plan to become. Doing so will allow you to make a careful analysis of your financial resources and lead to a realistic estimate of how long it will take you to improve them enough to shove off. Modify your plan based on an honest assessment of your personal situation and that of anyone you expect to accompany you. Your age, health, responsibilities to children and other family members, your personal resolve and fears are all things to consider in addition to your ability to raise a fat kitty (see chapter 6).

Next—and this is extremely important—give considerable thought to the living standards you expect to maintain while cruising. We have met cruisers living on tattered old boats kept afloat with love and seizing wire, eating boiled noodles and rice three times a day, earning money any way they could, and loving every second of it. And we have met cruisers on floating palaces equipped with every modern convenience who never missed an opportunity to voice their displeasure with their boat, their surroundings, the guidebook, the port captain, and life in general. There is a very real and interesting correlation between the size and luxury of cruising boats and the inability of their crews to handle the cruising life.

I will discuss this irony a bit later, but for now if you think you want to try an austerity cruise, you have to realize beforehand what you are getting yourself into. Similarly, if you know you require a certain minimum lifestyle, and this applies to nearly all middle-aged and older cruisers (including your aging-but-able author), then make sure you are providing for enough of a financial cushion so you can achieve this lifestyle without worry or anguish. If you are forced by circumstance to live below your minimum standards, you run the risk of making yourself and those around you miserable and wrecking your cruise.

Once you have completed this initial assessment, you should be able to come up with a preliminary time for departure. If you don't have a substantial start on your kitty, or don't receive a retirement income or some other continuing cash flow and you are starting from zero, you can plan on about five years of hard work and lean living (more or less depending on your earning power and the living standards you expect).

Five years is long enough for most people who are serious about going cruising and not building their own boat to plan on getting underway—some can do it in as little as two years; others will require more time. The average seems to be closer to 10 years from the time the idea first takes hold to when the docklines are cast off, but this usually involves about five years of hemming and hawing. You are way past this stage or you wouldn't be reading this book. But beware: we have met more than one would-be cruiser who has spent a lifetime planning a cruise never taken. Don't let yourself become so engrossed in the planning process that you never leave.

Who Is Going with You?

For most married couples or those involved in some other permanent relationship, the decision about who you are going to cruise with is an easy one—you'll cruise with each other—and further discussion on the matter is moot. On the other hand, many otherwise sound relationships have ended when one partner wanted to go cruising so badly that the cruising life was more attractive than the continuation of the relationship. We have some good friends who faced this problem just before we left Marblehead. He wanted to go cruising and she wanted to move to the Berkshires and raise Saint Bernards. Today, he is cruising and she is in Chicago as an important executive with a huge multinational drug company (funny how some things work out), and they send each other cards at Christmas. It's a sad story, but when the desire to cruise is stronger than the desire to continue a relationship, it is much better to work things out early on than to suffer the agony of trying to dissolve a relationship while living on a boat.

Poor George

If you are single, but you would rather not try to sail alone, you are advised to find your cruising companion well in advance of the time you leave on your cruise. Consider the following tale.

When Susan and I were looking for a boat in which to pursue our dreams of the cruising life, we heard from many sources that Charlotte Amalie Harbor in the U.S. Virgin Islands was chock-full of cruising boats for sale at bargain prices, so I took a couple of days off and flew down to take a look. There were, indeed, dozens of boats on the market and I spent three days checking them out, but only one sticks in my mind.

It was a lovely CSY 44 of the older "walkover" type that had been rebuilt from Windex to worm shoe by professional boatwrights. She was owned by a man named George who had dreamed his whole life of cruising around the world. Unfortunately, his wife didn't share his dream, so they separated, and George sailed off alone looking for the sun and a new mate with whom to share his boat and his life. He dropped the hook in a small harbor on the back side of St. Thomas and began dating every single woman on the island. He advertised for female crew in all the cruising magazines and in the lonely hearts classified in every major city. He even answered an ad that read "Meet Hundreds of Lovely East European Women for Only 25 Bucks." Alas, either his standards (or, more likely, those of the ladies he met) were too high or his luck was bad, because after two years of diligent searching, George gave up and went home to his wife's geranium farm, leaving his for-sale boat as a memento of his failure.

The sad ending to this touching tail holds a simple lesson for all single men and women who yearn to cruise: the cruising life is ready-made for lovers and dreamers, but unless you really want to sail alone, select your cruising companions before you go, and then leave enough time before departure to get to know each other.

In our travels we have gotten to know many singlehanded cruisers, but we've met only one or two who were really happy about sailing alone. Off the top of my head, I can name four successful singlehanders whom I came to respect for their formidable sailing skills and strength of character. Two were men and two were women, but all four were remarkable people; three of the four would rather not have been sailing alone.

Singlehanding is romantic and exciting, but it is also dangerous. Of the five boats lost while *Sultana* was crossing the Pacific, two were singlehanders. And, of course, singlehanding, like bumblebees flying, is technically impossible. International conventions require a constant watch when sailing on the high seas, and singlehanders just can't provide one. Common sense and an instinct for self-preservation also require a constant watch in heavy-traffic areas, and singlehanders can't do that either.

If you get the impression that I'm not comfortable with singlehanded cruising, you're right.

Family cruising is the way to go

The overwhelming majority of successful cruisers we have met are married couples or family groups. Couples with small children are particularly good at adapting to the cruising life because, I think, with their focus instinctively on the welfare of their children they are motivated to make all the right decisions and choices. They tend to be much more cautious in choosing when and where to sail than do couples without children, and they are more careful with the kitty. All of these are factors that make for a happy and successful cruise.

Right after married couples with children in the hierarchy of cruising success stories come married couples without children, then unmarried couples who have known each other for a while, and finally come same-sex crews.

Mixed crews can be a disaster

Several years before we left on our cruise, a young woman friend from Boston came to me all aflutter with exciting news. She had accepted a position as cook on a 50-foot cruising yacht that was being moved from San Diego to Sydney. In addition to

Tiffany, the experienced but nonprofessional delivery crew would be made up of the owner's college-age son and two of his friends. It would be a dream cruise through the South Pacific with no time or budgetary constraints to detract from an entire sailing season of fun in the sun. I sent her off with best wishes and a smile, but if I had known then what I know now, I would have begged her not to go.

I heard through the grapevine that the cruise ended in disaster after only two months. It seems that all three of the lads had fallen madly in love with Tiffany and their rivalry for her favors came to a head in Papeete. Fisticuffs erupted, two of the lads were hauled off by the gendarmes, and the third went for a brief stay in the hospital. Tiffany flew home in tears, and the owner had to fly in a professional crew to complete the voyage.

Mixed crews can and do work very well—we have met several that were efficient and effective—but they seem to work best in a professional environment with a strong and resourceful captain at the helm.

Mixed crews made up of two cruising couples can also work, but here, too, there is a danger of discord. I haven't met any crews where two couples share the cost of a boat to go cruising, but I understand that the practice isn't uncommon and that it has a mixed level of success. I do, however, take every opportunity to talk to the crews and service people in the charter yacht industry, and these folks all have juicy tales about mixed-couple crews who embark as friends and return bitter enemies. Of course, boat charterers aren't cruisers (I'll discuss why later on), and though the lesson here is neither salient nor profound, it is clear: if you are contemplating a mixed-couple or mixed-sex cruise with other than family or life companion, be careful.

And Why Are You Going?

I never miss a chance to make the acquaintance of any cruiser who anchors within hailing distance of *Sultana*'s cockpit. As soon as the opportunity arises, and it always does, I'll ask him or her what it was that motivated the big jump from shoreside life to cruising, and the answers I get are as varied and fascinating as the cruisers themselves. Some have dreamed all their lives of sailing off on a boat to see the world, and many of them are living their dream on a vessel they built (and often designed) themselves, having spent 10 or even 20 years in the process. Others have sailed on impulse, having been shocked into a realization of their own mortality by a close call with a dangerous illness or the untimely death of a close friend. Probably the most common answer to my question, "Why did you do it?" is this: "When I turned 40, I realized I wasn't going to live forever, and that there was a lot more to living than sitting at a desk shuffling papers."

Many others, however, honestly don't know the answer to this most basic question. "I often wonder about that myself," is the usual response, while others seem to have never thought about it. To them cruising is something that they just had to do so they did it.

I think there is a romantic notion that many people go cruising for the same reasons that people used to join the Foreign Legion or seek solace in the bottom of a whiskey bottle—to escape a troubled life or the heartbreak of a lost love. This is nonsense, of course, and I have yet to meet a successful cruiser who is cruising to avoid some unpleasantness. Cruisers are seekers, not runners. Nearly everyone I talk to is looking for something, not running away from it—a fuller life, perhaps, or adventure, or the infectious camaraderie of the high seas. But often the reason people give is even more mundane: they cruise simply because they love boats and sailing; others cruise just to see the world. There are hundreds of good reasons for choosing the cruising life; let's review a few of them.

It's an option to the rat race

Cruising full time is one of the last great options to the pressures and influences of modern society. That doesn't mean that cruising doesn't come with its own pressures and anxiety-inducing situations, but it is fascinating to see how many cruisers come from high-intensity business careers or from law practices or the advertising industry. Wherever cruisers congregate you will find a lot of people who led Type-A lives ashore: doctors, lawyers, dentists, accountants, computer programmers, stockbrokers, and writers—lots of writers. To many of these formerly highly paid denizens of the pressure cooker, the laid-back easygoing pace of the cruising life is a welcome relief; it can even be a lifesaver. We've met several cruisers who gave up their frantic lifestyles on their doctors' orders, and I've often heard the comment, "I hadda get away from sales (marketing, advertising, Wall Street, Fleet Street, etc.)" or "The doc said my blood pressure was going to do me in for sure."

That said, there seems to be plenty of room for the Type-A personality in the cruising community. Many cruisers are sailing on schedules—indeed, many people can't seem to get by without them. There are people frantically sailing from harbor to harbor trying to see as many places as possible within some arbitrarily established time frame, and there are others, a lot actually, who are sailing around the world in a year or two. Some need to get back to jobs before their leave of absence or sabbatical expires, while others need to get home before their welfare runs out (really), and others are doing it just for the challenge of beating the clock. But even the most frantic Type-A, if exposed to the cruising life long enough, will gradually and painfully come to endorse the mañana principle—that pervasive and universal belief among residents of the tropics that there is nothing so important that it can't wait until tomorrow—and learn to stop and smell the banana blossoms, kick back, and relax.

Cruising is a cheap way to see the world

Modern men and women are great travelers, and the tourist industry is one of the largest service industries we have. Thousands of workers look forward to their week or two in the sun on the beaches of the Caribbean every year, cruise liners attract thousands of others, and organized groups travel to the ancient cities in Greece, Egypt, and Israel or to the great capitals of Europe. Lately, the concepts of adventure travel and ecotourism have taken hold, and we find dental assistants from Vancouver digging Inca artifacts in the mountains of Peru and schoolteachers from Dallas studying pelagic fishes in the Bering Sea.

But these activities are expensive, and for many of us a week in Acapulco isn't enough to satisfy a yearning for adventure and faraway places. Bora Bora, in French Polynesia, was one of the loveliest places *Sultana* visited on her voyage across the Pacific, and we stayed there nearly a month, scuba diving, snorkeling in the lagoons, and hiking and bicycling around the island. It was easy to imagine the gloom of those who save and then spend thousands of dollars to get there, only to have to return home shortly after recovering from jet lag.

Many places aren't accessible to even the most dedicated tourist. The outer islands of the Marqueses in French Polynesia, and the Kermadecs that lie between Tonga and New Zealand, aren't served by the normal tourist industry and can only be reached by horribly expensive special charter or by cruising sailboat. And even places closer to the U.S., like Colombia's lovely San Andres Island (about 300 miles north of Panama) and the uninhabited and desolate Vivarillio Banks just off Cabo Gracios a Dios in Nicaragua, aren't readily accessible to American tourists. San Andres is a favorite destination of tourists from Colombia and other South American countries, but to get there from North America you must first fly to Bogotá. The Vivarillio Banks are two days against the wind from the Bay Islands of Honduras, and none but the cruisers and shrimp boats that use them for refuge ever get to see them.

Leisurely voyaging by boat is one of the few practical ways for those of us who aren't wealthy to travel the world, and it is one of the major reasons many of us give for adopting the cruising life.

The cruising life is adventurous

Who among us hasn't thrilled to the thought of trudging to the top of the Himalayas at the head of a column of trusty Sherpas? On a less vicarious level, adventure sports like parasailing and white-water rafting are attracting an ever-growing cadre of aficionados and participants, while mountain-bike racing and heli-skiing are attracting thousands of others. If you play by the rules and use your head, you can participate in these sports without undue risk to life or limb and still derive all the excitement that any normal person would ever want.

Many people love adventure, but real adventure is getting hard to find. Well, how about buying a boat and sailing around the world? Sure, thousands of people have done it, and sure, it's not even unusual any more, and sure, it's easier today than ever before and bound to get even easier, but ocean voyaging is still an adventure in every sense of the word. In fact, it's one of the last true adventures open to most of us.

It can even be dangerous if you want it to be

Did you ever wonder what attracts people to extreme sports like rock and ice climbing and base jumping? ("Base" is an acronym for Buildings, Antennae, Spans, Earth. It is an insane activity too extreme to be called a sport. To participate, one flings oneself off the tops of high places with nothing more than a parafoil to prevent oneself from splattering the landscape. It enjoys a casualty rate only slightly lower than the Normandy invasion.) Psychologists tell us that humans as a species (or at least many of us) seem to have a high requirement for risk and uncertainty in their lives, and many of us find participating in these ultrahazardous activities to be quite satisfying.

Anthropologist Ruth Benedict, a contemporary of Margaret Mead's, argued in her 1934 classic book *Patterns of Culture* that a society free of any dangers to its members will always find a way to inject it artificially—and she used several South Sea island cultures that were free from any natural danger as an example. They were isolated from any belligerent neighbors, had plenty to eat without having to work for it, and there were few dangerous or poisonous creatures to worry about. They compensated for this boring lack of natural peril in a unique manner:

they all had a shaman, or religious leader, who was empowered to sneak up behind anyone at any time and bash their brains out with a large ceremonial club.

A more pertinent example might be in New Zealand, which has constructed one of the safest societies on earth. Here too, there are no dangerous animals, and the islands' isolation has all but assured its safety from nearby enemies. New Zealanders enjoy lifelong security with free medical care for everyone and a welfare system that is one of the most generous on earth. "No worries, mate," could well be a national slogan rather than a beguiling bit of vernacular slang. Yet it is New Zealand that has developed and popularized many of the adrenaline sports mentioned above. Bungee jumping and base jumping were invented there, and rock climbing and mountaineering are developed to ever higher standards of difficulty on the icy slopes of the Southern Alps. In a one-week period, four young people jumped to their deaths from the tops of waterfalls after a popular soft drink distributor featured the "sport" in its TV ads. New Zealand is a safe place to live, but not entirely—many a proper and sedate New Zealander turns into an animal behind the wheel of a car, ensuring a horrific road toll. The automobile has become the New Zealander's sacred club and the fearsome accident rate is no more necessary that a shaman bashing in peoples' heads.

Although ocean voyaging is not in itself a dangerous undertaking, there's no denying that it offers elements of danger. Many of us have read the books and heard the stories of boats being sunk by whales or caught in typhoons and hurricanes or of crew lost overboard or of boats and crews that vanish without a trace—and that's not even counting the stories of attacks by pirates, desperadoes, loonies, and drug runners. Such tales are staple fare at any cruiser gathering. In fact, cruising is as dangerous or as safe as we want to make it. The cruising adrenaline freak will find plenty of thrills challenging the weather by sailing in the dangerous zones during cyclone and hurricane seasons or by treks into the roaring forties, the North Atlantic, or the South China Sea. Meanwhile, the rest of us can plod along following the established routes and staying well clear of the major weather systems, but even so we will experience enough thrills and chills, spiced with an occasional moment or two of stark terror, to ensure a ready supply of exciting stories for the folks back home. While I know of no cruiser who will intentionally put the boat in jeopardy, facing danger with impunity, even if it's only perceived danger, is a thrill from which few cruisers are immune—I know I'm not.

Cruising creates self-reliance and independence

If the absence of fear in the face of danger is stupidity, then courage is the ability to function in the face of fear. Self-reliance is the confidence in your own abilities to make the right decisions under adverse conditions tempered by fear. Millions of dollars each year are spent by corporations to send their executives to confidence-building courses where they learn to confront their fears by jumping off cliffs, swinging on ropes across ravines, handling frightening creatures (snakes and spiders and such), and performing other death-defying feats designed to make them better and more effective managers. Likewise, the Outward Bound program has trained thousands of youngsters and young adults to stand tall in the face of adversity simply by building faith in their own abilities and teaching them to handle their fears.

If you quail at the thought of heading out on a two-week passage on a blank piece of ocean where storms rage and there is no refuge outside the strength of your vessel and the determination of the crew, then join the club. Even lifelong cruisers experience a bit of trepidation and personal doubt in the face of a long and difficult passage. Is the boat ready? Did I check the masthead fittings? Are the spreader bolts tight? Do we have enough food? Is our safety gear in order? And the list goes on. There isn't a cruising skipper alive who gets a good night's sleep on the eve of a major departure.

But we go, and when landfall is made and the hook is buried in the mud, cruisers feel much more than a sense of relief that the passage is safely done. They enjoy a sense of accomplishment unlike any that noncruisers will ever experience. Long ocean passages in stormy conditions are challenging, true tests of courage, and genuine builders of self-confidence.

It's educational

Before we left Marblehead on our world cruise, I probably read about Vava'u at least a dozen times, but nothing I read really registered. I knew it was in Tonga, but I wasn't even sure where Tonga was located and I certainly didn't know how to pronounce Vava'u. Now having been there and spent a few memorable weeks sailing among some of the loveliest islands in the Pacific and having made friends among the inhabitants, I not only know where it is and how to pronounce the name, (say it with an adagio tempo as if it were three words like "How are you?"), but I know what the people are like, their religion, their language, their dress, their fears, and their ambitions. I know what they eat and how they live, and I'll never forget any of it.

Both my kids can tie a bowline with one hand, find any place on earth with a sextant and a watch, speak several languages, are accomplished divers, keen observers of the natural world, world-class sailors, and are miles ahead of many of their former classmates. But as proud as I am of their accomplishments, I can't brag because they are just average cruising kids. Except for those classes that require special facilities, such as music, physics, and science, cruising kids tend to be scholastically equal to or even ahead of kids ashore.

The educational potential of cruising just can't be denied. Children and adults both benefit by the simplest of actions. Just dropping anchor in a new and strange harbor, rowing ashore in the dinghy, and spending the afternoon in the port captain's office offers an enormous insight into the character and nature of the place you are visiting, and you'll learn whether you want to or not. The popular correspondence schools (Calvert and the University of Nebraska) do a fine job of keeping their students up to speed in the scholastic disciplines (readin' and writin') and all the other stuff just flows in. World travel offers educational opportunities that aren't available any other way.

Cruising fosters togetherness

An ancient bit of cruising wisdom says that if a couple (married or otherwise) can survive life together on a small boat, they can live together anywhere. I suppose it's true. Marital strife certainly isn't unknown in the cruising community—we've met several couples who have quit the cruising life and gone their separate ways. But the vast majority of cruising families that we have met will concede, without reservation, that they are much closer for the experience.

So if you are a fairly typical Mom or Pop working away at your job 40 or 50 hours a week, spending most of your spare time at the club, talking to your kids during the TV commercial breaks, and you think that there must be more to family life, then try cruising. Cruising, even weekend coastal cruising, is a genuine way of sharing your life with your spouse or children or others who cruise with you.

Cruising fosters friendship

We were tied up at the Marinatown Marina in Fort Myers, Florida, waiting for the weather to clear so we could continue our journey to Mexico via Key West, when Susan made one of her typically profound observations: "We've been cruising full-time for only six months and we've already met more interesting people than in the 10 years we lived in Marblehead." It was true—wonderfully, irrefutably true. Scoundrels and saints, rich and poor, black and white, we had met dozens of fascinating people in those few short months, and the more we cruise the more people we meet and the more friends we make. And please don't take this to mean that there aren't lots of interesting people in Marblehead. There are, but like most shoreside communities, folks are hard to meet and get to know if they are outside your own social circle. Among cruisers there is only one social circle—the one comprising cruisers.

A delightful camaraderie exists in the cruising community that attracts interesting and exciting people into a club that is at once exclusive and, at the same time, open to anyone who can follow the rules and pay the dues.

One of the basic concerns parents of young children have when contemplating a world cruise is the fear that their kids won't find enough friends in their age group to allow the normal socialization process that is such an important part of growing up. This was certainly one of our most pressing worries when Susan and I were planning our trip, and we agonized over it. We consulted educators and read everything we could on the subject, and it turned out to be a non-problem— Sarah and Phillip seldom were in a situation where there weren't plenty of kids around to provide all the companionship they needed. And we made another interesting discovery: in most neighborhoods ashore, kids tend to form cliques and exclusive groups of friends, but this doesn't seem to happen as much among cruising children. Also, age differences are less important at sea than they are ashore. Children raised on boats are often unusually mature and responsible. Phillip learned to start the 25-horsepower outboard on the inflatable at the age of 10 and could operate it so safely and responsibly by the time he was 12 that we had no compunctions about letting him take it to go exploring or to visit his friends.

Cruisers don't need formalities or introductions to make friends. If there is a potluck supper on the beach, all are welcome; if a boat drags anchor in the night and needs help getting off the mud bank, everyone pitches in to lend a hand; if an emergency arises and help is needed, it's only a VHF call away. Many of the popular anchorages, especially those in the Caribbean, have daily VHF nets so the entire fleet can stay in touch with each other and current on what is happening in the harbor. Newcomers are treated as friends from the day they arrive; by the second or third day they're almost family. If you are the kind of person who enjoys meeting people and making new friends, then cruising might be the life for you.

The cruising life is a spiritual life

No, cruisers don't tend to be more religious than other people. Some individuals do, of course, but when the cruising community is considered as a whole, the religious bell curve is probably skewed away from formal and organized churchly concerns. But when it's your watch at 2 A.M. and the sails are full with a favorable breeze and the stars look like they're close enough to touch and the gurgle of the wake is whispering, "all is well, all is well," it's hard to deny the feeling that there is a power, a benevolent watcher or guardian, if you will, that is making it so.

And when you're hove to 300 miles from nowhere with the wind screaming through the wires like a hellion on a leash and the waves are crashing on the deck and the crew is huddled on the floor of the cabin because even the strongest lee cloth won't keep them in a bunk, a great many cruisers report a feeling of peace and tranquillity that throws logic and reason into the face of dire circumstance.

Not many cruisers will admit to adopting the cruising lifestyle for spiritual reasons, but considering the frenzied life many of us leave ashore, I believe that the cruising life is much closer to the way the forces that created us, be they spiritual or natural, intended for us to live, and that living the way we were intended to live makes us much more sensitive to the presence of those forces. No, ocean voyaging won't do anything to convert the heathen, not this one anyway, but if the heathen is a spiritually aware person, that person will feel closer to The Great Navigator while cruising than at any other time or in any other activity.

The cruising life is a simple life

When we lived in Marblehead, Susan and I owned a large house in a good neighborhood, two cars, three or four TVs and VCRs, a computer, a garage full of power tools, a kitchen full of appliances, and our kids' playroom contained enough toys to fill an FAO Schwartz catalog. That we were living the good life, the American dream, was undeniable, but there was a basic problem: we were working so hard to earn the money to buy more stuff (and to pay for the stuff we had bought on credit) that we had little time to enjoy the stuff we already had. We certainly had little time for each other, and the care of our children was entrusted to a full-time nanny.

All that changed when Susan decided we should chuck it all and go cruising. Our transition from an average shoreside family to a decidedly below-average cruising family took a few years, and we encountered our share of adjustment trauma. We bought *Sultana* and moved aboard. We sold Susan's car and my beloved pickup truck and sold most of the rest of our worldly goods, stuff that we thought we couldn't live without, at my sister's yard sale. Treasured family heirlooms and things we couldn't bear to part with, such as my collection of books and Susan's china (she has enough plates to serve a small army at one sitting) went into a storage bin. Now our entertainment center consists of a tiny TV with a built-in tape player (which we use to watch educational videos and rental movies when they are available); we allow ourselves one backpack each into which all our clothing and personal effects must fit; all our tools fit into one locker under the pilothouse steps; and our small but efficient galley is a tiny fraction of the huge kitchen we left behind.

We didn't have a lot of money when we decided to buy a sailboat but we did have some savings, a lot of equity in our house (about $100,000 worth), and a retirement fund that would not be touched while we were cruising and that was adequate to ensure our survival through old age, however long it might be. When we left Marblehead, our primary income was from the rental of our house and a small portfolio of stocks and mutual funds (which at the time was worth about

$50,000). This left us with an annual income of about $20,000, which was about 25 percent of what we were accustomed to. It wasn't quite enough for us to live on, but we didn't know that until we had been cruising for about six months. We were lucky, however, because in spite of a drastic cutback in our material lives and a shortfall of cash, we were able to muster enough of our resources to get underway in only two years. If you already have a substantial kitty, you may be able to get going more quickly than we did, but more likely you are going to have to start from a smaller base with a five-year plan, as I'll discuss in the rest of this book.

Most people would consider the vast reduction we took in our material goods and living standards to be a huge and unacceptable reduction in our quality of life, but in fact it was just the opposite. Learning to live in a small space with as few material goods as are necessary to live comfortably can reorder your value system on a scale you never thought possible and thereby constitute a significant increase in your real standard of living. There is no question that the cruising life, at its best, is a simple and basic life that appeals to simple and basic people—people like you and me.

The cruising life is an economical way to live
The subject of what it actually costs to live on a boat while cruising is vastly misrepresented by the popular cruising and boating press, and the prime reason many new cruisers become disillusioned and abandon their cruising plans. I'll have a lot more to say about the economies of world cruising in following chapters, but for now it's enough to say that the cruising life can still be an economical way to live when compared with life ashore, and therefore remains one of the big reasons people do it.

The Nays
In spite of all the good reasons for adopting the cruising life, just a few of which are outlined above, we have met far too many people who have chosen the cruising life for the wrong reasons. Most often these cruises end in failure, the crew disillusioned and bitter. I won't spend a lot of time on this subject, but I would be remiss if I didn't mention at least a few of the most common wrong reasons people go cruising.

Cruising is not an escape
Cruising has an understandable appeal to people who are fed up with the lives they are living ashore and who long to escape to the simpler life afloat. I previously said that cruising is an important alternative to the stress and anxiety of modern society. However, it isn't a contradiction to say that cruising is not a way to flee from that life.

If you think that cruising is a way to escape a bad marriage, debts, addictions, the county sheriff, injustice, or a life that isn't going just the way you think it ought to be going, think again. If your life has reached a dead end or you face what seem like insurmountable problems and you are looking to the cruising life for salvation, it is critical that you confront and resolve the conditions that are causing your problems *before* you depart. These problems, whatever their complexity and nature, won't go away, and will, in fact, be much more expensive and difficult to handle from a cruising boat than from shore. Often, simply acknowledging your circumstances will carry you more than halfway to a resolution and halfway to the day you can depart on your cruise with a free mind and clear conscience. In addition, by learning to look your problems right in the eye without blinking will strengthen your already strong character—and strength of character is one of the most important cruiserly attributes.

Cruising isn't a way to find happiness

This one is easy. If you are miserable and unhappy ashore, it is likely that you will be even more miserable and unhappy afloat. The advice here is the same as above: you must deal with the conditions that are causing your misery before you depart. Whenever I offer this bit of wisdom in a group, someone always asks, "What if I'm just unhappy because I'm not cruising?" My answer is always the same. Contentment (a better word than happiness) comes from introspection, not from external circumstances. The belief that your lack of happiness stems from the fact that you're not cruising (or not wealthy or not a rock/sports/movie star or not whatever) is a mask for a more profound spiritual need that you must discover before you can ever be at peace with yourself. Find it and you'll find contentment whatever your external circumstances.

Cruising is not a way of dropping out of society

Actually, it is much more common to find disgruntled escapees from industrialized societies among the community of expatriates that inhabit many of the most popular cruising stops, but once in a while you will find one on a cruising boat. The reason for leaving is always the same: "I just got sick to death of greed and corruption and commercialism." So saying, they move to a place like Panama where greed, corruption, and commercialism are so deeply entrenched they comprise the very fabric of society. There are many expats who live in foreign countries for the excitement and adventure that it offers, but the malcontents, be they ashore or on a boat, tend to be a sad and bitter lot eaten alive by resentments and anger at demons they can only vaguely identify. If you find yourself with this sort of burden, deal with it first, then reward yourself with a world cruise.

Cruising isn't a way to find romance

It is surprising how many singlehanders we have met who are looking for a cruising companion. And although there are many wonderful and heartwarming stories of happy couples who meet while cruising, the sad fact is that the odds are against it happening. Nothing can describe the joy of cruising with a like-minded companion, but you'll be a lot better off if you can find that companion before you leave home.

Cruising isn't a way to fulfill a hyperactive ego

My definition of an egotist is anyone who is motivated by the desire to convince others that he or she is as wonderful as they think they are. Fortunately, cruising egotists are not too common, but you will run into one from time to time, usually in a waterfront bar regaling the regulars with tales of their derring-do on the high seas, or at the chart table busily writing press releases of the same to the hometown newspapers. Of course, there's nothing wrong with telling tales in bars—it's an important part of the cruising heritage—and an occasional press release and photo sent to the local news is a good way to keep the folks back home informed of the progress of your trip, but cruising egotists overdo it and are oblivious to the fact that many in their audience have done the same thing, only better, and the rest don't really give a damn.

Count your blessings

This one is tough to verbalize, but I'll try. If you have a good job and work that you enjoy, if you have a family and friends to look after and who look after you in return, and if you enjoy good health and the prospects for a long life, yet you find conventional existence slightly boring, don't turn to cruising as a solace to your ennui.

The holding is always better in the next harbor, the water is always cleaner, the palm trees are always shadier, and the beaches are always whiter and sandier, but you must first learn to appreciate the harbor you are in, before moving on to the next one will have any meaning. Boredom often comes with familiarity; it is synonymous with comfort. We who seek white sand beaches and palm trees swaying in gentle breezes can quickly become immune to the charms of the tropics, and after three years of subtropical cruising, I long for a frosty nose and the zing of my ski edges as they find an icy patch that signals I am about to be flung headlong into the nearest snow drift.

Before you can cruise with any degree of success, you must develop the habit of appreciating the good things that are yours now and learn to make the best of them. The joys of the cruising life are only obvious to those who can compare them with the joys of shoreside life. If you attempt to compare the pleasures of one lifestyle with the horrors of the other, you will find yourself wallowing in a trough of self-delusion, and you may be shocked when, one day, you realize that the true joys of the cruising life and of the shoreside life are one and the same—they are the joys of life itself, and you don't need a boat to find them.

And the Nay Nays

There are lots of reasons not to go cruising, the very best of which is that you just don't want to. As hard as it is for cruisers and would-be cruisers to understand, a lot of folks don't have any interest in setting off in a sailboat. And except for the fairly frequent (and always unfortunate) situation where a spouse is coerced into going along by a determined husband or wife, cruising is optional for all of us. However, there are a few good reasons not to go cruising even if you think it is what you really want to do. Here are some of the more important ones.

Cruising can be dangerous

Hold on there! Didn't we just list the aura of risk that's inherent in ocean voyaging as satisfying a perverse human requirement for danger, and therefore being a reason why some of us adopt the lifestyle? Yes, we did, and we're listing it here as a argument *not* to go for the same reason. Everyone has personal limits and, although some of us can handle a great deal of uncertainty in our lives—even thrive on it perhaps—others can't handle any at all. Cruising is a safe way to spend your life, but it's not as safe as staying home, and you are bound to encounter extraordinary circumstances that risk your life, health, and property. Unless you can accept the consequences of that risk, you probably shouldn't go cruising.

Cruising is expensive

Cruising doesn't require a lot of money, but it does require that you maintain yourself and your boat in presentable condition and that you not depend on the generosity of other cruisers for sustenance. It also requires a reasonable cash reserve for insurance against unforeseen expense and emergencies. If you are used to a comparatively lavish lifestyle, as were Susan and I, and you intend to reduce your standard of living, you must realize before you leave just what you are getting yourself into. Cruising on a budget can mean many sacrifices in material wealth, comfort, and security. The amount of money you will need for a comfortable cruise depends on your lifestyle and expectations, and I will try to help you determine how much that is in the following chapters. But for now, know that if you don't want to make those necessary sacrifices or if you don't have enough money to pay your own way, don't go cruising until you do. The large—and delightful—contingent of ragtag cruisers living from hand to mouth is unfortunately decreasing as the cost and popularity of cruising increases.

Cruising requires good mental and physical health
The cruising life is a physical and strenuous life; unless you enjoy robust good health, don't go. Even more important than your physical condition, though, is your emotional outlook. If you are a gloomy person by nature or if you are prone to neuroses and phobias that you can't control, you probably shouldn't go.

Cruising is a team effort
There is no way that the cruising life is as important as a sound relationship with your spouse or other life companion. If you are involved in a committed relationship with another person and that person doesn't share your enthusiasm for adventure on the high seas, don't go. In our travels we have met many cruisers who were going along for the ride just to keep their partner (usually, but not always, a husband) happy, with the inevitable result that the cruise isn't satisfactory for either. This is a major problem with cruising couples. I don't have any hard data to prove it, but I suspect that this lopsided enthusiasm for the cruising life is second only to finances as a cause of failed cruises, and it is certainly a major cause in failed marriages among cruisers.

Plan your cruise as a search for something you don't have but need—adventure, independence, broad perspective, understanding, spirituality, compassion, and time shared with those who care about you the most are a few good ones. Those who cruise to escape are doomed to fail because troubles follow like shadows that won't be dimmed by the miles—sail toward your goal; never sail away from anything.

4

THE DECISION TO GO

"I'd rather be sorry for something I've done

than for something that I didn't do."

–Kris Kristofferson, "I'd Rather Be Sorry"

Two Paths Up the Same Mountain

The decision to go cruising is a personal one that everyone approaches in different ways. I have known people who have dreamed of and prepared for the cruising life since they were teenagers. They acquire an encyclopedic knowledge of boats and designers and can quote statistic after statistic on gross weight to ballast ratios, sail areas, construction specs, and sailing performance. They spend their entire lives preparing to go cruising, and some of them actually make it. With others it is almost an impulse as simple as buying a new pair of shoes or stopping in to see Aunt Bessy because you happen to be in the neighborhood. For Susan, the decision was easy—she just decided that was what she wanted, and that was that. For me, the decision was a little harder. This is how it happened with us.

Mack Jellen and Haggar the Horrible

The four of us were sitting around the kitchen table one Sunday after church sharing the funnies from the *Boston Globe* as we ate a late lunch. I was halfway through "Haggar the Horrible" when Susan dropped a small bomb.

"I think we should buy a sailboat and sail around the world," she said without looking up from the gossip column in the magazine supplement.

I choked, and the resulting cough splattered coffee across the table and soaked the funny papers.

"You OK?" asked Susan.

"Yeah . . . choke . . . hack . . . yeah. I just thought I heard you say we should buy a new boat and sail around the world."

"You did. I've been thinking about it for a long time and I've read a few books on ocean cruising. You know how we enjoy our summer cruises in *Duchess* [the antique 38-foot powerboat we owned at the time]. It would kill me to part with her, but we could trade her in on a sailboat and do some real cruising. I think it would be very educational for the children."

"It would be educational all right. They'd learn how to perish in the ocean."

"I think sailing around the world would be a great idea," said Sarah, who was 10.

"Yeah, me too," said Phillip who was eight. "But it would probably take all summer."

"Didn't you guys see *Jaws*?" I asked trying to inject an element of reason into the conversation. "There are some big creatures out there that just love to take large bites out of small children."

"Your father is just being negative," said Susan. "There is no reason we couldn't sail around the world if we wanted to. Lots of people do it."

"Lots of people don't do it," I countered. "They think about doing it but most come to their senses and enroll in art classes or take up bridge or something sensible. The few that do it don't have kids in school and have tons of money they want to get rid of. You might have noticed that excessive wealth isn't one of our current problems."

"Mack Jellen did it," said Phillip. "We read about him in school, and I bet he had lots of kids."

"That's Magellan," said Susan, "and you're right. He was the first person to sail around the world."

"Yeah, but he got eaten by cannibals. How'd you like to be the main course at some cannibal luau?"

"Sir Francis Drake did it too and he didn't get eaten," said Sarah. "He got knighted."

"What he got was lucky. They would have eaten him if they had been able to catch him."

"Look," said Susan, "this is a serious discussion. If you don't want to participate, at least don't make fun of what the rest of us have to say."

"Right," I said properly chastised. "There are lots of serious reasons why we can't sail around the world."

"OK smarty, name one, just one, and don't say we'll get eaten by cannibals."

"I won't name just one, I'll name a bunch and you can take your pick. For one thing, a cruising boat big enough for the four of us would cost more than this house. For another thing, we couldn't afford it even if we did have a boat. It cost a fortune just to sail around Cape Cod, think what it would cost to sail around the world.

"And how about the kids' education? You can't snatch Sarah and Phillip out of school just like that." (Here I snapped my fingers in the air for dramatic emphasis while basking in the inner glow of my own glib logic.) "You don't want them to grow up illiterate any more than I do. I know . . . I know . . . you'll say we can educate them on the boat, but we're not teachers, and kids need other kids around. It's called socialization and without it they'll grow up to be socially deprived, reclusive misanthropes. They won't be able to get jobs, and they'll spend their lives as beachcombers or on welfare. Do you want our kids to be misanthropes?" I paused a moment to let the power of my argument sink in.

"Hurumph," said Susan.

"And what about me? It would take years to sail around the world. I'd be an old man when we got back. I'm too young to be an old man."

"Double hurumph. You're already an old fart."

"Tut . . . tut . . . no personal attacks, remember? This is a serious discussion." I decided to change the focus of my argument from the subjective to the objective. "What about all this stuff we own? We have a responsibility to our possessions, you know. Do you realize we own five TV sets, three VCRs, two cars, a state-of-the-art stereo, hundreds of CDs, two video game machines, two computers, and an electronic coffee pot with a built-in AM/FM radio? Who would take care of all that stuff if we sailed around the world?"

"Yard sale," said Susan without looking up.

"You mean you'd sell my Jimmy Buffett tapes?"

"Not all of them. You can take a few with you if you like."

"Gee, thanks, and what about the cat? I suppose you plan to sell poor Mr. Cat, or are you just going to mosey over to the neighbors and say 'Would you mind watching poor Mr. Cat while we sail around the world? We'll only be gone about five years.'"

Susan looked up from her magazine, closed one eye and glared at me with the other like a sniper sighting a target. I moved on quickly, spoiling her aim and preserving the spotless luster of my argument.

"And what about our commitments? I promised Bernie Shultz that I'd install a teak deck on his new boat by spring. You have your job—you just can't quit after 20 years, ya know—and Sarah has her music lessons. You wouldn't want her to walk out on Beethoven just when she's about to conquer 'The Moonlight Sonata,' would you?"

"How many reasons is that? Six or seven? I've lost count, but there is one more biggie: it's irresponsible. Responsible people don't just chuck everything and sail off on a boat." I paused again, leaving Susan speechless in the wake of my verbal juggernaut before returning to "Haggar the Horrible." I began cleaning the coffee from the last few frames.

After a lengthy and pregnant silence, Susan said, "Just as I thought."

"What's that?"

"Not one good reason."

I knew that further discussion was futile, and I retreated behind the privacy screen of the funny papers. The last frame showed poor Haggar, his eyes blackened and teeth missing, standing in the doorway, all shot full of arrows and spears with a large battle ax embedded in his helmet. "It's just been one of those days," he says to Helga.

"I know how ya feel, pal," I muttered. "I know how ya feel."

Dick and the flying meatloaf

By that Wednesday the subject of world cruising had largely been forgotten as I drove over to pick up Dick Welsh, a longtime friend with whom I had a standing weekly lunch date. We usually went to Dube's Bar and Grill in Swampscott where the meatloaf-and-mashed-potato special would curl your toes—if any of it ever got past your waistline. We talked of many things at these lunches: the moods of women, the philosophies of man, and the mysteries of life were all popular subjects, but mostly we talked about boats. Dick has been a sailor all his life, possesses an incredible storehouse of nautical know-how, and had for years been planning to sell everything he owns and become a full-time cruiser when he retired. (Dick left Marblehead on his 32-foot sloop, *Real Gusto,* one year after we did and is now somewhere in the Caribbean.)

Dube's is one of those dark, comfortable neighborhood bars that smells of cigarettes and stale grease, where the TV and air conditioner are always turned up too high, and that sports a few regulars who don't seem to change from the 8 A.M. opening to the 1 A.M. closing. Molly, the waitress, was waiting with our coffees as we took our seats at our regular booth in the back corner, and when she spilled a little on the table it reminded me of the exchange with Susan the previous Sunday.

"Susan wants to sail around the world," I said, just to get the conversation off on a nautical note.

"Great," bellowed Dick slamming the table with the flat of his hand hard enough to make the cutlery jump an inch and slop more coffee into the saucers. "That's terrific news. When do you plan to leave?"

Dick is a large man without any fat anywhere. He was a linebacker for the Holy Cross football team, looks like he could still handle the job, and habitually expresses himself with sometimes startling physical gestures. He is also a bit hard of hearing, and it is necessary to speak loudly and clearly for him to understand what you are saying. Like many partially deaf people, he reciprocates by talking very loudly himself. The staff and regulars at Dube's were quite accustomed to being included in our most intimate and personal conversations.

The service at Dube's is amazingly fast, and I paused as Molly placed our orders on the table.

"I don't think Susan is serious, Dick. As soon as she sees how complicated it is, she'll forget full-time cruising. After all, people don't just quit their jobs in the prime of their lives and go sailing off around the world."

Wham! went the hand on the table, up jumped the cutlery—this time accompanied by my meatloaf and mashed potatoes. A quick stab with my fork speared the meatloaf in midair, but the mashed potatoes landed with a plop on top of my green beans.

"Of course they do," he shouted. "They do it all the time." Every head in the bar swiveled in our direction. "Lemmy ask you this," and he lowered his voice to that of a drill sergeant addressing first-day recruits. "Have you ever heard of any guy on his deathbed say, 'I should have worked harder?'"

"No . . . no I haven't," I admitted.

"And what's the worst thing that could happen to you?"

"Well, my editor cuts out all my best jokes because she thinks they're silly. I really hate that."

"No, worse than that."

"Susan finds out about that crazy brunette over at the yacht club who keeps asking me to crew for her?"

"Nope, worse."

"What could be worse than that?"

"Only one thing."

"Well, I suppose I might get sick and die. That's the only thing worse than Susan finding out about that brunette."

"Right. And what's going to happen to you in the long run anyway?"

"You mean in the really big-time, long-term long run?"

"Right."

"Well, I suppose I'm gonna get sick and die."

"RIGHT." Bam went the hand, up jumped the silverware and my meat loaf. This time the mashed potatoes were a total loss. "So why in hell don't you just go sailing with Susan and the kids?"

"Yeah, man, go for it," said the drunk in front of the TV.

"You know, you really shouldn't let the children miss an opportunity like this," said Molly as she mopped up the remains of my mashed potatoes.

"Ya gotta do it," said Ralph, the bartender.

Traffic jams and the voice of reason

Several months came and went without further mention of world cruising, although the Wednesday lunch with Dick always raised a few questions, and Susan seemed to be spending a lot of time reading boating books, of which the Marblehead Public Library and Dick seemed to have an inexhaustible supply. Then one cold winter day while returning from an errand in Boston, I found myself crawling along in the endless traffic jam that clogs the Callahan Tunnel and the road home. I glanced around at the expressions of rage and frustration on the faces in the cars near me and then let myself slip into a state of reverie and introspection that has for years been my first line of defense against traffic jams. I force my mind to empty itself of any idea of where I am going or when I must be there, let the car creep along with everyone else, and have a little chat with the voice in my head that always seems ready to discuss things profound and obscure. Some would say that I am talking to myself, but it is more than that. The Voice is real and can, at times, be a brilliant conversationalist. Our chats render me oblivious to the erratic meanderings of the cars in front and the mindless honking of the fools behind.

Occasionally I'll pop a Jimmy Buffett tape into the stereo, and the Voice and I will sing along as best we can. At other times we explore together the higher pastures of thought where our minds can graze on the new grass of fresh ideas. But not this day.

"Today," announced the Voice with that irritating sanctimonious tone it sometimes uses when it wants to lecture me, "we will discuss our future. It seems that you have squandered most of the first 50 years of our life. Let's see if we can save some of the 20 or so that we may, with luck, have left to us." The squandering of years gone by was a favorite topic of the Voice and not one to which I readily conceded.

"Can't we talk about politics?" I pleaded.

"Twenty years is quite a lot of time if we start now," said the Voice, ignoring my attempt to change the subject. "As I see it we have a choice between continuing to squander the time allowed us or we can spend that time in the pursuit of some useful goal. Which will it be?"

"Well, obviously, a useful goal is preferable."

"OK then," continued the Voice. "Let's consider what's available in the way of goals. You must agree that the ultimate goal, as our friend Dick pointed out just the other day, is death, correct?"

"Correct," I said. "However, we are talking about a goal for the remaining productive years of our life, and while death may be the ultimate end, it isn't a goal we should be working for, is it?"

"Of course not. Life, at best, is but a temporary inconvenience that passes quickly enough, and there is nothing to be gained by rushing it. No, our goal for the next 20 years must be life itself, but how best to spend that life? That's what we must deal with here."

This made me pause. The life that Susan and I had forged for ourselves was going as well as could be expected considering the numerous rocky places and two or three major washouts we had encountered in the matrimonial road. We had a comfortable home in a good neighborhood and the children seemed to be thriving. Marblehead is a major suburb of Boston but it retains a small-town quality that makes it an excellent place to raise kids.

"One thing's certain," I said. "Whatever goals we come up with must be group goals that include the entire family. In my misspent years, my goals were solitary ones selfishly motivated, and that is very hard on loved ones. So this time, let's make sure everyone is included from the start."

"Excellent," said the Voice. "Then it is resolved that our goals must be group goals. So what will these goals be?

"The goals of youth are nearly always selfish (as you well know) and revolve around an important job, a house in the 'burbs, two cars in the garage, and a TV with a bigger screen than the one on your neighbor's TV. In middle age, the usual goals are to achieve security in old age. The goals of old age are to somehow enjoy the fruits of previous goals realized.

"These are acquisitive, consumption-driven goals, and the problems with them are that, while they are highly stimulating to national and world economies, they can be hollow, superficial, and—once stripped of the mantle of materialism—meaningless. If you want proof that this is true, just look into the faces of your fellow traffic jammers. Their expressions of empty despair, which long ago transcended the quiet desperation of Thoreau, are a direct result of this mindless pursuit of valueless, materialistic goals."

The Voice can get unbearably preachy at times, but I glanced into my rearview mirror and, sure enough, the guy behind me in a snazzy new sedan didn't look any happier than the guy beside me in a battered old pickup.

"Which," continued the Voice, "leads us away from the objective goals of acquiring prestige and property to the subjective goals of acquiring knowledge and ideals. Thus the ultimate goal of life can't be security in old age, which is a ridiculous oxymoron, any more than it can be death. It must be the pursuit of truth and enlightenment. And since mankind is a social animal that cannot be happy alone, the search cannot be a solitary introspection but must be an external group effort of the family rather than the self."

"YES . . . YES," I shouted with excitement at the sudden realization that the Voice was right. "We will cast off the fetters of crass materialism and sally forth into the wilderness of worldliness in pursuit of truth, enlightenment, and the quality of life that has eluded mankind since Adam and Eve blew it in the Garden.

"But now we have the problem of how to best pursue this goal. It's one thing to say we're going off to seek the truth and enlightenment, but it's another thing to actually do it. I can see how we could easily get carried away with the whole Don

Quixote, King Arthur-and-the-Holy-Grail routine of tilting at windmills and chasing dragons."

"Must avoid that, by all means," said the Voice. "The first thing we'll need is a compact and mobile environment in which the family group can function during the trip."

"Sounds good," I answered. "First we create a collective environment wherein the group can pursue truth and enlightenment—figuratively speaking, of course."

"Well, actually . . . er, no. Not figuratively speaking at all. Actually . . . oh dear, I don't quite know how to put this."

"You mean we need an actual physical environment?"

"Quite so," said the Voice.

"But that makes no sense. Why would we need to create a physical environment for the merely metaphorical pursuit of truth and enlightenment?"

"Merely metaphorical? You really don't understand do you? A metaphorical pursuit of our goals would never do at all. We must pursue our quarry in the real world like a hound after a hare. We must depart on a great journey of discovery and enlightenment and track that rabbit of reality into its den—if necessary, to the very ends of the earth."

"You're starting to sound as crazy as Susan and Dick. You want me to dislodge my family from our comfortable home and go stumbling around looking for ambiguous qualities like Diogenes looking for an honest man? That's out of the question. I won't do it."

"Very well, then, that brings us back to the first option."

"Which is?"

"Squander what's left as we have squandered that which has gone before. Just be aware that you will rapidly become one of them."

"One of whom?"

"Look around you."

I looked at the drivers in the cars all around me. "No," I cried. "You wouldn't let me become one of them, would you? Please, anything but that."

"It may be too late, anyway," said the Voice. "Look at yourself sitting there babbling away at the top of your voice to no one at all. You've got that poor guy in the next car scared out of his wits."

"NO . . . NO, it can't be. I'm not one of them—I'm not. You win. I'll do it. I'll do anything. Just don't let me become one of them." As soon as I said it I felt better and the old euphoria flowed back over me like an ebbing wave returning to the beach.

"That's more like it," said the Voice.

"We'll need a van," I said, "a minivan big enough for the whole family. Or how about a camper—a Winnebago, maybe?"

"Won't do," said the Voice. "We must cross oceans to far continents and pursue our quarry where there are no roads."

"An airplane, then?"

"Too expensive."

"Camels—donkeys?"

"Too smelly."

"What then, for Pete's sake?"

"How about a boat?" said the Voice.

epiph·a·ny (i-'pif-ə-ne) *n., pl.* -nies.
3. a. A sudden manifestation of the essence
or meaning of something

Thus, Susan and I came to realize that while our life together in Marblehead was a good life, it wasn't particularly fulfilling or exciting for either of us, and we were ready to look for something better. The decision to go cruising was first made by Susan, and for her the decision was an easy one that was made practically on impulse. For me the decision was more painful and required much introspection and uncertainty. My slightly dramatized dialogue with the "Voice" of reason actually took place, as did many other conversations just like it. It was months before I was comfortable with the idea of full-time cruising. It was a year or more before the combined arguments of the "Voice" and Susan, with a lot of help from Dick, finally convinced me that, yeah, we could do this thing . . . we could really do it. Then, we were on our way and nothing was going to stop us; we had seen the light and were heading for it with the resolute tenacity of Hillary heading for the Himalayas. We had reached epiphany.

Epiphany is the word I use to describe the decision to go cruising wherein you discover that the cruising life is the life for you and you become a cruiser. It is a spiritual crossroads and it is the point at which you stop merely dreaming about going cruising and start working toward doing it. When you reach epiphany, cruising ceases to be something you would like to do and becomes something you must do.

Epiphany can come upon you as slowly as springtime in New England or as suddenly as a well-thrown brick; you must not rush it with hasty and ill-formed decisions, but you must be ready for it when it comes. It is an emotional catharsis, a cleansing and purifying of the soul that will be among the most important turning points of your life. It's crucial that the decision to go cruising be based on a sound analysis of your ability to handle the cruising life and not on daydreams and fantasies, but it is just as crucial that the big decisions be made before the onset of epiphany because, after it arrives, reason and judgment are unalterably changed forever.

You don't have to leave at epiphany if you don't feel ready, and you can keep working if you need to save more money for the kitty, but you must understand that once epiphany arrives, you will become a different person. You will become disdainful of your previous existence, and the beckoning call of the distant horizon will become irresistible.

One-sided epiphany

Susan and I are lucky. Although our going cruising was Susan's idea, once I came around to her way of thinking we were both equally committed to the cause, and our combined efforts and enthusiasm meant that we were able to get our lives in order and get under way in record time. Not all couples are this fortunate. In fact, I believe that a one-sided epiphany is the second most common cause of failed cruises—right behind finances (which we will discuss later).

We meet a lot of cruising couples where one half is a dedicated sailor and determined cruiser and the other half is going along to keep peace with the first half. Sometimes this works, but more often it doesn't, and what starts as mild discord deteriorates into bitter acrimony which eventually destroys the cruise. Contrary to my preconceptions, in many cases of one-sided epiphanies, the driving force behind the cruise is the woman, and the man has gone along either thinking that he will eventually come to terms with the cruising life or that she will eventually see the light and agree to go home. (I don't know why this surprises me, since Susan was the driving force behind our voyaging life.)

Rarely, however, does a reluctant partner turn into a gung-ho cruiser. In one particularly sad case, a couple with whom we had become close friends canceled their plans to sail around the world, put their lovely traditional ketch on the market, and headed home to Canada when he found he simply couldn't deal with the idea of long ocean passages.

Some couples resolve a one-sided epiphany with compromise. We met Heddy and Steve on *Clearwater II* on the Intracoastal Waterway and our paths crossed several times before we made the big jump to Mexico. Steve is an ex-helicopter pilot who, for a good part of his adult life, had dreamed of going cruising when he retired. Heddy, however, loved gardening (a hobby you definitely can't pursue on a boat) and couldn't have cared less about boats and cruising. But they did care about each other, so they agreed that they would buy a boat and cruise for a year or two, after which they would move ashore to a piece of waterfront property they owned. There he could have his boat and she could garden to her heart's content and they could both live to ripe old age in contentment and harmony. Let's hope so anyway.

In the shipyard in Ipswich, Massachusetts, I got to know another couple who cruised by compromise. They both loved to travel, but his life revolved around cruising sailboats (he owned a lovely Dutch-built steel sloop), while she preferred to travel in a more conventional manner—you know, airplanes and such. Over the years, they had worked out a system: he sailed singlehanded to a new and exotic destination, she flew to the same destination, checked into the best hotel in town, and was waiting on the dock when he pulled in. They had been doing this for years and they really couldn't imagine any better way to live.

What should you do if the specter of one-sided epiphany raises its ugly head in your cruising plans? First, remember that epiphany arrives, if it arrives at all, for different reasons and at different times for different people—as it did for Susan and me. Now I can't think of living any other way, and we plan to cruise at least 10 more years before we hang up our Topsiders and retire to that little cottage in the country. Will something like this happen in your case? Well, to employ a bit of hackneyed phraseology that is always appropriate: Who knows? Only time will tell, so hang in there, and don't give up the ship.

Don't Commit Yourself until You Have to Commit Yourself

Remember in chapter 1 when we talked about the large number of would-be cruisers who change their minds and decide not to go? It is critical that you realize early on that you, too, might be among that majority of people (99 percent by some estimates) who decide they might be happier if they stayed home. The arrival of epiphany can cause a lot of personal excitement, and you will want to announce your plans to the world. If you do, you will learn the hard way that most of the world doesn't care, and the rest will think you're nuts.

Susan and I were astonished at the yawns we received from boat brokers when we explained that we were looking for a boat in which to take our family on a world cruise. We quickly learned that people involved in the boating and cruising industry (especially boatbrokers and salespeople) had encountered so many unfulfilled plans about cruising around the world that most simply didn't believe us. We were unceremoniously relegated to that vast body of tire kickers who drive brokers crazy by looking at boats they have no intention of ever buying, so we simply stopped mentioning our plans. After a while we told everyone who would listen that we were looking for a sturdy vessel capable of extended offshore cruising and left it at that—a tactic that greatly extended the attention span of the brokers.

Talking about your plans with friends and casual acquaintances may be a way of gaining the courage to make a major change in your life, but it's the wrong way to do it. The courage to make the change must come from *within,* not from outside pressures of those who are expecting you to leave. You should not announce your decision to go cruising to any but those who will be involved and your family. If you or your companion decide not to go, you want to make it as easy as possible to back out right up to the last minute. The planning process should be a private celebration of joy to be shared only with those with whom you share your life.

The decision to sail must be a joint decision made by all who are involved. The trick is to understand from the start just what cruising is and to get your personal life sorted out before you commit yourself.

5

CRUISING WITHOUT A BOAT: MEET THE CRUISING KITTY

"Money is the route of all cruising."

−*Ancient cruising proverb*

1. You've had the epiphany and you're going to go cruising. You'll need money.
2. Cruising is a comparatively Spartan lifestyle, and it would serve you well to experience that lifestyle while there's still time to change your mind.
3. Voilà! Put #1 and #2 together and start living the cruising lifestyle while you're still at home. Practice doing without, and save money at the same time. Kill two birds with one stone.
4. If you ultimately decide NOT to cruise, you will have saved some money (always good) and perhaps simplified your life in positive ways.
5. But first—What's a "cruising kitty"?

Getting Gone

As the father of a teenage son who is addicted to the damn things, I am not particularly fond of video games, especially the ultraviolent ones that require no skills to operate and are pointless in their execution—you know, the popular ones. To me video games are in the same category as jet skis and ghetto blasters in that they serve no useful purpose other than the enrichment of a bunch of greedy people whom I don't even know and probably wouldn't like very much if I did. There is, however, one exception to my wholesale antipathy for electromagnetic entertainment: the spunky little guy with a mustache in the game called Super Mario (in any of its numerous manifestations).

Mario is a cruiser in every sense of the word. He spends his time bouncing happily through life visiting strange and diverse lands looking for adventure and excitement. He isn't out to cause any trouble or to inflict harm on anyone. He just wants to rescue the princess (I suspect he has his reasons) but nonetheless, he encounters the most amazing series of misfortunes. He is knocked down by strange creatures that look like ducks with turtle shells; he is blown up by mean little kids called goombas; he falls off cliffs with startling frequency; some ugly green guys throw hammers at him from a balloon passing overhead; he is forced to swim through an underwater labyrinth where he is pursued by sharks, electric eels, and poisonous fish; he is blasted by cannonballs; dumped into lava pits; and stomped on by a giant dog named Bowser. In short, saying that Mario is accident-prone is like saying that the Red Sox fade in the home stretch.

You would think that in the face of all this misfortune Mario would give it up and go home, but no. Mario is a true cruiser; adversity just makes him tougher. He learns to jump over the turtle ducks and to stomp on the mean little kids (they had it coming, folks). He dodges the cannonballs, outswims the sharks, leaps over the lava pits, and what he does to that dog gives new meaning to the word retribution. But the important thing isn't that Mario learns to handle tribulation, but how he does it.

Through all his troubles, Mario never once loses his good nature, his cool, or his sense of humor, nor does he complain that life isn't giving him a fair shake— not even once. When he gets kicked off a cliff, he bounces back with a big smile and the determination to avoid that particular cliff in the future; when he gets squashed by giant stone blocks 20 or 30 times in a row, he learns to develop his timing so he can run under them the next time; and when the dog stomps him into a mud hole and kicks him back to the beginning of the game, he runs the entire gauntlet all over again and then does it again and again until he finally wears the hostile hound to a nub.

Mario gets by with persistence, determination, and a lot of help from his friends: Yoshi, the dinosaur; Toad, the mushroom; and Luigi, his brother. All are fellow cruisers and are there to help out when he needs it the most. He learns by his mistakes and with everything he learns, he becomes smarter and more power-ful. Eventually he triumphs and rescues the princess. Together they go on to devel-op even bigger and better video games that further enrich the companies that sell them and further deplete the mental resources of the world's youth.

So what can you and I, normal folks who don't have to worry about mis-chievous goombas and homicidal turtle ducks but who would like to change our lives just enough to go cruising, learn from this hyperactive little Italian over-achiever? Lots of things. We can learn that keeping our goal, be it rescuing a princess or buying a sailboat, foremost in our mind at all times will calm the seas and flatten the hills more than any other thing we can do. We can learn that per-sistence in the face of adversity is critical to success and that failure is as much a part of success as codfish is a part of my Aunt Minnie's chowder.

Failure, the critical element
It sounds crazy to say that you have to fail to succeed, but this simple statement is one of life's truisms. If you can get a grip on this one concept more than any other in this book, you've just about got it made. Our hero, Mario, succeeds in rescuing the princess because he prevails over an immeasurable multitude of failures with-out letting them get him down. He might try a hundred times to make it over that lava pit only to make it across on the 101st try. Lava-pit leaping is something that probably none of us will be much good at on our first few tries, but if we let our

initial failures deter us we might as well let the princess rot in the dungeon and go home and watch "Brady Bunch" reruns. But Mario never gets discouraged. He doesn't say, "Aw shucks, that's 99 times I've been knocked into the fire, I'll never make it across this lava pit." Hell no, he doesn't. With a "tallyho Geronimo," he flings himself at the pit once again. When he blows it yet again he says, "Hey, this is great. That's one more failure closer to success," and has yet another go at it.

And so it is with your quest for the cruising life. Once you decide that you are going to do it you must consider each obstacle you encounter as an opportunity to advance toward your goal. If you try to stop smoking and don't make it the first time, try again. If you are on the way to paying off your credit card debt and freak out on a new stereo, don't let it get you down. Just keep making those payments and resolve to never let it happen again. Success and failure are like hot and cold. Both success and cold (called absolute zero by scientists) are the immeasurable and mostly unachievable ideals; heat and failure are the tangible and measurable stepping-stones to our goals. When the weather is bad we talk about how cold it is, but a thermometer measures only heat. In just the same way we measure the success of people by the failures they have overcome.

You're on Your Way

So now it's settled. You are going to become a cruiser. You have considered all the ramifications of a major change in your life and realize that you must proceed with the care of a bomb disposal squad and the determination of a thoroughbred on the home stretch. You are well aware that the cruising life on a budget is a difficult life fraught with toil, disappointments, hardships, and you are resolved to face them. You have reordered your priorities so that you can live the cruising life right now, even though you don't have a boat yet. You are living your life based on needs rather than wants—you are living the free-range life of a cruiser.

The free-range life

Have you noticed that free-range chickens and free-range eggs are all the rage these days? It's interesting how things come around—when I was a kid that's all we had. We didn't call them free-range, of course. We just called them chickens and eggs. The idea of buying either in a store would have seemed odd when we had a backyard full of the things. Today the distinction is made between the "new" free-range birds that are presumably allowed some degree of freedom and space to scratch and peck for food, the way chickens have been doing since the dawn of time, and the "normal" chickens that are raised in cages that are only slightly larger than the chickens. The chickens that we had when I was a kid had the freedom to go where they pleased, do what they pleased, and eat what they pleased. If they wanted to fly off into oblivion, as more than a few did, that was fine. If they wanted to go and get eaten by a fox or a bobcat or get themselves run over by the school bus, that was OK too. Most folks in our neighborhood considered losing a few chickens now and then far easier than trying to keep them in a coop.

The majority of the chickens, however, chose to stay in the backyard where they were provided with a first-rate chicken house with nesting boxes and wire on the windows to discourage all but the most persistent raccoons and skunks. In return for hanging around, they were also given a measure of grain every morning and evening, over which each chicken fought with every other chicken in the flock for its share. My first lesson in Darwinian survival came when I realized that the smaller and weaker chickens were the ones that ended up in the stewpot first just because they were the easiest for an eight-year-old boy to catch.

Cruisers are like free-range chickens in a lot of ways. No, we don't have to fight each other over scraps of food, but we have turned our backs on the chicken factory where we were warm and comfortable and fed regularly. We learned to become more confident in our own abilities and to rely on and trust our friends and family more than we did before we left on our cruise and if the price we pay for an increase in freedom is a chance encounter with a stoat or a skunk, so be it.

The Cruising Kitty

OK, so now you've got everything you require to go cruising except what? If you are anything like the rest of us, you have everything you need except money—a cruising kitty. Let's take a close look at the care and feeding of this, one of nature's most interesting creatures.

The cruising kitty is a quantity of money that you will have in a handy place (in a bank account, invested in mutual funds, or hidden in the chainlocker). You will use it to pay the day-to-day expenses of your cruise. Your kitty is much more than a savings account or an investment program—it is the very essence of your ability to go cruising rather than report to work every day.

Simply stated, the kitty is a tool that you will use while you are cruising—a tool made out of money you have accumulated by working as hard as you can while spending as little as possible. While you are cruising, your kitty will be working; ideally, it will pay all your normal expenses through interest and dividends earned plus value added through capital growth. Your kitty must retain a large and accessible reserve for emergencies, of course, but you will need another large reserve for non-emergency contingencies and unusual expenses such as canal fees, haulouts, or the bureaucratic requirement that you post a bond equal to the price of a return airline ticket for each member of the crew when you enter French Polynesia.

All cruisers have kitties; you can't cruise without one. But just as no two cruisers are alike, their kitties aren't, either. There are, however, enough similarities to permit some broad generalities; in the rest of this chapter I will explain the different types of kitties and how to fatten them up. You don't need to be rich to cruise, but you do need to be in control of your finances. The careful management of your kitty is the way to do it.

Of all the hundreds of things you must do before you can take off on your dream cruise, this one item, building your kitty, can take longer than all the others combined. Your kitty is the second most important factor in the cruising equation— after you and your crew. Without retirement income or a rich uncle who is willing to pay your expenses to get you out of his hair, you will need to spend a major portion of the planning stage for your cruise accumulating and organizing your kitty.

Richard and the Warm Cervezas

Of all the places we stopped to visit on the first leg of our cruise, the tiny Mexican village of Xcalac is one of my favorites. There is no electricity there, although there is a huge complex of wind-driven turbines not far away. The only telephone in town hadn't produced a dial tone in more than two months. There are no paved roads for 20 miles in any direction. There are no windows in the simple board-and-tin houses—only shutters—and very few doors, just curtains hung in the entrances. The people are friendly and open, like people are in Mexico, and they display actions and temperaments that northerners might mistake for laziness until they have been there long enough to learn that the airless heat of a 90-degree summer day is considered a cold snap. Midday physical activity is unwise in Xcalac.

We had been in Xcalac for several hours and, after completing the check-in conducted by the local military, we were looking for a round of ice-cold drinks to quench our growing thirst. We wandered down the main street, which was also the only street, when I noticed a man and a woman with three children, obviously a family, lounging in the shade of their porch. The man sat in a chair leaning back against the house with his hat pulled down over his eyes, while the woman and the children, two small boys and a pretty teenage girl, sat on the floor. The man never moved, but the woman fanned herself with a palm leaf while the girl swished her skirt back and forth in a futile attempt to stimulate a breeze.

"Buscando por una restaurante, por favor," I said to the porch, self-conscious of my bad Spanish and trying to roll my Rs without hesitating between words.

The woman glanced at the man and replied that this was a restaurant and wouldn't we please have a seat. So saying, she shooed the kids into the house and gestured to the floor of the porch.

"¿Que gustas?" she asked once we were settled.

"Queramos dos cervesas y dos cokas muy frías, por favor."

She seemed to think the "muy frías" part was pretty funny, but she disappeared into the house and there ensued a rapid conversation with the girl that was way past my ability to understand. Moments later the woman returned, and I noticed the girl running in back of the row of houses toward the only store in town. Five minutes later the girl appeared carrying a tray with two warm cokes and two even warmer beers. We spent a pleasant half hour or so sitting in the shade of the porch, sipping our drinks, and chatting with the woman in our limited Spanish. When it came time to leave I asked how much we owed. "Nada, señor," she answered. "Es un regalo" (a gift). We departed with a very good feeling about Xcalic and life in general. I couldn't help but think that this was what cruising is all about.

We stayed in Xcalac for two or three days. On one occasion we joined Richard, a clean-cut young man from Florida who was singlehanding his small sloop around the Caribbean, for dinner at the only real restaurant in town, a tin shack affair built on poles with a sand floor. When the bill came, after a lovely meal of grilled fish and fresh fruit, we paid for our share with pesos and Richard paid for his from a large wad of American one-dollar bills. This made the proprietor very happy, and it led us into a discussion of handling money while cruising.

"If you need some pesos, I can sell you some," I offered, trying to be helpful.

"No thanks," he answered. "Never use 'em. Just keep American ones handy and I never need anything else."

"You mean you never exchange money?" I asked. Money changing and exchange rates are major headaches for cruisers. Exchanging American dollars into any foreign currency is easy, but it can be expensive. In many countries, the best rates are obtained on the street where clip artists and con men are common. Banks often charge a premium but are usually honest about it, and you will know where to find them tomorrow. It's frequently impossible to exchange foreign currency for U.S. dollars when you leave a country, and getting stuck with a pile of Ecuadorian Limperia or Colombian pesos can be costly.

"Nope, I've never been anywhere that they wouldn't take my ones, so why bother?"

"Wouldn't fives and tens and twenties be more convenient?"

"No way. When you give someone a larger bill, they often don't have enough change. When they do, they insist on giving it to you in local currency, and you can get stuck with it. When you use ones, you get just enough change to use for tips and to pay the kids for watching your dinghy."

"Well, how much do you carry at one time?"

"Quite a bit actually. I usually carry enough for a couple of months. Then I get my mom to send me more from my savings account. I keep it hidden in the chainlocker where no thief will ever find it."

The Size of the Kitty

The size of your kitty is a personal matter determined by the type of cruise you are planning, your personal needs, and your ability to live an economical life. A fortunate few can live and cruise on just the interest from their kitties. Some people don't feel comfortable without a huge bank balance on which to draw, and stop to replenish it when the balance reaches a level that a lot of us would be happy leaving home with. Many others cruise until the kitty is so emaciated it is practically dead before they stop to revive it. It is all a matter of preference, tolerance, and nature, and you'll have to determine your own style before you go. Regardless of your circumstances, however, I know of no case where a small kitty is superior to a large kitty.

On *Sultana* we try to keep our working kitty at around $30,000, which is our budget for one year of cruising. This may sound like a lot, but it is just $7,500 per person per year, and it must cover all the expenses (food, clothing, education, travel, medical, and various favorite frivolities) for people unaccustomed to austerity, plus all the operating expense for a large and rapacious boat. In truth, our kitty is probably below average. Most cruisers we meet who are willing to discuss their finances seem to think that $10,000 to $12,000 per person per year is about right. We've met other cruisers to whom this amount of money is an unimaginable sum, and once their kitty has a few thousand dollars in it, they are off and cruising for as long as it takes for the bank balance to bottom out. One delightful couple cruising with their two children on a homebuilt trimaran were on a three-year cruise with a total budget of $30,000, or $2,500 per person per year. We met them in Samoa where they were eating a lot of peanut butter and banana sandwiches (one of the healthiest meals known to man, as well as one of the cheapest) and they seemed to be getting along just fine.

Of course, the cruising kitty is much more than a quantity of money in a bank account or a wad of bills in the chainlocker—it is a system of earning and saving and spending that cruisers approach a little differently than anyone else.

Three Types of Cruising Kitties

There are two basic types of cruising kitties, plus a third type that combines the first two. They are somewhat analogous to the types of cruisers outlined in chapter 2, but there are enough differences to warrant going through the list one at a time.

The ideal kitty

The ideal cruising kitty is large enough to be self-sustaining. That is, it pays enough through interest and dividends to cover all cruising expenses. It is the nirvana of kitty-land and the type all of us would like to have. Unfortunately, the ideal kitty will need about a quarter of a million dollars to provide two people with a basic cruising lifestyle and half a million dollars or more (sometimes much more) to provide any degree of luxury. A kitty of this magnitude is usually possible only for older people who start with substantial savings or, of course, lottery winners and fortune inheritors. The envious rest of us will either have to spend a major part of our lives accumulating such a massive kitty or we will have to learn to make do with something less. Let's proceed under the assumption that you, like most cruisers, will opt for the latter and leave the former with the folks back in the office.

The work-as-you-go kitty

The work-as-you-go cruising kitty contains enough money to pay the cruising expenses of the crew for a specific period of time, usually one year. Then, the crew goes to work for however long it takes to replenish the kitty. The work-as-you-go approach works best for younger people with skills that are in high demand, and no children, but this isn't always the case. Susan and I have met many working cruisers with children and many others who aren't engineers or computer programmers.

Some cruisers have found that their earning potential while cruising is limited by their lack of skills and by the dearth of well-paying jobs in the most attractive cruising areas. But instead of putting the boat in storage so they can fly home to build up the kitty, as do many working cruisers, these hardy folks learn to live within their meager incomes and make do. And some of them make do very well indeed. I've met a lot of cruisers living on low-paying shore jobs, by providing services to other cruisers, by luck and pluck, or by some combination of all these elements.

Although it's common practice to ignore this advice, the work-as-you-go kitty ought not be depleted below a level that won't cover emergencies and periods when work is hard to find. And because cruising work is usually less lucrative than conventional work at home, this is usually possible by strictly controlling your expenses.

This approach presents a few problems, however. Working in the countries that are the favorite haunts of the cruising community is becoming more difficult than it once was because many of these countries are enacting laws or enforcing old laws that are designed to keep jobs for their own citizenry. Most of the countries in Europe and Australasia have strict laws regarding jobs for foreign nationals, and trying to circumvent them can quickly get you an invitation to leave and even a stiff fine. In other places, the jobs that are available are unattractive and pay poorly. New Zealand and Australia, for example, waive work-permit requirements for foreigners who want to earn some cash picking fruit and other crops, and (at the time this was written) will look the other way when a cruiser with a visitor's visa finds work as a waiter, cook, or bus person, especially in popular tourist areas where seasonal workers for menial jobs are hard to find.

In other popular cruising grounds, especially in Third World countries, it is often possible for a skilled person to stay busy working under the table for other cruisers. Anyone skilled in diesel mechanics, electronics repair, canvas and sail repair, tutoring, and most other services required by cruisers are in demand wherever cruisers congregate. Some of the more oddball services being offered to cruisers by cruisers include haircutting (bound to raise a complaint from the local hairdresser if you're caught), aromatherapy, marriage counseling, dentistry, palmistry and horoscope analysis, typing and manuscript editing, and one enterprising lad in the Rio Dulce promised to cure all of your ills by rubbing the right spots on your feet for a small fee. (Susan tried a session and loved it.)

Unfortunately, this sort of clandestine work is technically illegal in most countries, although the officials will often look the other way if the local businesses and residents aren't complaining. You do such work at your own peril, however, because local officials can change their minds very quickly and start to enforce long-ignored laws with harsh penalties.

If you think it's worth taking a chance, be sure to get a feel for the current local conditions and the prevailing attitude of the officials before you hang out your shingle. Don't ever assume that the favorable conditions of a year ago are still valid or that the friendly port captain who let you set up your law practice for a $10 bribe is still in charge. Always ask other cruisers about who is getting away with what and then wait, watch, and draw your own conclusions.

There are several American territories where U.S. citizens can work legally, including American Samoa, Panama (at least until 1999), the U.S. Virgin Islands, and Puerto Rico. In each of these places, though, the wages for most jobs—even those for highly skilled professionals—are very low. We met several cruisers in Pago Pago working as teaching aides for $4 an hour and carpenters working in Charlotte Amalie for $6—a fraction of what these skills normally fetch.

For most cruisers, local work in foreign countries is appropriate for short-term jobs to augment the cruising kitty, but it's seldom enough to revitalize it. Most American cruisers who must periodically work to replenish the kitty either sail to the closest U.S. port or, more often, leave their boats in secure storage and fly home to work.

The combination kitty

Many cruisers combine the ideal and the work-as-you-go kitties. They keep the ideal, or self-sustaining kitty, in some type of secure investments where it earns a substantial return. These investments might be stocks and bonds, mutual funds, income-producing real estate, or ideally, a diversified portfolio combining several of these vehicles. This kitty is left alone to do its thing and accumulate dividends, and it is called upon only when the cruisers need ready cash to meet some emergency or when a large fixed expense, such as a periodic refit, comes due.

Meanwhile, the work-as-you-go kitty pays for day-to-day expenses and extravagances such as dining out and tourist travel. This kitty is large and fat at the start of the cruise, but is slowly depleted as the cruise progresses. It is kept in a savings account or in a money market fund where it earns some interest but is readily accessible. The combined kitty is by far the most popular type of cruising kitty because it can be accumulated in a reasonable length of time.

Sultana's kitty is just such a combination kitty, and now stands at about $150,000, which came from the sale of our house (renting it out didn't work, but that's another story), plus our savings. However, that balance will be depleted by $20,000 to $30,000 after *Sultana*'s current refit is complete. Our self-sustaining kitty is kept in a diversified portfolio (the details of which we will discuss in the next chapter) and is never used for anything other than major capital outlays, such as the refit, and for medical emergencies.

The income from the self-sustaining kitty goes straight into our working kitty where it is supplemented by other income (a small pension Susan gets from her 20 years of work, royalties, and odd-job income that I pick up doing electrical work and boat repairs for other cruisers), and it is the working kitty that we use to pay all of our normal day-to-day expenses. This system has worked well for us for five years, and it is similar to the systems used by many other full-time cruisers we meet.

The chainlocker kitty

Richard, the young cruiser with the one-dollar bills we met in Mexico, had a good system and, although I can't recommend it as an answer for most of us, (especially in the Caribbean where thievery is endemic), it worked for him. A lot of cruisers, however, do keep some U.S. dollars secreted about their boats somewhere, usually in some obscure hidey-hole (the chainlocker is far too obvious) or, even better, in several hidey-holes. Susan and I regard these dollars as our emergency reserve and never admit its presence or discuss it in any way with anyone who is not a member of our crew. We don't even declare it to the customs inspectors when we enter a country. This is illegal of course, but hey, so is the extra measure of gin in the bottle with the washed-off label in the bilge.

On *Sultana* the amount of money in the hidey-hole varies between a couple of hundred dollars to a maximum of a thousand or so, depending on where we are and what we anticipate our needs for cash to be. The amount of gin in the bottle with the washed-off label in the bilge varies with the climate and captain's temperament.

My grandpappy used to tell me "it ain't whatcha got but whatcha do with it that makes the difference," and nowhere is this more true than in the cruising life. Base the size of your kitty on what you need, not what others have or what you want.

6

FEEDING THE KITTY

"A feast is made for laughter, and wine maketh merry:

but money answereth all things."

—*Ecclesiastes 10:19*

The cruising kitty is the most important element of the cruising life. Without one, you can't go cruising, and the size and vitality of your kitty will have a larger impact on the success of your cruise and the extent to which you enjoy your new lifestyle than any other single ingredient. If you are an average aspiring cruiser, at least four-and-a-half years of the five-year period that we have somewhat arbitrarily chosen as a reasonable time for achieving the cruising life will be devoted to fattening and grooming your kitty. In this chapter, we will explore a few of the best ways for you to get your kitty purring with a minimum of effort.

Start Saving Now

If you are serious about cruising, or even if you only think you might be serious about it some day, start feeding your kitty without delay. This is much more important than any other aspect of the planning process, and it is imperative that you do it now. Start by establishing a savings goal as a percentage of your income. Your target should be to allocate at least 25 percent of your take-home pay to your cruising kitty. More is better, much more is much better. If you can't start at this figure, do the best that you can. Ten, or even five, percent will get you started, but increase it as you're able until you reach 25 percent or better.

How? The most obvious way to fatten your kitty is to work hard and earn a lot of money, but there is another, far more important and in many ways more difficult step you must take first. It is critical that you stop spending the money that you are already making, no matter how much money that is, on frivolous and capricious items and services that do nothing to advance you toward your goal. This is the biggest and most important step to the cruising life, and until you take it you won't be going cruising. Going cruising means stopping spending like a shoresider, it means becoming frugal and thrifty.

Minimalism—The Key to the Cruising Life

The term "minimalism" was first used to describe an artistic style of painting that eliminated all the distracting and unnecessary elements while retaining the beauty of the central idea. The early traditional forms of Japanese and Chinese art typify minimalism as do several modern schools. It is a simple and basic style in which the artist uses just enough paint and the minimum number of brush strokes to convey his or her vision without denigrating or compromising the final image. Our simple and basic approach to the cruising lifestyle is the perfect analogy to minimalism, wherein one acquires and uses only what one needs to live in reasonable comfort. There is no need to wait until you are ready to leave on a cruise to adopt minimalism; you can start living that lifestyle now.

The minimalist life is an economical life so there will be extra money for your kitty. It's a rewarding life, but it requires some practice. In the following few paragraphs I'll discuss how you can achieve minimalism—and even if you decide not to go cruising, you will find it to be a fulfilling way to live.

Dropping out of the consumer society

Most of us have become used to life in a society where we are judged by the kind of car we drive, the neighborhood we live in, the degrees our kids are accumulating, and the thickness of our pay envelope.

Consumerism has a few dramatically negative aspects, of course, and any society dedicated solely to the consumption of its resources will, like a band of overly enthusiastic cannibals, eventually consume itself, but it's working so far. From tiny family-run businesses in the jungles of Brazil to huge factories growing like mushrooms all over China, the world is focusing on cranking out enormous quantities of products that feed the voracious appetite of the consumer. The jobs thus generated are elevating the living standards of millions of previously poor workers around the world, and their prosperity is further fueling the demand for products. It is an upward spiraling whirlwind of ever-increasing demand, production, and consumption, and its end is not in sight. It's a wonderful system, indeed, but it isn't for us. We're going to drop out of the consumer society.

Dropping out doesn't mean we can't enjoy the fruits of consumerism. In fact, by taking advantage of the benefits that accrue to us by our inevitable proximity to shopping malls and car dealerships while refusing to participate in the actual process of commercialism, we can garner huge rewards that can elevate our lifestyle to a lofty altitude far above that of a typical high-flying consumer. We need to develop the will to live at a subsistence level in an environment where we are surrounded by abundance and luxury. We need to ignore the temptations of an overindulgent society, to do without things that don't directly affect our welfare and our survival. We need to do this for one reason only: to save the money we need to fatten our kitty just enough so we can buy a boat and go cruising.

Every year, the citizens of developed countries buy billions of dollars worth of goods and services that they don't need, mostly on credit, and as people fight to move up the socioeconomic ladder by acquiring better stuff. They are delighted to sell the old stuff, particularly ego possessions like cars and boats, for a fraction of their original cost. I know several racing skippers who buy a new set of sails every year because the old ones get "stretched." True, these sails aren't any good for cruising (most racing sails are now Kevlar or other fabrics that don't stand up well to the demands of cruising), but when they are sold it starts a chain reaction that results in a bargain somewhere down the line on sails suitable for cruising.

The same principle applies to cars. We don't want to be the second owner of a luxury car—still too expensive—but the sale of that car will cause a chain reaction and sooner or later we will be able to pick up a 10-year-old Ford or Chevy in great shape for almost nothing.

For we who would be cruisers, the path is clear. As we decline to participate in consumerism while practicing minimalism and maintaining our income until we are actually ready to leave, we will be able to amass a substantial excess in the bank account that we can use to reduce debt and fatten the cruising kitty.

Consumerism, conformity, and the wealthy cruiser

If you are a wealthy person, fear not. You don't have to forsake consumerism to go cruising, for consumerism—and materialism—is alive and well in the cruising community. Cruisers are, after all, human beings, and we lust for the bigger and better just like everyone else. The problem develops when this natural desire for improvement overrides our judgment on practicality and available resources. There are literally thousands of products on which the cruising sailor can spend money (my current stack of marine catalogs is nearly eight inches thick), so any of us predisposed to profligacy will find ample opportunity to exercise it in the cruising world.

Among cruisers who can afford to do it (and a lot who can't), there is a distinct trend to move up to bigger and fancier boats. Even beginning cruisers are showing up in 50- or 60-footers when a few years ago 35 feet was about average. But in boats, as in many things, bigger isn't necessarily better. Big boats can mean big problems and big expenses. And the third biggest cause of failed cruises, right behind people problems and money problems, is having too much boat. Cruisers who trade up to or start out with larger boats often end up with more boat than they can handle both physically and financially and they go home. It is always tragic to see dreams shattered, but when they are shattered by something as preventable as overindulgence it is particularly sad.

This trend toward more boat is good news for us little guys. The big boats can't get into the small anchorages that are most often the best and least crowded, and when rich folks buy their big new boat, they are often willing to sell us their little old boat at a bargain price. As I write this, Eric and Susan Hiscock's penultimate cruiser, *Wanderer IV,* is moored some two hundred yards from *Sultana.* She's way too big for two people to handle without a lot of trouble, and when they built their last boat, *Wanderer V,* she was a full 10 feet shorter on deck. Even then, the Hiscocks often missed the convenience of their little 30-footer, *Wanderer III.*

Meet Your New Minimalist Lifestyle

Your new minimalist life will affect all aspects of the way you live. Minimalism is the art of learning to spend just enough money to stay alive while maintaining your health and dignity at a level that will allow you to maximize your income. You can't live in the woods and eat dirt and expect any potential employer, or anyone else, to take you seriously, but you can reorder your life so that you spend money on just those things that you need to maintain yourself at an essential level of civilization and decency while forgoing unnecessary luxuries and indulgences. The necessary changes in your routine are not as difficult as you might think, but doing so will require concentration and effort. First you have to learn the rules, then you must learn to apply them one at a time.

Consider first your living quarters

If you are paying rent for your home or apartment and won't be leaving on your cruise for two or more years, consider buying a tiny house in a good neighborhood. Your rent is coming right out of your cruising kitty. Buy a house and make the equity part of your kitty, but don't make the mistake that many home buyers make—don't buy the biggest and most expensive house you can afford. Remember, you are living your new free-range life based on your needs, not your wants. Find a good neighborhood and buy the smallest and least expensive house you can be comfortable in that is reasonably close to your work and the other services you will need—because the minimalist life also means minimum driving. Minimum effort for maximum gain in all things is the watchword.

You need to get used to living in small spaces anyway, and a small, cheap house means small, cheap expenses—heat, insurance, and the like. If you buy wisely, the appreciation of the house will cover a portion, if not all, of the rent you would have paid plus the sales expense. It may even contribute to the kitty when you sell it. If you live in a metropolitan area, a small, inexpensive condo might be the answer to your housing question, but be extra careful of condos. In many suburban markets a condominium won't be as good an investment as a single-family home, but in the city a condo may be the only affordable option. This isn't always true in either case, so do some homework on your own neighborhood before you decide what to buy. It is important to proceed with extreme caution when buying any kind of real estate because the wrong move could easily end your cruising plans. If you have never bought a house before or if you are otherwise unfamiliar with the real estate market, you should consult a trusted professional, one who has no financial interest in your purchase of a specific property.

Fix it if you can

If you are handy with tools and know what you are doing, buying a rundown house in a good neighborhood and spiffing it up for resale while you are living in it is an excellent way to reduce living expenses and build the kitty. In fact, if the circumstances are just right, it can be the closest thing to a surefire ticket to the cruising life that there is.

Unfortunately, if you are inexperienced in home repair, fixing up an old house is just like fixing up an old boat, and it is much more difficult than the home-improvement shows make it look. Buying an old house and fixing it up to live in is hard enough, but the need to do it for a profit makes it that much harder. So, if you have never done it before or if you aren't a home-repair expert and you really want to go cruising, you might be a lot better off if you didn't try to start now.

If you are going to make a profit in the real estate market, the following must apply. (The first three items pertain to any house or condominium; the last two are specific to fix-it-uppers.)

- You must buy the house at a good price under favorable terms.
- The house must be in a good neighborhood.

- The real estate market in your area must be expanding; stagnant or down trending markets won't do.
- The project must be realistic and within your capabilities to do it in the time you have available. Many run-down old houses, like run-down old boats, are too far gone to be fixed up for reasonable money.
- Most areas will allow you to work on your own house, but you must be familiar with and comply with all building codes and licensing requirements.

If you already own a house

If you already own your own home and it is of reasonable size with a reasonable mortgage, terrific. You are halfway to the cruising life. However, if you own a large home with a large mortgage, and your departure is more than two or three years away, consider selling it and buying a smaller house for all the above reasons. If you think you can save some money by trading down to a smaller house, be careful to compute all of the costs involved in the transaction before you make up your mind. Make sure you factor in the legal fees, bank fees and points, commissions, moving expenses, and all the other little odds and ends that cost money so you know for sure what the true cost will be before you sign on the line.

Renting

I have been a landlord on three separate occasions and in all three cases it has been a most unsatisfactory experience. I am now convinced that the stereotype of the landlord as a greedy, conniving tightwad with a black hat and twisted mustache is spot-on accurate. If you don't fit this stereotype you're going to get your butt slam-dunked through the hoop of reality by the moral equivalent of the best of Michael Jordan and the worst of Attila the Hun.

I seem to have a genetic defect that manifests itself in a desire for people to like me, and I was born without a defense mechanism for dealing with hatred. And let's face it, people hate landlords. The tenants hate 'em, the local governments hate 'em, the courts hate 'em, and, hey, I'm no different than anyone else—I hate 'em, too.

Don't rent your home to tenants without thinking about all the ramifications. The tax, liability, and insurance problems of renting a private home are more than most cruisers want to deal with. Even if you are the personification of Simon Legree, finding and dealing with tenants can be time-consuming and expensive, all of which detract from the cruising experience.

Consider next your automobile

The last time I returned to the United States on a business trip, I requested the travel agent to have a rental car waiting for me at Logan Airport in Boston. Being a frugal sort and a true minimalist, I ordered the smallest and least expensive car they had available, a Chevrolet Geo. After a long flight that was delayed by weather, I finally landed a little after midnight on a Friday night. I collected my bags and took the shuttle to the rental yard—the very empty rental yard. There wasn't a Geo in sight. In fact, the only car they had left was a huge white Oldsmobile loaded with every goody in the book and less than 200 miles on the speedometer. Since I had a confirmed reservation, I got the white monster at the Geo rate, and I drove away a happy man.

The Geo would have gotten me where I was going just fine, but that big Olds got me there with panache. As soon as I slid behind the wheel I ceased being a lonesome and bone-weary wanderer and became a man of importance and substance. I sat on the polished leather seats and felt the power and prestige of a flashy new car flow from the wheel through my hands. As I drove, I observed with bemused disdain the envious glances of the common people in their Fords and Chevy Geos. I was once again a cool dude with a new set of wheels, and I loved it.

The automobile is the single most expensive item most of us own. (Your house might cost more, but it's usually less expensive than a car because you get most of your money back from a house when you sell it.) Western culture is a culture of automobiles, and most of us could not live the way we do without a car sitting in the driveway for every adult member of the family. Furthermore, our automobile defines who we are. It is the first important item many of us buy, and our place in society is broadcast for all to see by the type of car we drive. This is why many of us buy the most expensive car we can afford and will happily spend a year's earnings supported by a 62-month loan on a car. The monthly car payment is as much a part of the average worker's life as the daily commute; few of us even consider living without one.

Massive amounts of money are spent on advertising to capitalize on our tendency to derive our image from the car we drive. And if the advertisers can't convince at least 30 million Americans each year that the new models are the greatest thing to happen to humanity since cultivated wheat, the entire U.S. economy suffers. We are told our new car makes us sexy, young, exciting, vibrant, smart, and irresistible to the opposite sex, and we lap it up like kittens at a milk saucer. There is nothing inherently wrong with the lopsided importance of automobiles in our society—the car culture accounts for between 20 and 30 percent of the U.S. gross domestic product, depending on whose statistics you use—and it is one of the most important things that makes life as we know it possible. However, if you plan to go cruising, turning your back on the car culture is one of the first things you must do and an important first step in learning to lead a minimalist life.

Would-be cruisers have to stop looking at cars as status symbols and start looking at them as a convenient way to get around town. Most cruisers and all minimalists think of cars as mechanical devices for getting from one place to another in reasonable safety and comfort, nothing more. They don't care a fig about what the car looks like. This is a very dangerous attitude—if everyone thought this way it would lead to the collapse of the automobile industry, the closing of factories around the world, massive layoffs, and worldwide unemployment. But don't worry, the economies of the world are safe. The idea that the automobile is the source of all our well-being is so deeply ingrained that none but you and I and a few other cruising minimalists are ever going to believe otherwise.

If you own a car on which you still owe money, get rid of it and resolve never to buy a car or anything else except a house with borrowed money. If you can't sell the car for enough to cover the balance on your note, you're faced with a dilemma. Car dealers play a little game with people who are in this unenviable position—it's called "trade in." They offer you an inflated trade-in value for your old car then add the difference to the price of the new one. (Most dealers are candid about having separate trade-in and cash prices for the cars they sell.) Quite an effective ploy to inflate your monthly payment, isn't it? Usually the best you can do in this situation is sell the car at a loss then pay off the balance as best you can. If you buy a good old car, a minimalist car, the savings realized in the first year should be enough to cover your loss and get you back on track.

Aged but able

Thousands of perfectly good old automobiles are on the market for a few hundred to a few thousand dollars. Look for a basic model that is in great condition, 6 to 10 years old, with crank-up windows and no light in the ashtray, but one that you still see a lot of on the road. For the most part, a car is in good condition if it looks like it is in good condition, but have a trusted mechanic check it out for you. Most six-year-old cars no longer have any prestige value, and you may have difficulties finding parts and service for those over 10 years old. Your mechanic can advise you here as well.

Basic models without frills are much more likely to be cheap and easy to repair because they don't have as much stuff to break. The fact that you see a lot of popular models on the road is testimony to reliability and sound construction. If the car is a weird color and has a few dents, so much the better—bargain city here we come—but shun rust like a kid shuns boiled cabbage.

If you buy a perfectly good old car you will save much more than the interest on the loan. A good old car will have most or even all of the depreciation wrung out of it, so when it's time to leave on your cruise you can often sell it for about what you paid for it. In most states you will save a fortune by purchasing only the minimum insurance required by law plus, perhaps, a little extra liability. Car theft has reached epidemic proportions in many places, but few thieves are interested in our good old car. Maintenance is also much cheaper for an old car, and it's easier to do it yourself if you're so inclined.

Like most of our minimalist principles, these basic rules of good-old-car ownership hold true no matter what your lifestyle. By turning your back on the contrived status and symbolism of the new-car cult and driving a good old car, you can effect a huge increase in your real standard of living.

Of course, when you finally leave on your cruise, you won't have a car at all, so now is the time to get used to a bicycle.

Good cruisers eat good food

Now is the time for would-be cruisers (and any others who want to improve their lives) to learn to eat simple and basic foods in balanced portions and reject as much prepared food as possible. "Eat when you are hungry and stop before you are full" is a cliché that I plagiarized from somewhere, but it should become the first rule of the cruising diet. Planned meals at specific times are terrific social occasions and a mainstay of family life, but it is much better to snack and nibble your way through the day than to stuff yourself full at the dinner table.

The practical answer is compromise. On *Sultana*, when conditions permit, dinner is a time for our family to gather around the pilothouse table where we discuss the events of the day and the plans for tomorrow; where we tell jokes and reveal fears and foibles. The meals are balanced and tasty (especially when Susan cooks) with a variety that reflects local habits and available supplies, but the portions are small. Anyone who is hungry can munch on peanut butter, veggies, fruits, and the bread and crackers at any time between meals. Cokes and sweets and pastries are off-limits until Mom says when.

Few foods are improved by processing. Fresh peas, for example, are a wonderful source of fiber and vitamins, but canned peas have no nutritional value at all—it says so right on the can. All right, so they have a little fiber—so does pine bark. Eat fresh raw fruits and vegetables when you can. To cook fresh vegetables, simply drop them gently into boiling water for a few minutes—just long enough to bring out the colors and flavors and subdue a bit of the texture.

Ditch the junk food, eat everything in moderation and in balanced portions, and you will never need any fad diet.

Learn to cook

Simple and basic cooking is fun and can be learned by any simple, basic person who is willing to work at it a bit. If you don't already know the fundamentals of cooking, many junior colleges have adult evening programs that are almost sure to include a cooking class, or you can get a friend to teach you, or you can just get a good cookbook and keep experimenting until you get it right. It sometimes takes a while, but cooking is one of those skills in which the learning progress is obvious and continual—which is one reason why cooking is satisfying and rewarding. Once most people get started, they develop their own momentum and don't ever want to stop learning.

Concentrate on learning how to prepare dishes that require only a simple and basic galley. A few of every cruiser's favorites include one-pot meals (which are the basis for many meals afloat and come in handy for potlucks); easy and tasty soups, stews, and extra-spicy goulash; and quick breads such as pancakes, waffles, biscuits, and muffins. As a bonus, these are healthy foods, too. (See chapter 11 for more information about galley layout and design, and for a few of my previously top-secret recipes—the one for Captain Garlic's World-Famous Spaghetti Sauce is worth the price of this book alone.)

Don't worry about your cholesterol or your blood pressure unless your doctor tells you that you have a problem. Most basic foods are naturally low in salt and cholesterol anyway, and if you do have a health problem that requires a special diet, the minimalist cruising life is the best way to deal with it because it's the healthiest way to live.

Entertainment afloat

Television has been called the greatest evil of modern society. (I know, I called it that myself.) It is the glue that seals the fabric of consumerism to materialism, and it demands that we sit mindless and passive for hours as a barrage of advertisers tell us that if we buy their new cars we'll become popular and sexy and smart, or that if we feed Spot their enriched and fortified food, Spot will become the greatest dog in the land. Americans spend more time watching television than doing anything else, including sleeping, and our kids spend more time watching the damn things than they spend in the classroom.

Television is an addictive bad habit, and the producers know full well that they no longer need to worry about quality programming. Most of us will watch no matter how bad the shows become, and all they must do is bring out a clone or close copy of whatever other show is ahead in the ratings. The public will channel surf for a while and then zero in on the one that is the least (or most) offensive.

The best thing I can say about television is that the smaller ones fit nicely into the trash can. OK, OK, so this is a bit draconian. You don't have to throw away the TV if you don't want to; you can sell it if you like. The important thing is to get rid of it and put the money you were spending on cable service straight into your kitty.

Consider your health

Cancel your health-club membership and sell all your exercise machines (except, perhaps, a simple weight set). These things are bad for your health. If you're like about 80 percent of us, you paid for your club dues and your NordicTrack with a credit card. All that money for principal and interest needs to go into your kitty.

And if you're like about 90 percent of Americans, you're not using these things anyway. Every time you plan to go to the club for a workout, something comes up and you put off going until later, and the NordicTrack is collecting dust in the basement. (Come on, admit it. It's true, isn't it?)

Learn exercise techniques that don't cost anything. Buy a good pair of stout shoes (not special walking shoes, just simple crepe-soled shoes with leather uppers are fine), wear heavy socks, and walk everywhere you can, every time you can. Walk with panache and enthusiasm; head up, chest out, arms swinging. Hum a little tune if you like, and think what it's going to be like walking along the beach in Bora Bora.

Get your heart beating and your lungs working. If there are some hills or a long flight of stairs nearby, walk up and down them as often as you can. As you become more fit, start walking with a small backpack filled with the Sunday newspaper. Every week add a newspaper until you are carrying 30 to 40 pounds. Leave room for a bottle of water and a snack, but keep walking.

If you're a runner, great. Now it's time to quit. It's too easy to get injured while running. Tendons get torn, backs get injured, ankles and knees get twisted—none of which are compatible with cruising, and running isn't necessary anyway. A brisk walk gives you all the aerobic and muscular exercise you will ever need. So stop running and walk, walk, walk. (Keep your running shoes to walk in, though.)

If it's too far to walk, ride your bicycle. Biking is as good a cardiovascular exercise as walking and it's faster. If you don't have a bike, buy a cheap used one that's hard to peddle (an old three-speed is ideal); you'll save money and get more exercise. As you gradually move away from being a consumer toward becoming a minimalist you will be amazed at how little you need to live a comfortable and rewarding life, and you will be able to put excess funds into the kitty—your passport to freedom. Don't delay for a minute. The trick is to adopt the minimalist's lifestyle now to prepare for the cruising life.

Get rid of useless possessions

Start now to sell all your excess possessions, stuff that you won't be needing once you start cruising, and put the money straight into the kitty. Extra cars, sporting equipment, stereo gear, computers, those exercise machines, kitchen gadgets, televisions, and large power tools are a few things you won't need while cruising. If you won't need these things cruising, you probably don't need them now and will be better off without them. One of the hardest decisions for most beginning cruisers to make is what not to take with them. As a general rule, it's always better to take too little than too much, and the more you can do without the better off you'll be.

Store the rest

Not many people can get all their worldly possessions on a boat, no matter how big it is. Susan has a lot of family heirlooms and I have a lot of books, tons of books, that we can't bear to part with. Putting all this stuff in storage will get it out of the way and unclutter your life until your cruising days are done.

Cancel all your memberships except to the SSCA

Cancel or don't renew your memberships in expensive clubs and organizations—that's right, even the yacht club—and put that money into the kitty.

You may want to subscribe to a few sailing magazines in order to feed the dream while you feed the kitty. Two of the best in the United States are the *SSCA Bulletin* and *Practical Sailor*. The first you get free with a membership in the Seven Seas Cruising Association (or maybe you get the membership free when you buy the bulletin), an organization to which every cruiser and would-be cruiser should belong, and the second you get by sending a large quantity of money to the publisher. The *Bulletin* is a collection of letters written by cruisers from all over the world and is the best source of information there is about destinations and cruising conditions worldwide. *Practical Sailor* is well written, comprehensive, and a good value.

Credit: The Most Frivolous of All Frivolities

Several years ago, my good friend Jerry, who is a little eccentric, decided he had had enough of renting a place to live and approached a bank for a loan to buy a house. He was a hard-working guy who made a decent living in a small one-man business that taught scuba diving on an academic level to budding marine scientists at several area universities. He had learned early on that when you have a sporadic cash flow from a seasonal business it is wise to keep all your bills current and to deal on a cash basis with as many suppliers as possible. He was quite surprised when the first bank he approached refused his application for a mortgage on the grounds that he had never borrowed money and therefore had no credit history on which they could base their loan. He tried another and got the same story. He finally gave up after several more banks told him the same thing. Several years and a few credit cards later, he did finally buy a tidy little condo in a Boston suburb.

This isn't an unusual story and most of us can recite similar ones. It is ironic that you can't borrow money if you don't owe money, but it's true and a vivid illustration of the value our society places on debt and credit ratings. I know several people who have credit card balances that exceed their annual before-tax earnings and are happily paying exorbitant interest rates and annual fees using one credit card for cash to pay off others, and charging nearly everything they buy. Many people seem not to realize that when you use a credit card you are borrowing money. It is amazing how many people actually believe that someday they will pay off all those cards and be free of debt.

The credit system isn't all bad, of course, and easy credit at reasonable rates for the masses is one of the secrets behind the phenomenal growth in the Western economies since the end of World War II. Just read the newspapers around Christmas and you can get a clear picture of the importance of consumer spending on the overall economy. A slow shopping season can shake the very foundations of society with profound effects on unemployment, interest rates, the stock market, and that undefined but critical element called consumer confidence.

Banks, other lending institutions, and social planners all have elaborate formulae that compare debt, age, income, history, where you live, and the kind of work you do. These mathematical factors are used to determine how much debt an economically healthy family or individual can carry without getting into financial trouble. They work just fine for shoreside dwellers, but it's a different story if you want to go cruising. Unless you can be happy with a short cruise, you simply aren't a candidate for the cruising life if you owe a lot of money. With this in mind, let's take a look at the dark side of debt and consider how to get rid of it.

Consumer debt and the cruiser

Consumer debt is the lock on the gate to freedom. Monthly payments are like fence posts that surround us and keep us hammering away at jobs we don't like in situations we'd rather not be in, and the interest on those payments is the barbed wire that connects the posts and ensures that we don't do anything foolish like buy a boat and sail away. Before you can become serious about adopting the cruising life, it is critical that you start now to open that gate by getting out of debt.

Consumer debt is money that you borrowed to buy anything except your house. Credit cards are the most common form of consumer debt, followed by auto loans, lay-away plans, and equity loans on your house that you use for vacations or refrigerators. Consumer debt is a massive burden to many families, and for many it is the single most stressful element of modern life.

Debt and the cruising kitty

How do the foregoing comments on debt relate to those we made on the cruising kitty in chapter 6? Wouldn't it make a lot of sense to use all of our resources to pay off all our debt before we start building our kitty? In a purely economic sense, yes it would, because the interest you are paying on your debt is most likely to be much higher than the interest you will receive on the budding savings account that is the early stage of your kitty. But on a practical and emotional level, it doesn't make any sense at all. It is important that you get your kitty started before you do anything else because that kitty will quickly come to symbolize your commitment to the cruising life. It is a positive element in your life that you can view with pride as you watch it grow. Your debt, on the other hand, is a psychological millstone that represents nothing.

A payment schedule

Once you have your kitty growing, you must next add up all your debt exclusive of your home mortgage and calculate a payment schedule that will get you debt-free within five years. Make sure that you allow a comfortable margin to live on while you reduce your monthly payments and that you continue to build your cruising kitty. This usually means that you won't be able to allocate any more than 20 percent of your income to debt reduction, which may not be enough to satisfy some of your creditors.

Unhappy creditors can be a problem, and dealing with them will require some negotiating skills on your part, but if you are making an honest attempt to pay off an honest debt, most companies will go along with a reasonable payment schedule. Your first responsibility is to your family and the cruising kitty, not to the department stores and credit card companies, but you must remember that your bills are legally and morally binding commitments that you entered into on your own with a free will. You need a clear conscience when you go cruising so don't turn your back on your debts. Many communities now offer consumer credit counseling services free to the public. Counselors offer help in setting up a payment schedule, and their involvement will sometimes get creditors to accept different terms than they would otherwise.

Kill all the credit cards

The most difficult part of your debt-reduction scheme won't be making your monthly payments—you have probably been doing that all along—but will be in developing the willpower and discipline to stop yourself from accumulating more debt. Doing so could be the hardest thing you do to get you moving toward the cruising life. In some chronic cases, people simply can't stop charging stuff, and these folks need stronger medicine than they'll find in this book. The rest of us will find it hard enough, but if you really want to go cruising, you can do it, and as a first step you should cancel your credit cards.

As I said earlier, credit cards are a convenient way to borrow money and they are one of the factors that make the economic miracle happen, but, alas, they cost too much so they just aren't for us. You can't even necessarily avoid interest charges by paying your bill promptly anymore, because some credit card companies are charging a fee for the privilege of doing this. Cancel all your credit cards except for one that you will put away to be used only for life-or-death emergencies.

Many cruisers use credit cards for cash advances from ATM machines and banks, for renting cars, and for identification. In most of the first-world countries you will be visiting, you will hardly be out of sight of the ubiquitous money machines. Nearly all banks in developing countries are happy to deliver a bundle of local currency against your credit card. But a cash advance against a credit card usually carries the highest interest rate allowed by law and, unlike charges, for which interest isn't charged for 30 days, the banks start charging for cash advances the moment the machine or the bank teller hands you the money. Therefore, cash advances are the most expensive way there is to borrow money short of resorting to a loan shark. The answer is to use debit cards and pay no interest at all.

Debit cards are the only way to go

As credit cards and the corresponding debt levels proliferate, so does the number of people who, through indiscretion, lose their charge privileges. Also, a significant and growing number of people don't want a charge card or can't get one because they have never had one. So, about a decade ago a few banks began issuing debit cards to anyone who could pony up a minimum deposit of $500 or so regardless of past credit history.

The principle behind debit cards is simple. You deposit some amount of money over the minimum amount required by the bank into a special account earmarked for debit-card transactions. The bank issues you a plastic card from Visa or MasterCard (or both if you wish), that looks just like a credit card. When you use the card, the merchant places it in the scanner and enters the amount. The scanner is connected to your bank's computer and the amount of your purchase is immediately deducted from your balance. If you don't have enough money in your account (over your minimum balance) to cover your purchase, your request is politely denied. Likewise, withdrawals from ATM machines operate just like credit card cash advances but, once again, you are withdrawing your own money from your own account and there are no fees for the service.

Don't leave home without one or the other

Credit card use throughout the world is so pervasive that having one with you at all times is practically a necessity, and you should not try to go cruising without one. A debit card is an alternative and every cruiser should have one, but if you don't like the idea of debit cards, go ahead and take a few credit cards. Many people will accept them as identification and some countries, like New Zealand, will accept a credit card or a debit card as proof of solvency, which is a requirement for a visitor's visa. Although there are exceptions, you can just about forget renting a car if you don't have that little plastic slab.

When we were returning from our shakedown cruise to Canada, we pulled into Boothbay Harbor, Maine, and decided to rent a car to visit some friends who lived inland. Finding a phone booth by the public landing, we called the only local number in the Yellow Pages under auto rentals.

"Yup?," asked the voice that answered the phone.

"Do you rent cars?" I asked.

"Yup."

"Do you have one available?"

"Yup."

"How much is it?"

"Fifteen dollars a day."

"Do you charge for mileage?"

"Can't, speedometer's broke."

"We'll take it. Do you take credit cards?"

"Nope."

"What do you take?"

"Whatcha got?"

We finally settled on cash. The car, a surprisingly tidy late-model Chevrolet, was delivered to the dock with a full tank of gas. When we were finished with it two days later, I called the number and asked where we should deliver the car. "Just put the money in the glove box and leave her on the dock," said the voice.

Things like this happen all the time while you are cruising but they seem to happen more in Maine than anywhere else. Thus, coastal Maine is one of our favorite places on earth in or out of a sailboat.

Hesitate, don't consolidate

One other thing before we leave the vulgar topic of credit cards and move on to something a bit more nautical: In struggling to find a path through your financial labyrinth, don't fall for the "consolidation loan" scam. These tempting offers, which are familiar to anyone who has a credit card, involve borrowing money from one lender to pay off credit card debt—ostensibly to give you the convenience of writing one check each month and saving you the nuisance of writing a separate check for each credit card. What they really do is clear your balances on your credit cards to encourage you to charge more stuff. It's sort of like trying to save bullets by putting all your snakes into one box then shooting the box. It doesn't work; you still have to shoot the snakes. Unless the new interest rate and fees (don't forget the fees) for the consolidation loan will save you a lot of money (unlikely) and you have the willpower to never use credit cards again, don't even consider this type of loan.

Generally, the only "consolidation loan" that makes real financial sense is a second mortgage or home equity loan that will usually carry a much lower rate of interest than an unsecured consolidation loan. Such a loan can be an extremely cost-effective way to pay off credit card debt, if borrowers cut up their credit cards and throw them away, as well as every new credit card offer that comes in the mail—all of which is a lot harder than it sounds, so don't consider this kind of loan either unless you are sure you have the willpower to stop charging stuff.

Work to Live

If you are lucky enough to be earning a lot of money working at a good job, you have a tremendous advantage in your quest to fatten your kitty and complete all the dozens of other tasks that are necessary before you can shove off. But remember, once you begin cruising that income is going to stop and there will be long periods when you won't want to work or won't be able to. That job you left is going to look awfully good from the vantage point of a small boat in a faraway place, so make sure you are making the most of it while you've got it. You need to take advantage of the planning period to accumulate as much cash in the kitty as you can.

Change your working attitude

Many people who are working at jobs they aren't thrilled with find an eight-hour day at the office or at the plant to be exhausting. They collapse in front of the TV with a drink or two and hardly move except to eat dinner and go to bed. This was my routine for many years and I never had a hint as to why I didn't have any energy. Finally, in desperation, I went to the doc. He gave me several thousands of dollars worth of tests and decided that I was suffering from chronic fatigue syndrome. "Get plenty of rest and drink lots of liquids," he advised. "And don't worry about it—it's probably genetic."

The hackneyed expression "we are what we eat" is, like most hackneyed expressions, true. But it is also true that we are what we do. Most of us consider our job as our life's work—our career—and we identify ourselves with our employment. Thus, in our shoreside lives most of us focus on our jobs. We live so we can work, and if our work is dull, lifeless, and uninteresting, then we too are dull, lifeless, and uninteresting. In the cruising life, you will turn the tables on the system. You will begin to work so you can live, and this small change in attitude makes a mighty difference.

You will become animated and exciting because your life is animated and exciting even though your work remains dull and commonplace. What were once insurmountable obstacles are now mere bumps and minor potholes on the road to the cruising life.

An interesting transformation will take place once you decide to go cruising. You will likely become so obsessed with accumulating enough cash in your kitty to make cruising possible that your work might take on new meaning.

When your job focus becomes accumulating money for your kitty, you suddenly have new reasons for getting out of bed in the morning. This will change your attitude about work. And you will have reached another important turning point in your life; by making your job secondary to your kitty it becomes a means to an end—the freedom of the cruising life.

Don't fear losing your job

Thinking of your job as just a job instead of a career and knowing that you will be leaving soon unshackles you from the fear of losing that job; therefore, you become free to take chances and risks that would have been unthinkable when you lived for your work. It is very possible that your new freedom will manifest a measurable increase in the quality of your work, a renewed interest in what were once boring projects, and a new respect for your job, the people you work with, and the company you work for.

It is also possible that you will be fired.

Many upper and middle managers fear nothing so much as a motivated worker. This is especially true in government jobs and older industries with entrenched management, but it can happen anywhere.

If you have trouble coming to grips with the prospect of losing your job and having to look for another, perhaps this simple mind game will help. First, consider your job and all its advantages—write them down on a slip of paper if it will help. Your list might include security, health care, regular income, high income, fascinating work, promotion possibilities, and anything else that you might like about your employment. Next, we're not going to list the disadvantages; in fact we'll pretend that there aren't any. Remember in Chapter 1 when we found that cruisers (the good ones anyway) never ran away from anything? Well, we wouldn't leave a perfectly good job just because of a few trivialities, so if there are a few negatives in your job, just forget about them.

Next we want to contemplate humanity. That's right, all of it. You don't have to write it down, just think about all the people in the world in all their billions and in all their multitudes. Now consider the fact that the majority of those people don't work for the company that you do and are quite happy with that. Many don't do as well as you do, of course, but many do better, a few do a lot better, and all of them seem to be getting by. Does that make you feel more comfortable? Good, but we aren't done yet.

You probably know at least one person who was fired or laid off at some time. (It is important that it not be recent because it takes most of us a while to sort things out when we change jobs.) How is that person doing now? The chances are that person is doing just fine. (If the person you picked isn't doing fine, pick someone else and try again.) This fact should also offer comfort.

One of my neighbors in Marblehead was a guy named Ralph who had a great job as an air-traffic controller. He was making enough money to compensate for the high stress and rotten working conditions of the job and was content to work away at it until retirement, but President Reagan came along and spoiled the show by firing the lot of them when they went out on a very badly inspired strike.

Ralph went through the normal agony of denial and expectation of eventually being recalled that all the victims of that political boondoggle experienced, but he didn't mope around the house. He had always been a handy lad so he started fixing stuff. One thing led to another and today he is the owner of a thriving home-improvement business. Is he making as much money as he was as a controller? I don't know, and he isn't saying, but I doubt it. But he is content and relaxed—miles ahead of the way he was before he lost his job. The last time I talked to him, he and his wife, Rachel, had just purchased a beautiful cruising boat, an older Tartan 37, on which they were having a ball learning how to sail. I wouldn't be a bit surprised to someday hear the plop of an anchor in some remote and exotic harbor and look out to see that Ralph and Rachel have arrived.

Maximize your income while you can

With your newfound enthusiasm for your job you will find you are invigorated by your work, giving you boundless energy for additional work, but don't worry about becoming a workaholic. Workaholics are people who are driven to work at obsessive levels to compensate for something that is missing in their lives. We all know one or two of these unfortunate folks who hammer their lives away at compulsive levels to accumulate the wealth that they tragically mistake for happiness. With each success they gather more wealth but when it doesn't bring the contentment that we all seek they think this means that they haven't worked hard enough and redouble their efforts. Trying to satisfy greed with money is like trying to put out a fire with gasoline. The most we can hope for these folks is that when they die, the kids will have the sense to spend the money on something useful, like a cruising sailboat.

Because would-be cruisers are accumulating money to satisfy the urge to change their lives rather than to satisfy the urge to accumulate money, the toil makes more sense and doesn't use us up so remorselessly. We work our butts off not to garner wealth but to go cruising, and that makes all the difference—that makes us cruisaholics and that's better.

Become a cruiseaholic

Cruisaholics are people who are driven to work at obsessive levels so they can save enough money to go cruising and thus change their lives. It's easy to become one but you have to work at it a bit. Once you get your regular job in order and adjust your attitude so that it becomes the best damn job in the world, once you achieve the mental stamina that makes you show up for work half an hour early, eager to jump into the old harness and pull that damn wagon like it's never been pulled before, you're ready to branch out. Work overtime if you can, but get paid for it—remember, you don't care about brownie points anymore. Work two or three jobs if you can find them; wait on tables, grease cars, mow lawns, sweep floors, paint your neighbor's house, do whatever you can that is legal and moral to make more money. Often, working at something you enjoy for less money than you would make working at something you hate can pay more in the long run.

In addition to your regular job, try to get part-time work that will teach you skills you can use for yourself and other cruisers while cruising. Diesel mechanics, sewing, electronics, carpentry, teaching, welding, outboard-engine repair, bartending, and cooking are a few good ones. Take a job with a business that caters to the growing Latin American community as a way of brushing up on your Spanish while you earn the big bucks. Remember that once you leave on your cruise, most temporary jobs that will be available to you won't pay near what you think you are worth, so get what you can now, while you can.

Put Your Money to Work

A major mistake made by a great many would-be cruisers is to never start their kitty or to delay starting it until it is too late because, "I don't have enough money for a serious investment program." If you don't have the minimum for a brokerage account, don't worry about it, few of us do when we start. Keep your kitty in a pass-book savings account or in a money-market fund at the bank until you accumulate enough for a more sophisticated option. If you are employed at a regular job (as opposed to being self-employed) have your paycheck deposited directly into your account with as much as possible going into the savings. Start your kitty now no matter how much or how little you can put into it. Ten bucks will get you on your way to the cruising life. Remember, a cruising kitty grows like an onion with successive layers built upon a tiny core. Without that tiny core you and your kitty aren't going anywhere.

A humble supplication
I am not nor will I ever become, under any circumstances, a qualified investment counselor. The following advice on investing your kitty is based on my own experience mucking about with *Sultana*'s kitty and on observations I have made in 40 years of investment experience. I am relating a system that has worked for us, not one that I think will work for you. Investment counseling is far too complicated, and the variables too vast, for me to presume to advise you in any way on how your kitty should be invested. So please take the following as only a guide to the process of setting up an investment plan rather than a plan to be adopted blindly. For a cheerful, insightful, right-on-target overview of the fundamentals of saving and investing, read *Personal Finance for Dummies* by Eric Tyson. Tyson explains it better than I can and in far more detail, and his book isn't just for dummies. In fact, I think Tyson must be a cruiser.

If you do choose to take any of what follows as advice and in so doing you should lose some money, don't blame your humble but sympathetic author. And if in the even more unlikely event that you should be wiped out in the process, please don't sue. For one thing, it would make me feel bad, and for another it would be unlikely that you would ever collect anything because, as one who has developed the wretched habit of following his own advice, it is quite probable that I would be wiped out too.

The All-Service Discount Brokerage
All-service discount brokerage houses are financial institutions that offer a variety of monetary services that might have been tailor-made for cruisers. They offer savings accounts, brokerage services, investment advice, money-market funds with checking privileges, electronic funds transfer, margin accounts, and debit cards, all at reduced prices. All are useful services for cruisers. Most provide one monthly statement for all your finances, a service that facilitates bookkeeping on a cruising boat, and one number to call—sometimes on a 24-hour basis—if there is a question or problem. Don't confuse full-service discount brokerage houses with discount brokerages that offer securities trades for a rock-bottom fee. You can save a lot of money if you do a lot of trading with these discounters, but they offer virtually nothing else in the way of services. Most cruisers will find that the full-service discount brokerages, like Charles Schwab, are well worth the slightly higher fees.

This one-number, one-statement service, which would be a convenience under the best of conditions, is a tremendous boon to the cruiser. When you are traveling in remote parts of the world it is often weeks and even months before your mail catches up with you. A simple (albeit often expensive) phone call will inform you of the balances in your accounts. It is also a major advantage to have only one piece of paper to file every month instead of having a confusing flood of statements coming in from a half dozen or more accounts. On *Sultana* our bookkeeping system involves stuffing everything that arrives covered with columns of numbers on it into a folder for later action (that is, never). Stuffing one piece of paper into a folder every month is much easier than stuffing 8 or 10, and in the rare moments when we need to recover some information, such as the periodic nuisance of having to pay taxes (sorry folks, the IRS doesn't disappear just because you're moored in Mooloolaba), the required numbers are much easier to locate. Once we find the most current of the 12 monthly statements, we simply find the last number in the last column of the category we need, and that's the one we use. The old way involved trying to add numbers from dozens of unrelated slips and scraps—no wonder we never filed on time.

To open an account, swipe . . . er, borrow, that is . . . a copy of any financial magazine from your dentist's waiting room and call any of the brokerage houses or fund managers that advertise with 800 numbers. My current copy of *Fortune* magazine (which is only about four months old), lists a dozen or so. You don't have to call more than a few because these outfits trade names like the Red Sox trade shortstops, and you'll soon be inundated with tons of brochures and prospectuses from every manner of investment house. There are only a few of the full-service type, but read all the stuff anyway—it's an excellent education once you wade through the unreadable fluff that is the hallmark of financial brochures everywhere.

My choice was Charles Schwab, and they have offered excellent, if impersonal, service since we switched to them about two years ago. Do your own research, though, and make your own decisions—it's the key to successful investing. And take that magazine back, will you? Someone else might get their hands on this book and go looking for it.

Most mutual funds and brokerage houses have minimum amounts for opening an account that range from $500 to more than $25,000 (a few go into the millions), depending on the type of account and a lot of other factors. The minimum for a regular investor-line account at Schwab is $2,500 as this is written, but check for yourself because the number is bound to change. If you don't have enough money to satisfy the minimum, let your cash accumulate in a savings account at a bank until you do.

Grooming Your Kitty

Once you have accumulated a fairly substantial hunk of cash, say $5,000 more or less (it'll happen faster than you think), in your money-market fund or savings account, you will want to start thinking about more sophisticated investments. This is when you want to learn all you can about risk management, investing in mutual funds, and in the stock market. You don't need to become a financial wizard, but you do want to make informed decisions about investing your cruising kitty. The best source of information on investing is free from your all-service brokerage or from your local library. Here's a brief primer on risk and investment to get you started.

Risk Management

Risk management is a fascinating subject and one that is fast becoming a major focus of study in academic institutions. It is also appropriate to the cruising life because cruisers practice risk management every day in the normal routine on the high seas. Every time we are about to depart on a passage we carefully consider all the relevant conditions and weigh the risks involved in going against those of staying in port.

Let's say you are at anchor in Apia, Western Samoa, waiting for the weather to clear so you can make the jump on a passage to Suva in Fiji. This isn't a long passage, it only takes four or five days, but it is a dangerous one that demands clear weather and careful navigation to avoid intervening atolls and reefs. There is a strong cold front approaching, and you are trying to decide whether to go now or wait for the front to pass. Cold fronts, of course, are nearly always followed by clear weather, but they are also followed by flat seas and light winds. If you wait until tomorrow will you be able to catch the backside of the front and ride it into the forecast high and thereby reduce your exposure to the predictable light winds? What if you leave now? Will you be clobbered by gale-force winds when the front arrives, or will the winds moderate as they approach land and give you the boost to get most of the way through the high before it develops and the winds die? You must consider as much of the available information as is pertinent, but ultimately you must go with the feeling in your gut.

From the hypothetical to the real. . . . We were in Nuku'alofa Harbor waiting with about a dozen other boats for a clear weather window to start the trip to New Zealand when the catamaran *Sudden Laughter* pulled in after an extended cruise to Mururoa to protest the French nuclear testing. After a day or so of replenishing supplies and undertaking a few minor repairs, the ship was making ready to leave in spite of a huge weather system developing in the Tasman Sea.

"Haven't you heard the weather report?" I asked one of the crew.

"Never listen to the bloody things, mate," he answered. "All they do is scare ya."

"Hey, you're going to get the shit kicked out of ya on any trip to Kiwiland, so you might as well get it over with early on," added another member of the crew.

When we caught up with *Sudden Laughter* in Nelson Harbor several months later, I found that they had indeed gotten clobbered about two days after they left, but after the front passed they had an easy sail to Nelson. We, on the other hand, had taken a more cautious approach and waited another week or so for the weather to clear before we left. After suffering through light and variable winds for a week, we got hit by a southerly gale that had us hove to for two days, blew our main to shreds, and continued to howl for more than a week. Like the guy at the carnival roulette wheel says, "Ya pays yer money and ya takes yer chances."

The same approach to risk that we apply to our cruising decisions is appropriate for selecting among the dozens of ways you can invest your kitty, and the goal of investing is also analogous to the destination of a passage. We want the trip from where we start (at investment) to be quick and safe to our destination (our investment goal). We also want a smooth trip with no storms and rocky seas that make the boat bounce up and down, making the captain and crew fret and worry about the whole thing sinking out of sight forever. But storms are a reality of the cruising life just like falling markets are a reality of investment. While we will do anything to avoid trouble, we must be ready for it when it invariably arrives. Thus we have liferafts and EPIRBs and signal flares and radios and all manner of safety gadgets to ensure our survival should that sinking sensation suddenly set in. So too do we have safety nets for our kitty (which I'll discuss a little later).

Of course, risk is the easiest thing in the world to avoid. All you need to do is stay in harbor and never make the passage. You'll have plenty of company because we've never seen a harbor yet that wasn't full of shiny yachts that will never see an open ocean. Either they weren't fit for ocean travel or their owners didn't have the confidence to go offshore. The owner of one of the nicest cruising boats in Marblehead Harbor has his boat professionally delivered to Penobscot Bay in Maine every year (a passage of about 135 nautical miles). At the end of a two-week cruise, the delivery skipper takes the boat back to Massachusetts. Lots of boatowners (and investors) do the same thing even though it's expensive. And although it's safe and comforting to pay someone else to take the risks, you will also miss out on most of the fun.

You can likewise eliminate all the risk of cruising by simply not going. A few years ago I read about a man from Tennessee who, in the prime of his life, was relaxing in the cockpit of his sailboat with (we can presume) a nice tall drink, a cigar, and a good book. The boat was tied safely to a marina dock, and the guy was living a life that was about as risk-free as you can get. But his luck was running out. A plane flying high overhead lost a large bolt from the landing gear, and you know the rest of the story. That bolt fell 25,000 feet, crashed right through the awning of the boat, and smashed that drink all to hell.

The relationship between risk and return

To get people to accept higher risk, investments have to pay a higher average return over some time, otherwise we'd all have our money in savings accounts or ultra-safe government bonds. But that higher risk translates into periods of gains and losses that we hope will average out to a higher return (the classic upward-trending sinusoidal line of stock market returns). In investing and in cruising, we can choose to stay in harbor for a risk-free (but boring) existence or we can choose to risk heading off to sea and be rewarded with the highs and the lows of the cruising life (which for most of us who try it adds up to something better than the shoreside life we left behind).

The relationship between risk and time

To get that higher average return, the investment needs to remain in place through the cycle of highs and lows. For the stock market, most investment counselors say, this means five years. Larger returns might be made by moving quickly in and out of the market, but so might larger losses. Without excellent information (read, inside information) the average investor is more likely to get trounced than to make a fortune buying and selling stocks over short time horizons. And don't forget, every time you buy and sell a security, your broker will want to be paid for the service, and these fees will often negate any returns. So lacking inside information (an accurate weather forecast) your experiences during a two-day passage are likely to be more extreme than over a three-week passage. In two days you'll probably either have great weather or get trashed; during a three-week trip you'll see a bit of everything and come out closer to what the pilot charts call average weather for that passage in that season.

Diversification

Diversification is an integral part of risk management. It reduces the dependence of the overall return on a single investment by spreading portfolio risk across companies, industries, sectors and even countries. But there are two kinds of risk involved—systematic risk that is inherent in the system and reflected by the underlying (once national, now global) business cycle, and nonsystematic risks like the consequences of the legal action against Microsoft and the "New Coke" marketing debacle committed by Coca-Cola. While diversification will eliminate or reduce the effect of nonsystematic risks on your portfolio, you cannot diversify away systematic risks.

If a company like Coca-Cola does something stupid, like altering one of the most popular products in the world, or if the government rules against Microsoft, the reduced price of these stocks will not overly affect your average return because other stocks in your kitty will be going up enough over the long haul to offset these losses. However, the risks from global disasters such as a total collapse of the Japanese banking system or a nuclear war between Pakistan and India would affect all markets and cannot be diversified away.

From a sailing point of view, you can carry a variety of safety and maintenance equipment to help you handle anything from jury-rigging a mast to treating a sick crewmember, but you can do nothing to reduce the chances of a freak accident like running into a whale or being struck by lightning. The distinction here is important because the underlying business cycle plays a large role in determining overall market return. In other words, if you have a large part of your kitty in the stock market, you can lose money no matter what you do. International turmoil can make bank accounts look attractive again and keep Russians stuffing dollars into mattresses rather than investing in their new stock market. Since the late 1970s and early 1980s, the American stock market has not been negatively affected by these kinds of risks, and many amateur investors have come to believe that a bull market can be sustained indefinitely by Alan Greenspan and careful financial management. The fact is, we've had an astonishing 20-year period of peace paralleling a period of unsurpassed economic growth even as the markets have become so intertwined worldwide that what happens in Japan or Peking or London affects our stock market almost instantly. People need to understand that they are betting on two more decades of global peace and worldwide economic stability if they expect similar returns over the next 20 years.

The first and most important thing to learn about investing is that there is no gain without risk and that a risk can result in a loss; substantial risks can result in substantial losses as well as gains. There's no room for crybabies; if you can't take the loss don't take the risk—it's that simple.

Investment Vehicles

The following is a list, in order of increasing risk and increasing average returns, of a few of the investment options open to you once your kitty has a few thousand dollars available to get you started on a serious investment program.

- Bank (or passbook) savings accounts are, of course, the most common and the easiest way to save money. Savings accounts are available anywhere, they are safe as an investment gets, you don't have to worry about fluctuations in the financial markets, and you might even score a new toaster when you open one. The only creditable risk is that the interest you earn will barely keep abreast of inflation. A savings account will preserve your money, but it won't put the money to work.
- Certificates of deposit (CDs) are a way of investing money for a specific

length of time for a known dividend that you will collect at the end of the investment period. They carry low risk, pay a modest return, and are available from any bank and most lending institutions. The disadvantages of CDs are that your money is not accessible for the life of the CD without substantial penalty and the return is low compared to other options (though higher than a savings account). As long-term investments, CDs are appropriate for timid investors and those who don't care to take the time to learn about other avenues. They can also be useful as a place to "park" money you're likely to need at a specified time in the near future. A "basket" of CDs with staggered maturity dates (six months, 12 months, 18 months, etc.) can make sense in this instance.

- High-grade government bonds pay a fixed interest rate and have a value that fluctuates with prevailing interest rates and their maturity date. They deserve a prominent place in your cruising kitty, but they need to be selected with care.
- Preferred stocks are much like bonds. They pay a fixed return, but they have no maturity date. In the past investors would offset the risk associated with common stocks by buying bonds or preferred stocks, but the notion that bonds and preferred stocks can be used to hedge common stocks has taken a beating recently, with the stock and bond markets moving together rather than in opposite directions.
- Common stock funds are mutual funds with full-time managers who spend their days and nights buying and selling profitable stocks for you, the investor. The value of a common stock fund (called the NAV for net asset value) is determined by the average market value of all the securities in the portfolio (and this is often in the billions of dollars) divided by the number of fund shares outstanding. The manager does all the work of buying and selling while the diversification of the portfolio helps to smooth out the lumps and bumps of the market fluctuations. They are just the ticket for a large part of our cruising kitty. The good ones pay a healthy total return (growth in market value plus dividends), and they are easier to select and carry less risk than individual stocks. International stock funds are also available. These are riskier than domestic funds since they are affected by currency exchange rates as well as the fluctuations of the component stocks, but they represent a useful way to move some of your eggs into another basket.
- High-grade bond funds are mutual funds that specialize in various types of bonds, preferred stocks, and a variety of government issues. There are a great many of these funds and selecting just the right ones can be daunting for a person not familiar with them. It is worth a bit of study though, because bond funds should be an important part of your kitty. Like everything else, they must be selected with care, so consult a professional if you don't feel 100 percent comfortable with them.

Cruisers who don't want to take the time to get any more involved in the complexities of investing can stop right here by putting a big part of their kitty in a diversified portfolio of CDs, common stock funds, bond funds, and perhaps some ready cash in a money market account. The following vehicles are a lot more tricky to use, they require more time for maintenance, and the risk is proportionately higher than with the vehicles listed above. Therefore, most cruisers should probably avoid them simply because they require too much attention. We have better things to do with our time than fret over the machinations of a fickle stock market. However, the aggressive investor or the cruiser who is truly interested in following market swings will need to at least consider the next five vehicles.

- Individual common stocks, on average, have paid the highest returns for the lowest risk of any investment vehicle in the past 20 years. The key word here is "average" because even in a rapidly rising market there are always a few losers and in any kind of market it is just as easy to pick a loser as a winner. Selecting the right common stocks requires much study and more than a little luck. Mistakes can be costly. The value of a common stock is determined by the price someone else is willing to pay for it and little else. Thus the price of a good stock can fall quickly if it falls out of favor with investors, and a bad stock can skyrocket if it becomes trendy with the in-crowd of investors. Professional investors are very much like lemmings and tend to follow the person in front of them even if that person runs off a cliff into the sea. Even the most adventurous cruisers should never let the amount of money invested in individual stocks (as opposed to common stock mutual funds) exceed 25 percent of the total kitty.
- American depository receipts (ADRs) provide a means of investing in overseas companies through the U.S. stock exchanges. ADRs trade through the various markets just like stocks. They tend to be more speculative than stocks but can still be excellent investments. Only a small part (no more than 10 percent) of your cruising kitty should ever go into select ADRs, but that small part can return large gains (and, of course, losses). I like ADRs, but most investors would prefer to invest in global or foreign stock funds and let the fund managers do the choosing.
- Closed-end mutual funds trade on the exchanges just like ADRs and should also be approached with caution, but they also deserve consideration for the aggressive kitty. Closed-end funds are worth what somebody else is willing to pay for them, just like common stocks. Typically, they trade at a discount to the net asset value (NAV) of the stocks they own. Among these funds are some that specialize in stocks of one country; these represent a convenient vehicle for targeted foreign investments. Cruisers and cruisers-in-training should be long-term investors—but if you feel compelled to trade, you're less likely to lose your shirt trading closed-end funds than individual stocks.
- Low-grade bonds, sometimes called junk bonds, are speculative, and you should only invest money in them that you never expect to see again. Don't discount them entirely though; Xerox, McDonalds, IBM, Intel, and a lot of others got started by issuing junk bonds. If you buy junks, don't buy a lot of them.
- Junk-bond funds can be a hedge against a falling market because when investors (we're talking about the big boys and girls here) decide to get out of stocks, they often go into junk funds because, while they tend to be more speculative than high-grade funds, in a down market they tend

to return what these heavy hitters are used to getting from their stock funds.

There are a great many other vehicles with which you can make and lose money. REITs (real estate investment trusts), the commodities (pork bellies and such) market, and short selling are just a few. These are sophisticated investments, however, best left alone by cruisers and anyone who is not a full-time professional investor. In the early 1980s, I jumped at the chance to buy a small safe deposit box full of Kuggerands and Canadian Maple leafs (gold coins) at a mere $450 dollars each because "everyone" knew that gold was headed for $500 an ounce and was sure to go higher. Those coins are now worth a robust $285 each, proving once again how easy it is for a misguided amateur investor to turn a large fortune into a small one with hardly any effort at all.

Dividend Reinvestment Options

Automatic reinvestment plans will use the dividends you earn from a security to buy additional shares of that security, usually without any fees or commissions. If your broker offers this, be sure and sign up. Your cash dividends will go into your securities account rather than your cash account, where they won't earn as much (in the long term).

Your broker will ask if you are interested in growth stocks or income stocks. Tell him or her that all you want is more money at the end of the month than you had at the beginning of the month and whether they call it growth, income, or sea-weed soup doesn't matter a bit. (There are some differences in the tax conse-quences of growth and income stocks that you don't need to worry about until you build a large kitty or unless you want to really get into investing.)

Worry-Free Kitties

Investing your kitty is a lot easier than most professional money managers want you to believe. It is about 25 percent science and 75 percent gut feelings borne of familiarity, which means it is highly instinctive, which is why so many cruisers are good at it.

Read a few back issues of *Barrons* and *Forbes* magazines, or any other fi-nancial periodical, and a few books from the library (*Against the Gods* by Peter L. Bernstein is a good one on risk) to learn the mechanics of investing. Then stay cur-rent by reading an occasional copy of the international edition of *Business Week*.

If you do buy stocks, buy good ones in good companies that have a record of paying reasonable dividends and show potential for growth, then put them away and don't worry about them.

Don't Cry, Diversify

I've covered this once already, but I'll say it again because it is the most important part of your investment program. Diversification is the key to investing for the cruising life and the single best way to protect your investment in any situation. If your entire kitty were invested in one moderately risky investment, say common shares of a high-flying software company, it would be difficult to sleep at night. However, if your kitty were divided among 10 moderately risky common stocks in three or four unrelated industries in three or four countries, what happens to any one stock doesn't matter that much, so you don't have to worry about it as much. Also, by diversifying your kitty you won't have a lot invested in any one area so that the consequences of your mistakes won't be as dire. Thus you will be training yourself not to make mistakes at the same time you are learning not to worry about the ones you do make.

Right now, *Sultana*'s $150,000 kitty is diversified as follows: 25 percent cash (money-market funds); 25 percent high-grade preferred stocks (mostly financial institutions); 25 percent common stocks (mostly large caps); and 25 percent mutual funds. The non-cash portion is further diversified into about 75 percent domestic investments and 25 percent global and foreign investment (ADRs and mutual funds). It is even further diversified among several industries (technology, financial, and farming) and at several levels of risk (50 percent low risk, 35 percent moderate risk, and 15 percent high risk). Sound complicated? It really isn't; in fact, it's about as difficult as a hand of contract bridge or a round of pinochle.

Sultana's kitty is presently earning about 14 percent after all costs except taxes are deducted. This is great; I'd be quite happy with a 10 percent return and don't really count on more than 8. An 8 percent return is enough to pay for most of our day-to-day cruising expenses, but extraordinary expenses such as refits and travel have to come from another source (work, luck, or chicanery). The good years, like 1997, help compensate for the bad years when the kitty doesn't make as much or even for those rare (but never rare enough) occasions when it loses money.

Except for your cash, which should be kept in a money-market fund, all your investments should be for the long term, which means for five years or longer. "Buy 'em and forget 'em," is the watchword of the cruising investor. You don't have to worry about what's happening to your diversified long-term investments. Solid long-term stocks of large American and European companies ("large-caps" in street slang) and hi-cap funds carry moderate risk and have been almost foolproof for the last 10 years. (The operative word here is "almost" because there just aren't any guarantees.)

I check *Sultana*'s kitty every three months and make any necessary adjustments, which are usually very minor. In fact, an annual check would be perfectly all right. Select your investments with the help of a good broker, a little study, and a lot of common sense.

How Not to Buy Stocks

Don't ever invest in "tips" from your dentist or some guy you met in the boatyard, and ignore anything you might read on the Internet until you confirm it with your broker. Be especially leery of anything that you read in cruising books written by grouchy old guys with wooden boats. A huge resource of investor information and assistance is available on the Internet, but there is an even larger body of nonsense and more than a few world-class scams. Until you are comfortable with investing your kitty and convinced that secure and conservative investments are necessary, you must stay away from this stuff, or at least learn to take everything you hear and read that doesn't come from a trusted professional with a large grain of salt. Even articles in national magazines can contain bad advice about bad investments so you need to be skeptical about the most reputable sources of investment advice.

Especially beware of life-insurance salespeople. At our modest level of investing, most people who call themselves financial advisors or investment counselors are actually life-insurance salespeople—if they so much as mention the words "life insurance," walk away. There is nothing wrong with life insurance, but life insurance is life insurance not an investment.

Ignore trendy investments (as opposed to trends, which is another thing) and fads. You can't keep up with them from a cruising sailboat anyway. The media gurus and personalities (such as those who appear on Louis Rukeyser's show "Wall Street Week") who so love to predict what is going to happen to the market or to favorite stocks and funds are a great source of information on the current state of affairs and are whizzes at analyzing historical data that can help you make up your mind which investments you want in your kitty. These folks are professionals in a difficult and complicated field, and you should listen to what they say, but when they are trying to predict what is going to happen in the future, they are wrong so often that it's comical. One perfectly valid investment strategy is to find out what these gurus say is going to happen then do just the opposite of what they advise. As this is written, in summer 1998, the best minds on Wall Street have been predicting a major correction (read collapse) of the market for the past three years. The Dow just shed about 500 points after a year of spectacular increase, and it now looks like next year will see a return to more reasonable levels of growth or even slump for awhile. The important thing to remember is that if you've done it right with conservative long-term investments, you can sleep soundly with no need to worry about what happens in the market.

Planning for What Comes Next

Let's face it: you aren't going to cruise forever. The charm of distant anchorages in strange places may eventually wear thin. You might tire of the gypsy life and begin to yearn for some permanent dirt under your feet and a vegetable garden out in the back yard, or you may want to do other things you can't do on a boat. More likely, you'll just grow too old to keep up with the vigorous life of the active cruiser. Whatever the reasons you give up the cruising life, when you do it you're going to need some resources. The most common mistake cruisers who are returning to shore make is to count on the resale of their boat for retirement funds. Of course you can sell your boat when you give up cruising, but I guarantee that you're not going to get nearly as much as you think you'll get for it—but we have said that before.

The point is that cruisers are notoriously bad at planning for the day when they must hang up their Topsiders. As you design the financial strategy for your cruise, you must take these needs into consideration and plan for them accordingly. Beyond this caveat, I can't say much because individual circumstances, needs, and ages vary enough to make any specific advice useless. Susan and I are fortunate to have a satisfactory retirement fund that will become available to us once we reach the magical age of 65. This fund, which we started many years ago, has grown steadily to about a quarter of a million dollars—not a fortune by any means, but adequate to meet our simple needs in our twilight years with, perhaps, just a bit left for the kids to fight over. If you don't have this most important base covered, your best bet is to discuss your needs with a trusted financial advisor and implement the advice you get.

With investing, as in all things, when you are smart and earn money, people will say you were lucky. When you are stupid and lose money, people will say you were stupid.

7

PLANNING DEPARTURE

"Make a new plan, Stan."

—Paul Simon, "Fifty Ways to Leave Your Lover"

Uncle Freddy and the Pompadour Kid

My earliest sailing experiences were aboard my Uncle Freddy's 29-foot Herreshoff sloop *Mazuka*. She was a fine old boat built somewhere in New England sometime in the 1920s. If she looked a bit run down and shabby she suited our purpose just fine, thanks, and when I learned to sail on her she still sported hemp lines and cotton sails. Like most Herreshoff designs, she also sported an enormous sinusoidal keel and a draft of over 6 feet. In the shallow waters of the Chesapeake Bay this meant that a good part of our sailing time was spent waiting for the tide to come in and float us off whatever sandbar the keel had decided we would colonize that day. That pleased me to no end because it provided opportunity to cavort in the warm bay waters with my two cousins, chase tasty blue crabs through the shallows with the ship's long-handled crab net, dive for oysters, and pursue other activities more interesting to a 14-year-old than mere sailing.

Let's back up a bit. When I say learning to sail, that may not be quite accurate. Uncle Freddy was the undisputed captain of *Mazuka* and as such, he did all the sailing. I spent most of the time while under way on the foredeck practicing my sullen look and working on my pompadour. This was the early 1950s and my teenage world was firmly under the influence of the recently departed James Dean, and the sullen sneer, defiant squint, and Lucky Strike dangling from pouting lips (when my mom wasn't looking, of course) were critical to post-adolescent survival. It was a jungle out there, and if your pompadour didn't stand up just right and your sneer didn't intimidate properly you were doomed to a life of ignominy and disgrace. I never did master the sneer, but I had a terrific sullen scowl, and my pompadour and ducktail rivaled those of the upstart Elvis himself.

Anyway, I didn't learn to sail on my uncle's boat, but I did learn something about what makes a sailboat go and why it does the things it does. I also learned a lot about what you can't expect a boat to do, like carry a 6-foot draft through 4 feet of water or get you home in a hurry when you really need to get home in a hurry. I learned that sailboats are fun, that my life wasn't in danger when the thing heeled to a stiff breeze, and that if I kept in the lee of the main by the mast, I could avoid the wind enough to preserve my pompadour. In a word, I learned to like boats and to respect them, and that has changed my life.

Learning to Sail

We've assumed all along that you know how to sail. If you don't, don't worry. The basics are pretty easy to pick up, and you'll learn quickly once under way. It's quite amazing how many people who have no previous sailing experience become successful cruisers. It isn't at all uncommon to meet folks from places like Iowa and Nebraska and Arizona who had never so much as been aboard a sailboat when epiphany struck and they decided to become cruisers. In Belize we met a couple from Ontario who spent 10 years building a 50-foot ferrocement ketch and who had never seen a body of water larger than an inland lake until they launched in Lake Superior.

Of course, some of these people never do become adept sailors—in fact, some of the best cruisers we have met are klutzy sailors even after years of experience. In the Cook Islands we met a family on a salty old gaff-rigged schooner who looked the epitome of stereotypical mariners—striped jerseys and sailor hats and everything but the parrot. I spent several happy evenings talking traditional boats and how sailing used to be with the skipper of this fine anachronism. I gathered he knew just about everything there was to know about boats and how to make them travel—until I watched them try to leave the harbor. When they cast off it was obvious they were having trouble controlling the boat under power and they finally had to hire a local boat to escort them out the narrow channel. Then, like a couple of blinking amateurs, they stumbled off over the horizon with the main blanketing the foresail and the jib flapping useless in the breeze. I was astonished at their ineptitude but not really surprised when I heard through the coconut telegraph (one of the most efficient communication systems on earth) that they had reached Australia before most of the fleet after an uneventful and presumably enjoyable cruise—proving once again my contention that judgment on when and where to sail, navigation skills, and strength of character are far more important to the cruising life than sophisticated sailing skills.

Another group of cruisers lies on the opposite end of the cruising spectrum. These are folks who might become disenchanted with the cruising life because they know how to sail, but can't. Many people who develop sophisticated sailing skills on high-tech boats are not happy with the low-tech, outdated boats that are so common among budget cruisers. It must be frustrating indeed to possess the skills to make a lightweight class boat fly around the buoys at the head of the fleet and then be stuck with an overloaded under-rigged slow-moving cruising tub. We've met a few of these folks and they constantly like to talk about what they would do to the old girl if they had the money for new sails and rigging. This is fine, of course, and we all like to blue sky about ways we would improve our boats if we had the cash, but I'm convinced that some of these former racers who can't afford a high-tech boat would be happier staying home until the kitty was big enough to allow them to sail like they want to sail.

Sailing schools

It is important to get as much sailing experience as you can before you buy a boat, but it is even more important not to spend a lot of money getting that experience. Don't pay anyone to teach you how to sail. The sailing schools that have flourished in recent years are terrific and usually good value for consumers. But we're no longer consumers, are we? We need that money in our kitty. Besides, most of these schools use old Solings or newer J/24s or some other class of boats that is a dream to sail. It's great fun and a great way to develop respect for sailboats and to meet a wonderful bunch of fun and interesting people, but it doesn't teach you that much about cruising sailing.

Bareboat charters

Don't indulge in bareboat charters. They offer good value to consumers looking for an exciting vacation, and they are an entrée into cruising for a lot of folks with deep pockets, but they're too expensive for those of us struggling to build a kitty, and they don't teach much about cruising anyway. The boats are usually light-weight production models with cut-down rigs that would be inappropriate or even dangerous for offshore cruising. All the work, such as provisioning, navigating, and maintenance is done for you, and many charter companies even provide cooks. You are also restricted as to where and when you can sail. To add insult to injury, many charter companies actively discourage any contact with the cruising community, a fact that has always puzzled me and deserves a slight deviation from our stated topic.

I first became aware of a curious segregation between cruising sailors and bareboat charterers in the Virgin Islands when I noticed that boats sharing the same harbors would clump up like flocks of sheep and goats—all the sheep were at one end of the harbor, the goats at the other. It quickly became apparent that these two groups were looking for different things from their cruises. The cruisers were looking for peace and quiet; the charterers were looking for fun—and fun to charterers often means crowding 6 or 10 people onto a 35-foot boat, getting drunk, and making noise until 2 A.M. This helped explain why there was a lack of dialogue between the two groups, but it still didn't explain the obvious antipathy with which the two groups viewed each other, nor did it explain why the charter operators told their customers to avoid cruisers.

It wasn't until we got to Vava'u in Tonga that I discovered the real reason. Neiafu Harbor is home to a large charter fleet run by the Moorings Company. The manager is an energetic young man named Bill Bailey (no"Won't-you-come-home?" jokes, please—it's no wonder the poor guy lives in Tonga) and I wasted no time asking him about this phenomenon. He wouldn't talk, but I struck up a conversation with one of his crew who made it all clear.

"Hey," he said defensively. "Most of our customers come all the way from the U.S. or from Europe and pay thousands of dollars for a few weeks sailing in one of our boats. They think it's a bargain and it is when you consider the cost of running an operation like this. But then they see the damn cruisers in their junky old boats and find out that some of these guys sail around these islands for a whole year and don't spend any more money in a year than what they are paying for a few weeks, and it causes trouble. Suddenly they think we are trying to rip them off, and they want to know how we justify charging so much." He paused for a moment to get his emotions under control, but it didn't work. "We even had a couple from Seattle who had been coming here for years get friendly with a cruising couple. Now they come and stay on their friends' boat for nothing—can you beat that?"

Crewing at yacht clubs

If we can't spend money and we don't have a boat yet, how are we going to learn to sail? Well, if a yacht club is nearby, there's your answer. Posting a notice that you would like to crew often brings a flood of calls, but be careful who you crew with and don't just hop into the first boat that comes along. Be particularly cautious if you are asked to crew on a racing boat.

Many racing skippers possess intense personalities and emotions that are hard for others to understand and tolerate. Therefore, many races deteriorate into screaming matches that often carry over to the protest committee and even to the courts. This is fine because it keeps a lot of self-important and potentially dangerous people off the streets and in the committee rooms where they can't do any real harm. The problem is that the screaming and profanity are most frequently directed at the crew instead of the opposition. Punching your skipper in the nose for calling you a lamebrained idiot (the usual epithet is much worse than that) when you got the traveler car a quarter- inch out of position on the last tack teaches you nothing about sailing or cruising. (However, I imagine that it is a most satisfactory experience.)

If you agree to become a member of a racing crew, the skipper usually assigns you to one line to pull or one winch to crank when you are yelled at. It's possible to crew for years under skippers like this without having a clue as to what's going on, and the only thing you become good at is pulling one line and hating the skipper.

Crewing for friends

If you have a friend who owns a sailboat, no matter the size, hint around that you'd like to serve as crew; chances are that you'll find a willing teacher. It is much better to learn to sail on a small simple boat with a crew of two or three than on a large boat with a large crew. Small boats are harder to sail well than large boats but you will learn more quickly. The owner of a small boat will be much more likely to let you participate in all aspects of sailing than will the skipper of a large boat.

There is a limit to the small-boat theory, however, and I would suggest not trying to learn sailing techniques on sailing dinghies. The little boats are great for kids (Phillip learned on an Optimist and Sarah graduated to a Laser) but they aren't for adults, and the more adult you are the more they aren't for you. Dinghy sailing requires the agility of an Olympic athlete and the humility of a saint. You must squat on the floorboard of the boat like a frog looking for a bug and be prepared to fling your weight about in a reckless fashion to prevent the whole thing from flipping over on top of you. When you don't move quickly enough you capsize, and if you are anywhere near as proficient a dinghy sailor as your aquaphobic author, most of your dinghy-sailing time will be spent in the drink trying to right the damn thing so you can carry on into the next gust of wind and start the whole process over again. Cruisers like me are noted for our great agility of mind and spirit and less so for agility of body. My advice is to leave the dinghies to the young people and those few adults who are predisposed to strenuous physical activity and other forms of self-torture. Try to find a spot on a bigger boat.

Crewing for delivery skippers and singlehanders

One raw and rainy October night, I was working late getting our old powerboat ready to haul for the season when I heard a timid knock on the hull and a thin voice request permission to come aboard. When I assented, a woman in her early twenties climbed into the cabin and asked if I was preparing the boat to move south. She was visibly disappointed when I told her the boat was being hauled out for winter storage in the morning. Being reluctant to send her back out into the cold, I fixed her a cup of coffee and let her sit for a while.

Her name was Lisa and she had spent the past three years hitchhiking around the eastern U.S. and Caribbean on cruising yachts. She had, however, waited a bit too long and had missed the major southern exodus of New England boats. When I commented that hitchhiking about on boats seemed like a rather dangerous way to travel for a young person, she laughed heartily and said that there were advantages to being rather homely—not to mention her third-degree black belt. She had experienced only one or two unpleasant moments in her travels, and nothing she couldn't handle. She also said that whenever she was ready to move on, she almost always had her choice of several boats from which to choose and that her present situation was unusual.

Lisa finished her coffee and went off into the night looking for adventure and a ride south and since she never reappeared, I assume she found both. Since then, I have met several people doing just what Lisa was, and it seems to me that it's an excellent way for a single person or even a couple to learn about the cruising life without buying a boat or otherwise making a major commitment.

In any major harbor frequented by cruising sailors, there are usually several boats looking for crew to help on a voyage; often, the boats are large, fancy yachts, on which the regular crew doesn't feel confident or comfortable moving it by themselves. A crew's berth on a large yacht with a reasonable skipper can be a very pleasant way to travel while learning the ropes—but don't become spoiled! Although it is always great to see how the other folks live, we don't want the good life of electric winches, VCRs in every cabin, multiple heads, and state-of-the-art hardware to seduce us away from our stated goal: to become simple and basic cruisers.

Another possibility for a berth is to seek out singlehanders about to embark on a passage. Insurance companies quite rightly frown on singlehanded passage-making and often insist that the boatowner find crew. Many singlehanders, even those who carry no insurance, will welcome an extra hand to stand watch and provide conversation.

One of the best ways to get experience cruising and boat handling anywhere is by crewing for a delivery skipper. Hundreds of newly sold boats are delivered all over the globe by professional delivery crews, and if you can secure a berth on one of these yachts, you will be learning from a professional sailor whom you can usually count on as being one of the best. If you've made even a short passage or two as crew on a cruising yacht and can provide solid references, there's a chance that a delivery skipper will offer you a free berth; cooking skills give you extra leverage. If you're good enough, you might even get a return airplane ticket out of the deal, and if you are really good you might even get a small paycheck. Many people who purchase boats do their own delivery and might just welcome you aboard as cook or an unpaid deckhand.

Bear in mind, if you are thinking about seeking a crew slot on any boat sailing into foreign waters, that international maritime law makes the skipper responsible for the welfare of the crew, and crew can demand that they be returned to their homeport by the quickest means possible. Thus in addition to a valid passport and any necessary visas, you will also need a return airplane ticket from the country you are visiting. A ticket isn't likely to be provided by the skipper as part of the deal for your first few trips while you are learning the ropes, so he or she may insist that you hand over a ticket or a sum of money equal to the price of the return fare on departure. Naturally, this requirement has led to some dicey moments between captain and crew, so make sure everyone understands the situation before you commit yourself to a crew's slot. The other major requirement is that you be flexible enough to drop everything and take off for a week or more to take advantage of opportunities as they arise.

Boat brokers are the best sources of information on current deliveries. There is a comprehensive list of brokers in the advertising section of any sailing magazine; simply get on the phone and call around. Unless you are lucky, you will have to call several brokers before you get someone willing to help you, so be persistent.

Cruising World, SAIL, and the SSCA *Bulletin* all list "crew needed" advertisements. These ads are sometimes free and should bring quick results, especially if you offer to share expenses—but you may want to avoid the ones requesting a photo. You will usually be asked to kick in for the fuel and provide your own food, but make sure everyone understands who pays for what before you agree to go. Be aware that when a skipper accepts expense money from a crewmember, even for little things like a case of beer, the boat could be considered an unlicensed charter boat. In certain areas like the Virgin Islands and the Galapagos, where the licensed charter operators guard their turf like pit bulls guard their backyards, this can mean a world of grief for the skipper. In the worst scenario, the skipper and crew can be jailed and the boat confiscated—not something you ever want to be part of in any country.

Yet another approach to finding a crew berth is the one used by Lisa and most other maritime vagabonds. Simply hang out around any big marina where there are a lot of yachts and let everyone know you are looking for a crew berth. Check first with the harbormaster or other authority person extant (APE) and let them know what you are up to. APEs like to know what is going on in their territories and a pleasant one (quite rare, unfortunately) will even give you a few pointers. If the APE objects to you approaching boats directly, ask if you can post a notice on the bulletin board instead. Prospective crew have even been known to have flyers printed which they hand out in yacht club and marina parking lots.

One last point before we chuck the subject of crew berths into the wake and leave it behind forever. The foregoing advice is good and sound, but most of the cruisers I know who need crew seem to find them hanging around waterfront bars. I would not and could not in good conscience ever recommend that a person looking for a crew position take to hanging around in bars, but it does seem to work, and hey, who am I to argue with tradition?

USCGA and U.S. Power Squadron courses

So sailing off with some person you don't know to somewhere you've never been is a little too heavy in the adventure department? Well then, what else is there? One of the ways to learn the basics, and even more about sailing and boat handling, is to enroll in local evening classes. Both the U.S. Coast Guard Auxiliary and the U.S.

Power Squadron offer a series of excellent courses covering all aspects of boat handling, seamanship, and navigation (traditional and electronic). Most are free or carry a small charge for materials, and in my experience the quality of instruction has been excellent. The teachers are experienced sailors with a firm knowledge of their subjects. However, they are not necessarily experienced teachers and only a few will have had extensive cruising experience, but I have never found this to be a problem. The classes are usually small after the first few nights (there are usually a lot of dropouts for some reason), and a camaraderie quickly develops among the students and staff that makes the learning friendly and easy.

Learning about Cruising

You should, by now, have a pretty good idea of what you are getting yourself into, and you have probably decided, yep, this is it, I'm really going to do it. That's great, but don't quit your day job just yet. We still have a lot to do.

Cruising seminars

Don't spend money on cruising seminars. They can be entertaining and informative for noncruisers, but they can be expensive, and most of the people giving the seminars are no longer cruising. The speakers are often so busy giving seminars, they don't have time for cruising anymore. Worse, many of them are opinionated, a trait shared by many cruisers. (Thank God your knowledgeable but unbiased author has escaped such a fate.) Susan attended one, for example, where the lecturer insisted autopilots and wind vanes were useless.

Don't believe anything you're told about cruising or cruising destinations until you check it out yourself. As stated above, cruisers tend to be opinionated and base their opinions on their own experiences; a good experience for one is a nightmare for another. Fellow cruisers have often advised us to avoid a place where they have had a bad experience; we've gone there anyway and found a wonderful place to visit—for us. Other times we've been told that such and such a place was a paradise for cruisers only to find a place we were indifferent about. We rarely find a place we don't really like and it's usually close to a city, but this reflects our prejudice and preference for quiet rural areas. Other cruisers prefer the hustle and bustle of busy harbors, and we've even met some (quite a few really) who actually like Pago Pago.

Would you like to know where you can find a free cruising seminar almost every evening of the week? Head for the aforementioned waterfront bar. (Just watch out for the ones called pubs or those that have a gold-painted sculpture of a pineapple or a rooster instead of a name—they tend to be pricey and populated by yuppies.) Seek any group of cruisers therein, strike up a conversation, and offer to buy a round of beers. A single round should get you about three hours of uninterrupted cruising lectures, plus you will glean untold bits of useful information such as the IQ, dietary habits, and sexual preferences of the harbormaster, who snuck off with whom to do what, and which grocery stores offer the best discounts on case lots of Spam and Dinty Moore beef stew.

The Seven Seas Cruising Association (SSCA)

The SSCA is a large, mostly volunteer, worldwide network of cruising sailors and a superb source for up-to-date cruising information. The monthly *Bulletin* (which

I have already mentioned several times) is worth the price of membership, and because the association accepts no advertising, the authors of *Bulletin* articles are candid about products and services. Articles are written by active cruisers, so they are subjective and must be taken as opinion instead of fact.

Stay current with your SSCA *Bulletin*s and read the back issues for information on areas you might want to visit. The *Bulletin* has a good index, and back copies are available from the home base. If you read an article in the bulletin by a skipper with whom you would like to communicate, don't hesitate to write care of home base. Just allow at least six months for a reply—slow mail is a fact of the cruising life.

Unfortunately, however, there is only one real way to learn about cruising and that is by going cruising yourself. It is fine if you can afford to go as crew with another cruiser for a while, and your extensive reading will help equip you with the tools you will need in your new lifestyle, but what you will learn by cruising with others is how others cruise in their boats, and when you read you learn how the authors of those books dealt with the problems and situations they encountered. Cruising is a highly individual experience and no two cruisers whom I have met ever approach it the same way. You will want to find out what your cruising style will be, and the only way to do that is to cruise.

You're Almost Ready

We have pushed the fast-forward button and it's several years, perhaps five years, later. You're almost ready to go. You're living in a tiny house in a good neighborhood, wearing old (but neat and tidy) clothes; eating simple, basic, and nutritious meals; exercising regularly so you're a paragon of physical fitness; and you're out of debt. Your kitty has grown fat and healthy, and you've developed a harmonious relationship with your mate, your kids, and anyone else who plans to go cruising with you. What next? By now you have probably formed a pretty firm plan about where you want to do your cruising. If not, it's time to start thinking about it.

Susan and the Wonder Cruise

Many folks don't believe me when I tell them that Susan is the driving force behind our adopting the cruising life, but it is true. No, I wasn't exactly dragged into it screaming and kicking against my will, but I was at first skeptical of the basic philosophy of world cruising (it seemed a little decadent and a lot impractical), and I was a little reluctant to leave behind a lifestyle that could only be described as a good thing. But leave we did, and in spite of a few difficult times and a lot of amateurish foibles, neither of us has ever looked back or regretted for a moment our decision. Although we thought we had made very careful preparations and paid a great deal of attention to the specifics of what we were going to do with our cruise and where we were going to do it, the trip that transpired only vaguely resembled the trip we planned.

The first cruising scheme that Susan came up with was for us to take off as soon as the children were safely away at college, and this suited me just fine. At the time our youngest was eight, and I figured that the ensuing 10 years or so would be plenty of time for Susan to forget the whole thing and come up with something practical for us to do when the chicks had flown and the nest was empty. If my "yes, dear . . . of course, dear" approval of the idea rang a little hollow, it was at least approval, and that's all Susan needed. As subsequent revisions of Susan's scheme brought our departure date closer and closer, every hint of reluctance I voiced brought forth a "but you said you liked the idea."

It wasn't long before Susan decided that 10 years was too long to wait and that she didn't want to go cruising with some grumpy old guy as her only company, so she resolved to leave earlier and take the kids with us. "Great idea," I answered. "We'll leave in nine years instead." But then Susan decided that if we were going to go cruising with the kids at all, we had to do it now or the kids wouldn't be kids anymore. My comforting 10-year lead time had been reduced to a frantic two.

Once we had decided to leave while the children were too small to mount any serious opposition to our plans and I had decided that any further resistance to Susan's cruising strategy was futile, we settled on the idea of a three-year circumnavigation that would get us back to Marblehead in time for Sarah to graduate from high school. We would buy a boat, sail to Bermuda, then to Panama via the Virgin Islands, transit the Panama Canal, and cross the Pacific to Australia in the first year. In the second year we would pay a brief visit to Singapore and Sri Lanka, then blast through the Red Sea and spend the winter touring Europe by train. Our third year would see us across the Atlantic to the Caribbean then up the East Coast to home in time to get the kids back to school by September and for me to pick up the shambles of a normal life.

Even now I marvel at this lovely practical plan. In our naiveté, we didn't know any better. And we certainly didn't know that the size of our bank balance—which could only be described as small—would have such a large effect on our ultimate cruising "plan."

When we began looking at cruising boats we were shocked at how expensive they were. The first few brokers we talked to snickered when we told them how much we had to spend, and we quickly learned not to say that we planned a circumnavigation if we expected any response other than bemused indifference. The consensus among brokers seemed to be that we would need to spend at least $250,000 if we were going to get a safe and reliable boat that four people could live on for three years. This was rather disappointing because that figure was almost twice our budget for the entire trip. If we had found a boat for half that amount we still wouldn't have had any money left for the trip, and if we had set aside enough money for the trip, we wouldn't have had enough for a boat. "Ah well," I said. "It was a great idea but it obviously won't work, so I guess we'll just have to go back to spending the rest of our lives like normal people."

But neither Susan nor Sarah (who had become a staunch supporter of the cruising guru) would have any of this. Susan had gotten hold of Annie Hill's *Voyaging on a Small Income*, and Sarah had read about the Smith's adventures on *Appledore*, so every time I started to backslide, one or the other of them would whack me back on track with a quote from one of these books. I came to dread the sentence, "If they can do it, so can we."

Both of these books are about people who went cruising after building their own boats, and while I have worked with boats most of my life and would have felt comfortable enough building one for us, the minimum two or three years the project would have added to our getaway plans wasn't good enough for the girls. So we compromised again, and with the compromise came more changes in our plans. We would buy an old boat in reasonable condition and fix it up for our trip, which would, I figured, only add about a year to our departure time. That still wasn't good enough. Once we were resolved to leave, the whole crew wanted to go now. And even I, the reluctant captain (no one else wanted the job) of our expedition, didn't want to wait any longer than necessary.

Our first plan evolved into our buying an old boat, getting it into seaworthy condition with as little fuss and expense as possible, then sailing it as far as we could before stopping in some faraway and exotic land to fix it up enough to continue the voyage. Thus we rescued *Sultana* from under a pile of pigeon guano in a barn in Maine, got her hull repaired and her sails patched enough so that we could leave, and sailed off without the slightest idea of how far we could get before the need for major repairs would stop us cold.

When we left Marblehead, I figured that we would be lucky to make it to Florida before the old girl gave it up, but from Florida we made it to Mexico, and so it went from one stop to another until we found ourselves safely ensconced on the hard on the South Island of New Zealand. If it hadn't been for a major gale that destroyed the last of our sails and broke our boomstay, we would have easily made it to Australia. As I write this, *Sultana* is about two-thirds of the way through a major refit that will restore her to much-better-than-new condition and prepare her for yet another 41 years of world cruising. I wish there were a way to fix me up to go that long.

Our old boat, for which we had paid $25,000, just 10 percent of what the brokers told us would get us a minimum cruising boat, had made it nearly halfway around the world, and she had done it without a hitch. We experienced far fewer problems than many cruisers had on the same trip in brand-new boats. Does this prove that old boats are better than new ones? You bet it does, and that's a major part of what this book is about.

This chapter, however, is not about the relative superiority of old boats over new ones; it's about plans and how they change. Each time we met a hurdle to Susan's initial cruising plan we found a way to jump over it, but each jump meant a change in plans that often raised a new hurdle. The need to stop and effect major repairs to the boat shot the three-year plan all to hell, and the trip that has evolved from the initial plan bears no resemblance to it whatsoever, but it has been a great trip nevertheless. Our current plan is to have no plan at all, but this isn't working either; every time we talk to the folks back home they inevitably ask, "What's your plan?"

Destinations—The Long-Range Plan

Make all the plans you want, but don't make schedules. Plans tend to remain flexible and tentative right up to the last minute and as such are easier to change or back away from than schedules, which tend to become rigid and dictatorial. Schedules don't work in the cruising environment and they can actually be dangerous because they lead people to sail into bad weather when they otherwise would stay in harbor. On several occasions we met cruisers who just had to get someplace so badly that they were compelled to leave in the face of an approaching frontal system, or with the boat in less-than-perfect condition, or shorthanded, or with some other condition that made staying much more sensible than going. The usual reason for such hasty impropriety is to meet family or to pick up new crew or to get an existing crewmember to an airport in time to make a flight. It's called the I-got-to-get-to-Cartagena-by-Christmas syndrome, and it only happens with schedules, never with plans.

I've mentioned earlier that it's best not to announce your plans until just before or after you depart. Naturally, as the time for departure draws close, it would be cruel and inconsiderate not to tell family members and your most trusted friends that you are planning to leave and that you will be gone for quite a long time, but everyone you tell should be made to understand that cruising isn't like a trip to Disneyland. You can't have a daily itinerary, and you can't know just where you will be at any one time. Small changes in conditions or small events can require major changes in cruising plans, and you must remain flexible to take advantage of unexpected opportunities and to respond to emergencies and adverse conditions as they arise. After fighting gale-force headwinds for several days on our trip from the Tuamotus to Papeete, we simply decided we didn't want to go there anyway, changed course, and had a great sail to Raieatea. We never did get to Papeete, even though we had told everyone that it would be one of our major stops.

Tell Mom and Dad and the grown-up-and-moved-out kids what's up, but always bear in mind that unannounced plans are easier to change or back away from than announced ones. We've changed *Sultana*'s plans so many times that anyone trying to follow them would think she—and we!—were schizophrenic.

Reading your way around the world
One of the most important things you can start doing once you make up your mind to go cruising is read every cruising book you can get your hands on. By now you should be best pals with Slocum and Chichester and Hiscock and Tristan Jones, on speaking terms with the Pardeys, the Smith family, Robin Lee Graham, and Tania Aebi, and looking forward to meeting all the rest. Nigel Calder and Charles "Chappy" Chapman should be your trusted technical advisors; while Steve and Linda Dashew will keep you posted on how to cruise the good life once you finally hit the big one in the state lottery. (See "Recommended Reading" for titles and publishers.)

Don't neglect Melville, Conrad, Robert Louis Stevenson, Jack London, or John Masefield either. They may not have a lot of practical information to offer but they sure get the old sailor's blood boiling. They make you yearn for the salt spray on a heaving deck, a tarred queue, hardtack, and dead whales.

While we are at it, let's not neglect old Nathaniel Bowditch (even though we have no intention of reading the book named after him—I'm convinced that nobody has actually ever read *The American Practical Navigator*). But you should by now be familiar with the principles of navigation he refined. By the way, if you are ever sailing in Marblehead Harbor on a local boat, you will undoubtedly be shown Bowditch Ledge where the story goes that old Nathaniel, after navigating for several years around the globe without mishap, ran hard aground on his return. The story is complete fabrication, and all Marbleheaders know that, but it is too good a story not to pass on—proving once again that while truth might be stranger than fiction, fiction is often more fun.

Reading of the adventures and misadventures of hardy souls who have gone before acquaints us with the general areas that we might want to visit, but as we discovered in chapter 1, it's best to read everything with the author's point of view and the timeliness of the piece foremost in our minds. The cruising environment changes rapidly and much that is written is outdated before it is printed. Right now, for example, I am reading *The Small World of Long Distance Sailors* by Ann Carl because it was recommended as a good read that catches the flavor of cruising in the Mediterranean Sea. The book does just that and I am enjoying it in anticipation of getting there soon, but one entire section is devoted to the joys of cruising in Yugoslavia. Of course, there is no more Yugoslavia, and the area where it used to be won't be open to any but the most adventuresome (and foolish) cruisers for several years. As another example, most cruising books recommend avoiding Cuba like a sickness, but Cuba has discovered that cruisers carry greenbacks and so has laid out the welcome mat. What promises to be one of the greatest cruising grounds in the world is gradually opening up to all.

Deciding where to go

One of the popular misconceptions that shoresiders have of cruisers is that we enjoy the freedom of going anywhere we want to go as long as there is navigable water nearby. Although that may be true in a philosophical sense, in practical terms nothing could be further from the truth. Cruisers are not only at the mercy of the winds, weather, and world currents, they must be constantly aware of the political situation in any area they plan to visit. Most cruises progress from east to west because of the prevailing wind directions; hurricanes, typhoons, and cyclones dictate when it's safe to visit certain locales; crime and health problems may influence some cruising plans; and an uneasy political climate can make for an uneasy cruise.

All this means that we can't just up anchor and head off for anyplace we want to go. We must know where we are going, what we expect to find there, how long we can stay, and what is the best time of year for the voyage. Therefore, we must study and plan—and starting to do so about a year before departure isn't too early.

The beginning cruise planner will want to have four sources of information on hand. The first is a large world atlas as detailed as you can find. (Such an atlas is quite large and heavy, so the one at the local library is usually a good bet, or if you have a computer get one on CD). The second is a copy of Jimmy Cornell's book, *World Cruising Routes*. The third is as large a collection of the back issues of the Seven Seas Cruising Association *Bulletin* as you can amass (these, too, are available on disc if you have a computer). The fourth is a copy of Beth Leonard's book *The Voyager's Handbook*.

The practicality of any passage is often determined by the direction and strength of prevailing winds and tides, and many times a passage that looks like an easy run is, in fact, quite difficult. The trip from Bonaire to Cartagena, for example, is an easy albeit rough two-day downwind sail, but to sail from Cartagena to Bonaire by the direct route is a practically impossible bash to windward. Although the format is confusing until you get used to it, Jimmy Cornell's book is invaluable for his observations on problems such as this one and for computing distances, routes, and the times required for any given passage.

Each issue of the SSCA *Bulletin* is a collection of letters that active cruisers write, giving advice and information on specific areas they have visited. They tend to be wordy, the writer's point is often obscure, and the *Bulletin* is sometimes used by cruisers who have an ax to grind with a business or supplier, but even so they are invaluable. As you read through back issues, you will get to know a lot of cruisers before you meet them and you will get a good feeling for the flavor and atmosphere of a country or a specific harbor—all of which will help you decide about whether you want to visit that place. All the popular cruising areas and routes are well represented, and most issues include three or four in-depth letters by different correspondents. It is important to read them all to form a consensus based on the viewpoints of different correspondents.

Beth Leonard has an amazing ability to gather and analyze data, and her book is full of rock-solid advice on every aspect of cruising from buying fuel and food to how many comic books you should have in the head. She wrote *The Voyager's Handbook* during a three-year circumnavigation wherein she kept track of every item in meticulous detail. (Beth doesn't really write about comic books in the head—that's just something I made up. So who's perfect?)

Charts and Guidebooks

You might be amazed at the number of charts you will need for a world cruise. To get from Marblehead to New Zealand, *Sultana* used a stack that is 8 inches thick and weighs more than 30 pounds. So start now and make building your collection of charts and guidebooks a part of your planning process. Don't skimp here. Good charts and up-to-date guidebooks are worth the money you spend on them.

Outdated charts are fine as long as they are in good condition and you remember that they are outdated. Many weekend cruisers who have a steady income and need only a few charts are aghast at the idea of using outdated charts, but few cruisers worry about their charts being the latest editions. Charts are simply too expensive to throw out every time a new one is published, and new charts are usually printed with a few significant errors that make them outdated as soon as they are published anyway. New charts tend to foster confidence that isn't warranted and besides, using outdated charts makes you a more careful sailor. That charted lighthouse might still be there, and it might not, so you're going to keep a very careful watch.

Many of the hundreds of charts in *Sultana*'s collection are more than 30 years old; the set we used on the Intracoastal Waterway (ICW) was 20 years old. The ICW hadn't moved, but many conditions had changed. Lots of buoys weren't there anymore, and we were surprised to see how many areas that showed 15 or 20 feet of water on the old charts had shoaled to three or four feet at low water.

Many cruisers use photocopies of charts, which is fine and can save you a lot of money, but I'd much rather work with an outdated original chart than a copy of a current one, simply because the stiff paper is easier to work with and the color makes the details stand out. Yet another possibility is to buy a bound set of charts, such as *Charlie's Charts in the Pacific,* that are available for many popular areas. If you have a computer that you plan to take cruising with you (and you should), there are more and more charts available on disk which can be useful. They are available for heavily populated areas but not for remote ones—not yet anyway, but stay tuned—so their usefulness is limited. Naturally, you wouldn't even think of using them for your primary cruising charts. (I'll discuss this in more detail in chapter 12.)

The planning cruiser will find guidebooks specific to your intended voyage to be a great help. For the more popular cruising areas, such as the Caribbean and the Pacific, you'll find dozens of such books. Outdated guidebooks are fine for your preliminary planning. New editions are quite expensive and a complete, up-to-date set simply isn't necessary at the initial planning stage. Check your local library and used-book stores for older guides. Once you are committed to visiting an area, however, you should get the latest edition.

While you are at the library pick up any tourist guides for areas that you may want to visit. Fodor's, Frommer's, and Lonely Planet are all good noncruising guides, but there are lots of others. Tourist guides won't direct you to a decent spot in a harbor to drop the anchor or help you deal with the port captain, but they are invaluable in determining what to expect once you get ashore.

Popular areas to cruise

As your cruising plans evolve, remember that the most popular areas for cruisers are popular for good reasons. They are either easy to reach with good harbors and facilities, or they present attractions that make cruising there worthwhile. Other stops may be popular simply because they are on the way, convenient places for resting, or with easily accessible markets where you can replenish the larder. Popular spots also have the advantage of a local population that is used to dealing with folks on boats and who understand that we have needs and requirements different from those of "normal" tourists. The people who run the hotels at a few of the major tourist stops tend to resent cruisers because we don't show up with a thousand dollars to blow on a week's fun in the sun, but the local people around most popular anchorages have come to value cruisers for the solid and predictable contribution they make to the local economy. Generally, the more touristy a spot becomes the less appeal it has for cruisers anyway.

Of course, this doesn't mean that you shouldn't strike out on your own and sail into areas that aren't among the most popular—after all, that's what cruising is about—but if you rein in your adventurous zeal to explore until after your first year of cruising the beaten path, you will be better off. You will gain a wealth of information from hanging around experienced cruisers. It's an education through association that you can't get from any other source, and when you need assistance or advice, the old-timers are always there when you need them. So for the first year at least, stick to the most popular areas and save the more adventuresome stops for when you have accumulated a few barnacles on your bottom.

As you plan your cruise, keep in mind that you don't have to sail around the world if you don't want to. In fact, most cruisers don't. Many who set out on a planned circumnavigation never make it, not because they give up or run out of money (although that certainly does happen often enough), but because they reach an area that fits their concept of paradise and they decide to stay right there. Many boats in the South Pacific sailed here 10 years ago on a circumnavigation and are still here, and the same is true of the Mediterranean. The most popular cruising area, by far, is the Caribbean where thousands of cruisers spend their entire cruising careers moving from island to island, and between Central and South America, and wouldn't think of going anywhere else.

These cruisers don't stay in the Caribbean because the sailing is easier there, in fact some mighty tough conditions prevail between Cuba and Venezuela. But many Caribbean cruisers like the fact that they can get anywhere they want to go in three or four days, don't like the expense and changeable weather of the Mediterranean, and don't care to make the one- or two-weeklong passages required in the Pacific. More and more island governments and emerging countries in the Caribbean are becoming cruiser-friendly, and their growing economies are providing services and supplies where they weren't available just a few years ago. Although problems with crime, pollution, and poverty plague some of these countries, overall the Caribbean is a wonderful place to cruise and many cruisers consciously make the decision to go no farther.

Brownwater cruising

Not only do you not have to sail around the world if you aren't so inclined, you don't even have to go offshore if you don't want to or if your boat isn't up to bluewater work. Many cruisers never leave the ICW, the southern rivers, or the Great Lakes, and several thousand boats cruise between the Bahamas and Florida every year with never a thought of going anywhere else. One of the most interesting cruisers we ever met has sailed for more than 10 years and claims he's never gotten out of sight of land. Another chap we met in Florida sticks to the rivers; he claims that if one shore is good, then two are twice as good. "It shore does simplify navigation." (That's his joke, not mine.)

Preliminary plans

At this early stage you'll only want to make the preliminary plans about where you might like to visit, and there are two good reasons for this. One, the political climate for many cruising destinations is constantly changing. Right now the worldwide trend is toward improving conditions for cruisers. In fact, the political situation in many cruising locales right now is better than it has been in decades. Cuba, Borneo, and Madagascar, to name just a few, are becoming much easier for cruisers to visit, and closed areas such as the western Adriatic Sea show promise of opening up in the years ahead. However, with the recent crash of the Asian economy, certain areas of the South Pacific, specifically the Philippines and Indonesia, are shutting down as crime and anarchy rise. As you learn more about the different cruising areas through reading and talking to experienced cruisers, more specific plans will materialize.

The second reason for making preliminary plans is that, no matter how much study and reading you do and no matter how much sailing and coastal cruising you have done before you leave on your cruise, the environment you meet will never quite match your expectations. The conditions you find won't necessarily be better or worse than what you expected but they will most certainly be different. That's because we all have a different response to a given situation and paradise to one is hell to another. We were told by one seasoned cruiser, for example, that Belize was a boring place to visit because there was nothing to do. What he meant was that there were no nightclubs and casinos there, an enormous plus for cruisers like us.

The First-Year Plan

I know, I know. We haven't bought a boat yet. We'll get to that, I promise. But for now, let's concentrate on putting together a plan for your first year of real live cruising. I have no intention of trying to tell you where you should go, but I will make some suggestions about how you should proceed for your first year, regardless of your circumstances.

The first 12 months are a make-it-or-break-it period for many new cruisers. It is during this time that you learn what you have gotten yourself into and you will make more mistakes than in any other period of your cruising life. You will find out more about yourself and your companions than you ever thought possible and face both gloomy disappointments and cheerful surprises like never before. I'll never forget the first time we ran *Sultana* hard aground on a sandbar and had to be pulled off by our fellow cruisers. We were embarrassed and humiliated beyond measure to think that we could let such an amateurish thing happen to our wonderful new-old boat. Now, after having been aground dozens of times in all sorts of conditions, we realize that it is just part of the cruising life—and the more adventuresome you are the more your bottom paint suffers. We even run aground intentionally from time to time to anchor for a few moments on a rising tide or to careen the boat. To compensate, we have become highly skilled at getting ourselves off anything we get ourselves onto and only rarely require any assistance.

Full-time cruising is different from any other type of sailing you've ever done, regardless of your experience, and you should work hard at making it as easy and uncomplicated as possible. The first year should be a year of learning what you and your boat can do. A weeklong passage in rough seas is easy enough to read about in books, but many who try it for the first time without a few easier passages under their belts find that they never want to do it again. It's much easier on everyone if you make your first few overnight passages one-nighters. Then when you develop the confidence to handle a 24-hour passage, do a few two-nighters and so on until you can stand on the foredeck and look a week of rough water right in the eye without blinking. It won't take long, I promise you, so resist the natural tendency to fling yourself straight into the bluewater environment with a cruise to Hawaii or Bermuda. Go instead to Santa Catalina or Block Island and when you get there, spend a few days enjoying the sights and sounds of a new harbor. After all, cruising isn't about passages. It's about places and the people you meet in them—and one of the first people you will meet is yourself.

Start with coastal cruising
Even if you have had a lot of offshore experience, you need to build confidence in your cruising-life skills, and the best way to do this is by coastal cruising. Make the first six months to a year a series of short easy passages with long stops between them. Short day sails in an interesting area will let you get accustomed to life on a small boat. You'll have fun while you're learning, and if you do get into trouble and need help, it is readily available.

The Inland Passage of British Columbia and the Sea of Cortez are good destinations for beginning West Coast cruisers. Cruisers who start from the East Coast are a little better off because the Atlantic offers several attractive options for beginning cruisers. The Intracoastal Waterway, the Canadian Maritimes, and the Bahamas are topnotch cruising areas that offer protracted coastal cruising; it's possible to visit dozens of new and fascinating places in these areas with only an occasional overnight passage.

Leaving home
It is important to get out of your immediate home waters as quickly as possible, but it is a good idea to stay in a familiar geographical area. Does this sound contradictory? Well, it's not really. Getting out of your familiar surroundings quickly makes you feel like a cruiser right away and gives your ego and confidence terrific

boosts. However, staying in the same geographical area will keep the cultural and environmental shock of drastic change to a minimum. The ability to stay in touch with friends and family for at least the first few months with an inexpensive call from a phone booth is often comforting for all members of the crew, it will ease the fears of the folks at home, and if you have children, it is particularly helpful if they can chat with a friend at home from time to time.

Most of the anxiety and stress of the cruising life comes from the passages we must make to participate in it, but most of our time is spent at anchor, not on the high seas, and most of our happiest moments are while we are in harbor. The skills we will need to live on a boat at anchor are more difficult to learn and much more important than sailing skills. This isn't to say that sailing skills aren't important. They are, of course, but it's your living skills that will determine how satisfying you find your new lifestyle. All cruisers learn to sail, but many never learn how to live on a boat. Thus you should devote most of that first year to learning all the intricacies of life on a small boat and save the easy stuff, like learning to like long passages, for later.

Sultana's first cruise after we left Marblehead was up the coast of Maine into the Canadian Maritimes. Then we cruised down the Intracoastal Waterway and spent several months sailing among the Florida Keys. In our first six months of full-time cruising we made only two overnight passages. By the time we were ready to head across the Gulf of Mexico to Isla Mujeres we had been cruising for nearly a year and were just beginning to feel like competent sailors. We were ready for what was to be our first real bluewater experience.

Don't Become a Liveaboard

Many "experts" advise living on your boat for at least a year before you depart on a major cruise, and while I hate to risk the derision of my fellow cruisers (especially them that's experts), I believe that this is very bad advice. There are profound and fundamental differences between cruising sailors and people who live on boats while maintaining shoreside lifestyles—those we call "liveaboards."

People often confuse the two, but they aren't the same thing at all. "Liveaboard" is a collective term that describes people who live on boats instead of in houses and who remain in one place or in one area for long periods. Some live on boats for economic reasons, some like the romantic image that living on a boat imparts, and others just love boats. Most liveaboards lead normal lives with regular jobs, kids in school, nice autos in the marina parking lot, and a plugged-in TV and stereo. The only difference between them and shoresiders is that they live on a boat in the water instead of in a house on land, which means that most of them require all the comforts that all other shoresiders require. Liveaboard boats become so encumbered with power cables, water and sewer pipes, cable TV hookups, and telephone lines that they frequently become permanently moored to a pier or wharf and few ever do any sailing.

Cruisers, on the other hand, are people who live on boats so they can travel from place to place. They seldom have regular jobs, their children are often home-schooled, and they hardly ever own automobiles. Where liveaboards tend to congregate at docks in marinas, cruisers tend to anchor out and shun the amenities of shore hookups.

There is nothing wrong with liveaboards, of course, but in some areas, particularly in the southern U.S., the liveaboard fleet has gotten very large and their propensity to pollute harbors and their reluctance to pay property taxes has caused some communities to retaliate by enforcing strict anchoring laws, which directly affect cruisers.

Because the two lifestyles are so different I strongly advise people who are interested in trying one to not get involved with the other. It's nearly impossible to maintain a normal job and other shoreside frills and responsibilities while living like a cruiser, and if you try it you will likely become so frustrated and disenchanted that you will quit the cruising life even before you start. The gulf between liveaboards and cruisers is just as wide as that between your shoreside life and your cruising life. And the leap from the shoreside life to the liveaboard life is just as upsetting as the leap from the liveaboard life to the cruising life. Who needs two traumatic changes in two years? So please, don't try to live on your boat for an extended period before you take off on your cruise.

The transition from the shoreside to the cruising life can be difficult and traumatic, and when approached improperly it can end your cruise before the first dockline is cast off. The trick is to make the first year afloat, your transition year, a success by making it as simple and basic as you can.

8

LIFE
ABOARD

"Follow in my wake, you've not that much at stake.

For I have plowed the seas, and smoothed the troubled waters."

—Jimmy Buffett, "Barometer Soup"

An Incident at Aitutaki

Have you ever noticed that when you make an exceptionally seamanlike maneuver in a boat there is hardly ever anyone around to appreciate it, but when you do something that is extraordinarily stupid, half the population of China will be on hand to watch the disaster unfold? I am convinced that inscribed in some cosmic lawbook is an otherwise unwritten law stating that foibles must be witnessed by vast multitudes of bystanders while triumphs go unnoticed. Perhaps this is as it should be because it helps to slow the natural progression toward arrogance among those fortunate few who enjoy more than their fair share of spectacular achievements. But for us klutzes who enjoy only an occasional minor triumph, it is manifestly unfair.

Some 25 years ago when Susan and I bought our first sailboat, a sleek 23-foot production boat that had popped fully formed from a mold in some factory in Florida, we set off from the Ipswich Bay Yacht Club on our first real cruise up the coast of Maine without knowing too much about what we were doing. We were, in fact, as green as new lettuce, but our enthusiasm more than compensated for our dearth of sailing skills, and we had a wonderful time cruising among the inlets and islands of Casco Bay and Boothbay Harbor. When it was time to return home, however, disaster struck. As I pulled the starter cord on our brand-new Chrysler long-shaft outboard, it rumbled to life with a throaty purr, then coughed a few times, made a few clanking noises like there was an elf in there with a hammer trying to get out, expelled a single puff of black oily smoke, and died, never again to function as anything more dynamic than a very large and expensive paperweight.

We were a little panicky and despaired of ever getting our new boat back to our homeport when a local lobsterman rowed over in his dinghy to see what the fuss was all about.

"Dang outboards," he began after we explained our plight. "Never trusted 'em myself. Good thing ya got yer sail up there and don't need no outboard. Never had no use fer tha dang things anyway." He then rowed away, leaving us staring at each other and thinking, "Why didn't we think of that?"

We sailed off the mooring with just the main, then got the jib up and had a delightful sail into the large harbor that was our day's destination, and dropped the anchor for the night. The next morning we were off at the crack of dawn, and after a few hours of being becalmed among a sprightly pod of pilot whales, we had another day of perfect sailing conditions. When we reached the mouth of the Ipswich River, a difficult entrance under the best of conditions, a strong south-easterly was blowing a semi-gale with a flooding tide. We blasted over the bar with both wind and tide in our favor, going about as fast as our little boat had gone since she was dropped off the delivery truck. We practically flew up the river skipping across the tops of the waves, but as we approached the club floats to which we wanted to tie up, we were faced with a slight problem. We were traveling far too fast to stop. If we had tried to round into the wind, the current would have carried us past the floats as soon as we dropped the sail and we would simply have continued traveling upriver backwards. We only had one chance and if we had missed it, it would have been hours before the wind and tide changed enough to allow us to get back to the floats.

With only a few seconds to decide what to do, Susan moved to the bow and lowered our big Danforth over the bow roller until the flukes were just barely in the water. Then, 200 feet from the floats, I rounded smartly into the wind, Susan let go of the anchor, and I hopped onto the cabintop and dropped the main with a clatter onto the deck. The boat hesitated for a moment, the jib luffed frantically, and then we began to drift backwards. When we were opposite the floats Susan snubbed the rode on the deck cleat, the anchor grabbed the sandy bottom, the boat stopped cold, and the current swung us ever so gently up to the floats. As our gunnels bumped lightly against the fenders, I stepped off the boat with the springline and made it fast.

A master stroke of nautical genius. We had executed with perfection what was undoubtedly one of the greatest maritime maneuvers ever pulled off by two greenies with a new sailboat. After a moment my hands stopped shaking and I looked around, ready to bask humbly in the admiring glances of the gang of hangarounders who were always hanging around the floats on Sunday evening. Much to my horror the dock leading to the floats was empty, the clubhouse was shuttered, and the only car in the parking lot was ours. Our shining hour had gone unwitnessed, unheralded, and unremarked. And Susan didn't care. She was a little miffed at the jib for flapping as she tried to deal with the anchor line, and all she could think about was home and a hot bath.

If witnesses for our few triumphs are scarce, then those for our many foibles are correspondingly plentiful. We had been anchored in the tiny harbor at Aitutaki, New Zealand, for several weeks, enjoying the beaches, making new friends, and exploring the outlying islands in our inflatable, but now it was time to haul anchor and move on. Bright and early on the day of departure a large group of well-wishers and onlookers gathered on the harbor quay to see us off. The channel that led through the forest of coral heads and out through the surrounding reef was narrow and shallow, but we had come in with no trouble, and

I didn't anticipate any trouble getting out. *Sultana* has poor visibility from the helm so our normal procedure for negotiating a narrow channel is for me to take a position on the bowsprit, for Phillip and Sarah to stand by the port and starboard shrouds, while Susan takes over at the wheel. I signal minor changes in course to keep us in the channel or to get us around encroaching coral heads, and Sarah and Phillip relay the signals to Susan. We have done this many times and have evolved a set of hand signals so there is no need for verbal communication. As we headed out of the anchorage I gave the power-up signal, indicating I wanted Susan to give *Sultana* some juice. With all those people watching, I wanted our departure to be smart and seamanlike.

All was going well as we motored along with a good turn of speed. The channel at Aitutaki makes a sharp zigzag as you leave the anchorage and enter the main channel. You must zig sharply to starboard and head directly toward the quay; then, just as collision with the rocks is imminent, you must zag to port. I should have realized that Susan, or any thinking person for that matter, would be reluctant to point the bow straight into a pile of rocks, but I was familiar with the channel and assumed that she was, too. When we approached the zig I signaled that Susan should slow and turn to starboard, but since she could see nothing to starboard except the rock pile, upon which stood lots of happy waving people, and to port she saw nothing but open water, she naturally turned to port away from the perceived danger. Her maneuver elicited a frantic response from me and the kids; the three of us took to hopping up and down like a bunch of bungee-jumping monkeys while gesturing violently to starboard. I even succumbed to my racing-skipper friends' nasty habits and began screaming in a piercing shriek.

"Starboard . . . STARBOARRRRRD . . . STARRRRRBOARRRRRRRD. . . ."

We struck the reef halfway through the last starboard. We all heard a sickening grinding sound, the deck heaved, I flung arms and legs around the furled jib to avoid being hurled to my doom, the bowsprit rose to point heavenward, and we stopped. Susan shut the engine down and I just sat. I plopped my butt down on the top of the deckhouse and stared in stunned silence at the people on the quay, all of whom were staring in stunned silence back at us. Finally one of our friends, a Maori lad from New Zealand named Mike, dove off the quay and swam to *Sultana*'s rail.

"Looks like you might be stuck, Mate," he said in a tentative voice.

I continued sitting and staring in dazed disbelief while wondering why all those people on the quay couldn't find something better to do than stare at us. After a while I decided I had better do something useful, like maybe crying, but then I thought better of it and sat and stared some more.

It was Mike who got things going again. He recruited a local fishing boat to pull us off, but even with her twin engines and *Sultana*'s diesel in full reverse we didn't budge. Finally, Mike swam back to the quay, dragging our two spare 100-meter nylon anchor lines tied together and secured the bitter end to the trailer hitch of an onlooker's car, and with that extra boost we managed to slide *Sultana* back into deep water.

Fortunately, and in profound testimony to the advantages of a full keel and a strong hull, there was no damage—not to the boat, anyway. The skipper's ego was smashed to a fare-thee-well, however, and as I continued to sit on the cabintop in a state of mute introspection, Mike and Susan took *Sultana* out through the channel without further incident. When we cleared the fringing reef and were safely on our way, Mike gave a cheerful salute, did a back flip off the bow and set out to swim the quarter mile or so back to the island. We never saw him again, but he is high up there on the list of the hundreds of wonderful people we have met while cruising, and we will never forget him.

Some months later the incident at Aitutaki was almost forgotten, the splints and dressings had been removed from the skipper's pride, and except for some massive residual scar tissue, it looked like a full recovery was imminent. I was sitting in one of the many waterfront bars that line the harbor front at Nuku'alofa in Tonga sharing a beer with a new acquaintance who had just arrived from Fiji. We were discussing all things nautical and naughty that strangers talk about in waterfront bars all over the world when the conversation stalled for a moment.

"Say," said my new friend. "Did you hear about the jerk who ran his boat up on the reef in the Cooks?"

I lowered my head and hunched my shoulders so he couldn't see my face, formed my arms into a protective circle around my glass, then slurped some of the head off my beer without lifting it off the bar. He couldn't see my half-crazed expression or my teeth bared in a vicious snarl. "No, no I haven't heard that one yet," I lied.

"Well, ha, ha, ha, not much to it really. This guy has his whole family on board so he, chuckle, chuckle, puts his wife at the wheel then, snicker, snicker, orders her to run the boat full steam right up on the reef, ho, ho, ho. Stupid jerk probably didn't know where the channel was, yuk, yuk, yuk, not that it's not marked or anything like that—whole damn town was there to see it too—guy in Suva told me about it. Amazing some of the people out here in boats these days, ain't it?"

"Hey," I answered, further hunching my shoulders. "There was probably some logical explanation, like maybe the throttle stuck or the rudder broke or somethin' like that."

"No way, the boat was in perfect condition. Sometimes I think they should give an IQ test to everybody who wants to buy a boat. Dumb ass, could'a drowned his whole family pullin' a stunt like that."

"Slurp, slurp. . . I bet the sun was in his eyes."

"Naw, the guy was just a jerk."

"Slurrrrrp, slurp, slurp . . . I bet the throttle stuck and the rudder broke and the sun was in his eyes all at once—yeah, that's probably what happened. Poor guy couldn't help it, really."

"You know the best part?" my gleeful friend continued. "The boat is so far up on the reef that they can't get it off with a towboat so they run a line ashore, and you know those junky Russian cars called Ladas? Well, they tie the line to a Lada and he gets them off. Can you imagine the humiliation of running aground like that in the first place, and then having to get towed off by a Lada?"

Cruising Skills

I've said several times that life skills are more important to the cruising sailor than are sailing skills, and there are several reasons why this is true. When many of us decide to go cruising, it's only natural that we study everything we can get our hands on about boats. But we gloss over the dramatic changes in lifestyle that moving from a large immobile house to a tiny boat entails, or we assume that living in the confines of a boat is something that we will just have to get used to. But it doesn't happen like that. To become proficient cruisers requires developing two separate sets of skills: cruising skills will enable us to get the boat from one place to another safely and to maintain it in good repair; noncruising skills enable us to live a happy and rewarding life while residing on the boat.

I realize that this book treats critical skills such as sailhandling and anchoring in a rather cavalier manner, but there are already a zillion or so books out there, really good books, that discuss these things ad nauseam, and I am loathe to add to the pile. Earl Hinz wrote an excellent book that covers every aspect of anchors and anchoring, and in my current *Armchair Sailor* catalog there are no less than 27 books about sails and sailhandling. Anyway, we're going to learn these things whether we want to or not. The first time our anchor pulls out in a rainsquall at 3 A.M. we'll become experts at setting anchors, and the first time we nearly take a knockdown because we thought the cold front sneaking up from the south didn't have any wind in it, we'll become converts to the principle of reducing sail before the sail reduces us.

Navigating

It's amazing how rapidly technology can come upon us and change our lives. If it doesn't change our lives, technology at the very least affects the way we live significant parts of our lives. Some of us grouchy old codgers often have trouble accepting such dramatic changes. I, for example, am just starting to realize that perhaps these newfangled compact disc players do indeed have some small advantage over magnetic tapes, especially after having to plop most of *Sultana*'s extensive music library into a dumpster because the tapes had been eaten alive by a voracious mold.

When Loran first became available I thought it was exceedingly clever, but that it would never catch on because you could never beat the good old chart and compass. When GPS came along, however, its advantages were obvious even to traditionalists like me.

The advent of GPS is one of the most significant technological developments since the magnetic compass, and it has revolutionized cruising and cruising navigation. The lack of navigation skills and their perceived complexity kept many would-be cruisers safely in sight of the local lighthouse. Traditional navigation with watch and sextant isn't really that difficult (probably on par with high school algebra in complexity), but many people, when confronted with gadgets bearing scales and wheels, and books with columns of numbers and formulae, are convinced that such awesome apparatus requires a graduate engineering degree to master.

There is no way to know for sure, but I suspect that a lot of people who wanted to go cruising in the past didn't because of the perceived complexity of traditional navigation. Now anyone who can afford a $200 gadget and has minimal reading skills can become a world-class navigator with about 15 minutes of study and can navigate from here to anywhere with a mind-boggling accuracy that was unimagined just a few years ago. We can now navigate at night, in the fog and rain, with our eyes closed, from our bunk in the forepeak, or even while comfortably ensconced in the head. The cook can do it, the kids can do it, and with a little training, the ship's cat could probably do it too. Instead of a few miles accuracy that we got with traditional means, we can now navigate to within a few yards of any-where we want to go, and if the military ever gives up on selective availability, we'll get that down to a few inches.

And cheap? Boy, are they cheap. When Susan and I first began looking for a cruising boat, a good GPS cost about $1,000. When we left on our cruise two years later, we bought one on sale at West Marine for $500; and on my last trip to the States, I bought a tiny Garmin model that is so small I have to be careful when I clean the lint out of my pocket—it set me back all of $150. If this trend continues, we'll soon be able to get them as premiums for subscribing to *Time* and as prizes in boxes of corn flakes.

Don't forsake the sextant

All this electronic wonderfulness has a downside, though, especially to us hoary curmudgeons who enjoy the challenge of doing difficult tasks with style and dash and actually liked things the way they used to be. With every new technological advance a thin layer of the mystique of life is stripped away, and I firmly believe that our short stay here on earth is diminished by that. When I was in school, a slide rule peeking out from a shirt pocket symbolized an active intellect—and even though I kept mine out of sight so it wouldn't interfere with my carefully cultivated James Dean image, I was proud of my ability to use one. Then along came elec-tronic calculators and shot the mystique of the slide rule all to hell. Now anyone with one finger and the hand-eye coordination to hit a half-inch square with it can perform complex mathematics.

Is this sour grapes coming from a grouchy old-fart reactionary, as Phillip and Sarah claim? Not a bit. I wouldn't even consider for a moment trading my Shakuhachi ultra-programmable, solar-powered, maxi-scientific Model XL747 Stretched Super Deluxe pocket calculator for anything—especially not for a slide rule. That sucker has 96 buttons, about a hundred functions, and an instruction manual thicker than the Manhattan phone book. After a year of intensive study I've finally discovered how to turn the damn thing on, and if I can ever figure out which function is the plus button, I'll soon be able to add two numbers together using only one finger. Hot damn . . . maybe there's hope for humanity after all.

GPS became a necessity for every offshore sailor as soon as it hit the market. Its universal acceptance was instantaneous, but the tendency to forsake the sextant is dangerous. I repeat, traditional navigation methods are not as difficult as you might think, and they're fun besides. But many cruisers don't know beans about navigation and rely on the little box to do everything for them. I've even met long-time cruisers who have sold their sextants, thinking they will never need them again.

Let's hope they're right, but the ability to find a speck in the ocean like the Galapagos Islands with our sextant, watch, and Almanac is much more than just an emergency backup to the GPS. It is one of the few useful links with tradition that dates back to the Middle Ages. Indeed, skill with a sextant has long been a symbol of the cruising life. Just look on your bookshelf and notice how many covers of your cruising books are adorned with a photo of the author hanging from the shrouds while taking a shot with the sextant. If there isn't one on the cover, there'll be a photo of a sextant inside for sure. Can you imagine a cruising book whose cover shows some befuddled clown with a quizzical expression punching buttons on a box? Probably not.

Knowing how to use a sextant gives an enormous boost to self-confidence, sets you apart from the hoard of newcomers who consider navigation skills in the same category as the sounding lead (amazing how many boats don't carry lead lines any more) and the cat-o'-nine tails. (What? You don't have a cat-o'-nine aboard?) Besides, a basic knowledge of the principles behind traditional navigation gives you an understanding of what's going on when your GPS tells you what to do to get somewhere. To follow an electronic readout blindly without understanding what it's trying to tell you is an exercise for fools and children. Relying on a single technology when you are in a hostile environment is a serious mistake because it always leads to over-reliance on the technology which, in turn, leads to panic when the technology fails. And trust me—it will fail. It's much the same as the pilot of a small plane who hasn't stayed current with engine-out procedures because "I haven't lost an engine in 30 years of flying." At that, the engine craps out. There have been several instances of cruisers panicking and setting off their EPIRBs when their GPSs went on the blink. I know of at least one documented case when a skipper and crew abandoned their boat when their electronic navigation (a SATNAV) failed.

The Columbus Method

A more basic means of navigation has also become a lost art—the Columbus method, also known as the sail-in-the-general-direction-of-where-you-want-to-go-until-you-see-something-then-try-to-figure-out-what-the-hell-it-is method. This is the method by which I first learned to sail, and it has always served me well when all else has failed.

Once while crossing Massachusetts Bay on a foggy pitch-black night in the late 60s with my cousin Steve, we motored all night through an oily black sea, using only a Boy Scout compass and a map on the placemat from the restaurant where we had enjoyed our dinner. At about 3 A.M. we spotted a lighthouse. After consulting our placemat we determined that it had to be either Halifax, Nova Scotia; Gloucester (our destination); or Marblehead. After eliminating Halifax as being out of range, we resolved to sail toward the light until we spotted a boat. If the boat were a grungy fishing boat covered with rust, we would be in Gloucester; if it were a palatial yacht with a uniformed flunky on the bow prepared to fend off any idiots in sailboats who might emerge from the fog, we would definitely be in Marblehead. As it turned out the first boat we came across was neither a fishing boat nor a yacht, but a Coast Guard cutter looking for pot smugglers. "Close enough," said Steve. "This has to be Gloucester. Marblehead would never tolerate pot smugglers—Cabernet Sauvignon smugglers maybe, but never pot smugglers."

Watchstanding

Much nonsense has been written about watches and the necessity of keeping them, most of which might have come right out of Captain Bligh's handbook. Rigid watch schedules are a major pain in the butt on most small cruising boats, and crews who try to initiate them often have morale problems. It is much better to maintain a flexible watch schedule that simply ensures someone is on deck anytime the boat is under way. Obviously, much more diligence is required in places like the Yucatan Channel (where an average of three or four freighters are in sight at any one time) than in the middle of the Pacific Ocean where you can sail for weeks without seeing a sign of another boat.

Many cruisers don't stand regular watches and singlehanders, by definition, can't. On *Sultana* we have developed a standardized schedule based on preferences. During daylight, someone must be on deck at all times—and that person never leaves the deck while the other three are below without asking to be relieved.

At night things get a little more formal. Phillip takes the watch from 1800 to 2100; Sarah is a night owl so she takes 2100 to 2400; I take over and go to 0300, then Susan takes over until 0600. If she wakes up, that is. Susan does all the cooking on our passages, so if she doesn't wake up and if I'm not about to fall asleep at my post, I'll keep the watch until she does wake up. It really isn't self-sacrifice and consideration for my mate that keeps me at the helm, it's hunger. A sleepy cook is a worthless cook, and by letting Susan sleep through her watch, I ensure myself a sumptuous breakfast and, with a little luck, lasagna on Friday.

Noncruising Cruising Skills

Earlier, I mentioned a few skills that cruisers find useful either as a means to achieving self-sufficiency or as services to sell to other cruisers as a means of prolonging the life of the cruising kitty. These are skills that don't have anything to do with sailing or boats but they will make your life afloat more enjoyable and maybe even profitable.

Cooking—the most important skill aboard

This isn't an exaggeration. A crew that eats well is well, and a continual supply of nutritious food is a critical element of a successful cruise. It is so important that all of chapter 11 is devoted to food and the galley.

Mechanics

Early in my youth I was classified as a hoodlum. I was, of course, thrilled with this designation, but tragically, inasmuch as I had never done anything really wrong other than wearing my Levis too low, snarffing a few Luckies in the boy's room, and wearing my hair too long, I was never a candidate for reform school—an exalted institution to which all of us James Dean wannabes aspired. As a compromise, I was sent off to what is now called Vocational Arts but was then known as Trade School. Simply stated, Trade School was a Reform School where they let you go home at night.

After gaining admission to the hallowed halls of Bladensburg Trade School (BTS), I was given a battery of tests that revealed my previously unknown aptitude for automobile mechanics. (The fact that automobile mechanics was the only class that had space at the time was pure coincidence, I'm sure.)

The courses I took at BTS turned out to be some of the most valuable that I have ever taken in that they definitively proved that I didn't possess even a hint of mechanical aptitude. After my graduation, my dad let me do a valve job on his nearly new 1953 Chevrolet station wagon. When I got the lifters in upside down, thereby necessitating the replacement of the entire engine, he was quite good about it really. That was my last foray into the field of auto mechanics. After finishing college (which I attended solely to avoid ever having to work on cars for a living) I took a desk job with the telephone company and actively avoided any contact with automobiles other than with door handles and steering wheels.

My phobia of things mechanical carried over to the cruising world. When we began our cruise I felt qualified to fix just about everything on the boat except the engine. However, after being billed $75 for an oil change at a marina run by a guy with the amazingly appropriate name of Captain Rob, I resolved that a renewed interest in things mechanical was in order.

I spent the next few months reading and studying everything I could get my hands on about diesel engines. I even went so far as to climb down into the cramped and dark engine room and check out our old Ford four-banger. I sat on the transmission and read the entire section on diesel engines in Nigel Calder's *Boatowner's Mechanical and Electrical Manual,* and when I climbed out, I felt competent to fix just about anything that ever showed the poor judgment to break. In fact, way down deep inside, I may have secretly hoped that the engine would blow up just so I could have a go at rebuilding it.

Unfortunately for my ego, diesel engines are among the most reliable mechanical contraptions ever invented, and *Sultana*'s old clunker is among the best. It wasn't until we were off the east coast of Mexico that I got a chance to try out my newfound mechanical skills. We were a mile or so off a lee shore in a 25-knot breeze with about a 4-foot sea on the beam when things got dicey enough for me to resort to artificial power. *Sultana* motorsails like a dream and we can often gain about 10 points on the wind just by starting her engine. In this instance, I felt we could clear an approaching headland without tacking if I used a few rpm's of the prop for a boost.

Needless to say, this was a dumb thing to do. Just as we were clearing the headland, no more than 100 yards from the reef, and right after I said to Susan, "Boy are we in trouble if the engine quits," the engine stopped dead. Naturally the first thing we did was panic and in so doing lost enough way so that we couldn't tack. This forced us to wear ship, which brought us within a few heart-stopping feet of the reef, but it did get us going back the way we had come and away from those threatening fangs of coral and rock.

Once we were clear of the reef, I plunged into the engine compartment, tool kit in one hand, Nigel Calder's book in the other, and attacked the enemy. Four hours later, battered and bruised from being flung about in the engine compartment and soaked in diesel fuel, I located a fuel line that had been blocked by sediment kicked up by the rough seas. I got the engine running again. Today, after spending what seems like half a lifetime in that engine compartment and thumbing my copy of Calder's book to a tattered rag, I believe that it would take me all of 10 minutes to clear the same obstruction and get old Betsy back on line. In fact, I could do it in my pajamas with one hand tied behind my back while wearing a blindfold.

My purpose here isn't to brag but to illustrate my point that, no matter how much of a mechanical klutz you might be, you will learn to fix diesel engines if you are to survive as a budget cruiser. It's much better that you do it now in night school or in home study than to wait until you are on a lee shore off the coast of Mexico with four footers bouncing you around like an olive in a martini shaker.

Electronics

When I started sailing all those many years ago, a knowledge of electronics would have been superfluous because the electronics inventory on Uncle Freddy's *Mazuka* stopped at the running lights—and they never worked because the battery was always dead. Today, however, *Sultana* needs hundreds of amp hours of battery power just to find her way out of the harbor, and her main circuit breaker panel has more toggle switches than an airliner's cockpit. We have radios, depthfinders, radar, navigation devices, masthead strobes, autopilots, and even a curious little round thingy under the floor boards that promises to beep cheerfully just before we are to be blown to bits by propane leaking into the bilge. And that's just the "necessary" stuff. If I started in on the VCRs, computers, video games, the new CD player, and all the other paraphernalia that we might be able to suffer through life without, I'd need the rest of this chapter just for the list.

Cruising yachts today rely on their electronics just as much as they rely on their diesel engines—but diesel engines are rather primitive and simple contrivances that most of us can come to terms with after a little study. Understanding electronics, however, requires nothing less than a pact with the devil. Only a select few will ever comprehend what goes on inside all those boxes when you push those buttons. In short, unless you have made said pact with Lucifer in the form of extensive electronics training, you can forget about fixing your own electronics. To make things worse, a single drop of saltwater, or even humid tropical air can convert thousands of dollars of electronic apparatus into worthless pieces of junk in seconds. A lightning strike can turn every transistor and resistor on your boat into a miniature firecracker.

Electronics are at once essential and sensitive to breakage and impossible for those without special tools and training to repair. The best we can do is carry a spare of the essential ones (a VHF radio and a GPS) and train ourselves to carry on without the others when necessary. After all, Magellan didn't need electronics, and neither did Drake, Columbus, Slocum, or my Uncle Freddy.

Electrical equipment

Although you can't fix your own electronics, every cruiser should have an intimate knowledge of electronic circuitry and Ohm's law. You should know how circuit breakers and fuses work, be able to find short circuits and track down the source of stray voltage, be proficient at chasing circuits from the battery to the device and back to ground, and be familiar with the mysterious workings of your digital electrical multimeter and your test light. You must know how your generators, alternators, and inverters work. You should understand that your batteries are reservoirs of power, the very life blood of your electronics, and that they must be replenished or they will dry up and become useless. You must understand that the green powder that collects on your electrical terminals is your enemy whose goal is to deprive you of your most valuable equipment—and the enemy pursues it with the fervor of an evangelist chasing sinners. You must understand the guiding philosophy of galvanic action, how it can destroy a boat, what you can do to prevent it. And you must know all about bonding circuits.

Unfortunately, this book is nowhere near long enough to go into the details of the electrical troubleshooting skills that you will need to become an effective cruiser, and I'm not really qualified to write about it anyway. But if you already have a basic knowledge of electrical theory, you don't have to go any further than your copy of Nigel Calder's book, wherein you will find several hundred pages of clear and concise information on the subject. If you don't have even basic knowledge of electrical circuitry, you could do a lot worse than taking a course on electronics at a community college or night school.

Carpentry

One of the things I like to do best is work with wood. I swoon to the sound of a jack plane zinging off heaps of golden curls from the surface of a pine board or the seductive rhythm of the bow saw as it rips a mahogany plank into something useful or beautiful or both. Wood is my thing, and if I do say so myself, I am good at making it into stuff we need. While you don't need to develop this degree of religious fervor about woodwork, a few basic carpentry skills will be worth the effort on any boat, and if you happen to be among the fortunate few who are blessed with a wooden boat, they will be essential.

Again, a few hundred bucks dropped on the cashier's desk at a community college is an excellent place to start, but if you do take this path to woodworking proficiency, make sure that you take classes that emphasize the use of hand tools. Skills with a thickness planer and an 8-inch jointer are going to be marginal on a boat, but the ability to sharpen and use a chisel, plane, and handsaw will be invaluable. Once you get the basics, pick up a copy of Fred Bingham's book, *Boat Joinery and Cabinetmaking Simplified,* read it cover to cover, practice with a few basic projects using nothing but hand tools, then make it a permanent part of your cruising library.

Housekeeping

Everyone knows that when two or more people live together in the confines of a tiny boat, everything must be picked up and put away when it isn't in use. "Everything in its place, and a place for everything," is our watchword. On *Sultana* every item on the boat has a designated storage spot that belongs to that item alone, and there is not a single item that doesn't have its place. When a new item comes aboard, the first thing we do is assign it a storage spot, then we make sure the entire crew knows exactly where that spot is. Each of us scrupulously returns each item to that designated spot the moment it is no longer being used. Everything on the boat is neat and tidy, and the hideous specter of unsightly clutter never raises its ugly head. Not on our boat. Nosiree Bob . . . I wish.

The only reason that I mention housekeeping as an acquired skill (it's confession time here) is that the crew of *Sultana* are so wondrously bad at it. We are a boatload of unrepentant slobs with gear and clutter everywhere, and if anyone were ever to just once put something back in the place it came from, Susan would be right there with the ship's thermometer from the first aid kit. But that's not the worst part. In those rare instances (only slightly more frequent than the appearance of Halley's comet) when we get so fed up with all the junk laying around and actually clean the place up, we go for weeks and months without being able to find anything.

"Where's the can of corned beef I was keeping here in my underwear locker?" asks Susan the day after a major cleanup, or "What happened to the dead squid I was dissecting for my science project?" asks Phillip. Once, on San Andres Island off the coast of Colombia, I used my nifty little low-angle block plane and my whizbang ratcheting screwdriver to fix a loose plank in the cockpit, then put both tools away in a special place where they wouldn't get lost. Just the other day, two years later, as I was tearing out a storage locker to refinish it, I came across rusted remains of the block plane—but I still haven't located the dang screwdriver.

We do try to be neat and tidy and we will continue to fight the good fight for order and organization, but I have noticed a curious phenomenon on some other people's boats. You may not believe this (it came as quite a shock to me), but there are some boats out there that have achieved the high degree of tidiness to which we aspire. Their decks are meticulously laid out with all the gear properly stowed and secured and their interiors are orderly to a fault. But there is a curious problem here. Those skippers and crew who have mastered the art of neatness seem to have also mastered the art of being consummate twits, and their neat and tidy boats have all the warmth and charm of freshly cleaned goldfish bowls. Meanwhile, those boats that maintain a certain degree of clutter or have that lived-in and homey look (and my friend Mauri's aptly named ketch, *Goatlocker,* comes to mind here) are warm and comfortable. So the lesson is clear: be neat and tidy and keep everything as shipshape as you can, but don't forget that people are *living on the boat* and with people comes a degree of disorder and confusion. Learn to love it; it's life.

While a degree of clutter and disorder down below is a normal part of living on a boat, it's a different world on deck, especially during a passage. Here, clutter is more than an unsightly nuisance, it's dangerous and can even be lethal. Loose lines can fall overboard to foul the prop and rudder, unsecured gear and equipment can be lost overboard in rough seas or can shift violently causing damage to people, items secured on the deck walkways can trip crew who are trying to tend sails. Even at anchor, a little thing like an unsecured halyard can drive you crazy with its slapping on the mast when the wind comes up at 2 A.M.

On *Sultana* we are learning the hard way to keep the decks clear and gear tied down. So far we have lost the staysail when it was blown overboard in a gale because the sailbag wasn't tied to the deck, and two jerry cans have gone by the boards. Don't learn the hard way; keep the deck clear and everything thereon secured.

Personal hygiene

While we are on the neat and tidy subject, a few words about personal hygiene while cruising: its importance is highly overrated. While talking to groups about cruising someone will always come up to me and say, "Oooooh, how can you stand to go that long without a bath?" To which I usually answer, "It's tough, but you get used to it." But this is a cop-out. The real answer is that there is no problem keeping clean on a boat. A liter of hot water in a bowl with a lot of soap and a washcloth is more than enough to keep the most finicky cruiser clean. Except on the longest passages where water conservation is important, I like to shave every other day or so. I know it doesn't fit the scruffy world-class cruiser image I should be cultivating, but it makes me feel good, so I do it.

Skills You'll Need Ashore

Sultana's first stop at a foreign port was at the lovely Mexican island of Isla Mujeres in the Yucatan Channel where the Caribbean meets the Gulf of Mexico. There we had our first encounter with the terror of Third World bureaucracy, the port captain, and learned firsthand the importance of diplomacy.

Diplomacy

In its simplest form, diplomacy is the art of getting someone to do something you want them to do; in its most complicated form, diplomacy is the art of getting someone who hates your guts to do something you want them to do. Diplomacy goes hand in hand with tact and common sense, and the importance of these three skills in dealing with officials of foreign governments, especially Third World governments, cannot be underestimated. And in my observation, the cruising community is unequivocally bad at all three.

The port captain's office in Isla Mujeres is in a plain cement building—somewhat like a concrete bunker—with no glass in the windows and no proper door at the entrance. When the four of us from *Sultana* entered the bare waiting room, around which were scattered a few rickety folding metal chairs, another American cruiser was there ahead of us. We could see the port captain in an adjacent room, which was also bare of any adornment, sitting at a metal desk reading a newspaper. The American skipper sat fidgeting in his chair for a while, then jumped up to glare first at his watch then at the captain. Finally, he stuck his head into the captain's office and asked in a loud voice, "Excuse me, but could we puulleeeze get some help out here?"

"Minuto, minuto . . . asiento," said the captain in an angry voice gesturing the skipper back to his chair.

Perhaps 15 minutes later, the captain emerged from his office, took one brief look at the skipper's papers and told him, in florid Spanish, that he needed to go to the police station first and hustled him out the door. The American obviously couldn't understand a word of what was said and stumbled off down the street muttering under his breath.

On hearing this I got up to leave since we hadn't yet been to the police station either, but the captain caught my eye and I felt I should say something.

"Buenos dias, señor Capitan. Necetamos voy a el policia tambien."

"Oh, I think we can handle that for you right here, amigo," said the captain in broken but perfectly legitimate English, "have a seat."

Ten minutes later we were back on the street with our passports stamped and ready to enjoy what was a very enjoyable port indeed. The good captain even took the trouble of correcting my deplorable Spanish. (It's *Él Capitana* in Mexico, never *Capitán*.)

We have witnessed this same scene unfold in port offices halfway around the world. It is amazing how many cruisers have chips on their shoulders as they enter into negotiations with port officials and try to bully or intimidate officials. It never works. What does work is a polite, even obsequious, smile, patience, and a head nodding in assent of everything the official says. You need to keep in mind your objective—to get the appropriate stamps in your passport and a *zarpe* in your pocket, not to make a statement for human dignity, fairness, or to indulge in macho posturing or a contest of wills. Swallow your pride and bob your head, and if you are kept sitting in a drafty office for half a day, sit with a happy smile on your face. Nod your head every now and then as if agreeing with what the official is thinking. It's tough but it works. Only once in all our stops did we ever lose our cool—that once cost us a hundred bucks.

A word here about bribes. Graft and bribery are a major part of the culture in many parts of the world; in Spanish America, giving small gifts to officials is a normal part of daily life. Public officials in most Third World countries are woefully underpaid, and it is unlikely that our friend the port captain in Isla Mujeres made enough from his yearly salary to pay for the wristwatch at which the American skipper was glaring. If port captains are to support their families, they must make up the shortfall of income from graft. Usually this graft is built into the fee schedules and the officials skim their take off the top, but in a few countries, especially those not visited by a lot of yachts, the graft is on top of the normal fees.

That being said, we have found the best policy is to never mention a bribe unless you are specifically asked for one, act surprised and confused by the request when it does come, then offer no more than half the amount requested. Many progressive governments recognize entrenched graft and greedy and corrupt officials as being a major hindrance to healthy economic growth and are trying to stamp out these practices. When you approach officials for the first time, you have no way of knowing if they are good guys or bad. If you boldly offer a bribe to a good guy you could find yourself in an embarrassing situation or even, in an extreme case, in front of a magistrate. By pretending naive ignorance of any requirement for a bribe, you can often avoid the matter entirely. If you are braced for a bribe and can't avoid it, just pay it and get on with your life. Don't insist on a receipt and don't take a Polaroid of the offending official (a suggestion I read only recently)—just smile and hand over the money. We were forced to shell out extra cash only in Belize and Panama, so if you handle it right, bribes are not a problem.

Psychology

Sometimes I think I'd like to be a psychologist when I grow up because I get a kick out of watching people and trying to figure out why they do some of the things they do. I particularly enjoy watching tourists in some of the more touristy places we visit. In the Virgin Islands one time I was strolling along the waterfront in downtown Charlotte Amalie when I was confronted by a solid wall of humanity rushing toward me.

"Is this the way to the shops?" asked a frantic woman in a big straw hat who appeared to be the leader of the mob. I nodded my head in assent. "Oh, wonderful," she gushed. "This way gang," she proclaimed to the multitudes behind her, and about 1,000 people charged off in the direction of the shopping district. I later learned that the cruise ships dock for only two hours in Charlotte Amalie and that the stores feature bargain prices for emeralds. The result is a feeding frenzy of shoppers scooping up millions of dollars worth of emeralds. Some find true bargains, but most shoppers end up with low-grade stones that they could buy in any discount jewelry store in the mall back home for much less. The docks are more than a mile from town and there are nowhere nearly enough buses and taxis to ferry the thousands of passengers that emerge from the bowels of a single large luxury liner. Consequently, the stampede of zealous emerald shoppers is a regular occurrence in Charlotte Amalie.

My psychological dabblings are more than mere personal entertainment, however. Over the years, I have made a careful study of the cruisers who have been mugged in the Caribbean and have discovered that the cause of 90 percent of all muggings is shorts. Although I don't have any hard data, I can make a pretty good case for my argument. Most Latin American males, particularly those in the lower socioeconomic levels who are more prone to such marginal activities as tourist mugging and cruiser bashing, consider men who wear shorts to be sissies and, thus, easy marks for a mugging. Few Spanish American men would be caught dead in a pair of shorts, so they naturally consider any tourists who wear them to be effeminate wimps.

The lesson here is clear. If you are among the vast majority of us who wish to avoid getting mugged by misguided people who are ignorant of the latest in summer fashions, simply wear long pants (dark trousers with a loose-fitting, light-colored shirt are best).

Language

It is amazing to me how many cruisers there are in the Caribbean who never make an attempt to learn Spanish. We have met people who have cruised there for years who can't count to 10 in the native tongue, which is not only disgraceful, it's stupid. Most people I have met who aren't interested in learning even the basics of Spanish say that it's not necessary because there is always someone nearby who speaks English, and it's true, there usually is. But try switching roles for a moment and pretend you are the proprietor of a store in downtown Halifax, Nova Scotia, and a Spanish-speaking person comes in demanding that you provide an interpreter. Would you do it? Probably, if there was enough money at risk. Would you resent it? You bet. Would you charge a little extra for the trouble? Hell no, you wouldn't, you'd charge a lot extra for the trouble, and that is just what will happen to you if you venture forth into the Spanish-speaking world without making an effort to learn a little Spanish.

Remember our experience at the port captain's office in Isla Mujeres? The ability to use just a few basic Spanish phrases changes your entire relationship with many public officials. Just a simple "Good morning" ("Buenos dias, señor") and a brief apology for not speaking proper Spanish ("Lo siento. No hablo español muy bien. ¿Habla inglés?") will likely change an indifferent or even hostile official into a friendly one. Likewise, knowing how to count and ask the price of an item in a shop ("¿Quanto es esto? Por favor.") will go miles toward getting you the best price, and maybe even making a new friend.

Of course, if you are headed on an extensive cruise, Spanish isn't the only language that you should become familiar with. The French particularly respond well to attempts to communicate in their language, and on Bora Bora I had one official refuse to respond in English until I made an effort to break the ice in exceedingly bad French. If you intend to visit any French-speaking countries, a basic knowledge of the language is well advised.

Skills to Sell to Other Cruisers

I am not enthralled with the idea of cruisers selling services to other cruisers for several reasons: It seems a bit mercenary and it detracts from the idea that we are all in the same boat, helping each other out as our abilities and needs dictate; commercial activity by visitors to foreign countries is often illegal and must be conducted on the sly; the quality of work by itinerant cruisers fluctuates from the acceptable to far below substandard; and finally, most trades and professions today require a substantial investment in specialized equipment, and few sailboats have the space to use this equipment even if they do have it aboard. We have met several cruising sailmakers, for example, who do acceptable work with an onboard sewing machine, but a sailmaker without a loft is at a serious disadvantage. Likewise, a diesel mechanic without a machine shop or a dentist without a proper chair and drill is going to be handicapped in providing excellent service.

Because it is difficult to judge the degree to which itinerant craftspersons are qualified to do a job, people are often reluctant to hire them. We hired a guy in the Rio Dulce who called himself a marine engineer and claimed to be a qualified rigger to help install a new roller furler. He got the forestay about 4 inches too long and instead of recutting it, he compensated by taking up on the bobstay and backstay. This threw the whole rig out of balance and eventually led to the failure of the bobstay. I have probably wasted more colorful language on that particular self-styled engineer than on any other person we have met. I thought of him all the way across the Pacific every time we tried to get the main to set properly.

That being said, cruisers with skills that are in high demand will find a ready market in harbors and ports frequented by other cruisers around the world, and doing such work is a popular means of kitty renewal. Here is a rundown of a few of the favorites.

Mechanics

If you are a qualified diesel mechanic and wish to sell your services to fellow cruisers, you will find no scarcity of work in most of the popular harbors around the world. The question of the legality of pursuing your trade is a matter between you and the local officials as most large harbors have a ready supply of mechanics who could become vociferous if they discover you are competing with them.

While in the Rio Dulce we had some engine work done by an enterprising young man named Frank who was cruising with his wife and small daughter aboard their meticulously reconstructed Chinese junk, *Concubine*. He billed himself as Doctor Diesel and was quite aggressive in soliciting work. From all outward appearances he was operating a successful business and seemed to have as much work as he could handle, and the work he did for us was first rate.

Sewing and sailmaking

The ability to repair sails is always in demand, of course, but there is also a steady market for dodgers and cockpit shelters, sailcovers, and all manner of canvas stuff. If you can make the ubiquitous canvas tote bag with loop handles, you'll find buyers. If they are monogrammed with the ship's name and hailing port, they'll sell like hot dogs at the ballpark. The absence of a sail loft makes major sail repairs on a boat somewhat difficult, and making new sails for anything larger than the dinghy is out of the question, but it is surprising how well some shipbound sailmakers learn to handle small repairs on large sails in the confines of a cockpit.

Fiberglass repair

Repairing gelcoat and fiberglass damage to fiberglass boats is a natural trade to sell to other cruisers, but it isn't as easy as it might seem. Many cruisers don't get too concerned about cosmetic damage to the topsides and let the dings and dents that are a normal part of cruising accumulate until it is time for a major refit. Of course, any major damage such as structural failure or holes in the hull mean the boat will have to be hauled. Any yard equipped to haul a cruising yacht is also most likely equipped to make major repairs and isn't going to take kindly to outsiders scooping off their work.

In U.S. and Canadian ports, as well as in other countries where it is legal, however, a skilled fiberglass worker can usually find hourly work at local boat-yards and with boatbuilders. Skills in making invisible gelcoat repairs (more an art than a skill) are particularly desirable where there are a lot of expensive yachts.

Carpentry

Because most serious cruisers are passable carpenters themselves, there isn't a big demand among the sailing community for woodworkers. However, if you have house-building skills, you can make a lot of money in a short time if you find your-self in the right place at the right time. When we were in Charleston, South Carolina (one of our favorite stops on the East Coast), the downtown was still re-covering from a major storm the year before, and skilled finish carpenters who could help restore the grand old Victorian mansions were in high demand and pulling down top wages. Likewise, there was a building boom in Fort Lauderdale where experienced framing carpenters found all the work they wanted.

Varnishing and painting

Like carpentry, most cruisers can handle whatever painting and varnishing chores that come along. Again, however, if you find yourself in a U.S. or Canadian port where there are a lot of local yachts, passing around a simple flyer or posting a no-tice on a yacht club or marina's bulletin board might bring some responses.

Teaching and tutoring

Enterprising people with teaching skills might find themselves with a steady, if not large, income. Most cruisers who have children use homeschooling or correspon-dence schools for educating the little darlings, and if you possess knowledge in sub-jects that parents often find difficult—language, math, science, or music—you will often find work for an hour or two a day. The pay won't be great, but it's reward-ing work, a great way to meet people, and you'll seldom find any problem with the local officials.

Arts and crafts

When we first got to Tonga we were approached by a distinguished-looking gen-tleman with a short white beard and the patina of a long-time cruiser who asked if we were interested in buying any of his authentic Maori jewelry. He had several display cases full of stylized fishhook pendants, broaches, and rings and bracelets carved from whalebone, tortoise shell, exotic rainforest woods, and all manner of politically incorrect materials.

We declined to buy anything but we did have a chat. It turned out the guy was from Marblehead, and until about 10 years earlier he had lived about six blocks from where we did. The irony of traveling halfway around the world to buy authentic native jewelry from a guy who was practically a neighbor was too much to take. Collecting native handcrafts from around the world (molas from the San Blas Islands, carved masks from Guatemala, tapas cloth from Fiji and Tonga) is a major pastime of cruisers, but I prefer to buy mine from natives, not from guys from Marblehead.

However, if you happen to possess artsy-craftsy skills and are visiting any port where large cruise ships dock, you can make a lot of money in a short time just by setting up a simple stand somewhere in the path of the disembarking hordes. Usually there will be an area where artisans gather and often you can just set up and join in. At other times, in more organized areas, you will need to get clearance and perhaps pay a small fee to the designated authority person (DAP) to secure table space. In some places, because you are a foreigner your participation will be restricted (or even illegal), in which case you can count on paying a large fee to the DAP.

We have met several cruisers who supplement their incomes with handcrafts, and there are one or two who do so well at it that they don't have to do anything else.

Skills to Sell Ashore

In many places, particularly in third-world countries where the wages for skilled workers is measured in a few dollars a week, trying to find a job in the local economy isn't worthwhile, but there are a few exceptions. Most of the skills listed above as appropriate to sell to other cruisers may also be sold ashore, but some are appropriate only for the shoreside domain.

Food-service skills

Any experience you might have had in restaurants, cafeterias, bars, or other divisions of the food-service industry will stand you in good stead in the cruising life. In fact, waiting on tables, bussing them, or washing dishes is practically a tradition among budget cruisers. The work at these menial jobs is often hard, and the hours are long, and the pay is low, but the jobs are available nearly everywhere. These kinds of skills are particularly valuable in resort areas such as Key West and Honolulu, and a job in those places can be yours for the asking. The big hotels are likely to be controlled by unions, but there are plenty of smaller places that are always looking for help.

In New Zealand and Australia there is such a shortage of dedicated help in many of the tourist areas like the Bay of Islands and Cairns that even though it is technically illegal for foreigners to work in these countries without hard-to-get work permits, the officials look the other way, at least during the busy tourist season when the demand is highest. This same situation exists on many islands in the Caribbean and may be the case in Europe. I don't know, I'll let you know when we get there.

Food-service jobs are easy to get in the U.S., too. If you are planning to work on your cruise and will be depending on shoreside employment for income, you are well advised to take a part-time job in a local restaurant or bar and learn all you can about waiting tables, food preparation, kitchen management, and bartending. The work is there whenever you need it.

Engineering

I'm not sure what engineers do but they have been defined as folks who try to figure out how to do with two bolts what most of us can do with one. I'm not sure what that means either, but I suspect it isn't very complimentary. We seem to meet all sorts of engineers on boats. I've met a civil engineer in Belize who was working on a water project of some sort or other, a computer engineer in Guatemala doing reprogramming of some hospital's computer system, a mechanical engineer teaching local technicians how to use sophisticated welding equipment in Honduras, and a self-styled marine engineer in Guatemala who made a career of destroying other peoples' boats for money.

Like I said, I don't know just what it is that engineers do but apparently whatever it is, they do it all over the world and seem to turn a pretty good buck doing it. If you are one—an engineer, that is—there is a good probability that you will find ample opportunities to exercise your skills. (By the way, what *are* your skills?)

Crop harvesting

With muscle and a little effort, you can make a few bucks while visiting Australia or New Zealand during the crop harvesting season. I'm not sure what it is about picking apples or berries or kiwi fruit or tomatoes that turns folks off, but it is gosh-awful hard to find people willing to do it. Perhaps it is the endless hours in the hot sun lugging a heavy apple bag, or mastering the back-breaking duck walk of the tomato picker, or enduring the painful spines of the kiwi plant, or the fact that most people who live in these countries can make more money by going on the very generous dole and staying home to watch the soaps on the telly than by working in the fields. Whatever it is, picking fruit can be a terrific way to spend a few productive months ashore. If you are good at it, crop picking can be quite lucrative. Our friend, Randy, on *Mariah,* works both the Australian and New Zealand seasons and makes enough money to spend the rest of the year cruising in luxury. I have heard of many other people doing the same.

The work is hard and the pay is low, but expenses are nonexistent, there is more work than you can ever handle (in season), it's outdoors and healthy beyond measure, and you are bound to meet some terrific folks. And isn't that what cruising is supposed to be all about? Isn't that what life is supposed to be all about?

Once you start cruising, you will be called on to solve an ever-changing array of problems that will challenge every skill you can muster. You can't call a plumber when you are 500 miles from the nearest land, and there is no hospital emergency room to which you can rush the victim of a medical crisis. You need to be able to handle these things yourself, and the more skills you have in your bag of tricks the better and safer your cruising experience will be. The trick is to acquire as many of these skills as you can before you shove off and to keep acquiring them once you are under way.

9

OK, LET'S BUY
A BOAT

"There's a good life had at sea . . .

Sail away Raymond, sail away."

—*Ringo Starr, "Sail Away Raymond"*

Delphus **and the Doofus**

After Susan decided she was going cruising and I decided that if I didn't want to live the rest of my life in hopeless desperation and lonely despair I had better go along too, the next logical thing for us to do was to buy a boat in which to pursue our insanity . . . er, fantasy. At the time we owned a large antique powerboat that we dearly loved, so after I convinced Susan that there was no way such a boat could make it around Cape Cod much less around the world, we began looking for a replacement.

The criteria for our ideal craft were simple enough: We needed a commodious boat that was livable and comfortable for four people, two of whom were growing at a frightening rate and who found a three-story, 14-room "post-Victorian" house with a three-car garage and a workshop to be barely adequate; it must be inexpensive to buy in boat terms (we figured we could spend up to a maximum of $125,000, and I will never be able to consider that much money to be inexpensive for anything, no matter what it is); it needed to be in good enough condition so that we could leave within a year of purchase; it needed to be seaworthy and safe for offshore cruising with a crew who didn't know a lot about offshore cruising; it need to be inexpensive to maintain because after spending that much money for a boat, we weren't going to have a lot left over for upkeep; and it needed to be as warm and homey and welcoming as our old boat.

This didn't seem like a lot to ask at the time but we quickly discovered that our list of needs, no matter how reasonable, eliminated about 99.99 percent of all the boats on the market that brokers touted as cruising boats (a brokerage term that means anything that isn't a hi-tech racing boat). Our search took us from the tip of northern Maine, where we had to chip ice off the winter covers of several boats, to the Virgin Islands where I suffered from severe sunburn. We looked at trimarans and catamarans and monohulls of every size and description, and we had several notable close encounters of the disaster kind.

In one case, in a fit of blind passion, I became determined to buy a floating monstrosity named *Delphus,* a huge Chinese-built ketch that had been used in the Caribbean charter trade. The problem was that I fell in love with the boat that was pictured in the listing that the broker provided. She was 54 feet on deck and of a style that might be called Asian Gothic, with teak taffrail and hand-carved trailboards on the bowsprit. She had an ornate, solid teak spiral stairway leading below decks to a paneled main cabin big enough for the next Democratic National Convention, and she sported enough bunks to sleep half the after-work crowd at Marblehead's Rip Tide Lounge.

This hulking heap of Chinese hostelry had been repossessed by the bank from the previous owner who had neglected to tender the agreed-upon sum to said bank at the end of each month, and the poor boat had sat at anchor in the hot tropical sun for more than a year. The bank had originally wanted $300,000, which was the assessed value of this treasure, but as the relentless Caribbean rays worked their mischief and the boat steadily deteriorated, they had steadily reduced their objective. The word was out that they were now prepared to accept any offer short of a giveaway and that wasn't so ludicrous as to attract the attention of the bank examiners.

Delphus was a mess. Inside she was dirty and moldy. Outside, the sun had eaten away every bit of varnish from the vast expanses of woodwork; the martengale boom had rotted away, thereby loosening the rig to the extent that it looked dangerous; much of the metal work was corroded; and the wooden spars showed signs of substantial internal rot. It should have been obvious that the boat needed a major refit and that to bring her back to a serviceable condition would cost about what the boat would be worth in a restored state. In other words, *Delphus* wouldn't have been any great bargain even if she had been given to us for nothing.

But I was in love. I was blinded by the fact that the base price for a new model of this particular make of boat was $750,000—so blinded that I couldn't see the tragedy that was right in front of my eyes. In a hypnotic trance of rapture I made an offer of $85,000—the amount that the broker thought was the minimum the bank would accept. I figured that would leave us $35,000 to get the boat back into condition. I know, I know . . . I should have known better, but don't forget, I was in love and a man in love is not responsible for his actions.

On the way back to my hotel room I thought of all the wonderful things I would do to make that boat a showpiece and all the terrific places we would go in it. I couldn't wait to call Susan and tell her the great news. But it was not to be. When I returned to the hotel, I received a message with an urgent plea to call the broker. "Great," I thought, "The bank didn't waste any time in snapping up my offer." But when I returned the call, the broker wasted no time in breaking my little bubble of self-delusion. It seemed some other guy had made an identical offer to the bank just a few hours ahead of me, and in a fit of hasty disregard for the prospect of additional offers, the bank had accepted.

I was desolate and staggered to the bar to drown my wretchedness in a couple of pints of draft lager. The Marriott bar in Charlotte Amalie looks out over the harbor, and I had a clear view of *Delphus* riding at anchor. From a mile and a half away, she sure looked fine. I was working on my third pint when a young man with the air of the sea about him sat down in the next chair, and I wasted not a moment in unloading my tale of woe.

"What!" he exclaimed. "The *Delphus*? You weren't thinking of buying that @#$% pig, were you?"

"Who? Me?" I was somewhat taken aback by the intensity of his vitriol. "Well, actually . . . you see . . . I thought that . . . maybe somebody could . . . er, fix her up or somethin' like that . . . maybe?"

"Fix *her* up?! They ought to fix her up into an artificial reef or somethin' like that." He was really on a roll. "Or maybe you could fix her up into a bonfire or somethin' useful like that. Ho, ho, ho. Anything to get that floating piece of @#$% out of the harbor."

As it turned out, the guy was a paid skipper on one of *Delphus*'s several sister-ships that were part of the crewed-charter fleet that used Charlotte Amalie as their home port. I bought him a beer and he gave me his opinion of these fine boats. They couldn't sail worth beans (he didn't say beans), they were top-heavy and under-rigged, and in three years of trying he had only once been able to tack the sistership without turning on the engine—and that had been in a howling gale when every inch of sail she carried was flying in an attempt to "scare the beans" (he didn't say beans) out of some particularly obnoxious charter customers. "We almost got her rail under and were making about 6 knots, which would have been great except we were going sideways. Damn boat always sailed sideways better than forward. I think that the only reason we were able to tack that once was because the wind shifted."

Later that night I called Susan. She knew I was looking at our dream boat and was waiting for my call.

"Did you buy it?" she asked.

"Naw," I answered. "I didn't like the way she looked, I think she was top-heavy and underrigged."

"No kidding. I thought you really liked that boat."

"Well, I did at first, but if you know anything about boats you can spot these things close up. She didn't look like she would sail worth beans to me. In fact, she looks like she would sail better sideways than straight ahead."

Looking at Boats

Assuming that you have groomed and nurtured your kitty to maturity, have made all the necessary changes in your attitude and outlook so that in searching for a boat you aren't seeking a measure of status or a symbol of prestige, and that you have otherwise gotten your head square on your shoulders and ordered your day-to-day existence so the cruising life looms large on the near horizon, let's go look at some boats.

It would be a great advantage if I could simply provide you with a list of which boats in each price range you should be looking at, but of course, I can't. I have no way of knowing what your minimum requirements are, your toleration for discomfort, or your personal resolve and resourcefulness, and all these factors de-termine what kind of boat will work for you. Even so, I can offer a few guidelines that will get you started in the right direction.

When Susan and I were looking for our ideal boat, we spent more than a year in the process and ended up buying one of the first boats we looked at. During that year we looked at big boats and little boats, fat boats and skinny boats, beautiful boats by famous designers, and ugly monstrosities "designed" up by someone with only a vague idea of what constitutes a proper yacht. It could be argued that since we ended up with a boat we saw and liked early in our search, looking further was a waste of time. That was not the case. The year we spent groveling through boat-yards up and down the East Coast was an education, and although *Sultana* was the third or fourth boat of several hundred that we looked at, it took us a full year of hard work, heartache, hysterics, and heroics to learn that she was just the boat for us.

We learned a great deal about cruising boats in that year, but we learned even more about ourselves and what we wanted out of our cruising life. We learned some things about others too, things that we would have just as soon left alone. We learned that among a few friends and associates, and even family members, the active pursuit of a dream can engender anger in those who may not approve of the decision to live what can only be called an alternative lifestyle. Even worse was the envy and resentment from those who had developed a keen desire to do something meaningful with their lives but lacked the resolve to act on their desires. One close friend in Boston, for example, refused to acknowledge any of our cards or letters for more than two years because he thought that taking the children out of school to go sailing was egregiously irresponsible and would doom Sarah and Phillip to a life of illiteracy and sloth. Fortunately, we are now friends again, but there are others with whom we aren't.

These lessons came hard, but it was the accumulated experience and knowledge that gave us the confidence to finally make our choice and buy our boat. You'll learn too, and although there is no shortcut to this learning process, you may graduate from the school of hard knocks more quickly than did Susan and I.

Sneaking a peek

In spite of my remonstrances against worrying about the boat until you are ready to leave, you have been sneaking off looking at them anyway, haven't you? Not only that, you already have a pretty firm idea of your ideal cruiser, and it's most likely a Stinkley Blue Water Maximum Magnum with jacuzzis in the heads and Voxy Blaster stereo throughout. That's just fine, I kind of like that one myself even if it does remind me of *Delphus,* but even if we combined our kitties we couldn't make the down payment on the starboard winch handle. And remember, we are resolved to pay cash for our boat.

No room for error

We have already discovered that the importance of the boat in our cruising plans is often overrated and that any well-built and seaworthy craft can be made to do the job. However, this bit of philosophy does not hold true for the buying of the boat which in itself is the most important element of your preparation for the cruising life. A serious mistake in the purchase of the boat in which you are going to cruise can, as it has for many others, end your dream forever.

I will be eternally grateful to my unknown savior who beat me to the bank with his bid for *Delphus* because if we had bought that boat, as I was determined to do, we would never have gone cruising. We would have been stuck with a white elephant that would have drained away our meager resources like a ditch drains a swamp—just getting her home would have consumed a major part of our $35,000 reserve. Today, Susan and I would both be working trying to accumulate the cash required to repair her spars and rigging enough to just get her going again.

A few resolutions

Before you venture out into the field and begin looking at real live boats, let's make a few resolutions that will help avoid expensive and disappointing pitfalls. Divine Providence is a wonderful lady when she is on your side, but she is a fickle lover, and to depend on her to keep you out of trouble would be foolish and irresponsible. The boat-buying jungle is rife with the alligators and boa constrictors of poor judgment who are lying in wait to eat you alive, and packed with the quicksand of overindulgence that's waiting to suck you down.

The best lessons are those we learn from the mistakes of those who have preceded us, so let's start with a list of problem areas encountered by others who were a tad less cautious than you will be.

Buying too early

Many would-be cruisers buy a boat too early in the formative stages of their preparations because they misjudge the importance of the boat in their plans, and that's understandable. A lot of people planning to adopt the cruising life are lifelong sailors whose love for boats is the prime attraction to the cruising life, and it is very difficult to explain to these folks that their plans would be much better served if they did not own a boat until they were almost ready for departure. These people have likely owned a boat for years, and to be without one is unthinkable. But it is time to rethink the unthinkable, and if you own a boat and want to go cruising, get rid of the boat now. Buying another when you are ready to leave will, in most cases, greatly expedite your departure. Boats are sinkholes for cash and time, and by selling your boat now you will free up all the money you would be spending on it, plus you will have a lot more time for more important things like kitty building.

I have mentioned this problem before and perhaps it is starting to sound a little stale, but I'll repeat it one last time (I promise). Owning a boat during the planning process can double your time until departure and can even preclude your ever going cruising. Owning a boat large enough for successful and comfortable cruising is hopelessly expensive. I know of no instance when owning one during the planning stages is preferable to not owning one and putting the considerable money saved in your kitty and letting it go to work for you.

The trap is an insidious one, and owning a boat in which you plan to cruise exposes you to the risk of becoming an addicted planner and wasting all your resources on your boat when you should be concentrating on your kitty. We all know people who really want to go cruising but they can't, and the terrible irony is that they can't go cruising because they own a boat and must work night and day just to pay for it.

Buying too big

We have met many cruisers who have made the mistake of buying a big boat because big boats are more comfortable than small boats (I can't argue with that), just as long boats are faster than short boats. Big boats are also more prestigious than small boats, and many more cruisers than will ever admit it buy too big for this one reason alone. Furthermore, the idea that big boats are somehow safer or more seaworthy than small boats is a myth popular with new cruisers, as is the idea that there have been major advances in technology that make new boats better than old boats. Today's cruiser will be much safer at sea in a 30-year-old 29-foot Pearson Triton than in 98 percent of the new 40-footers being popped from molds in modern boat factories around the world.

People who buy big cruising boats find that they are as hard to sail as to pay for; that their access to ports is limited by a deep draft; that they need extra crew for difficult passages; and that, once in a comfortable harbor, they tend to stay there because getting them going again is so much work.

Small boats cost less to buy and much less to maintain. Dock and haulage fees, fuel, sails, storage, paint, and materials are all much cheaper for a small boat. A small boat that can be careened on the beach is an asset where the tide allows careening. Small boats can fit into small harbors, and the number of free anchorages is much larger for small boats. Large boats seem to prefer marinas where they can connect to shore power and water and where they can get rid of some of that extra cash they all seem to have. Repairs on small boats are easier and quicker and you will be better able to manage them yourself. But the strongest virtue of a small boat is the very fact that it is small and as such epitomizes the concepts of freedom and flexibility that are the essence of the simple cruising life that is your destiny. With a smaller boat you have fewer worries and a lot fewer problems.

We have known many cruisers whose plans came to a premature conclusion because they bought a boat that was too big for them, but only a few who have had problems because the boat is too small; don't you make the big-boat mistake.

How small is too small?

Of course, the concepts of too big and too small are relative terms. Some time ago, I met a woman in the Caribbean who had been raised on a 32-foot sloop with four other children. I come from a family of seven also, but my early years were spent in a large farmhouse in the country, and even there things were a bit cramped. But this woman (her name was Gertrude) claimed to have lived a happy childhood and can't remember conditions being crowded at all—which shows that small to one person is large to other. The important thing is to select a boat in which *you* can be comfortable. However, it is even more important to buy a boat that is no bigger than the smallest one in which you will be comfortable.

If this sounds tricky it's because it is tricky. We have met many cruisers whose plans ended prematurely because their boat was too big, and several who gave up because their boat wasn't tough enough to stand up to cruising conditions, but I can't recall meeting even one who gave up because his or her boat was too small. If you must err, it is critical that you err on the side of too small rather than too big. You can live with "too small" for a while or correct it for a price that won't kill the kitty, but too big is often deadly.

Buying too expensive

One of the biggest pits of quicksand that lurks in the swamp of boat buying is the one that beckons from the covers of glossy brochures found in brokers' offices. No matter how much money is in your kitty, never be tempted to spend any more of it than is necessary to get a boat that will do the job. Again, this will mean different things to different people. Let me relate a case history.

While in the Caribbean we met a delightful older cruising couple who were veterans of some 20 years on the water. They began their cruising career in Seattle and sailed south in an old wooden boat to enjoy many years of cruising the South Pacific. They wrote a book and several magazine articles about their adventures, and after the book enjoyed a modicum of success, they decided it was time to move up to a better boat. They sailed back to the U.S. where they sold their boat and went to work ashore (he was a homebuilder and she was a schoolteacher) to build the kitty they needed for their dream boat. After many years of hard work, meager living, and onerous savings, they purchased a lovely 40-foot Shannon—a boat that, for my money, is one of the best cruising boats on the market.

But Shannons are expensive and a new one is not really a candidate for the average cruiser. Who knows what they were thinking. Perhaps they overestimated their earning potential as cruising authors (a common failing among writers, I've noticed), or maybe they anticipated other revenues that didn't materialize, but whatever it was, they spent the major part of their resources on the boat, bought insurance through a plan sponsored by the Seven Seas Cruising Association, and sailed off in their shiny new boat to the Pacific where they hoped to resume the happy and carefree cruising life they left so many years before.

Halfway across the Caribbean the insurance underwriter went belly up, their policy was canceled, and their plans were ruined. They had so much of their lives invested in the new boat that they were terrified of losing it, so they scuttled from one safe harbor to another agonizing over their plight. They were not willing to risk their uninsured boat in a crossing of the Pacific, and they couldn't afford insurance from any company that was willing to let them make the passage. After several years of hiding out in hurricane holes they relented, sailed back to Seattle, sold the boat, and moved ashore. And the cruising community lost two of the nicest people we have ever met.

We met another delightful couple who had sailed their new Beneteau from California to New Zealand's Bay of Islands. While the rest of the cruising fleet spent the 6-month cyclone season touring the countryside and making new friends among the locals, these two spent the entire time anchored far away from the other boats, practically hysterical that they would drag anchor or spring a leak or that some other disaster would befall their new boat. Their concern for the welfare of their boat made it impossible for them to enjoy their cruise.

The majority of budget cruisers go without insurance because it is too hard to get, too expensive when they get it, and too restrictive. The most inexpensive cruising boat you can find is going to cost a lot of money, and when you cruise without insurance there is always a possibility of losing the boat, thus losing your investment. By minimizing your investment, you minimize your potential loss, gain considerable piece of mind, and enhance your ability to enjoy your life.

Buying prestige

We all like to own good stuff, and the old saw that you get what you pay for is nowhere more true than in the cruising life. This desire for quality, however, has been corrupted by the consumerism that drives so many of us to buy expensive things not so much to get quality, but to earn what we perceive to be the admiration of our fellows. We have already discussed how ownership of material things equates to self-esteem in our society and that none of us is immune from the desire to impress others. But you must fight this desire for the admiration of your friends with all your resources lest you spend the time you could be cruising in a reasonable boat working your life away trying to support a very expensive mistress.

Most people who matter in this life will be much more impressed with your ability to get by and live a happy and productive life while practicing a low-impact minimalist existence than will be influenced by your ownership of a flashy yacht.

A Liability, Not an Asset

Many cruisers think of their boat as an asset (an asset in accounting terms is something that will make you money) and this is a dangerous delusion because it serves to seduce us into spending more on the boat than we should. Try to think of the boat you are about to buy as a financial liability (something that is going to cost you money) and don't ever justify the purchase of an expensive boat with the argument that you will be able to recoup the money you spend by selling the boat after the cruise is over.

In the late 1970s the U.S. tax laws were changed at the behest of pleasure-boating interests to allow boats that were large enough to be lived on to be treated as real estate. These laws were important to the boat lobby because the industry was then in a deep recession, and the changes allowed buyers to apply for 20-year mortgages on boats, deduct the interest as a second home, and depreciate the capital if the boat were chartered. The most important change, however, was psychological in that it encouraged people considering purchasing a large expensive boat to view it as an investment in the same category as a house or other real estate, an amazing bit of economic voodoo that worked wonders for new-boat sales. Many buyers were led to believe that their new purchase would even appreciate in value, a phenomenon we haven't seen outside of a few go-go years in the early 1970s.

Some cruisers buy boats expecting to sell them for the purchase price when they get home. I know of a Marblehead cruiser who left on a three-year circumnavigation on a popular and expensive yacht only to find that when he returned the market for used sailboats had slumped and his boat, now pretty beat up from the rigors of the trip, was worth about a quarter of what he paid for it. I've also heard of a wealthy southern accountant and her husband who sold their family mansion and sunk all their money into a new 55-foot cruising palace. The boat was way too big for two people to handle and their dream turned into a nightmare. The cruise ended after about 18 months, during which time she estimated the boat lost about $100,000 in value.

And finally, in an almost unbelievable instance of self-delusion, a man from Portland, Maine, convinced his wife that if they sold their house and sailed around the world, he would write a book about their adventures, the boat would become famous (presumably along with him), and they could thus sell the boat for a tidy profit. The voyage progressed as planned, but the last I heard, the book remained unpublished, the boat remained unsold, and the wife hadn't been seen for awhile.

Your boat as durable goods

Even though the tax laws may let you treat a boat like real estate, it is much smarter to consider your boat "durable goods" as the economists call it. As such your boat is in the same category as a car or refrigerator, and its value will steadily decrease until it becomes worthless and you have to pay someone to haul it away.

Considered this way, your boat is something you are going to use up over the life of your cruise, and anything you get for it when the cruise is done is extra.

A surprising number of people who are considering becoming cruisers are also considering becoming subsistence farmers. The 20-acre spread in Idaho or Kentucky where you can grow a crop of organic alfalfa and free-range chickens while you enjoy the good life living off the land has a similar attraction as the cruising ketch with a crop of free-range barnacles on the hull. Thus, the farming fantasy is much the same as the cruising fantasy, and the appeal of returning to a simple life is identical. My advice to anyone who would ask is always the same: If you need to get your money out of your investment, go for the farm every time.

Pay Cash

Here's a quick exercise for determining if you have enough money in your kitty to go cruising. Take the total amount in your kitty, deduct the maximum you think you must pay for a suitable boat (and again "suitable" means different things to different folks), and deduct a little extra for any changes you need to make. If one-half the remaining kitty is enough for you to live on for about two years, you have enough to go. The remaining half is for emergencies and contingencies, one of which will surely be that you underestimated the amount you will need to live on for two years. (Don't fret about this last item. It's a fact of life and it happens to everybody; plan for it now and it won't be a problem.) No matter how much money you have, however, it would be irresponsible to have any more than 15 percent of your total net worth wrapped up in a cruising sailboat; 10 percent would be even better.

Do not ever under any circumstances borrow money to buy a cruising boat. (Am I starting to repeat myself? Good, this is one message that needs repeating.) If you do you'll spend the rest of your life or a substantial portion thereof paying off the loan and not cruising.

If you really want to go cruising you can work hard and save the money in one quarter of the time that it will take you to pay off a loan.

Any amount of money borrowed for 10 years at 15 percent annual interest will cost the borrower twice the principal to repay. Thus, if you borrow $15,000 to buy a boat with 15 percent interest, you will have paid $30,000 by the time you have paid off your loan. Your monthly payment would be about $242. If you take that $242 and invest it at an average return of 8 percent, due to the miracle of compounding (the return you earn on reinvested returns), you will have almost $20,000 ($19,326 to be exact) in your kitty after five years. If you keep saving for 10 years (the same length of time it would take you to pay off your $15,000 loan with a $242 monthly payment), you would have nearly $50,000 ($48,157) in your kitty. So instead of having a worn-out and practically valueless 10-year-old boat for which you paid $30,000, you would have 50 grand with which to buy a fine cruising boat—and that's even before you consider the huge savings in maintenance, storage, and insurance you will realize by not having a boat to spend your money on. Maintenance items can easily double the cost of a boat, so now you have $100,000 to spend after 10 years, and $40,000 to spend if you can't wait that long and want to get going in five years.

Lenders and salespeople have learned to make borrowing money easy and painless, which is why millions of credit card users are happy to pay 16 or even 18 percent on consumer debt. They'll even try to make it sound like the smart thing to do by letting us believe that we are getting such a good bargain that it justifies buying now and paying the interest.

There are several reasons you don't want to borrow money to buy your boat, over and above the cost of interest discussed above and in chapter 1:

- Lenders will be reluctant to lend you money on the good old boat you are looking for anyway, and will ask for additional collateral that you probably don't have or don't want to tie up.
- The mortgage holder will insist that you insure your boat for the amount of the mortgage and name the mortgage holder as beneficiary.
- The mortgage holder will insist on a periodic (usually two years, sometimes one) survey by a certified surveyor to verify the condition and value of the boat. You will be required to make repairs and improvements the surveyor recommends, as well as pay all the expenses of getting the surveyor to and from whatever port you happen to be enjoying at the time.
- The mortgage holder may restrict the area where you sail as a condition of the mortgage.

Never forget that the "mort" in "mortgage" means dead, which is what your cruising plans will be if you borrow money to buy your boat. If you can't pay cash for the boat you want, you aren't ready to go cruising. Either lower your sights and buy a less expensive boat or go back to work and earn some more money.

Insurance

Insurance for old boats is hard to find, and when you do find it, it's so expensive you'll wish you hadn't. Insurers will dictate where you can sail without losing your coverage, and may insist that you hire a professional delivery skipper or extra crew for what they consider difficult passages. It is possible to get good coverage through companies such as Lloyds, of course, and SSCA members are eligible for coverage through that organization, but even then it is expensive and restrictive. Not too long ago, it wasn't at all unheard of for insurance companies to deny coverage to boats less than 40 feet that were headed offshore with fewer than three people as crew. (And it's not unusual for requirements to get tighter after major storms result in increased claims.) Singlehanders can almost never get insurance without hiring crew or lying to the insurer.

A lot of people believe (and your adventuresome-but-never-reckless author is right there among them) that going without insurance makes for a better and safer sailor. Susan and I have owned two boats that each experienced hurricanes, and the difference in our attitude in each case is representative of my point. In the first case we owned a Hunter 23 that was insured to the hilt. When a major hurricane was predicted to hit the north shore of Massachusetts, I took off the sails, doubled the anchor lines, went home, and slept well, secure in the knowledge that if disaster struck we would be getting a new boat. If it hadn't been for my basically intact personal integrity, I may have even been a bit disappointed when the storm shifted south and cleaned out Rhode Island instead.

In the second case we were cruising the coast of Maine in *Duchess,* our old wooden powerboat, a craft no insurer in his or her right mind would even think of covering, when Hurricane Bob blew in from the Caribbean. I wasn't about to try to ride it out with my family aboard, but I put out all three anchors with every bit of rode we carried, and spent most of a day securing everything I could. Then we were hustled off by the National Guard to a makeshift shelter in a local high school gymnasium while the storm howled through. In the morning we walked to a bluff that overlooks the bay where *Duchess* was anchored. I'll never forget the sense of relief we felt when we found her safe and sound several hundred yards from where we left her.

I don't have any hard data to support these assumptions, but when we talk to cruisers who have decided to spend the cyclone season in Tonga or Fiji, both of which get slammed by major tropical storms every few years, rather than make the run to Australia or New Zealand, the majority seem to have hull insurance. Those who do take the more prudent route and clear out, don't. I think you will find the same situation in the Caribbean. Boats that are left there to be turned into kindling by storms like Luis and Hugo are nearly all insured, while many boats that seek the havens of Venezuela, the Rio Dulce, or Roatan are uninsured. If this is the case, and I believe it is, the cruising community and boatowners in general can direct their thanks for the problems of getting and paying for hull insurance right at those who insist on leaving their boats in the northern Caribbean and mid-Pacific then wrack up enormous claims when storms blow through these cyclone- and hurricane-prone areas.

One more interesting phenomenon about insurance claims. It seems that the majority of the boats sunk by whales between Equador and the Galapagos turn out to be older boats that are fully insured with a lot of extra survival gear aboard. Hmmmm.

A Few Things to Look for in Your Cruising Boat

I have already said that I can't give you much guidance about what specific boat might be best for you, any more than I can tell you how much you should spend on it (outside of a few standard guidelines for quality construction and sea worthiness). However, there are a few features that every cruising boat should have. Here are the ones I think are the most important.

Heavy-duty construction

Whatever you do, don't fall for the line that lightweight boats are faster than heavy boats. They *are* faster, but the added speed in no way compensates for their drawbacks, which are many. To sail well, a light boat must be kept light, which means inadequate tankage and inability to carry a decent supply of stores and equipment. Many light boats today must rely on watermakers because they can't carry enough water—which means they spend most of their time in port waiting for the repair parts for the watermaker to arrive. The math is simple: If you have a 10,000 pound boat and carry 2,000 pounds of stores you have increased the weight of your boat by 20 percent and she'll be a pig to sail. If you have a 30,000-pound boat and you bring on 2,000 pounds of stores, you've increased the weight less than 10 percent, and since she is probably less than a sprightly sailer anyway, she won't even notice the extra weight.

A heavy boat is also much more comfortable and easy to handle in a seaway than a light one and is considerably safer in most cases. In any price and size range, go for the heavy boat over the light boat every time.

Solid construction

Akin to heavy construction is solid construction—but the two criteria aren't the same thing. Many quality boats were built with cored hulls as a means of thickening the hull and correcting some of the obnoxious qualities of fiberglass boats, notably noise and internal condensation. Also, many decks were strengthened by laminating plywood or balsa cores into the fiberglass. This is not a sign of inferior construction, just the opposite in fact, but cored and laminated hulls are prone to water saturation that can ruin a perfectly good boat. Later boats that were cored with Airex or other artificial ingredients are usually OK, but be particularly careful of those built with endgrain balsa cores. When water infiltrates a laminated deck or a cored hull, the repair costs are often more than the boat is worth, so if you are considering one of these boats, make extra sure it passes survey without reservation.

Solid polyester boats from southern waters can also have saturated hulls and the fix can also be expensive although the consequences aren't as dire. Your surveyor should catch any problem. It is an excellent idea to ask your surveyor to specifically state on the written survey report that the hull has been checked with a moisture meter and has been found to be free of water saturation. If your surveyor won't do this, you should probably pass on the boat.

A known design

Some wonderful boats are out there cruising that were built and designed by the cruisers who are sailing them, but yacht design is a complicated technical field that is part science, part experience, and part innate artistic ability. The beautiful creations of L. Frances Herreshoff, John Alden, and many others sport lines that are identifiable from across the bay (but unfortunately, so do most self-designed boats). Other designers such as Bruce Roberts and Phil Bolger specialize in practical designs that are less lovely to some eyes but are nonetheless excellent and seaworthy boats.

Unless you are a trained and experienced boat designer, you have no way of judging how good or bad a particular design might be except by the designer's reputation and work. Quality of construction is fairly easy to spot after a little experience, but quality of design is best left to the experts—and even many of them get it wrong. Go for a quality built boat from the board of a known designer and leave the home-designed or heavily modified boats alone. Bear in mind, too, that a respected design holds resale value better than an unknown one.

A full keel

Here's one that is good for an argument from any high-tech yacht owner, but I am convinced of the superiority of a well-designed full keel with a cut out port for the prop over any other design. Bolt-on fin keels particularly are an abomination in the cruising environment. I have already related how we ran *Sultana* onto a reef in the Cook Islands with no more damage than a few scratches on the bottom paint. If we had tried that particular trick with a boat that had any kind of bolt-on keel, we would still be there. Modified full keels with a cutaway forefoot and a skeg-hung rudder are OK too, even though they sacrifice some control under power because the prop is usually too far away from the rudder, and the prop is slightly more vulnerable to damage. The most important thing to look for is a boat with an integral keel. If the ballast is bolted onto the keel that's fine, but the keel should be built right into the boat.

Keel-stepped mast

I have seen quite a few cruising boats with deck-stepped masts—particularly ferro-cement boats—but you should restrict your search to a boat with the mast or masts supported at the cabintop or deck by partners with the butt end of the mast steeped directly onto the keel. Such an arrangement sacrifices a small amount of cabin space and usually produces leaks around the mast boot, but this is a small price to pay for the added strength and security of setting the mast right on the keelson. Of course, there are exceptions to this rule. The Westsail 32, one of the strongest cruising boats ever built, has a deck-stepped mast, as does the Allied Seabreeze yawl, which is another fine cruising boat, and there are undoubtedly others.

I would also enjoin you to look for a boat with wooden masts over aluminum ones, but I realize that it would be a losing argument. Wooden masts are superior to metal ones because you can fix them yourself if they should break, but they are getting scarce and are very expensive to make properly. Aluminum masts seem to do the job OK even if they do look like hell and make a terrible racket when the wind blows.

A central galley

The galley is the most important part of the boat, and it is important that it be located as near to the center of gravity as possible. Some larger boats built in the 70s (notably Gulfstar) had what's called a "galley up" configuration ("Alley Oops" to their many detractors) that put the galley up in a pilothouse, I suppose so the cook could see out the window. This was a great idea for motoring around in the protected waters of Florida Bay or Sarasota Sound, but you wouldn't want to even think of trying to prepare a meal in such a galley while sailing. On many other boats the galley is too far aft to be comfortable in a seaway, and on some really old boats the galley is in the forepeak, which would almost be as bad as the galley up.

I'll discuss the layout of the galley in chapter 11, but for now just remember that the closer to the center of gravity you can keep the cook, the less effect the thrashing around of the boat will have on the omelets and Béarnaise sauce. The more comfortable the cook, the better the meal. The better the meal, the better the cruise—it works without fail.

New Boats versus Old Boats

Often my brilliant arguments that old boats are better than new boats are brushed aside and discarded as the incoherent ramblings of a disgruntled old cruiser who sails in an old wooden boat because he can't afford a shiny new boat. I will admit that there just might be a modicum of truth there, but just a modicum, no more. Some beautiful boats are being built by first-class yards today, better than anything that has ever been built before, and I am the first to admit it. Companies like Hinckley, Shannon, Pacific Seacraft, Morris, and many others build cruising boats that are stronger and safer than any of those built in the years past. And new wooden cruising boats are being built by several yards on both coasts of the U.S. that specialize in high-quality, all-natural-ingredients, ultra-expensive craft. The problem, of course, is that the stripped-down economy version of these new glass or wood boats costs the better part of half a million bucks before the hull gets wet, and even a good used one goes for a quarter million or so—not something that most of us are interested in.

And although new boats are being produced in the lower price ranges, consider a few of the "improvements" that the production-boat industry has given us in the last 20 years:

- Reverse counters, which manufacturers claim are stylish and increase the waterline length, while what they really do is decrease the deck area for a given waterline length (and make the boat cheaper to build).
- Ultralight displacement construction, which they claim makes the boat faster and more responsive. It does both these things, but it also makes for a fragile boat that is hard to steer (and much cheaper to build).
- Water ballast, which is supposed to make the ultralight hull stand up better but in reality only makes the boat cheaper to build.
- Reduced sail area, which got rid of such nuisances as bowsprits and boomkins because they weren't needed with the ultralight displacement hull.
- Bolt-on fin keels, which reduce wetted surface dramatically but also make the boat hard to steer, vulnerable to a grounding, unresponsive under power (and cheaper to build).
- Molded hull liners, which are supposed to reduce maintenance (but are really just cheaper to build).
- High-aspect-ratio single-stick sail plans that increase windward performance over multimast rigs (and by the way, are a lot cheaper to build).

I could go on and on with this list of modern improvements, but to do so would risk being labeled a grouchy old fart by Sarah and Phillip and I think that I have listed enough items so that the careful observer can see a common thread running through all these advances in yachting technology. You are way ahead of the cruising game in an old Pearson Trident, Allied Seabreeze, or any similar old-fashioned boat than in any of the new boats being produced in the "affordable" category.

In all fairness to modern production boatbuilders, most of the economies dressed up as improvements that are listed above are necessary in today's world of astronomical production costs for any product, and boatbuilding is a tough racket to be in. Just look at the list of builders who tried to build quality boats who aren't with us any more—Pearson, Allied, Bristol—while others, who spent more money on advertising gimmicks than on lay-up schedules, are still around. Some of these boats make adequate coastal cruisers, but as the inventory of good old boats is depleted, more and more budget cruisers are turning to these lightweight production boats for offshore cruising, and this is a dangerous trend.

Let the Search Begin

As you look for your cruising boat, always bear in mind that you are looking for a bargain. You aren't trying to cheat anyone, but you must find a good boat at a reasonable price if your cruising plans are going to work out. The better the boat and the more reasonable the price, the better your cruise will be, and it is the universal nature of those who sell their boats to overestimate the value of their craft. Most boats you look at that haven't been on the market for at least a year are going to be overpriced. It takes at least a year for many sellers to become pragmatic about what they are going to get for their boats. As you begin searching for your ideal boat, it is important that you look at as many boats as possible, but always pay especially close attention to those that have been on the market long enough for the owner's expectations to become a little more realistic.

Try to resist the natural tendency to focus on a specific type or style of boat. As a budget cruiser, the more flexibility you can retain in what you are looking for, the greater the chance you have of finding your bargain boat. It's amazing how hard this basic truism is for people to understand. All the boat brokers I know confirm that it's always the people who have little or no money who show up with a long list of requirements that specify the builder, style, sail plan, hull material, galley configuration, and even the color of the hull. Thus, this type of "client" is classified as a tire kicker, and is the primary reason why many brokers won't list boats that are asking less than $100,000.

Likewise, prospective buyers who announce at the top of their lungs that they are looking for a boat in which to sail around the world are greeted with a yawn and inched firmly but politely toward the door. If, however, you sit down with a good broker and tell that broker that you only have so much money to spend, that you are looking for a sturdy bluewater-capable boat, that you don't care what shape it's in as long as it's a good value and repairable, and that you are looking for a bargain (leave out the part about sailing around the world), you'll find brokers who are interested and helpful. Good brokers can be your best allies because they know what is available and where, and they can greatly reduce the time you waste looking at boats that aren't suitable.

Of course, many boats you will be interested in looking at are never listed with brokers. Going from boatyard to boatyard in places like the Chesapeake Bay; Newport, Rhode Island; Marina Del Ray, California; or almost anywhere in Florida, will uncover dozens of unlisted boats whose owners have despaired of selling them, at least one of which might be exactly what you are looking for.

And don't forget to poke around boatyards for south-end boats. They're the ones you'll find at the south end of a north-facing boatyard back along the fence where the owners have put them to get them out of the way after trying to sell them for a year or so. They are old and dirty and moldy and forlorn and just what you're looking for. A few of these south-enders could become great cruising boats once a few layers of crud and neglect are stripped away, and they will be available for prices only a fraction of what a well-cared for boat of the same type would cost.

A simple and basic boat

As you look at boats and become familiar with what is on the market and at what price, remember that as a simple and basic cruiser you are going to want a simple and basic boat. This means a boat that is easy to sail and comfortable to live on, a full keel or a modified full keel with a cutaway forefoot, and a deck that is free of spinnakers or complicated sail inventory. In fact a good cruising boat should be able to carry the entire inventory except for the storm jib and trysail on the spars where they belong. Any extra sails will just eat up valuable storage room. Avoid complicated and fancy sail rigs, especially spinnakers.

The trick is to find a boat whose owner doesn't want it around anymore. In fact, the more the owner is anxious for the boat to go away, the better off you're going to be and the better your chance of finding a real bargain.

Also remember to look for the smallest boat you think you and your crew can be comfortable in, but don't overdo it. Make sure you have enough boat so that your crew doesn't become so cramped that all they can think of is going home. Look at as many boats as you can. The perfect boat for you is out there somewhere, waiting just for you. But you have to find it, because it isn't going to come to you.

Necessary travel

Unless you are lucky, finding the right boat will involve some travel (and therefore expenses), because the number of good cruising boats in a specific price range is small and they will be widely scattered. Fortunately, many places where you will be most likely to find boats are also fun places to visit: Panama, the Rio Dulce, the Virgin Islands, and Venezuela are a few prime examples. Treat travel to these areas like a working vacation and enjoy yourself.

A few places are famous for being where bad cruises tend to come to an end—resulting in a concentration of bargain boats. Charlotte Amalie Harbor in the U.S. Virgin Islands and the Pedro Miguel Yacht Club in Panama are two. Call or write to brokers in these areas before you go, though.

Fix-it-up boats

A fix-it-up boat is a great way to get on the water without spending a lot of money, but watch out. Make sure you know what you are getting into, especially if you have never tried it. Boat work is a lot more difficult than it appears. Inexperienced buyers tend to underestimate the cost of repairs, even minor repairs, by a factor of at least four. Experienced boatwrights find estimating the extent of repairs to be the most difficult part of any job.

One of the dangers in fixing up an old boat is that the repair project can become an end in itself and the potential cruiser becomes so involved in getting the boat ready that the actual cruise never happens. Another more insidious danger is that the potential cruiser will get involved in an overambitious restoration and suddenly the kitty is empty and the boat is still not ready for the water.

Badly conceived and poorly executed restoration projects, like boatbuilding projects, can stretch out for years beyond the original estimates and are probably responsible for killing countless kitties. I've seen this happen more times than I care to think about, and any drive through the country within a hundred miles or so of any coast will reveal the rotting hulks of someone's cruising dream sitting in a field surrounded by weeds and wildflowers.

Even with a fix-it-up project that is more realistic, it is easy to spend more time and money repairing an old boat than you would have spent on a better boat in the first place. It is possible to start with a junky $10,000 boat, spend $20,000 on repairs and upgrades, and end up with a very nice $10,000 boat. You will see many boats on the market that look good on the outside but have, in fact, come to the ends of their useful lives and are worthless. One of these can easily empty even a large kitty before it is close to being ready to go in the water. It is critical that you not be suckered into buying a derelict boat because if you do, your cruising plans are over.

Ignore the extras

As you appraise the value of an old boat, concentrate on the boat itself and ignore the extras—at least in the beginning. It is easy to become blinded to the obvious faults of a bad boat by a plethora of fancy gear that is included in the deal. That long list of stuff is great to have, but don't pay much for it unless it is still in the box it came in. The electronics (radios, radar, GPS, depthsounder, etc.) are guaranteed to be outdated and worthless, and many that have remained installed on a boat that has been in storage for a few years will have deteriorated beyond repair. Much electronic apparatus that has been abused in this manner will work for a short time, then need replacing, so even if a piece of gear like an SSB or radar seems to check out OK, don't add anything to the price you pay for the boat because of it. Sails and running rigging may be strong enough to start you off but they, too, will probably need to be replaced within a year or so.

The Hull

Cruisers, like all sailors, love to argue the merits of the various sail plans and hull materials, but neither really matters that much when you are looking for a south-end boat. Be open to any sail plan and any hull material as long as the boat is a bargain.

The sail plan is a matter of personal choice anyway. I like *Sultana*'s ketch rig for two reasons: because that is the rig she has and we're stuck with it whether we like it or not, and because of its flexibility and balance. But all traditional sail plans are good as long as they match the boat.

Among 20-year-old south-enders, the most desirable hull materials in decreasing order of desirability and reflecting a slight authorial bias are:

- Steel—The world's greatest cruising boats are made from steel, and the Dutch-built boats are the greatest of the great. Most of the real old-time cruisers we have met—those who have circumnavigated many times over—sail steel boats. Steel boats suitable for offshore cruising are expensive, though, and a good used one is hard to find in the U.S.
- Aluminum—Similarly, aluminum is also an excellent hull material. It is also expensive and hard to find.
- Wood—A traditionally built wooden boat is probably the best value available to the budget-boat shopper, provided the buyer knows something about wooden boat construction and has the skills to do fairly major repairs such as fixing or patching frames and planking. Lots of run-down wooden boats are on the market, many of which are structurally sound and available for a fraction of what you'd pay for an equivalent steel or fiberglass boat. Make sure you hire a surveyor who specializes in wooden boats, and don't buy one if you can't do most of the repairs yourself.
- Fiberglass—Fiberglass isn't a very good material with which to make boats, but it is so much cheaper and easier for the builders that the majority of cruising boats are made from one or another form of plastic resin and fiberglass. The older boats, those built before the concept of ultralight displacement hulls and fin keels took hold, are far superior to the newer boats and are cheaper, of course. Pay particular attention to boats that were built for but never used as charter boats such as the CSY 37 and 44 and the Morgan OutIsland 41. One of the best deals in a solid bluewater cruiser is a Valiant 40 with a blistered hull. (I'll talk more about all three of these classics later in this chapter.)
- Ferrocement—During the 1960s and 1970s, hundreds of future cruisers

were working away in their backyards building reinforced cement boats. Many, perhaps most, of these boats were never finished and remain as monuments to the folly of unfulfilled fantasy. Many of those that were finished are sleek and beautiful, while others are lumpy and bumpy and so ugly they look like floating warthogs. Nobody wants these home-built boats anymore because it's impossible to evaluate the condition of the hulls. Some surveyors won't even look at them. The dilemma is that many of the ugly boats are very well made and good for a lifetime of cruising, while many of the sleek and pretty boats are ready to fall apart—and there's no way to tell which is which. Consequently, ferrocement boats represent the biggest bargains on the market, but they are a risk and I wouldn't consider one that wasn't practically given to me.

The most readily available hull materials, in decreasing order, for south-end cruising boats are

Fiberglass
Wood
Ferrocement
Aluminum
Steel

The least expensive south-end cruising boats, in increasing order, are made from

Ferrocement
Wood
Fiberglass
Steel
Aluminum

The Engine

The specific hull material and the design of the rig aren't that important, but the engine is another matter. You need a good diesel engine of adequate horsepower to drive the boat into headwinds and through large seas and to move the boat for long distances when there is no wind. Many cruising boats, especially older and less expensive ones, are underpowered for safe and effective cruising. You should figure at least two horsepower per ton of displacement. Three is better, and four is a lot better.

If the boat you are looking at has a gasoline engine, especially an Atomic Four, or if it has an older diesel without enough power, this doesn't mean you shouldn't buy the boat. Changing engines is a common and fairly easy thing to do, although not easy enough for you to try it yourself unless you have done it a couple of times on other peoples' boats. Several manufacturers make replacement diesels for the ubiquitous Atomic Four (by far the most popular gasoline engine of the pre-diesel era) that bolt right in, and in many cases you can use the existing exhaust and transmission. However, engine changes are expensive. A new one usually runs between $10,000 and $15,000; the cost is somewhat less for a reconditioned one.

Do *not* consider heading offshore with a gasoline engine (see below).

An exhausting task

Speaking of exhaust, I would caution you to be extra careful here. Offshore cruising boats need a high-lift wet exhaust system with a good siphon break to guarantee against water incursion from a heavy following sea. As a large sea overtakes a boat, the stern squats and submerges the exhaust, sometimes to a depth of several feet. This forces seawater down the exhaust, and in the case of an inadequate installation, through the manifold and into those cylinders that stopped on the exhaust stroke when the engine was shut down and thus have valves open. When you try to start the engine, a slight amount of cranking closes the valves and creates a rigid hydraulic lock. If the seawater isn't cleared from the cylinders quickly, the engine will be ruined. This is a common cause of diesel engine failure in cruising sailboats.

Don't assume that just because a boat has lived 25 or 30 years without any evidence of exhaust problems that you won't have them either. The vast majority of large sailboats, even those used in the charter fleet, go for many decades without ever being subjected to heavy weather. Most coastal cruisers and charter boats head for shelter when the seas get much over 3 feet, but cruisers don't have that luxury. When the 20- or 30-footers come rolling in from the Southern Ocean, you'll just have to hunker down and enjoy them while you can, but you must make sure you still have an engine when things calm down. If you aren't familiar with terms like "water lift" and "siphon break" get out a good manual and read the section on exhaust several times before you look at any more boats. If your boat needs a replacement exhaust, you can figure on spending up to about $5,000 on it, so this is not an area to be taken lightly.

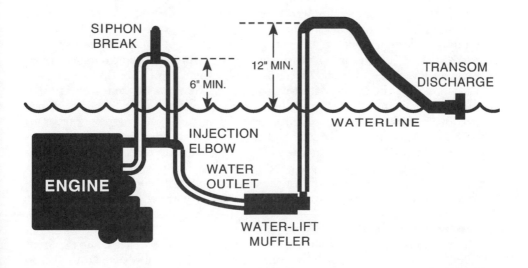

The water-lift exhaust system is one of the most important systems on a cruising boat. The 6-inch and 12-inch elevations shown are minimums; distances should be as great as possible.

New diesels are better than old diesels

Modern diesels have evolved from the huge and cumbersome monsters of a few years ago into compact and amazingly reliable powerhouses. The old Ford four-banger in *Sultana* is a case in point. It is about 30 years old, possibly more, runs like a watch, and is rated at about 50 horsepower at 2,200 rpms—more than enough for her 14 tons gross weight. Parts are available anywhere in the world for this old workhorse, and the engine is still being made by Ford. The new version looks much like the old one, a lot of the parts are interchangeable, and the only real difference is that the new version produces 85 horsepower instead of 50. All of this extra horsepower is due to increased efficiency made possible by a long list of internal engineering and design improvements made over the years.

Ask a lot of questions about the make of engine in your prospective purchase. Many older or oddball engines are difficult to find parts for. Volvos have a particularly bad reputation for expensive parts and frequent repairs, while Ford and Perkins are top-notch. There are dozens of others so don't reject a boat just because you've never heard of the engine brand. Ask around and talk to a few marine mechanics, and you'll soon have a wealth of information on which to base your judgment.

The age of a diesel engine isn't nearly as important as it is with a gasoline engine. *Sultana*'s ancient Ford is more reliable than many newer engines in our friends' boats. Except in extreme circumstances, I wouldn't refuse to buy a boat just because it didn't have just the engine I wanted, but it's important to know what you're getting into. Diesel engine repair is one of the must-have skills for the successful budget cruiser, and an engine that is accessible, easy to work on, with parts generally available, and that can be removed with the main boom is a real asset.

Motorsailers

The designation "motorsailer" really isn't valid today. That term came into use when the distinction between powerboats and sailboats first became evident at the beginning of the century. Back then a typical engine in a sailboat was a hand-start one-lunger with just about enough guts to get the boat in and out of her slip and that was it. Any thought of moving the boat from point A to point B under power or using engine power to counter heavy seas and winds was out of the question for two reasons: one, the motor wasn't up to it, and two, it wasn't considered gentlemanly or yachtsmanlike to move a sailboat for a long distance under power. When an extrastrong boat was built around a large engine, up to 50 horsepower or so, or when a keel, sails, and a rig were fitted to a powerboat, they were called motorsailers. Today, however, with modern lightweight diesel engines with high horsepower ratings, any sailboat with a good engine and adequate tankage will have a range of hundreds of miles with just the engine, and most engines are capable of moving the boat into adverse seas and winds with or without the help of the sails.

Gasoline engines

Don't even look at a boat with a gasoline engine unless the seller allows about $15,000 to change it to a diesel. Gasoline engines are impossibly dangerous and no amount of bilge blowers, sniffers, and other specialized safety gear can reduce the danger to the extent that a gasser can be operated offshore. In many parts of the world, gasoline is expensive—averaging more than $5 a gallon, and can be hard to get. Gasoline engines are nowhere near as reliable as diesels, and they are harder and more expensive to get fixed. There is not one single advantage of a gasoline engine over a diesel engine except the initial price—and even that is illusory.

Cruising without an engine

Don't be tempted to try to go cruising without an engine in your boat. A boat that can't get out of the way is a big hazard to navigation in parts of the world where there is a lot of traffic. It is quite possible for a large vessel to run down a cruising yacht without ever being aware of it, and several such tragedies have happened recently. A cruising boat anchored in the Mississippi was run down by a barge at night, and another cruising yacht was struck and sunk by a log carrier off the cost of New Zealand. In neither case were the crew of the larger vessel even aware of the collision.

In many parts of the world and anywhere on the open sea, any yacht interfering with a fishing boat is fair game, and some skippers will try to push a smaller boat out of the way rather than interrupt a trawl. Our friends Ruddy and Don aboard the 27-foot *Chamois* reported being rammed at night off the coast of Ecuador by three men in a powerboat. Naturally, they were terrified and thought they were being attacked by pirates, but I think it is much more likely that they had accidentally sailed into an area where nets had been set by people who were protecting their turf in a hostile and inappropriate manner.

Would you be in the right if you found yourself in any of the above situations? You bet you would—technically—but the bottom of the sea is littered with the bones of many technically-in-the-right boats, and you don't want to be one of them. When you find yourself in the path of any large commercial vessel with any possibility of collision, the first thing to do is get on the VHF and confirm that the captain of the oncoming vessel sees and can avoid you. If you can't make contact, you must get clear of the danger zone immediately without the slightest regard of who has the right of way, and that often requires an engine.

Skippers of engineless boats often tend to be just a tad hypocritical; they are quick to sing the praises of life without the nasty, noxious, and noisy engine—and they are just as quick to cop a tow in and out of harbors, either from other cruisers, which is a nuisance, or from the authorities, which can be expensive. The days when the arrival of a small engineless boat was cause for a celebration or even considered unusual are long gone.

As a cruiser, you must be self-reliant and independent. This means you must have the ability to move your boat against the wind, and when there is no wind, if for no other reason than to keep out of trouble. In many parts of the world popular with cruisers, particularly the Caribbean, Asia, the East Coast of the U. S., and the Mediterranean, yacht rescue is a growing industry. In the U.S., Sea Tow charges $300 dollars and up for a basic tow off a sandbar. In other parts of the world, cruisers have been gouged thousands of dollars for simple tows, and in extreme cases, rescuers have claimed salvage rights to the vessel. It is critical that when you get yourself into trouble you be able to get yourself out of it, and having a big reliable engine is one of the best insurance policies you can buy.

After saying all this against the idea of going cruising without an engine in the boat, I have just finished reading *My Old Man and the Sea* by David and Daniel Hays, the firsthand adventures of a father and son who sailed around Cape Horn in their engineless 25-footer, *Sparrow,* and all I can say is well done, lads, really well done.

What's Your Price Range?

How much you end up spending on your boat is a personal decision that must be made by you in consultation with your kitty, and no one else can really help you much. Acceptable cruising boats are available in all price ranges and you might even see one listed in the "Free Boats" section in the classified pages in the back of *WoodenBoat* magazine. Here are a few of my personal thoughts about what you can realistically expect in each price range.

One of the handiest tools for searching for your boat is the Internet; you can search through thousands of boats for sale with just a few clicks of your mouse. Many of these ads are outdated and, when you call you will find that the boat sold months ago, but it is an excellent way to get an idea of what's on the market and where. You can also post notices on various bulletin boards that will bring you e-mail from around the world. In among the junk, you just might find the answer to your dream.

Under $10,000

If you only have a small amount of money to spend on a boat and don't (for whatever reason) have any prospects for earning more, or perhaps you feel that you just have to get on with it right away (such as how Susan and I decided we had to get underway before our children grew up), you may take heart from the fact that there are a lot of cruisers out there in boats that were purchased from the very bottom of the cost spectrum. Lack of money shouldn't keep you from the cruising life if you want to go badly enough and can endure the hardships of living in a tiny boat with little income.

We met several boaters in the lower socioeconomic category on the Intracoastal Waterway (ICW) who seemed to be getting along just fine. If you are determined to join them you should, perhaps, look for an older outboard-powered production boat 23 or 24 feet long that is in good enough condition to preclude heavy repair bills. Then restrict your cruising to sheltered coastal areas such as the ICW or the protected rivers. To be more ambitious would invite disaster either from wasting valuable resources trying to resurrect a worn-out larger boat that has deteriorated beyond the point of practical renewal or from succumbing to the temptation of asking your craft to deliver more than it can and attempt passages that it can't safely handle.

Very small and very light boats tend to be very uncomfortable boats, and living on them can be more like camping out than cruising. Living on a tiny boat full time can turn into an endurance contest, and then the danger is that the experience will quickly exhaust your kitty and sour you toward the cruising life forever. Therefore, the best advice for anyone with such a limited amount of money is to bite the bullet and go back to work for a few years and earn some more. Better yet, sell the bullet and put the money into your kitty. The patient and persistent approach is certain to work out better in the long run and you will actually end up saving time.

$10,000–$25,000

A lot of good boats are available for $25,000 and less, but very few of them are good offshore cruising boats. If you are limited by this sum you should look for an old-but-sound wooden boat (presuming, once again, that you have the skills to effect repairs yourself) or look for a well-built ferrocement boat about 30 to 35 feet long. Yet another alternative is to look for a larger and cleaner production boat that is too light for offshore work and restrict your cruising to coastal and sheltered waters.

When Susan and I were looking for a boat, we came across a lovely 45-foot Alden ketch on a mooring in Beverly Harbor, Massachusetts, that the desperate owner was advertising for sale at $15,000 or best offer. She was truly a lovely boat with classic lines, a trim white hull, a panel full of new electronics, and a sail inventory that was worth as much as the asking price. The only problem was that the hull was made from ferrocement, and we were resolved from the start not to buy a ferrocement boat. There is a good possibility that this boat was sound and ready for a lifetime of cruising, and for someone with a little gambling blood in their veins and a limited kitty, it may have been an excellent value. But remember that a gamble presupposes the possibility of losing and a loss in a critical maneuver like buying your boat will be catastrophic to your cruising plans. We opted to pass on this boat, and I'm glad that we did no matter how much a bargain it might have been.

We eventually found *Sultana* in a barn in Maine and bought her for $25,000. Even after having substantial hull and engine work done on her we still had a lot less than $40,000 invested. This was largely luck because we were prepared to spend much more, but the fact that we did not have to empty our kitty to buy our boat has been one of the big reasons why our cruise has been such a resounding success.

$25,000–$50,000

If you can hold out long enough to accumulate $50,000 to spend, you will find yourself with enough money to buy a decent, if not posh or grand, cruising boat. Don't be discouraged if you don't see a lot of boats advertised in this price range or if a lot of brokers aren't enthusiastic about showing these boats; sellers advertise for the price they would like to get, not what they will accept, and the good brokers will be quite helpful once they learn you are sincere and have some cash in your jeans. Let the word out among brokers and yard operators that you are seriously looking for an inexpensive boat, and call the banks and finance companies that offer marine mortgages to see if there are any repossessions available. Good repos aren't as common as some would have you believe, but when you do find one, it can mean a real bargain. Such boats are nuisances for the banks, who often want to just get rid of them for what they have in them, regardless of the book value. In extreme cases, like the *Delphus*, they will even accept a substantial loss just to get rid of the boat.

A blistering bargain

I have looked at hundreds of boats with horrible cases of the boat pox, but have seen only one or two where the blisters were anything but a cosmetic blight. In most cases the blistering is limited to the gelcoat below the waterline. But because blisters are profoundly ugly and very expensive to repair, buyers shy away from blistered boats the same way they avoid ferrocement boats. However, there is little risk here—blistered boats can represent some of the best bargains afloat. Blisters are caused by, among other things, exposure to warm water, so the southern U.S. states and the Caribbean are good places to start looking.

If you are one of the favored few who appreciate the aesthetics and other virtues of wooden craft, the under-$50,000 price range is where you will start to find some wooden boats worth looking at. Look for one-off boats built in the 50s or 60s by professional builders or skilled homebuilders to plans from well-known designers such as Sparkman & Stephens, John Alden, Bud MacIntosh, and Eldridge McGinnis. (There are a lot more, of course.)

For the most part, I would advise staying away from wooden production boats built during this period because many builders were then trimming costs while coping with spiraling wages and competition from the new plastic boats. Wooden boats built then can be poorly constructed and difficult to repair. *Sultana* is, of course, a production boat, but she is an exception in that she was one of the early boats built and heavily constructed in a traditional manner. Later Newporters weren't nearly as well made as the early ones.

$50,000–$75,000

If you are looking for a large boat with a lot of room (in spite of my remonstrations to keep it small) and you have about 75 grand to spend, you could do a lot worse than looking at some of the better (but older) examples of the William Garden- or Bill Crealock-designed Taiwan-built boats. These boats have well-deserved reputations for heavy construction, sloppy workmanship, and inferior hardware, and there are thousands of horror stories about them. I have seen chainplates pull out of hulls, turnbuckles snap while being routinely tightened, and whole sections of teak trim simply fall off because they were glued on with no mechanical fasteners. However, if you look for one that has been used as a bluewater cruiser for 10 or 15 years, most of the problems will have been discovered and corrected by the previous owners.

I would not consider one of these boats that has seen extensive use in the charter fleet unless it was in obviously good condition and available at a bargain price, and I would caution you to spend a lot of money on an exhaustive survey. Many of the older Taiwan-built boats have laminated plywood and fiberglass or cored decks under teak and when fresh water gets in there (often through fastener holes), the boat is quickly rendered into junk because it will cost more to fix the decks than the boat is worth, even if you do the work yourself. Any sign of sponginess in a laminated deck should be a sign for instant rejection of any fiberglass boat.

Your options open up when you have $75,000 to spend. Older fiberglass workhorses include the Allied Seawind ketch, earlier Cape Dorys, Pearsons, the Tartan 37, and the Cal 39.

$75,000–$100,000

If you are able to come up with more than a hundred grand or so for your cruising boat, consider yourself lucky, but you are about to leave the price range to which this book is dedicated. That's OK, the rest of us less fortunate folks wish you well, but we will also entreat you to reconsider your decision to spend this much money on something as ephemeral as a boat. Thousands of adequate cruising boats are available for less than $100,000, and if you work hard and find one with which you can be happy and put the balance of that money back into the kitty or use it to fix up your less expensive boat to get it just the way you want it, you will be buying peace of mind and contentment on a level unavailable to those who sail in pricey boats. You will also come to know the real joy of living well with less—a joy that is becoming so difficult to find in our consumption-obsessed world.

Once you break the $75,000 barrier, you will find a lot of fine cruising boats on the market. You might even get lucky and find a well-built steel or aluminum boat whose owner is willing to entertain offers in this price range, and well-worn, older Bermuda 40s, a fine cruising boat by Hinckley, sometimes go for under $100,000. Many of the large Taiwan-built boats are in this category, some of which will be offered with extensive inventories of spares and gear.

One thing that $100,000 will not buy, unless you are very lucky, is a large cruising boat in pristine, sail-away condition. Smaller plastic boats in the 30- to 35-foot range and larger wooden boats might be ready to go, but most boats in any category (even new ones) will need a little cosmetic work, perhaps a new sail or two, and a thorough stem-to-stern, windex-to-wormshoe check of every component in the boat—and that's after your surveyor gets done with it. It's reasonable to suppose you may spend 50 to 100 percent of the purchase price on your first-year refit to put the boat into safe, comfortable, sail-away condition. I'll discuss how to go about doing this economically in the next chapter, but first let's take a look at a few of your humble but keenly observant author's favorite boats.

Some Favorite Boats

Keep foremost in your mind that any full-size (40 feet or so) cruising boat you find under $100,000 will have had a lot of water under its keel and be nearing the time for a major refit. However, there are plenty of these boats that will have a few years of carefree cruising left in them before this happens, and this is just what you need to get you on the water and exposed to the cruising life. If you buy right and exercise care in your choice of a boat, when the time does come for the refit, you will know just what you want and will have enough money left in your kitty to get it done without strain or worry.

Outside of a few general guidelines listed above, I'm not trying to tell you what you should be looking for in a cruising boat, but if I were looking for a boat today and I wanted to stay under the $100,000 figure, here is a sampling of classified ads from various sources that I would be interested in pursuing.

35' Southern Cross, 1982, one owner, cruise equipped, $53,900
42' Sparkman & Stephens, 1975, fiberglass ketch, center cockpit, $69,000
39' Concordia yawl, upgraded classic, one owner, $75,000
50' Murray Peterson Gaff Schooner, mahogany on oak, $71,000
43' LOD Alden Schooner, 1980, heavily built, 100 percent sound, $125,000
   (This one is more expensive than I would consider, but what the hell, I'd like to take a look anyway—asking prices are asking prices.)
45' Davies pilothouse ketch, Douglas fir over oak, $80,000
30' Bud McIntosh-designed and -built ketch, Atomic 4, recent upgrades, $15,500

Naturally, these listings reflect my bias for wooden boats as well as an irrational passion for wooden schooners, just as your list will reflect your own personal bias and prejudice. The point is that there are a lot of good old boats out there and one of them is just the boat for you.

As you review the endless parade of boats that are offered for sale, you will quickly develop a fondness for certain types, designers, and builders. In our year of

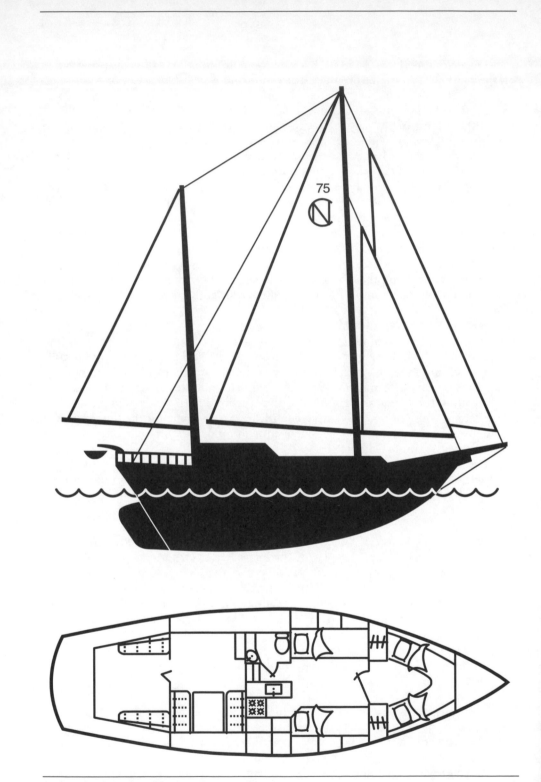

Sail and cabin plan, Newporter 40

looking at everything that came on the market that was even close to our price range, we learned as much about what we didn't need and what we could get along without as we learned about what we just had to have to get by. Here are a few specific makes and models that we liked or at least came to respect; they may not be the type of boat for you, but they represent the sort of value in boats you should be looking for.

Old wooden boats

If Susan and I should ever become wealthy in material terms (we are already wealthy beyond measure in immaterial terms), which is about as likely as our cruising to the moon, I can see us finishing out our cruising days in that big John Alden schooner listed above. Naturally, we would have it done over first, in Maine by craftspeople of our own choosing, and I can easily envision the bill for this do-over exceeding the million-dollar mark. (It would be the binnacled pool table in the main salon that puts it over the top.) But short of this idealistic and highly improbable occurrence, we will keep plugging away on *Sultana* which, once the current refit is complete, will be ready for at least another 35 years of world cruising.

Old wooden boats have a peculiar attraction for certain folks like your peculiar old wooden author, and I find it hard to imagine sailing in anything else. It's not that I wouldn't sail in a plastic boat, I most certainly would, and I am the first to admit that there are many fine fiberglass boats from first-rate designers, just as I will freely admit that wooden boats aren't for everyone. I am simply more comfortable in a wooden boat—even one made of plywood—than in boats built from any other material. (My bias has much to do with my years of wooden boat restoration experience, which gave me all the woodworking skills I need.)

Newporter 40

Because *Sultana* is a Newporter 40, I have developed a fondness for the design even with its several major drawbacks. The Newporter was designed and built by Ack Ackerman who made a lot of money during WWII building gunboats for the military. After the war, he built a schooner, sold his boatyard, and went cruising in the South Pacific. But alas, after a few years in paradise, he decided he liked building boats better than cruising in them. Ack returned to Newport Beach, California, where he designed the Newporter based on what his cruising experiences taught him the perfect cruising boat should be like, and he nearly got it right. He only designed this one boat; eventually he built more than 300 of them, a huge number in the early days of mass-produced sailboats.

In its day the Newporter was the yacht to have among the "in" crowd, and several were bought by movie stars and other wealthy people looking for status symbols. Gary Moore, of *To Tell the Truth* fame, had one named *Eastern Way* that he kept at his summer home in Somes Sound, Maine, until his death in 1995. (He also had a powerboat that he named *Western Way*—folks that live up around Mt. Desert Island in Maine will understand the pun.)

Of the 300 or so Newporters built in the late 50s and early 60s, many are still around and occasionally come on the market at reasonable prices. Precious few of the reasonable ones are in good enough condition for world cruising, however, so choose carefully. I have seen marginal Newporters needing a lot of work offered for as little as $10,000, and a good one ready to cruise might be had for about $50,000, but expect to pay about twice that for one in pristine condition.

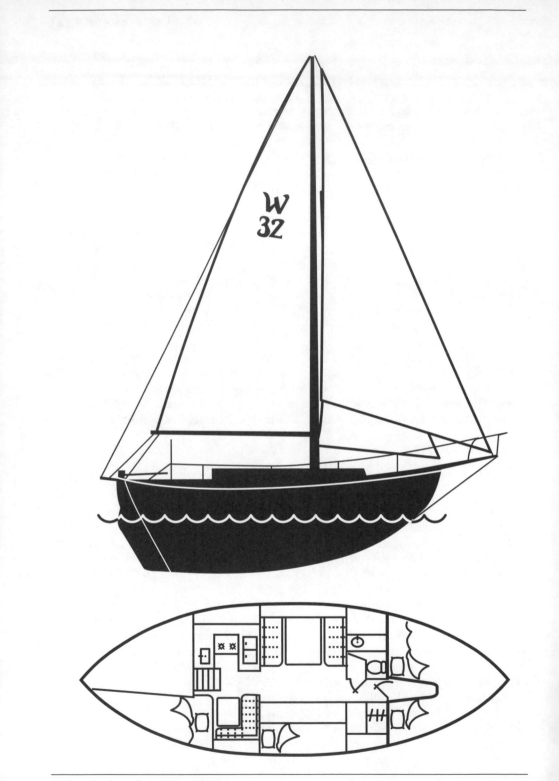

Sail and cabin plan, Westsail 32

There are a few serious drawbacks to the Newporter in addition to those that are inherent to all wooden boats. The fiberglass and polyester skin on the hull and deck is an abomination that has destroyed many boats by trapping rot-inducing rainwater under the skin. This skin should be removed and a good two-part paint, such as Awlgrip or Imron, applied directly to the plywood. If you can afford to do it, you can replace the polyester with fiberglass and epoxy, and there is one Newporter in New Zealand that has had the plywood replaced with conventional planking.

Another problem is the huge, poorly draining cockpit that fills with sea water every time we get pooped (it's happened twice so far). This isn't as dangerous as it is in some boats because of the enormous reserve buoyancy on the stern, but repeated poops aren't something I care to think about. It is distressing when a thousand gallons or so of the South Pacific finds its way into the bilge. The large deep cockpit also makes visibility from the helm a problem (Old Ack, at 6 feet 4 inches, could see right over the pilothouse roof). The large glass pilothouse windows will need to be replaced with overlay windows of thick (10 or 12 mm) acrylic or polycarbonate strong enough to withstand the full force of a beam sea.

Westsail 32

This classic boat has an amazing number of detractors. Most anyone will be happy to tell you the Westsail 32s are hopelessly slow (their nickname is "wet snails") and don't really make good cruising boats, but very few of these detractors have ever been aboard one and I bet none has actually ever sailed one. What they mean is that Westsails look slow and cumbersome because they look like a turned-over turtle.

In truth, the number of these little boats that have successfully circumnavigated is probably now in the hundreds. They have survived pitchpoles and knockdowns and come up smiling with the rig intact and they can keep sailing in the most incredibly bad conditions—long past the point where larger but lesser boats are hove-to or lying ahull. With their heavy displacement, tiny but secure cockpit, and simple sail plan they are one of the safest boats afloat, and their extreme beam makes them more comfortable than many boats with 5 or 6 more feet on the waterline.

A lot of Westsail 32s were built, more than 800 I believe, before the company called it quits, so there are usually several on the market at any one time. A lot were sold as kit boats with the interior finished by the owner, many of which were beautifully done with exotic hardwoods, and the quality of finish far exceeds anything a factory could have produced. However, even more were poorly done with a superficial plywood interior that would be very easy for a handy person to remove and redo, and if you can find one you may have found a real bargain. Poorly finished kit boats that are in otherwise top condition often sell for less than $25,000. Westsail 32s in sail-away condition can be had for $50,000 to $75,000.

In the later years of production, Westsail brought out several larger boats up to 44 feet that were also built like a steel ball, but there were far fewer of them built and good ones usually go for well over $100,000.

Morgan OutIsland 41

I don't like Morgan OutIslands much. They are ungainly, almost ugly to my eyes, and they are miserable creatures to get to sail well. Not only that, they have

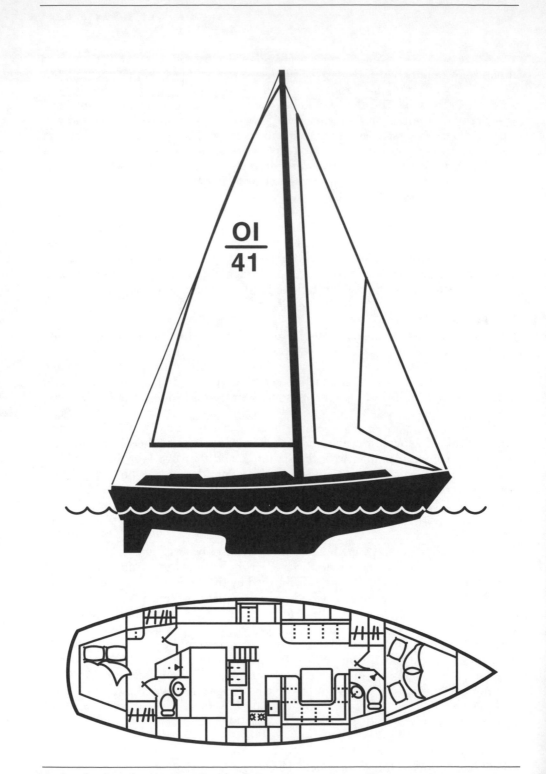

Sail and cabin plan, Morgan Outlsland 41

carpeting on the floor, and I would never sail in a boat that has carpeting on the floor—that's where a proper wooden cabin sole should be. In fact, I wouldn't even mention the Morgan OutIsland in this book if it weren't for the fact that there are a lot of them available and the people who are cruising in them seem to love them. They will defend the lousy sailing qualities to the death, and some even claim to like that stupid carpeting.

I do have to admit, however, the old Morgans seem to be better sea boats than they ought to be, and once you are in harbor they are very comfortable with lots of interior space and a commodious center cockpit big enough for the entire fleet to enjoy a major potluck feast. And, their shoal draft opens up an entire world of shallow bays and rivers where a deep-draft boat will never be able to venture.

A pretty much worn-out Morgan OutIsland can be found for about $50,000, but a real good one will still be under $80,000, and yes, if I had to, I could learn to love one, after I ripped out that stupid rug and installed proper flooring, that is.

CSY 44

For about a decade from the mid-70s to the mid-80s, the CSY Company (originally Caribbean Sailing Yachts) dominated the bareboat charter industry with major operations in all the most popular cruising grounds. To ensure a steady supply of rugged and safe yachts to man its fleets, and operating under the adage that if you want something done right you have to do it yourself, CSY designed and built its own boats. The resulting CSY 44 is one of the most sturdy cruising craft ever constructed from fiberglass on a production basis.

Most of the boats were sold as leasebacks to investors who had a lot more money than they needed but who needed a tax dodge to keep from giving any of it to the government. (The change in tax law that partly closed this loophole is one reason why CSY went out of business.) Quite a few CSYs, though, were sold as private yachts.

Most of the boats sold to investors for charter were built with an abbreviated rig and a reduced sail area to keep the customers, most of whom think they are Phillippe Jeantot, out of trouble. These boats with the abbreviated rigging are only marginal sailers, but they are adequate for cruising, and the full-rig versions sail very well for a boat that weighs in at well over 30,000 pounds.

The old charter boats that you find on the market are often worn-out and require more to get them going again than they are worth, but there are a few of the older walk-over type (newer ones are called "walk-throughs" because the forward and aft cabins are connected) that have been refurbished that might succumb to an offer of $60,000 or $70,000 once the owner has had the boat on the market for a year or so at half again that amount. Clean, never-chartered CSY 44s with the full rig and deep keel usually go for over $100,000.

You might see a few CSY 37s on the market, but I really don't know too much about them except that they embody the same heavy construction as their big sisters, that they are one of the ugliest boats ever built, and that quite a few of them are in the cruising fleet whose owners are very pleased with them. You will also see a few CSY 50s, a huge bathtub of a boat with a skimpy rig. These boats, which were built by Gulfstar in Florida, are CSYs in name only and bear no resemblance to the other two.

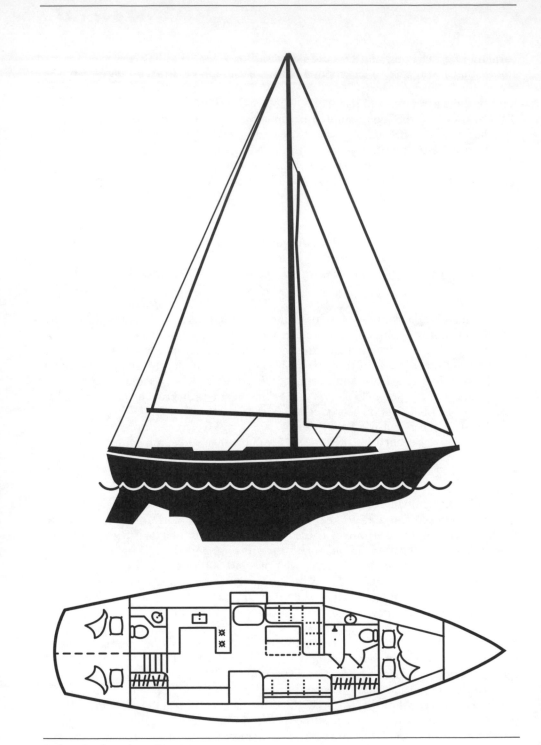

Sail and cabin plan, CSY 44

Valiant 40

One of the best deals around for a classic cruising boat of proven Bob Perry design and quality construction is an older Valiant 40 built by Uniflite of fire-retardant resin. This resin, which was used by the builder in a noble attempt to combat the tendency of fiberglass boats to burn like blast furnaces when they get going, proved to be particularly prone to blistering, and not just below the waterline. The gelcoat of the old Valiants bubbles up everywhere. Some have more blisters than a toad has warts and the blisters go deep, often involving several layers of cloth. It's also not clear if these blisters can ever be fixed; some evidence indicates that they will just keep popping up no matter what you do to try and stop them.

But even so, an older blistered Valiant (hulls with the worst blistering are numbers 101 to 259) sells for about half of what a newer unblemished one sells for, and much less than a third of the $300,000 or so that you would pay for a current version. A few years ago, you could buy a blistered Valiant in sailable condition for about $40,000. Today, the word has gotten out and most of these super bargains have been scooped up, but you still might find one for around $60,000 if you persist and aren't shy about making offers. That 30 or 40 grand difference between a blistered boat and a clean one is a lot of money to save for a little bit of ugly and a lot of class.

Actually, you might be too late for this one. When Susan and I were looking at boats there were several blistered Valiants on the market with anxious owners willing to consider offers under $50,000, but a recent search on the Internet could locate no Valiant 40 on the market for less than $280,000. Take a look anyway, you might get lucky.

Tartan 37

This boat has been around since 1967 and has proven to be a capable and comfortable cruising yacht able to get you anywhere you want to go. It's not my kind of boat (it's too plastic and I hate that ski-slope stern that wastes deck area), but if I found myself with a choice between this boat at a bargain price and the boat of my dreams (whatever that is) for a lot of money, I could learn to be very happy in a Tartan. Because the design has been around so long, there have been a lot built, and there are usually quite a few on the market. The older ones are excellent values.

With a little looking, you might find a usable version of the Tartan 37 for under $50,000, and even an up-to-date version with modern electronics can be had for well under $100,000.

Outside of the foolish "racer-cruiser" styling from the 60s and 70s (which I admit doesn't seem to bother most people), the biggest problem is that Tartans are considered small by today's standards (which can actually be a big plus), and the centerboard, like most centerboards on cruising boats, can be noisy as it slats back and forth in a cross sea. Also, the centerboard trunk tends to get clogged with mussels and barnacles and other sea creatures. I have seen several Tartans whose frustrated owners have glassed over the centerboards, choosing to sacrifice a bit of windward performance for the peace of mind that comes from not having a centerboard to worry about.

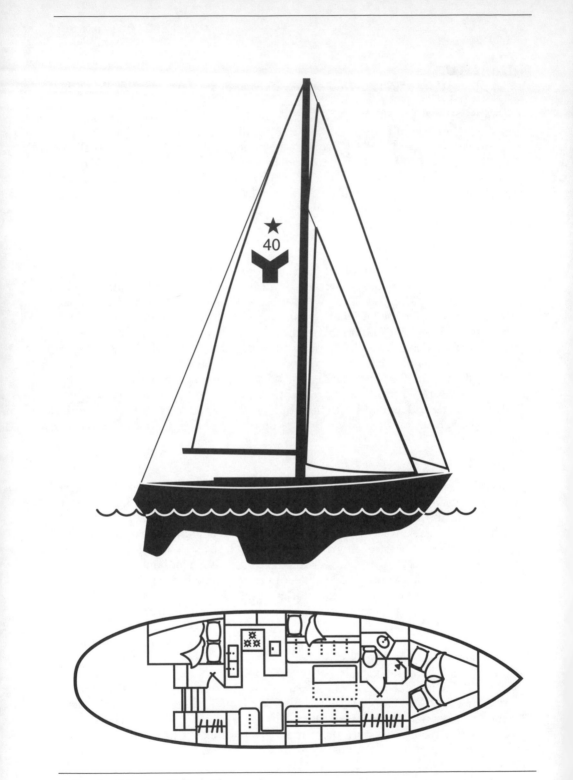

Sail and cabin plan, Valiant 40

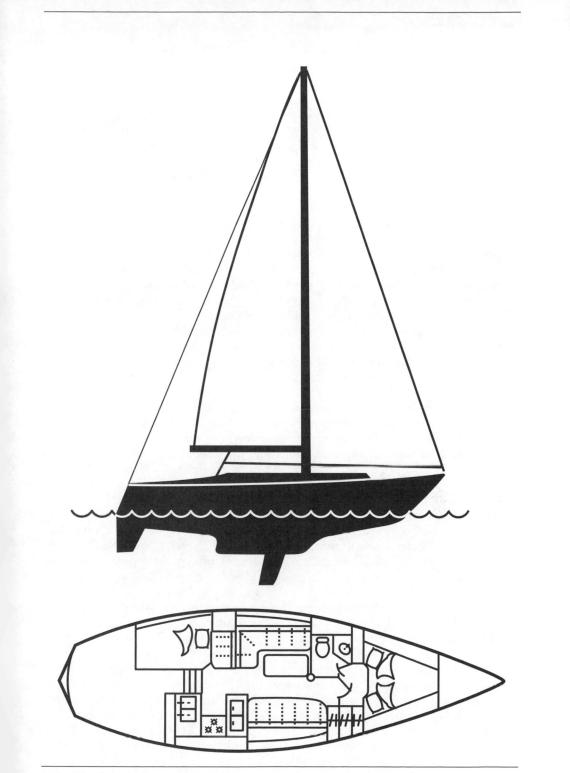

Sail and cabin plan, Tartan 37

Making an Offer

When you finally find the boat you want, the first thing you must do is to go away and think about it for awhile. How long is awhile? That depends on you, but it should be long enough for you to make sure you are proceeding in a rational rather than an emotional manner. Don't forget that a good sales effort can pluck your heartstrings like Jimmy Buffett plucks his guitar, so go somewhere quiet and spend an hour or a day or a week asking yourself the questions we've discussed above: Is the boat too big? . . . too small? . . . too expensive? Can we get her in the water with a minimum of effort? . . . time? . . . expense? Will she be seaworthy? . . . safe? . . . easy to sail? . . . easy to maintain?

Don't worry if it isn't the perfect boat for you, there's no such thing as a perfect boat anyway. Just make sure she will do the job you want her to do without strangling your poor little kitty. Don't worry about the asking price. Make your offer based on what you think you can pay, even if it's only a fraction of what the seller expects to get. Don't worry about the actual value of the boat either, as long as you know your offer is lower. The only thing that should concern you at this point is how much you can pay and what the seller will accept.

There is often a psychological advantage in offering about 10 percent less in your first offer than you can pay in the end. Doing so allows the seller the face-saving option of rejecting your first offer while imparting a feel-good attitude about talking you up to a higher price. You'll get the boat at a price you can afford and everyone will feel better about it.

Don't be astonished if your offer is rejected and don't be intimidated into offering even a little more than you want to pay. If the seller is indignant or offended by your offer, be polite and make sure that everyone understands that you've offered as much as you can and that your offer will stand for awhile. If your first offer isn't refused, you've probably offered too much anyway.

Get a Survey

The importance of getting a survey on any boat you are considering can't be overemphasized. Even the simplest craft is a complex creation of many diverse disciplines. Literally thousands of things can be amiss that even knowledgeable boat people can overlook. True, the majority of these potential problems are minor and no boat is free of all of them, but others can be both hard to detect and fatal. A bad deck-to-hull seam on a fiberglass boat, for example, is invisible in dry weather, but it can cause leaks that make life aboard a misery at best. At worst the seam can fail in heavy seas and sink the boat. Intergranular and crevice corrosion in an aluminum or steel hull and in major hardware components is likewise invisible and hard to detect, as is rot in a wooden boat; all of these problems and many more can mean the end of a boat that looks just dandy on the outside. Hundreds of other items such as poor engine mounting, water saturation, stray electrical current, or inadequate wiring are common and repairable, but the repairs can be expensive, and you want to know about those expenses before you buy the boat.

When you find a boat you are interested in, first agree on a price with the seller, but make the price contingent on the results of a good survey. If you are using a broker, the broker will undoubtedly recommend one or several surveyors, but you are better off getting one yourself based on recommendations of other boatowners in the area who are not involved in the boat-selling industry. The convention is that the broker is working for the seller (in some states, brokers are required to tell the buyer this) and the surveyor is working for you, the buyer. In reality, the broker is working for the broker who is trying to sell boats, and the surveyor is working for the surveyor who is doing surveys, and you are left to look after yourself. Even the most honest surveyor may be reluctant to kill the sale of a broker who sends in a lot of business.

Because the buyer pays full price for the survey, you can order just what you want. Some surveyors specialize in certain kinds of boats (steel, wood, luxury yachts, commercial vessels, etc.) so try to find a surveyor who specializes in the type of boat you are looking at, and spend a little extra on a full survey. That means the boat is checked in the water and out, with a full engine run-up and a test sail thrown in for good measure. Whatever you do, don't trust a survey that was done last month on the same boat for some other potential buyer even if the seller or the broker offers it for free. Such an offer is unethical at best, and in many areas it may even be illegal.

Once the results of the survey are available, you can decide not to buy the boat if catastrophic difficulties are discovered, or you can renegotiate the price to get it into line with what the repairs would cost. As a third option, you can request the seller make the repairs before you buy the boat, but make sure your purchase is contingent on a new survey if the repairs are major—or at least contingent on the approval of the original surveyor if the repairs are minor.

Surveys and the surveyors who do them are negative by nature and tend to reveal the bad things about a boat and ignore the good things. The final price should always be renegotiated based on the worst items discovered in the survey and what it will cost to repair them. When we bought *Sultana* the surveyor came up with a list of 52 items that he deemed critical enough to require immediate attention, and that list knocked a full third off what we ended up paying for the boat.

Building Your Own Boat

Although I have never built a cruising boat, I know lots of people who have. There was the man in Ipswich who spent the better part of 10 years building a lovely Tahiti ketch on the banks of the Ipswich River, only to discover that his wife was terrified of tipping over when the boat heeled in a breeze. And then there was the young man on the south shore of Boston who started building a 40-foot Bruce Roberts ketch in his backyard when he was 17 years old. We met him when he was 29 and the boat was still nowhere near complete.

Many backyard and part-time builders of cruising boats I have known over the years never finish the boats they are building even after 10 or 15 years of work, and of those few who have, most have never gone cruising. There seems to be some fundamental difference between the type of people who are good at building boats and those who are good at sailing and cruising in them—it is rare to meet someone who is good at both. Of course there are exceptions to this statement and those exceptions shine like diamonds in a fist full of pebbles.

The most successful boatbuilders are those who cruise long enough to know exactly what they want in a cruising boat, then go to work full-time building just the boat they want. On Hunga Atoll in Vava'u we met the crew of the steel ketch *Sammy Ley,* who had cruised in their first boat for many years, then gone ashore in England. Keith, the skipper, spent two years designing and building

Sammy Ley, one of the loveliest and most comfortable cruising boats I have ever been aboard.

What can would-be cruisers learn from these somewhat casual observations of the building machinations of our fellows? Well, perhaps not to undertake a boatbuilding project unless you have a very long time between now and your expected departure, and then only if you have already built several boats and know exactly what you are doing. Even in that ideal situation it is wiser to cruise for a few years on a small and inexpensive boat so that you will know just what you need when you do go ashore to build your dream boat. For most of us it makes much more sense to go to work and sedulously save our shillings for the kitty, then let the kitty build our boat.

Ours is a free-range life in an artificial world, and to be successful at simple and basic cruising we need first to shake off the standards of behavior that society uses to keep us tethered safely to the dock. We need a good old boat that doesn't cost a lot money to buy, outfit, and maintain. The trick is to find just the right one by looking for price and condition rather than for style and features.

10

COMMENCE CRUISING

"I gotta go where there ain't any snow . . .

I gotta go where it's warm."

—Jimmy Buffett, "Boat Drinks"

I have argued (with a great deal of conviction, of course) in the preceding chapters that the type of boat you go cruising in doesn't matter that much but that the purchase of the boat is one of the most important steps on the road to the cruising life and the logical culmination of the planning process. I bared my soul relating the horror story of our near-death experience with *Delphus,* and I have beseeched thee not to buy any boat larger or more expensive than the minimum that will get the job done for you. Now you've gone and done it, and it's too late to look back now. Good cruisers never watch their wake anyway, just the bow and the horizon ahead.

Let's Get Going

OK, so now you have bought your boat and a beauty she is indeed. True, the gelcoat or the paint is a little dull, and the sails are more gray than white, and the VHF is 10 years old, and the Loran-C, which was state-of-the-art only a few short years ago isn't going to be much good once you get south of Cuba, and the old double-sideband isn't legal to use any more. But what the hey . . . you're going cruising.

Now that you have a boat, what are you going to do with it? The surveyor came up with a long list of things that need to be done, like those deck fittings that need to be rebedded and have backing plates installed, the winches that need to be upgraded to a larger size, and the standing rigging that needs to be replaced simply because it's the same age as the boat. If there is any money left over, you will be able to get a good roller furler for the jib and maybe even a radar, but these things can wait for awhile—at least until after you finish upgrading the electrical system. The important thing is that you bought yourself a good solid boat with a sound hull, and that old diesel sounds as if she is good for another 20 years or so.

But before you start fixing stuff, even the important stuff, let's take a few days and just look around. Have a trusted ally crank you up the mast in the bosun's chair. Throw away that old board and rope contraption that came with the boat and get yourself a decent bosun's chair that has a strong crotch strap and a good back support. (West Marine sells a dandy.) Spend about an hour becoming thoroughly familiar with the masthead hardware. Go over every item one piece at a time until you know what every shackle and bolt is for, what it is supposed to do, and what is going to happen if it fails. On the way down notice how the spreaders are attached to the mast and check everything else that is attached to the mast to make sure it is bedded and fastened properly. Check aluminum masts for any sign of corrosion, especially galvanic corrosion caused by dissimilar metals; check wooden masts for any discoloration around fittings that might indicate water incursion. Check every fitting you encounter for any sign of excessive wear or stress, but more important make sure you know why it is there. Go over the entire boat like this, pausing at every item you encounter. If its purpose isn't obvious at first, consult your manuals or ask someone who knows about such things. It's not until you are intimate with every screw and rivet and block that you can say the boat is truly yours.

There are precious few boats available for less than $100,000 that won't require at least a little work to get them ready to go, and even a brand-new boat will require extensive preparation for a world cruise. Let's assume that your new old boat is structurally sound with a solid hull and a good engine, and revisit some of the areas where most boats will require some attention. First, though, consider where you want the work to be done.

Foreign boatyards

Boat work in the United States and Canada is very expensive, even though materials and equipment are as cheap as you will find anywhere. However, the quality of the work you can expect from most boatyards is spotty at best. There are some great craftsmen and women in both countries, certainly, but there are many more hacks and semiskilled laborers who call themselves artisans. If you are not able to do much of the work that needs to be done on your boat yourself, you should consider doing just enough work to make the boat safe enough to get going, then sail to a foreign port to get the work done. This can be an attractive option even if you intend on doing most of the job yourself. Foreign yards often offer skilled craftspeople at wage rates that are only a fraction of those in the U.S. and Canada, and the workers are likely to be appreciative of the chance to help you.

Naturally, there are dangers associated with having boat repairs and upgrades done in a foreign port, and you must be extra careful where you go and who you select to do your work, but this is true anywhere. One of the major jobs currently underway on *Sultana* is the redoing of the epoxy/fiberglass skin on her bottom that was installed only five years ago by a large U.S. boatyard at a substantial cost. They used a polyester filler under the epoxy and the whole thing is delaminating. (The epoxy sticks to the polyester just fine, but the polyester pulls away from the wood and traps water in the resulting voids.)

The most popular places for inexpensive refits are Venezuela and New Zealand, but Argentina and Southeast Asia are also reported to be good destinations. The back issues of Seven Seas Cruising Association *Bulletin*s are full of advice and warnings about specific areas, and many will even give the names and addresses of individual workers who are recommended for quality work.

I have already related how we ended up sailing *Sultana* to New Zealand for her first complete refit in 35 years. That refit is well underway as this is being written, and so far everything is working out just dandy. There is a peculiar conundrum that the government here has gotten itself into. Most cruisers have heard of the infamous Section 21 whereby visiting yachts that don't meet certain safety requirements won't be allowed to leave until the unsafe condition is corrected, while immigration will normally allow a visitor from the U.S. to stay for only one year (nine months plus one three-month extension) on a tourist visa. Thus, an amusing situation: one branch of the government, Immigration, says you must leave because your visa has expired, while another branch, The Department of Marine Safety, says you can't leave until you bring your boat up to its standards. The situation could be further complicated by the Customs Department, which has the power to slap you with a 32 percent import duty once your initial temporary import permit expires. Fortunately, we haven't experienced any trouble with the authorities, both Customs and Immigration are accessible and pleasant to deal with, and they all seem quite willing to stretch their own rules as long as we are honest and direct in our dealings with them. They even seem pleased that we are here, but there are some interesting possibilities in this bureaucratic paradox.

Highly skilled and certified (the New Zealand government certifies everything from boatbuilders to propane tanks), boatbuilders are available here for about $15 per hour (U.S. dollars) and the quality of work is as high as I have ever seen. Kiwi boatbuilders are a little sloppy when it comes to time commitments—they like to take lots of breaks and occasionally don't show up when they say they will—but they are conscientious workers, most are honest to a fault, and when the work is done it will be done right. Even though I'm doing most of the work on *Sultana* myself, it looks like the final bill will be less than half of what it would have been in the U.S. even with the huge shipping bills from having materials and gear sent from the U.S. Even this is less of a problem than it used to be. With the recent slip in the value of the Kiwi dollar against the U.S. dollar, it is becoming more economical to purchase most things locally than to import them. Kiwis love their boats (I'm told that New Zealand has more boats per capita than any other first-world country) and have a national passion for high-quality merchandise (check out the uniform and unblemished New Zealand apples in your local supermarket), so most of the boat stuff manufactured here starts at excellent and goes up from there.

Another argument for delaying any work that for safety reasons doesn't need to be done right away is that you can commence cruising right now instead of waiting until the work is done, and by delaying renovations for a year or so, you will have a much better feeling for just what you need in a boat—a feeling borne of solid experience.

The Rigging

When you buy an old used boat, you can assume that you are also buying old used rigging, and rigging has a few peculiarities that make it worth spending some time on it.

The standing rigging

Your surveyor will have gone over your standing rigging, and you, of course, have gone up the mast at least once to get familiar with all the parts and their functions (and to get used to going up the mast, which can be scary if you haven't done it before). If any cracked or corroded terminals or swages are found or if there are any broken strands in the wire, you'll have to replace all the standing rigging. Inadequate rigging isn't something that you can mess around with in a cruising boat. It is one thing to snap a shroud while daysailing a few miles from home and quite another to lose that same shroud while hove-to in a gale 500 miles from nowhere. You must not give in to the temptation to try and save a few bucks by replacing rigging piece by piece as it begins to show signs of stress or failure. As often as not the piece that fails and takes the mast by the boards will not have given any warning anyway.

Even if your rigging passes survey without a hitch, you must pay careful attention to its age. Old rigging is like a glamorous movie star grown long of tooth. She can be fixed up to look just fine from a distance, but underneath all those tummy tucks and facelifts she is still an old movie star. If your standing rigging is more than 20 years old, you have an old movie star on your hands, and you should consider replacing the lot no matter how good it looks.

Norseman and other screw-on terminals make doing your own rigging work possible, but these terminals are expensive, and cutting wire to the right length is a tricky business. Swaged terminals are cheaper and better and stronger if they are done right, and an experienced rigger is often worth the price. If you do replace your rigging, keep your old headstay, which is most often the longest piece of wire on the boat, and a few of those screw-on terminals and stow these items somewhere handy. Then if you need an emergency replacement for any wire on the boat, you can cut the old headstay with a hacksaw, attach the terminals, and be underway in no time.

If you can wait until you are underway, rigging is one area where you can save a lot of money when you get to a foreign country. *Sultana*'s rigging was replaced in its entirety by Nelrig, an outfit in Nelson, New Zealand, for less than half of what the same work would have cost in the U.S., and considerably less than what it would have cost me to do the job myself using screw-on terminals.

Oversized wire

Many cruisers have oversized wire installed at the same time they have their standing rigging replaced, believing that this gives them an extra measure of security against rigging failure in heavy weather. I suppose it does do that, but oversized wire also increases windage aloft and adds a lot of weight above the decks right where you don't want it. I personally think it is a waste of money because most rig failures are caused by broken terminals and hardware, not by broken wire. If you want oversize, spend your money on stronger turnbuckles and thimbles, and use the wire size recommended by your rigger.

You might find that your rigging is made up of wire of two or more sizes. The upper shrouds might be heavier than the lowers or the mizzen might be rigged with smaller wire than the main. In this case, changing all the rigging to the largest size might make sense. For one thing, it will be a lot easier to carry just one size of spare wire and terminals, and you might be able to save some money buying a lot of wire in one size rather than buying smaller quantities of two or more sizes.

Chainplates

While you're looking at your rigging be sure to check the chainplates, and if you question their integrity, replace them. Broken chainplates probably account for more lost rigs in the cruising world than any other single factor except turnbuckles, and they are particularly vulnerable in older boats where they are often hard to get at. Chainplates are subjected to incredible force and stress, so even a little surface corrosion can weaken them to the point of sudden failure. Also, some production boatbuilders have a tendency to try to save a few pennies on items they think the boat-show crowds won't notice, and one of their favorites is skimpy chainplates. That they are just about the most important pieces of hardware on the boat seems lost on them. While you are checking, make sure the clevis-pin hole hasn't become elongated both in the chainplate and the masthead hardware.

My feeling is that chainplates on a cruising boat should be on the outside of the hull where we can keep an eye on them. Of course, most modern rigs use inboard chainplates to allow the jib to be sheeted flat, to allow leaks to develop in the deck right where they will be the biggest nuisance, and to keep them out of sight where you can't see how skimpy they are. If your chainplates are out on the rail where they belong but are embedded in or installed behind the planking or hull, the simplest replacement procedure is to grind off the above-deck portion of the old chainplate and install new ones on the outside. Drill right through the old chainplates and bolt the new ones in place using the old ones as backing plates. On *Sultana* I was able to simply double up the chainplates so that I didn't have to grind off the old ones. The combined thickness of the ¼-inch original plate and the ¼-inch new one makes a plate that is a ½-inch thick. Overkill, yes, but I won't have to expend a lot of energy worrying about breaking them. Additional oak blocking on the inside of the hull where the chainplate bolts come through is usually in order, and 1-inch by 4-inch oak strips under the new chainplates on the outside of the hull give your boat a cruiserly look while it widens the base slightly, which serves to further strengthen the rig. Naturally, you would not want to do any of this if the internal chainplates pose no problem and external chainplates would spoil the look of your boat.

Running rigging

Running rigging is a lot easier to deal with than standing rigging; if it looks like it needs replacing, it does. Frayed lines should be changed right away, but discolored, stained, or weathered lines are usually fine.

The best procedure is to keep a 300-foot spool of the most popular sizes of high-quality braided Dacron on hand and learn how to use a Uni-Fid for splicing. Get the largest size rope you will need, then use this same size for all your sheets and halyards where it will fit through the sheaves. When a cold front moves in and things on deck start to get dicey, big rope is much easier to handle than small rope. Replace all your wire halyards with rope—there isn't any significant advantage to wire with the new low-stretch Dacron rope that is available—and don't worry about color coding your lines. After a few months of cruising, you'll be so familiar with your rig you won't need color coding anyway.

The Electrical System

It's the rare production boat that leaves the factory with adequate wiring. Wiring isn't one of the things that sells boats so it's right up there with skinny rigging as a

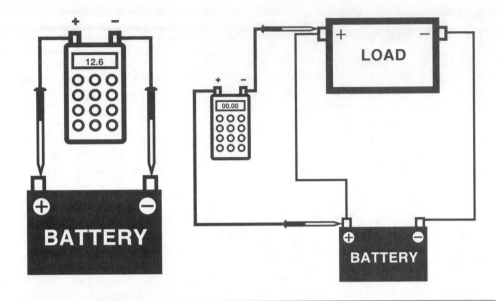

Basic voltage tests for a DC circuit. If checks #2 or #4 show any voltage at all, even at the lowest meter setting, check for a short circuit or dirty terminal. If check #3 shows a lower voltage than check #1, look for a faulty load. 1.(left) Check voltage across battery terminals. The meter reading will reveal system voltage; 12.6 volts is about right. 2. (right) Check voltage drop between the positive terminals of the battery and the load with the load switched on. There should be no reading. *(continued page 175)*

way for boat factories to save a few bucks, and the problem has been made much worse by the way modern boats are assembled from the inside out. A typical production boat is wired before the molded hull liner is installed. Usually the wire is stapled to the liner itself, the liner is dropped into the hull, then the deck is pop-riveted and glued in place ensuring that the wiring and other critical components are totally inaccessible.

Rewiring a boat is very expensive even in a foreign port, and hiring a qualified electrician to do this job is usually out of the question for most of us. This means that you must be your own electrician. Even if you can afford to have it done, doing the rewiring yourself will assure the job is done right and you'll end up being so familiar with your electrical system that finding any one component will be as easy as finding the head in the middle of the night. Once again, if you don't feel comfortable with electricity, take a basic course in night school then read your manual through a few times.

And folks, please pay attention to this: household alternating-current (AC) voltage is the second most dangerous thing on a boat, second only to gasoline and propane fumes; it can kill you deader than a stomped-on squid and just as quick. Until you become a competent electrician and have gained a thorough understanding of what is going on with those little subatomic particles zipping back and forth through their little racetrack circuits, restrict all your efforts to the 12-volt DC systems, and never attempt electrical work on a boat that has any high voltage aboard. Unplug the shore power and disconnect the inverter every time you do any electri-

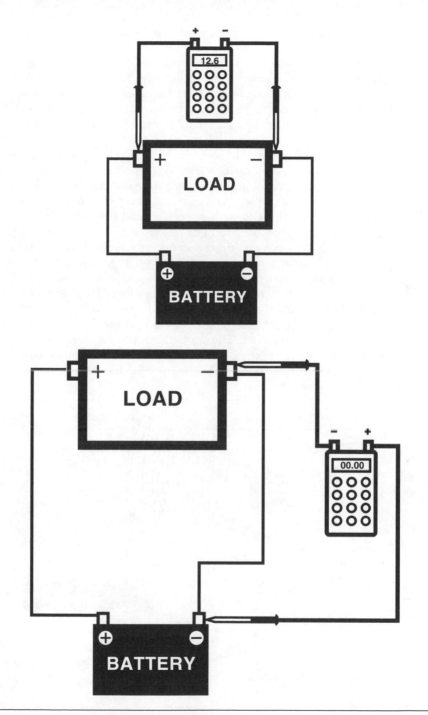

(continued from page 174) 3. (top) Check the voltage across the load terminals with the load running. Reading should be the same as system voltage (same as #1). 4. (bottom) Check the voltage between the negative terminals of the battery and the load. There should be no reading.

cal work. On many inverters, the switch merely turns off the circuit while the unit itself is still live. To be safe you need to disconnect the 12-volt leads to the set and open the circuit breaker. Even then you will invariably grab onto the right end of the wrong 12-volt capacitor at some point and get a new hairdo out of the deal.

Once you think you have a handle on the basics of electricity, it's time to try a few basic jobs that will put your new skills to work. Get yourself a good digital multimeter (Fluke is recommended as a reliable brand, as are the more expensive ones at Radio Shack) and a test lamp. Start at your battery (you *have* unplugged the shore power and disconnected the inverter, haven't you?) and chase down the entire DC circuit for the forepeak reading lamp or some other easily accessible circuit. Turn everything off but this one circuit and use your test light at each terminal. Remove each connector as you come to it and clean it to bright metal with a small scrap of emery cloth. (I use Susan's disposable nail files when I can get away with it.) Once you have cleaned every terminal on the circuit (don't forget the bases of the lightbulbs and your battery ground connection), check for voltage drop. Acceptable drops of 3 percent for critical circuits, bilge pumps and such, and 10 percent for noncritical circuits is a good rule of thumb to start with. If you find that the drop is excessive, as you most likely will in any older boat and even in a lot of new ones, try replacing the old wires with new wires of the proper size. The size of wire in a DC circuit is determined by the amperage the circuit is expected to carry and the length of the wire. Thus, a light located on the top of a 50-foot mast that draws 5 amps will need a 10AWG (American Wire Gauge) wire, while a light in the cabin that draws the same but is only 10 feet from the distribution panel will work fine with an 18AWG wire.

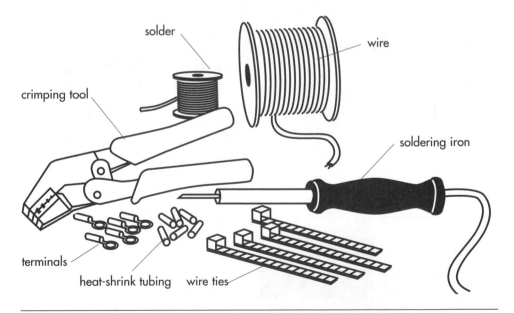

Basic components of shipboard wiring kit: terminal kit, good ratchet crimping tool, soldering iron, heat-shrink tubing, plastic wire ties, wire, and rosin-core solder. As your skills grow, your kit will grow with them. Your kit will ultimately be a highly personal collection containing many more items than shown here.

You will need a 100-foot spool of standard, tinned wire of the correct size. If you don't have the correct size, it is perfectly OK to use the next larger size, but never use a smaller size. You will also need a terminal kit (Jamestown Distributors has a good one) and a quality crimping tool. The pliers-type crimper that comes with the kit is handy for cutting bolts and stripping wire, but don't use it for crimps. Get a good ratchet crimper that produces a double compression crimp. You will also need a soldering iron with rosin-core solder, an assortment of heat-shrink tubing, a set of colored electricians' tape for color coding wires, and a bunch of plastic wire ties of various sizes. Don't try to buy all the correct colors of wires—there are way too many of them, and the colored tape works just fine. The American Boat and Yacht Council (ABYC) specifies 13 different colors of wire on a properly wired yacht, but with a minimum of three sizes needed for some colors, such as the orange accessory-feed wires or the dark blue lighting wires, you would need about 20 spools of wire to do the job properly. Just put a loop of tape at the beginning and end of each wire and more loops at strategic places along the run or get a few sheets of the peel-and-stick numbers that electrical supply houses sell for keeping track of circuits. Use any color wire you happen to have on hand, except white, as long as it is the right size. For your safety, use white wire only for the hot (positive) side of high-voltage AC circuits—never use it on a DC circuit. This is to prevent dummies like you and me from getting our cookies fried when we tap into an AC circuit thinking it is part of a DC circuit. It is also an excellent idea to keep AC circuits isolated and in their own conduits whenever possible.

Start by double-checking to ensure there is no high voltage aboard from any source, then disconnect the 12-volt current by removing the positive leads from all the batteries or by turning the battery switches to "Off." Now unbundle the first section of wire you want to replace. It may be tied with string or with plastic loops or, in older boats, with insulated metal loops. (If you find any of these, get rid of them. The insulation on the loop will deteriorate and the metal can chafe through the insulation on the wire causing dangerous short circuits and fire.) This unbundling can be a challenging job, and if you have a molded hull liner you may have to cut the wire you want to replace to get it out. Don't leave the old wire in place if there is any way to avoid it; unused wiring can be a nightmare if any stray voltage should get aboard.

Next, decide where you want to run the replacement wire. Sometimes you will want to put it right back where you removed the old one, but if you think about it a bit, you might hit upon a direct route that makes more sense. Some builders, in defiance of the laws of nature and common sense, like to run bundles of wires through the bilge as a means of saving a few more pennies, and any you find there should be moved. Naturally, you should make all runs of wire as short as possible (without going through the bilge) because it saves expensive materials and makes the circuit more efficient.

Now cut the new wire to length and solder terminals to each end. Use loop terminals instead of the spade type wherever you can. I'm not really hung up on soldered terminals because I've always had good luck with proper crimped terminals, but soldering is a necessary cruiserly skill that is only acquired with practice, and these first few projects are a good place to practice it. To solder a terminal, first crimp it, then put a drop of solder right where the tip of the wire shows through the terminal loop. The solder will flow back up the wires and seal out any

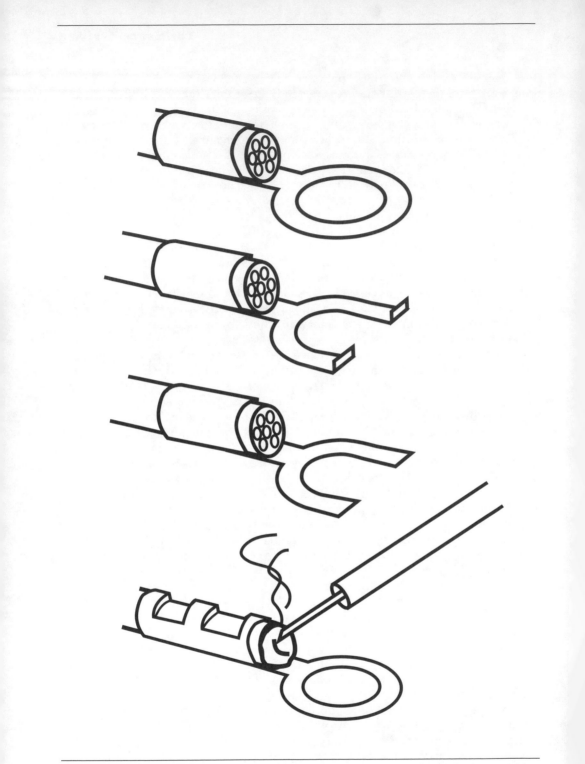

Top to bottom: ring terminals are great, eared spade terminals are OK, but spade terminals are NFG (no flippin' good). Solder terminals only after they are crimped by flowing solder into exposed ends of cut wires. With a proper crimp, soldering terminals is optional.

moisture in addition to strengthening the terminal. It is much easier to solder terminals to the wire before you install it, but if the wire must be fished, this is sometimes impossible. Whenever you can, avoid the common practice of attaching the old wire to the new one and using it to pull the new wire into place. The insulation on adjacent old wiring can be fragile and can be damaged by the new one as you pull it through, and it is hard to get a neat job. Those molded hull liners can have razor-sharp unfinished edges in back of the panels where you can't see them, which can strip a wire to bare metal without your being aware of it. Of course in some cases, like when replacing wires inside a mast, pulling the new wire in with the old one makes a lot of sense.

As you replace the new wire, upset the threads of any screw connectors with the serrated jaws of a pair of Vise-Grip pliers to help ensure that they stay in place or, if you can get at the back of the terminal, a light tap with a spring-loaded center punch right where the male and female threads meet will do the same job. As each section of wire is replaced, turn the juice back on to check that all is in order. I make it a habit to listen and sniff every time I activate a circuit I have been messing with. If you have a short, you'll often hear it first, smell it second, and see the smoke third; quick action in turning the juice back off can save a lot of aggravation and extra work. If the light works, turn the juice off again, bundle all the wires, and move on to the next section.

You will find many light fixtures and other electrical apparatus that have been permanently installed or potted leads that are often several sizes smaller than the recommended wire size. Makers of popular submersible bilge pumps do this as a matter of practice. (They aren't stupid, they just think we are and won't notice.) The appropriate wire size for a given amperage (or "draw") is determined by the distance the wire runs from the distribution panel to the device and back to the panel, and it is beyond me how manufacturers presume to know what this distance will be. While we are grinding this particular ax I will also mention that not only are these wires too small in most cases, they are also too short, thereby necessitating splices in inconvenient and inappropriate places (like the bilge). Because you can't replace these wires, cut them as short as practical and splice the shortened

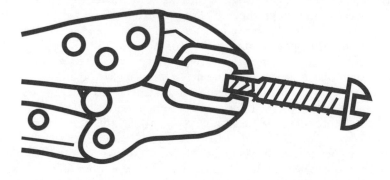

Lightly crimp the threads of electrical terminal screws with a pair of Vise-Grip pliers to help prevent screws from loosening.

leads into the new properly sized circuit; solder the splice and protect it with heat-shrink tubing or, better yet, use the new waterproof barrel splices made by Anchor Electric (available from West Marine).

Speaking of splices, my favorite trick is to forget to put the heat shrink on the wire before I solder it. Susan says that this is because I am getting old, but Sarah thinks it's because my heat-shrink brain has been greatly reduced by three years of exposure to the tropical sun. Naturally, you wouldn't shorten any wire that has been calibrated by the manufacturer as are those on some antennae, depthfinder transponders, and other sensitive monitoring apparatus. In the case of critical components like bilge pumps, a far better practice is to just not use products that come with inadequate leads.

After all the wires in the circuit have been replaced, check for voltage drop once more. See? There it is right within acceptable limits. Doesn't that make you feel like you have accomplished something? And you have a lot more to show for your efforts than more efficient lights in the forepeak. You are now a functioning electrician and can use these same procedures to cure at least 90 percent of all your boat's electrical problems.

Test for stray voltage

Another test you should learn to do with your new multimeter is a stray-current test. When there is an electrical leak into a boat's ground or bonding system the damage to hardware caused by galvanic corrosion can be catastrophic. Even a tiny leak of a fraction of a milliamp can cause significant damage over time. Fortunately, the test for stray voltage is easy. First, pull all the fuses or turn off all the circuit breakers for every piece of equipment on the boat. With the battery switch or the isolation switch closed so that the battery is connected to the distribution panel, remove the positive battery cable from the battery and tap the cable end against the battery post. If there are any sparks at all (do it at night when you can see the sparks), you either have a solar panel that you forgot to disconnect (if it's daylight), a piece of equipment that is running still connected, or you have a leak to ground somewhere.

For a more comprehensive test, connect a multimeter to the circuit with the positive lead on the cable and the negative lead on the battery post and check for voltage by clicking through the voltage scales from the highest to the lowest. Any reading, even a fraction of a millivolt, means there is a leak somewhere between the battery and the open circuit breakers or fuses. To find it you will have to disconnect and reconnect every piece of wire that is connected to this section of the wiring system one at a time until the meter shows a zero reading.

If there is no reading (and there shouldn't be), reconnect the circuit breakers or fuses one at a time for each piece of equipment with the equipment itself turned off and check for voltage. (Don't connect the inverter, though, unless you know for certain just what you are doing.) If there is any reading, first make sure you are not on a memory circuit that is hot all the time (such as is found on bilge sniffers, some GPS and radar equipment, and most AM/FM automobile-type radios), and double check that the equipment is off. If you still have a reading you have a leak and will have to break the circuit at each terminal, starting with the one closest to the battery on the negative side, until the meter reads zero and you have isolated the leak.

A few hours spent looking for unwanted voltage drops and checking for stray voltage is a great way to get to know your new old boat and your new multimeter while performing an essential check of your electrical systems. If, after reading this, your manuals, and Nigel Calder's book, you still don't feel comfortable with DC electrical circuits, either take a course in basic electricity or ask among the local cruisers and try to find a friendly "sparkey" (all cruising sparkies are friendly) to show you how to do it. As a last resort, hire a pro, not to do the job but to show you how to do it. Electrical skills, like cooking skills, are among the most valuable you can have on a cruising sailboat and are well worth whatever it takes to acquire them. Eventually you will acquire the exalted title of "sparkey" yourself. Then, wherever you go you will find that you are one of the most popular cruisers in the harbor.

Batteries and Charging Systems

This is a subject that deserves its own chapter, and a book could easily be written about your batteries and the various ways of keeping them alive. Come to think of it, there are already several good books out there on the subject, and one of the best is the section on electrical systems in *Boatowner's Mechanical and Electrical Manual* by Nigel Calder, which I've already referred to several times. (No, I don't get a cut on the sale of this book, and I don't even know the guy who wrote it. It's just the best book ever written on marine maintenance is all.) So, if you will read this material, you will save me from repeating a lot of stuff that others have already covered a lot better than I could anyway. There are a few details on your 12-volt and charging system that are specific to the cruising life, however, so let's go over them here.

Batteries

For active cruising and liveaboard use you will need a lot of battery power. I'm not going to try to tell you how much because it will depend on your specific needs, but *Sultana* carries about 400 amp hours in the house banks for her modest array of electronics (which are listed in chapter 12), her refrigeration, and her somewhat greedy autopilot. Our starting battery is a 125 amp-hour heavy-duty (not a deep-cycle) truck battery, which is more than enough for our 50 hp Ford. In five years of cruising, we have never had to switch to the house banks to start the engine, which leads me to believe that the traditional battery selector switch is a vestige of another day when batteries, charging systems, and diesel engines were not as reliable as they are today. Thus, I am removing the selector switches and replacing them with simple two-position isolation switches (explained below) with no provision for cross-connecting to the house banks other than a handy pair of jumper cables.

A lot of simple and basic boats are out there with no refrigeration or radar or autopilots, and if you can be happy in this category, God bless your spare existence. Your need for batteries will be at a minimum, and it is a proven fact that if you can be happy without a lot of electrical gadgets on your boat, you will be a lot happier than those of us who can't be happy without them. It's too late for me, however; I like my autopilot, microwave oven, pop-up toaster, and all the other old familiar simple and basic amenities.

Regardless of your needs, you should have enough battery power to live comfortably without ever having to plug in to shore power. This means lots of amp-hours of capacity in the batteries and in the charging system. Batteries on a

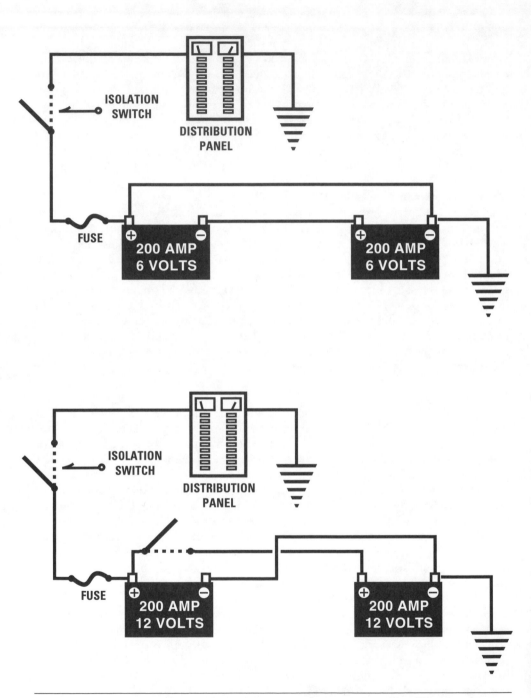

Each bank of two 6-volt, 200-amp-hour batteries wired in series yields 12 volts and 200 amp-hours *(left top)*; wiring two 12-volt, 200-amp-hour batteries in parallel yields 12 volts and 400 amps *(left bottom)*. Two banks of two 6-volt, 200-amp-hour batteries, each wired in series to

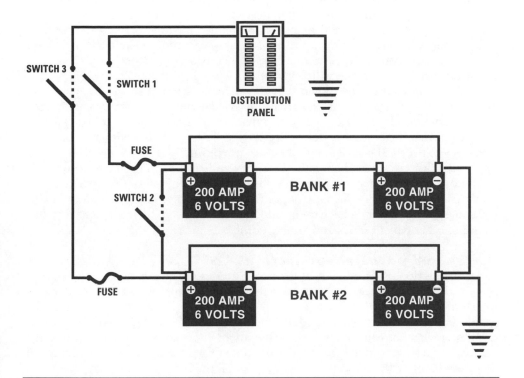

yield 12 volts and 200 amp-hours, can be combined in parallel to yield 12 volts and 400 amp-hours *(right)*. Closing either switch 1 or switch 3 alone delivers 12 volts and 200 amp-hours to the distribution panel. Closing switches 1 and 2 together delivers 12 volts and 400 amp-hours to the panel.

cruising boat should be of the wet cell type just because they are cheaper, more reliable, and more generally available than gel cells. Gel cells are a great idea for part-time cruisers who must leave their boats unattended for long periods and for day-sailors, but wet cells are the way to go for cruising sailors. The trick is to have enough capacity so that with normal use and considering static charging devices (solar panels) your batteries will never be discharged to below 12.5 volts.

All batteries must be tied down in their own locker separate from the engine compartment. Say that again . . . tied down. Got it? Tied down. There is no excuse for any cruising boat to have batteries, wet or dry, that are not isolated and TIED DOWN.

Regarding the type of batteries, we started out on *Sultana* with golf cart batteries, switched to 8Ds in Panama, and are now in the process of switching back to golf cart batteries, mostly because I'm sick and tired of trying to hoist those 8Ds in and out of the battery compartment. I only have to do it about twice a year, but moving an 8D is like moving a piano, only the piano is easier to lift. Golf cart batteries are per-amp-hour cheaper than 8Ds, and if you need more capacity, just clamp another pair in series and you've got it.

Series and parallel connection

Series connection (the terminals of the two batteries are connected positive to negative and positive to negative) increases the power or voltage of a battery bank by the sum of the voltage of all the batteries so connected. Thus, two 200-amp-hour 6-volt golf cart batteries connected in series equals one 200-amp-hour 12-volt battery bank. Parallel connection (the terminals of the two batteries are connected positive to positive and negative to negative) increases the capacity or amperage of a battery bank by the sum of the amperage of all the batteries so connected. Thus, two 200-amp-hour 12-volt batteries (or two banks of 6-volt batteries connected in series) connected in parallel equals one 400-amp-hour 12-volt battery bank.

This may sound confusing if you haven't encountered it before, but it is exactly how the battery banks on most cruising boats are wired, so it is important that you understand the principles. It is not really that hard. Read these few paragraphs through a few times, study the drawings, and you should have it.

Battery charging

One of the true joys of modern electronic innovation is found in the efficient charging devices that drastically shorten engine-running times even with an increase in battery capacity. In the good old days when we all had automobile alternators and mechanical regulators, the engine had to be run for hours just to keep the light in the head bright enough to find the top to the toothpaste. If you had any kind of refrigeration with the typical underinsulated ice box of the day, engine running was pretty much a full-time deal. Today, we run *Sultana*'s engine about three hours a day in the tropics, which gives us plenty of power from two Balmar 100-amp alternators with three-step electronic regulators and shunted gauges to let us monitor charging rates. Once we finish installing our new array of solar panels, I hope to cut that engine time in half.

One good trick on a cruising boat is to get rid of those old three-position battery switches and install three high-capacity toggle switches instead, one for each battery bank and one for crossover. These switches will give you more positive control than the old battery switch, and you are much less likely to leave the batteries connected by mistake. If you have dual alternators or one dual-output alternator, you can even get away without the crossover switch and just use a pair of jumper cables to start the engine from the house batteries if you have a battery failure (very rare if you take care of your batteries) and need the house bank to start the engine.

One thing we don't have on *Sultana* is a wind generator. They are dangerous and noisy, and we have found that there is no need for them if you have adequate solar panels and charging capacity. A good cruising friend, Captain Dick Bunker on the S/V *Sans Souci,* once sailed his dinghy into his wind generator in the Bahamas, and the ensuing fallout of busted wind generator and dinghy parts is still being talked about. Fortunately, parts of Captain Dick were noticeably absent from the debris—but only just.

The inverter

A good cruising boat needs a good inverter to convert batter power to AC voltage. We use a Pro Watt 1500 that supplies most of our 120-volt needs without breathing hard; it even works my pop-up toaster although it doesn't like it that much. During our New Zealand refit I added a second inverter, a Pro Watt 800, that produces 240-volt AC current just to handle the assortment of electrical stuff we have purchased in countries where this is the standard voltage. These Pro Watt units use the newer modified sine-wave technology that is a lot lighter and more efficient than the older square-wave sets of just a few years ago. The modified sine wave also lets you use microwave ovens and appliances with heating elements like pop-up toasters. A good inverter lets you use small electric fans from Wal-Mart or Sears that work a lot better than the 12-volt ones you buy in the marine stores, and they

A standard ground-fault circuit interrupter (GFCI) should be installed at the first receptacle in each AC circuit even if there is another on the inverter, generator, or shore power feed.

are a lot cheaper. Look for the ones that are made out of plastic with plastic blades and blade guards. They won't rust and they are easy to clean.

In addition to the main inverter, we have two or three of the small 100-watt units that plug into a cigarette lighter outlet. These are great for running low-demand items like the laptop computer upon which I'm writing this eloquent verbiage, Phillip's video games (no, you can't escape video games just by going cruising), and the portable stereo. Using these small units means that we don't have to activate the big unit when we only need a few amps. Just don't try to run your pop-up toaster on them.

Never forget that the household voltage from even a small inverter is lethal. If you install your own and you are not a qualified electrician, be sure to have it checked out by someone who is before you try to use it. Don't be lulled into complacency by the fact that most modern sets come with a ground-fault circuit interrupter (GFCI) already installed. These things are designed to automatically shut off the juice right after it kills you, thus ensuring the safety of those who come to claim your body; they are great to have but don't rely on them. Speaking of which, even if your inverter does have a GFCI, install another one as the first outlet in each circuit someplace where it will be easy to test, then test it every time you activate your set. GFCIs can fail closed so that you can have the juice without the protection. You need to push that test button every time you use your inverter.

Shore power

With a modern and efficient battery and charging system, you should never have any need for shore power. In fact, *Sultana* doesn't even have a shore-power outlet any more; I took it and the battery charger out.

The Engine

Assuming your surveyor has given your engine a clean bill of health, one of the first things you should do is to change the oil and filters. You should have an instruction manual for the engine; if it's missing, try to get one from the local dealer for the type of engine you have, and while you're there, order a shop manual and a parts list. These two things can save a world of grief if you need work done or parts in some faraway place.

The fuel system

Before you do anything else on your engine, first locate and identify all your fuel filters. Start with the primary fuel filter, which should be the first large filter between the fuel tank and the engine. It may have a glass water-separator bowl with a drain on the bottom, and it is probably made by Racor. If it isn't a Racor, consider changing it to one as soon as is practical. Racor filters are effective and filter elements are available everywhere there are cruisers; elements for other makes can be hard to find. While you are making the change, consider adding an inexpensive vacuum gauge to the outlet side of the filter or anywhere in the line between the primary and secondary filters. Any increase in vacuum reading in this gauge during normal engine running will indicate that the fuel pumps are laboring to draw fuel through the filter, which usually means that it is time to change the element.

After you have located the filter, cleaned the separator bowl, and changed the element in the primary filter, follow the fuel line until you find the secondary filter. It's usually smaller than the primary and located on the engine itself, and it is usually a spin-off type similar to, but smaller than, your auto oil filter. If it is the older canister type with an element inside a fuel-filled reservoir, consider changing the entire filter to the newer CAV type. They're easier to change, less messy, and their elements are readily available. While you are at the secondary filter, notice the two screws in the top that don't appear to be doing anything; there should be one each near the inlet and outlet couplings. These are your bleed screws and you will need them later.

Continue following the fuel line until it disappears into a little cylindrical protrusion, usually located on the side of the engine block, with a curious little lever on the bottom or side. This is the lift pump that supplies fuel to the injector pump. There may be a screen filter on the top of this pump that won't require cleaning unless you experience a major contamination of your fuel (such as when buying it in Mexico), but you should check it now just to get aquatinted with it.

The next item on the fuel line is the injector pump, which supplies fuel under high pressure to the injectors where it is vaporized and exploded into the force that spins the prop and drives you through the water when the winds fail to blow. The only thing you really need to know about this pump is where it is and where the bleed screws are located. Some of these pumps have a separate oil reservoir that needs to be topped off and changed when the engine oil is changed.

Bleeding the fuel lines

Once all the fuel filter elements have been changed or cleaned, you will need to bleed the system to get every last bubble of air out of the fuel lines. The bleed procedure varies with different engines, but generally it involves cracking the bleed screws—while operating that curious little lever we discovered earlier underneath the lift pump—until the bubbles stop and clear fuel runs out. This is a messy job and any attempts to catch the fuel are usually frustrated by all the other apparatus that get in the way, but try to catch it anyway. Start at the Racor filter and work toward the engine. Open the top of the filter case and fill the reservoir full of clean fuel. Then secure the top, making sure there is a good seal at the gasket. Move on to the secondary filter and crack the first bleed screw and pump until the bubbles stop. Tighten that screw and move to the next one and so on until you have bled them all. If your engine doesn't have bleed screws or if you can't find them, you can do the same job by cracking the coupling nuts at each fitting.

You may read in some cruising books about electric fuel pumps, in-line outboard-motor (bulb-type) pumps, or other gadgets that are supposed to make bleeding the fuel lines unnecessary. None of these that I know of worth the trouble; it's just one more thing to break, and it's guaranteed to break right when you need it the most. Bleeding the fuel lines should become a second-nature response to any engine failure, so just go ahead and get good at it; it's not that hard.

Congratulations! Once you have successfully bled your fuel system you know enough to fix about 85 percent of all diesel engine problems. When a diesel cranks at normal speed but won't start, you can almost bet air is getting into the fuel lines, and you can further bet that it is getting in through that little pump with the lever on the bottom. Make sure that the filter cover is tight and that the diaphragm isn't leaking. If that isn't it, check that all connections are tight (a cross-threaded connector is another source of air) and if that isn't it, check for restricted fuel lines.

The oil system

Failure to change the oil and oil filters probably does in more diesel engines than anything else. In fact, if you keep your fuel and oil clean and the engine running at the right temperature, you can expect many diesels to outlast you and your boat.

Changing the oil in a boat engine is essentially the same as changing the oil in an automobile engine except that the oil will usually have to be pumped out because there isn't enough room under the oil pan to drain it through the sump. Many newer engines have a built-in pump for removing the old oil, but most older ones can be pumped through the dipstick port. Several electric pumps are on the market that make this job easier or you can use most any hand pump with an intake hose small enough to fit into the opening. The best advice is to ask the previous owner how he or she did it, then do it the same way.

Changing the oil filter is a straightforward procedure provided, of course, that it is the spin-off type. If you don't have the spin-off type oil filter, consider changing it, and while you are at it, if the filter is in a hard-to-reach spot, like 99.99 percent of all marine oil filters are, consider installing a remote filter that is easier to reach. You need to make the oil-changing procedure as quick and easy as possible so you will never be tempted to delay the job when the time comes.

Change your filter every time you change the oil no matter what the manufacturer recommends. The filter might be fine but there is often nearly a liter of dirty oil in there we want to get rid of and besides, filters are cheap—bearings and piston rings are very expensive. There is no excuse for dirty oil or filters on a boat. While you are changing the oil, don't neglect the injector pump if it has a separate oil supply, and check the level of the transmission fluid while you are at it. Oh yeah, don't forget to clean and oil your air-intake filter now, too.

The cooling system

All you really need to know about your cooling system is how to check the fluid level, how to change the thermostat, and how to change the engine zincs. If you don't already know how to check the level of the cooling fluid in the header tank, you might want to reconsider your decision to go cruising or at least look around for a more mechanically inclined crew to take along.

The thermostat is usually a two-bolt-and-gasket affair located somewhere under the header tank. If your engine runs OK but takes a long time to reach operating temperature, it may mean your thermostat is stuck open; if it overheats and runs rough, it could mean it is stuck closed. Stuck open is OK and a nuisance at worst; stuck closed can be dangerous and lead to major repairs. Some cruisers in the tropics remove the thermostat to improve coolant flow, and if your engine runs a bit hot even with a functioning thermostat, this might be worth a try.

By the way, if you can't find your header tank, you may not have one. This would not be good news because it means your engine is cooled by raw water or, more unlikely, that you have an air-cooled engine. If you have a raw-water-cooled system it should have been called to your attention by your surveyor because, unless all your cruising is done in the Great Lakes, a raw-water-cooled engine will have a much shorter life expectancy than a freshwater-cooled engine. Of course, you shouldn't ever put only fresh water in your freshwater system—use cooling-system fluid from an auto parts store. I've only seen one air-cooled diesel on a boat, so I can't say too much about them except that the one I saw had more ductwork than a commercial air-conditioning unit, and it isn't something I'd ever want on *Sultana*.

Manufacturers delight in making engine zincs hard to find and harder to change. Your boat should have at least two zincs—one in the engine block somewhere where it will protrude into the water jacket, and another in the heat exchanger. There may be a third in your header tank. Check these zincs often and change them when they are about 25 percent gone. A rapid increase in the rate of deterioration in these zincs is a sure indication of electrical system leakage, and you must stop everything until you find what is causing it.

Be particularly diligent about your zincs while tied to a marina, even if you are not connected to shore power. Stray current from the boat next door can be climbing all over your boat without your ever knowing about it. The best advice is to avoid marinas altogether and anchor out with the real cruisers. The air is cleaner, the water is clearer, it's quieter, the companionship is more companionable, it's cheaper, you'll be doing what cruisers go cruising to do, and you can always get to the marina bar in the dinghy.

The raw-water system

The function of the raw-water system is to cool the coolant in the freshwater system, and on some boats, to cool the oil and transmission fluid (see above). Seawater is circulated through a large, coarse filter by an engine-driven pump, then through the heat exchanger and any other coolers, and then pumped into the exhaust system where it exits the boat through the exhaust pipe. Each of these elements is of critical concern to the cruiser, so let's go over them one at a time.

The raw-water filter

The raw-water filter should be located somewhere adjacent to your raw-water seacock where it is accessible and convenient; it should be fitted with a large glass sight bowl. Some cruisers install two raw-water filters on a Y-valve so if one becomes clogged with seaweed it is a simple matter to switch to the secondary filter without shutting down the engine. It is also important to operate the seacock at least once a week to make sure it's working because when a component in the raw-water system fails, it can sink the boat. Many fine yachts have been lost because a seacock was frozen open. The filter element needs to be cleaned whenever you can see foreign matter accumulating in it.

The raw-water pump

The raw-water pump is located on the engine right where the hose from the raw-water filter attaches. Most of these pumps have a rubber impeller that will self-destruct in about two seconds when the supply of seawater is shut off. It is critical that you keep a supply of these impellers on board and that you become skilled at changing them. If yours is a Jabsco pump, and it usually is, there will be six screws holding a flat plate onto the end of the pump that are removed to expose the impeller. Remove and replace this impeller now just to get familiar with the procedure. I can guarantee that when you really need to change that impeller, you will need to change it quickly and you won't have time to mess around with an engine instruction manual.

Every time an impeller fails it sheds a few blades that will be forced downstream to lodge where they can restrict the flow of raw water. You should follow the line and look for traps where these stray blades can hang up. Elbows and sharp bends in the line are likely places; some smaller bits will make it to the heat exchanger. Don't be tempted to leave these broken-off impeller pieces in the system because, even if they are not doing any harm now, they can become dislodged and move to a new address where they will start to raise hell right when you least need it.

The heat exchanger

The heat exchanger is the marine equivalent of the automobile radiator and it works on the same principle except that excess heat is carried away by water instead of by air. Raw water circulates through tubes in the exchanger that are surrounded by coolant from the freshwater system that is being circulated by the engine's water pump. You already know where the heat exchanger is located because you had to find it to change the zincs. Some heat exchangers have removable plates that give access to the cores that can be cleaned using a bronze cleaning brush designed for cleaning rifle bores. Usually a .30 caliber brush will do the job, but if you have a larger or smaller caliber heat exchanger, the guy at the gun store can help you find the right size.

The only other thing you need to know about heat exchangers is that they are critical to an engine's operation and that they are prone to unannounced failure. Heat exchangers are a lot like rigging in that the older they get the more likely they are to fail when you need them most. They can fail without giving any warning, and a failure can be catastrophic. We had ours let go in the Cook Islands where it soaked the engine compartment with a fine high-pressure spray of seawater. Before we discovered the problem it ruined a $600 Balmar alternator. After a dozen tries at a temporary patch we just gave up on the engine and hoisted the sails. We were able to reach Pago Pago although it took awhile when the wind died for a solid week. The total bill for replacement parts came to more than $1,000, all because of a pinhole leak that was barely visible when the engine wasn't running. (One good thing about Pago Pago, perhaps the only good thing, is that they have great UPS service from West Marine. OK, so there is a good Costco grocery store, too.)

Many cruisers carry a spare heat exchanger, and it's a good idea to install a new one just before you leave on your cruise, then keep the old one as an emergency spare. That's just what we're going to do—next time.

Sea Trials

Chances are you took your new old boat out for a trial sail before you bought it, but it really doesn't matter. I am convinced that unless you are experienced in the type of boat you are buying, the pre-purchase sea trial is a classic case of form versus function and is not that important anyway. Boats exhibit such a wide variety of behavior under sail that it is difficult to make any judgment on the sailing characteristics of any one type of boat until you have covered many miles of ocean in it. Your surveyor would have used the sea trial to check out the engine, rig, and the sails, and to check for any obvious structural defects—but once around the harbor is plenty of time for most surveyors to do this. Even if you went along, it is doubtful you learned that much. It's hard to spot problems when your eyes are full of stars and your imagination has you dropping anchor next to the ghost of Captain Cook's *Endeavor* in Moorea Lagoon instead of returning to the dock at Podunk Creek.

Once the boat is yours, however, you're going to need to learn how to drive it, and the first thing to learn is how to bring it into dock. The crew of *Sultana* has evolved a foolproof method for docking. Sarah takes the bow with the bow line ready to throw, Phillip stands on the midship rail with the springline, and Susan stands next to the pilothouse where she can keep an eye on things. As honorary captain, I am at the wheel. We begin our approach from about 100 yards out and at a 45 degree angle to the dock. When Susan yells "Lookout, we're going to crash," I know it's time to throttle back and start to lose way. When she screams "Arrrraghhhh," and covers her eyes with her hands, I shift to neutral and start to turn the bow away from the dock. When she falls to the deck and covers her head with her arms, I put it in reverse, put the wheel hard over opposite the direction I want to move the stern, and punch in a good jolt of power. The old boat drifts into the dock as gently as an oak leaf drifts to the ground in an autumn breeze. When the fenders touch the dock, Phillip steps ashore with the springline, and Sarah either passes the bow line to a bystander or waits until Phillip can come and get it. I shut down the engine, secure the stern line, then reassure Susan that we have miraculously survived another landing. The crew works together like a well-practiced drill team, and we never (well, practically never) fail to impress the dockside hangarounders.

This technique works every time, but it wasn't always that easy. We left a series of gouged docks and loosened pilings from Marblehead to Key West while we practiced. My favorite trick was to forget about the bowsprit, which I can't see from the cockpit, and use it to either sweep the dock clear of all bystanders or get it trigged between two pilings; I've even made several attempts at removing dock-side fuel pumps using this procedure. Fortunately, we never did any serious damage to anything more important than the skipper's pride, but if someone had been along with a camera, we would have been a hit on that TV show that features the world's most embarrassing videos.

Our docking procedure works for us, but unless you have a crewmember with Susan's remarkable depth perception, you will have to develop your own technique, and the time to do it is now, not after you get underway. The first thing to do is to motor around the harbor a few times making tight turns to port and starboard. Then try the same thing in reverse and notice how well the bow tracks the stern. You should notice the boat moving slightly sideways while in reverse, depending on which way the prop is turning (to port with a clockwise prop and to starboard with a counter-clockwise prop) and you can learn to use this movement to great advantage when docking. Once you have a good feel for the boat under power, find a remote dock somewhere where there aren't a lot of bystanders and practice approaching and leaving. Even if you are an experienced skipper, you will find that all boats respond to the controls in different ways, and you will need practice before you master this important technique.

Once you have mastered the boat under power you can take her out of the harbor and try sailing. Pick a good day with a gentle breeze and flat seas, and start gradually with a simple reach. If you are new to sailing, it would be a good idea to have a friend who is experienced with your size of boat. A dinghy skipper might be fun to have on board but isn't going to be a lot of help. If you can get the previous owner to go along for the first few trips, that would be ideal. Sailing a large sailboat is not a difficult thing to learn how to do, there is little need to learn complicated maneuvers, and after just a few trials, you will start to feel like an old hand.

Heavy weather

One of the important bullets all bluewater cruisers have to bite is learning to handle heavy weather. Our coastal cruising brethren can deal with big waves and high wind by scuttling into port and would be quite foolish not to seek shelter when the weather turns nasty, but you are not always going to have that luxury. I can recall one instance when we were becalmed after leaving the Tuamotus on a particularly clear and brilliant day and watching a most mammoth and spectacular frontal system approaching from the south. It was a solid wall of ominous black misery that stretched from one horizon to the other. It promised to make a sincere attempt at blowing our socks off and there was no way we could avoid it. When the front hit, the winds rose from zero to about 50 knots in just a few minutes and the waves built to the point that they were washing the decks. By the time the first gusts hit, however, we had everything secured, were safely hove-to, and were down below engrossed in a lively game of Monopoly. (Phillip plays Monopoly with a ruthless disregard for anything but winning and refuses to quit until he has acquired every last hotel and property, has wiped out everyone, and has left the board in a hopeless shambles. He should do just fine in international finance once he gets ashore.)

As you become more and more familiar with your boat you should take advantage of every opportunity to learn how she handles when the gales start to howl. Then, instead of scuttling back into port when the winds rise, sail offshore where there is a little sea room and practice your heavy-weather maneuvers. Don't wait until there is a full gale in force, but watch for the small-craft warnings to go up and start practicing in 20 to 25 knots of wind before you venture out into anything stronger. Foul weather can be a terrifying experience for the uninitiated and a bad experience in a storm has turned many would-be cruisers into dedicated landlubbers.

There are four commonly accepted methods of handling nasty weather: lying ahull, heaving to, running off, and lying to a sea anchor or drogue. These are all important enough to warrant our going over them one at a time.

Lying ahull

Lying ahull is the simplest of the four maneuvers and, depending on your boat, may be one of the most useful. All you do is take down every scrap of sail, lash the helm in the neutral position, and go below to enjoy the ride. All boats ride differently when left to their own devices. *Sultana,* like most full-keel boats, tends to ride beam to the sea, which means she wallows a lot if the wind against the rigging isn't strong enough to impart stability. In about 35 knots of wind she lies ahull very nicely with little rolling noticed below. With the wind less than 35 knots, putting up just a scrap of mizzen turns her into the wind and greatly improves the ride even though it could be argued that we are no longer lying ahull. Full-keel boats will often ride better than those of other designs, and deep fin keels can be deadly. Of all the boats dismasted in the notorious 1994 Queen's Birthday storm between New Zealand and Fiji, most were fin-keel boats that broached, tripped on their keels, and rolled. It is important that you learn how your boat will ride the waves and wind with no sails set, so give it a try in 20 to 30 knots of wind. Make sure you have plenty of sea room, of course, and don't try it in shipping lanes.

Heaving to

Heaving to is a little more complicated and a little more work than lying ahull, but it is a much more useful maneuver, is usually safer, and nearly always more comfortable. Once again, each boat will react with its own characteristics, so it is critical that you practice before you leave on your cruise. Generally it involves flying just enough sail to impart stability and keep the boat moving into the wind at headway speed. Usually a scrap of jib is sheeted against the wind (backed), the deeply reefed main or the trysail is sheeted nearly flat, and the rudder is lashed or locked to windward. The idea is to get the boat to move forward, then round gently into the wind until the main stalls enough for the jib to push the bow back to lee, filling the main and starting the cycle all over again. On *Sultana* this means a backed storm jib and a double-reefed main and a furled mizzen with the wheel lashed hard to windward, but it is bound to be different for your boat. This procedure is nowhere as difficult as it sounds and you should have it down pat in one or two practice sessions.

Again, light displacement boats with fin keels are miserable creatures to get to heave to. They usually respond to attempts to trim the sails by alternately broaching and luffing. If you have one of these boats, you may find that this particular maneuver doesn't work and you will be safer running before the wind.

In practice, the time to heave to, or lay ahull for that matter, is any time you become uncomfortable sailing the boat or when you need some rest. Never wait until the situation deteriorates to the point of being dangerous before you take action to protect yourself and your boat.

Running before the wind

Running before the wind is just what it says, and was the favorite foul-weather maneuver with the old square-riggers. All you need do is take in the sails and steer the boat in the direction in which the wind wants you to go. The trick is to maintain just enough speed to soften the effects of a following sea without the hull surfing down the forward slope of the wave as it passes. Often it helps to drag an anchor or another drogue on a long warp off the stern at least two wave lengths behind the boat. Some light displacement boats don't run well because they are difficult to keep from surfing and broaching in the troughs. We have never used this technique on *Sultana* because we have never needed it, but I can envision us using it as a last resort.

Life's a drag

Well, not really, but if you want to get a lively discussion going among any group of bluewater sailors, bring up the subject of sea anchors and drogues then sit back and enjoy the fireworks. The first argument . . . er, discussion . . . will be over the definition of these two devices. One group will maintain that sea anchors are always deployed off the bow and drogues are always deployed off the stern. Thus a sea anchor deployed off the stern becomes a drogue and vice versa.

The second and equally vocal group will insist it is a matter of size. A sea anchor is large and intended to stop the boat cold, as a normal anchor would do, or as nearly so as possible. A drogue, on the other hand, is much smaller than a sea anchor and is intended to slow the boat to manageable speeds and improve maneuverability. I, of course, as a trained journalist (I took Journalism 101 in college and quite nearly passed) remain completely neutral here even though I do admit to a slight list toward the brilliant arguments of the second group. For our purposes you can deploy a sea anchor anywhere you like, even from the head handle, and it remains a sea anchor. A drogue is a drogue no matter how it's dragged. Deploying a drogue off the bow in anything but moderate conditions (when it will act like a sea anchor and stop the boat) is considered bad form by most bluewater sailors. Without adequate resistance, the small drogue can allow the boat to move backwards with the wind, which can impart unacceptable stress to the rudder even at slow speeds.

Regardless of what you call these two devices, they are both designed to either slow or stop your boat under extreme conditions and the proper use of either involves the highest degree of seamanship and heavy-weather experience. Sea anchors and drogues are extremely complicated devices and the dynamics they set up when deployed are often misunderstood by experienced sailors. Sea anchors and drogues are most often deployed under extreme conditions of high winds and huge seas, conditions that can be terrifying to even an old hand. A novice faced with these conditions and the need to deploy a hundred pounds or so of complicated gear from a heaving wet deck is in a tough spot to say the least. Fortunately, few of us who confine our cruising to the middle latitudes seldom encounter these conditions so we don't need these devices often, and the majority of cruising boats don't carry them. Lightweight high-tech boats (especially multihulls) need them more often than a heavy boat with a traditional full- or semi-full keel.

Right now *Sultana* does not have either a sea anchor or a drogue aboard, but this deficiency is constantly under review. My problem with them (other than their cost—about $200 for a drogue and $500 for a sea anchor) is the amount of room they take up in the cockpit lockers. For example, a Jordan Series Drogue for a boat of our size requires a minimum of 100 meters of ¾-inch line (more is better), a 25-pound anchor, a buoy, and a trip line. That is a lot of stuff to keep handy when you will probably only need it once every 10 years. However, if we ever decide to sail offshore higher than 45 degrees north or south latitude, we will most certainly have one or both aboard.

With the above second definition fresh in our minds, let's review these two sea brakes one at a time.

Drogues

Technically, a drogue is anything you can throw overboard secured to a line (warp) that will create drag and slow the boat's progress. A drogue can be one or more long warps of line, your anchor and rode, an unused sail, buckets, or anything else you can induce to go over the side and stay attached to the boat. Commercial drogues are currently available in three general types: the delta drogue, which, as the name implies, is shaped like a triangle; the series drogue, which is a long line festooned with cloth buckets that look and act like underwater wind socks; and the parachute drogue, which is shaped like a small parachute. All three types have their vocal advocates, which leads me to suspect that any of the three types will do the job if deployed correctly.

Drogues are normally streamed from the stern and the most common use for them is to slow the boat when running before the wind under bare poles. They also are supposed to keep the longitudinal axis of the boat perpendicular to the wave crests, offering minimal surface area to an overtaking wave. The danger is that a boat under bare poles (particularly a light boat with a fin keel) will build speed to the point where it wants to broach as it races down the face of a large following sea or it wants to jump off the top of a sea that is being overtaken. In either case, the drogue is designed to slow the boat enough to prevent these things from happening.

Drogues pose several dangers over and above the complicated deployment procedures. Unless the drogue is perfectly matched to the boat, it can cause the boat to yaw and sail back and forth on the face of a wave; in so doing it can actually increase the danger to the boat. Many users of drogues report a loss of rudder control, and I have heard one firsthand report from a skipper who had to cut the drogue free to save his boat when the drogue caused a broach in a heavy sea. Another obvious problem is that with the stern held into the seas there is an increased tendency for the cockpit to fill with water. One can only imagine what would happen with the sugar-scoop sterns currently in vogue with the racing set. These two problems point to a third, more insidious, problem: until you practice these techniques you will have no way of knowing how your boat will react to them, and it is almost impossible to practice because the severe conditions that are needed just aren't encountered that often. Practice under moderate conditions is always a good idea, but bear in mind that your boat is going to take on a whole new personality when the weather gets nasty enough to need a drogue.

There are a few other uses for drogues that don't involve heavy weather. They are a good way to steer a boat that has suffered damage to the rudder. To do so, stream a small drogue from the stern on a bridle so that pressure on one or the other of the lines will direct the boat. Drogues can also be deployed to help hold a position outside a harbor while waiting for the weather to clear or for daylight to enter, and they can be streamed behind a boat being towed to keep it from riding up on the stern of the tow vessel. A great trick when towing a dinghy in a sea is to drag a small drogue (a small plastic pail on a bridle with a short section of chain added for a weight works well) behind the dinghy.

Sea anchors

Sea anchors are just like drogues only bigger. They are usually shaped like a large parachute. In fact, many boats carry a surplus military or cargo parachute as an economical sea anchor. One popular design is shaped like a deep parachute made of webbing to limit resistance and reduce the shock to the warp. Many products sold as drogues will make fine sea anchors if you simply buy one that is one or two sizes larger than the one recommended for your boat.

Sea anchors are usually deployed off the bow and are large enough to practically stop the boat, or at least slow it to a half knot or so. Since they are anchors in every sense of the word, all the rules for normal anchoring with your standard ground grabber apply. You will need adequate warp with 100 meters being about minimum. If you deploy with your all-chain rode as a warp, you will need an adequate snubber, and catenary is just as important as when you are ground anchoring in a storm. All the cautions listed above for drogues is true in spades for sea anchors: they are complex devices, difficult to deploy properly, and even more difficult to predict and understand without actually using one in severe conditions.

The big danger in using a sea anchor in severe conditions is that it will not be big enough to stop your boat or slow it to a safe speed. Thus, many boats have found themselves proceeding downwind backward, which can be scary under the best of conditions. The forces on the rudder can break the lashings (the rudder is always lashed in neutral when deploying a sea anchor) or even break the steering mechanism so the rudder slams hard over and causes a broach. Rudders have also been lost, which may just be the more desirable thing to happen under these conditions.

The idea of deploying a sea anchor outside a harbor to wait for tide change or daylight to enter safely is, I believe, another example of cruising mythology that is never actually practiced by anyone in the cruising community. Deploying and retrieving a sea anchor is an enormous amount of work, and I can't see anyone doing it just to keep the boat stationary for a few hours—not when there are lots of easier options such as sailing in circles under reduced sail, lying ahull, or just drifting for a while. Deploying close to land with any current running would certainly be a bad idea. Furthermore, if a large ship should come along while you are tethered to a sea anchor off the mouth of a busy harbor, you could find yourself in a dire situation where you had to cut loose a lot of expensive gear to save your boat. I have never heard of such a thing happening, which further reinforces my belief that cruisers simply don't do this sort of thing.

Reducing sail

OK, so there are five heavy-weather techniques instead of four, but reducing sail is not really a heavy-weather maneuver. You will learn to reduce sail for many reasons, including to slow the boat enough to time the arrival at your destination at dawn so you aren't hanging around the mouth of a dangerous harbor in the dark, or to make the boat a little more comfortable. A boat that booms along with the rail under day after day will get there a lot quicker than one sailed with a more vertically inclined mast, but the crew will be worn to a frazzle by the experience and the captain might just end up sailing as a singlehander some day.

Some boats still rely on hanked-on jibs, which are changed every time the sail area must be reduced or increased. This can be a dangerous procedure for two reasons. One is obvious to anyone who has ever changed a headsail in a heavy sea and high wind; keeping the thing under control and yourself on board the boat throughout the procedure is a definite art. If the headsail is out at the end of a long bowsprit where it belongs, changing it becomes even more dramatic. Being washed off the foot ropes while working headsails was often the cause of a premature trip through the pearly hatchway for thousands of sailors in the old days, and it can still happen today. Under the best of conditions, fumbling with those little bronze hanks with numb fingers while green water is breaking over the bow is not one of the joys of cruising we read so much about.

For these reasons and others, roller-reefing headsails are almost universal these days. *Sultana* will have both headsails on oversized roller-reefing gear when she next gets her shiny new bottom wet, and it is not uncommon to see boats with three roller-reefing rigs forward of the main mast. On the big-money boats, motor-driven reefing systems are becoming common even on the main and mizzen. Not that roller-reefing systems don't present their own set of dangers. Once in a mild blow on the way to the Marqueses, we were sailing with *Sultana*'s big genoa reefed down to a nub and a double reef in the main when the reefing line pulled out of its jam cleat, thereby releasing the entire 320-square-foot sail. We got it under control quickly enough, but not without a great deal of excitement, and it could have taken the mast down if the wind had been a little stronger. The lesson here, of course, is to never trust jam cleats—run the reefing line through the jam cleat, take three turns around a winch, then secure the line to a regular cleat. You might need the turns around the winch to help if you need to take in more sail, and if the jam cleat does slip, you will need the winch to get the line off the regular cleat. The best policy is probably not to reef headsails in heavy weather. *Sultana* will have her 320-square-foot 130-percent Genoa on the forestay and the 175-square-foot staysail on the baby stay. We should be able to use the big Genoa by gradually reducing the area until the winds reach about 20 knots, then roll it up and run out the staysail, which, because of its low center of gravity, is a good heavy-weather sail. When the winds reach 40 knots, it's time for the storm jib, which laces over the rolled-up staysail.

When to reduce sail is always a dilemma for cruising sailors, and the old saying that the time to reduce sail is when you first think about it doesn't work for us nervous types who think about it all the time. Reduce sail before the sail reduces you, is a more appropriate way to look at it. Anyway, reducing sail is a pain in the butt and there is a natural inclination to avoid it until the last minute, which can be dangerous, of course; if you reduce sail too early and find yourself lolling along at 2 or 3 knots in a fresh breeze, you're going to feel like a fool.

On *Sultana* our standard procedure is to reduce sail at the first sign of a rising wind, sit there going nowhere for about an hour, then shake the reefs out just in time to get clobbered by a half gale. I have the added problem of what I call the Sarah factor. Sarah likes to go fast, and she firmly believes that the proper place for the sails is up and the normal place for the lee rail is about 6 inches under the sea. Every time I decide to slow down by taking in sails, I have to contend with, "Aw dad, what are you doing that for? We were just starting to get going."

Once you get your new old boat in the water and move aboard, get ready for a long period of adjustment and learning before you are comfortable. Be patient and your boat will eventually learn all your wants and needs and idiosyncrasies and will gradually transform itself into everything you ever wanted a cruising boat to be. It will become your home and when that happens, you are cruising at last.

11

FOOD
AND THE CRUISING GALLEY

"We can cruise without poetry, music and art;

We can cruise without conscience, and cruise without heart;

We may cruise without friends; we may cruise without books;

But civilized cruisers can't cruise without cooks."

—Apologies to Owen Meredith, "Lucile"

The Most Important Part of the Boat

In the first chapter of this book, I enraged traditionalists and about 75 percent of active cruisers by stating (and proving by the force of logic) that the cruising boat isn't as important to the cruising life as most people think it is. That being so, what is the most important part of the boat? The engine? Of course not. Lots of boats don't have engines. How about the rig and sails? Close, but wrong again. "The galley," shouts the cook with the flour-smudged nose in the back of the room—and the cook is always right. No part of any cruising boat is anywhere nearly as important as the galley because no other single thing has as much of an impact on our contentment, stamina, mental outlook, and general sense of well-being as the food we eat. A cruising crew can be wet, cold, tired, and lonely, but if they have recently enjoyed a decent meal they will be ready to wrestle tigers. Conversely, a crew that is rested, dry, and warm, but hungry, will be largely worthless until fed. Centuries ago, some military megalomaniac who was fond of coining clichés observed that an army marched on its stomach. We can revise that to say that cruisers float on their bellies, and while it doesn't work as a cliché, it's true.

The quality of your diet will reflect the quality of your cruise more than any other single element of your daily routine. Regular meals of wholesome, nutritious, and tasty food makes cruising—nay, life itself—a joy, and food is much more than mere nutrition. Mealtimes, or at least one meal a day, should be social events where the crew gathers to discuss the events of the past, to plan and speculate on the events to come, and to confess fears and doubts and ambitions. Eating should be a cultural experience because nothing else you can do, besides learning the local language, will better put you in tune with the inhabitants of the lands you visit than eating the local foods.

The French cruisers you will meet on your journeys have a well-deserved and hard-earned reputation for holding the rest of us in haughty disdain. They are convinced that they are superior to cruisers from any other country because they eat so much better than the rest of us. The most distressing thing about this arrogance is that it's true; the French really are superior to the rest of the world. Eat a few meals aboard a typical French cruising boat and you'll find out why.

Can the cans

In spite of the lucid manner in which I present my case, not everyone agrees with my argument that to cruise well one must eat well, and many cruisers, particularly singlehanders, subsist entirely on canned food. This may be the very reason why singlehanders are singlehanders. Eating from cans is almost a cruising tradition, but it is one that dates back to the days when there were no grocery stores in the jungle and onboard refrigeration was considered as frivolous as onboard air-conditioning is considered today. Nearly all the old cruising books and a distressing number of new ones contain extensive narratives about laying in several years supply of canned goods, then spending a month or so removing the labels, marking the contents with a magic marker, and even lacquering the cans to keep them from rusting. Then there are usually another few paragraphs about the best ways to inventory the cache of cans and how to store them in the bilge. And while this sort of nonsense may have been necessary in the good old days, it is mostly a waste of time in these better new days in which you and I do our cruising.

For short-term cruisers who are too lazy to learn the principles of cooking, and racing crews who love to regale the folks back home with tales of how dreadful the onboard food was, the traditional canned stew, raviolis in that glutinous red syrup they call tomato sauce, and various objects that began life as vegetables are standard fare, but most canned food is dreadfully unhealthy. Even the favorites like tuna fish and corned beef contain heaps of chemicals and fat with hardly a trace of nutrition—just read the cans. Canned soups, sardines, and beans are handy for quick meals during rough passages; canned tomatoes are necessary for Captain Garlic's world-famous spaghetti sauce (see below); and canned corn, meats (chicken and tuna), mushrooms, and peas add interest to stews and goulash, but beyond that, try to limit the stuff you eat out of cans. Canned goods are available everywhere, so just buy enough to get you to the next stop and don't worry about the label falling off. Get rid of any cans that show signs of rust, and always listen for the little puff of air that signals the integrity of the vacuum seal. No puff of air, don't eat the food. It isn't worth taking a chance with botulism and food poisoning.

With 90 percent of all passages lasting less than two weeks, there is no excuse for a crew not having plenty of fresh wholesome produce on board at all times. I'm not saying that canned food isn't a boon to the cruising chef, but to overdepend on canned goods is unhealthy, unappetizing, and unnecessary. Too many cruisers waste too much time learning esoteric things about sailing, such as the relative merits of various brands of chart plotters or watermakers, when what they really need to learn is how to make a good omelet.

Provisioning myths

Some time ago I read an article in a cruising magazine about the correct way to provision a boat for a six-week Caribbean cruise. The article was illustrated with a photo of all the necessary foodstuffs, more than $2,000 worth, spread out on the dock. It covered all the standard cruising lore about coating your eggs with Vaseline, turning the big ends up, wrapping all the potatoes and onions in newspaper, marking all the cans with a magic marker so the contents can be identified when the labels rot off, and washing all the vegetables in bleach water to rid them of germs and cockroaches.

Unless you are intent on exploring the few remaining areas of the world that are truly remote, none of this nonsense is necessary. There are few, if any, areas in the popular cruising routes where good produce and foodstuffs are not available, and many previously primitive areas now sport modern grocery stores. We have bought Skippy peanut butter in the jungles of Honduras and Kellogg's Corn Flakes on Nuku Hiva, and the closest we have ever come to a food shortage was in Bora Bora when Susan couldn't find any pimento-stuffed olives for my martinis. *Sultana*'s rule of thumb is to have enough food for any passage so we can be out twice as long as we expect to be without resorting to emergency rations. That means a two-month maximum food supply for the one-month passage from the Galapagos to Nuku Hiva in the Marquesas.

Attempting to have large food stores on a boat guarantees wastage and spoilage that will drive the cost of your meals way beyond what you will save by buying in quantity in the population centers. The exception is for staples such as flour, sugar, baking powder, cooking oil, and such that can be bought in quantity for convenience and economy, not because they won't be available in the places you will be visiting. Even in the most expensive areas (and the most expensive place on earth to eat has to be French Polynesia) you will not save enough money to warrant the aggravation of trying to lay in supplies for anything longer than the next passage.

One large ketch we met in the Pacific had stocked up on beer and Coke and packed several cases of each in the bilge. A small amount of seawater got aboard, and when the crew reached Nuka Hiva, they had a bilge full of empty cans. The seawater had induced galvanic corrosion that had eaten a tiny hole in each can. All of the liquid had drained into the bilge, where it was pumped overboard without their ever being aware that anything was amiss. In Rangiroa Lagoon we met a German boat that had stocked up with two dozen cases of beer and several cases of rum in Panama; halfway across the Pacific the demons of the night visited the skipper, strongly suggesting that further indulgence in intoxicating liquids would rapidly bring his cruising plans to a halt. He heard the word and swore off the stuff; for several weeks thereafter he ran a mini-liquor store off the stern of his boat trying to get rid of his cargo—which was a great boon to the cruising community. (Your temperate but thirsty author scored two cases of Heineken out of the deal.) It was also, though, a very foolish thing to do. The French take their import restrictions on alcohol very seriously, and the mind boggles to think of what might happen to any yachtie, not to mention a German yachtie, caught selling illegally imported booze.

A word about roaches: "yuck"

Cockroaches come in three sizes: little, big, and gigantic. The closer you get to the equator the more gigantic and more numerous they become. Entomologists tell us that roaches are harmless, intelligent by bug standards, and ubiquitous; they are clean, carry no diseases (as do mosquitoes); don't eat enough to cause food short-ages (as do locusts); don't contaminate the food on which they nibble (as do flies); and don't make loud noises that keep you awake at night (as do crickets). What, then, you might ask, is all the fuss about? If you believed all you read about cock-roaches, you would welcome them aboard like old friends and thrill to the sight of their cute little pumpkin-seed bodies scampering around on your countertop, just like a bird-watcher thrills to the sight of buntings and finches hopping about on the birdfeeder back home.

In spite of the overwhelming evidence that indicates cockroaches should be our friends, we don't welcome them aboard at all. In fact, we will do just about anything short of burning the boat to get rid of the disgusting little vermin. With all their redeeming qualities, they have only one bad one and that is that they are one of the most revolting creatures on earth. It may be the squishy-crunchy sound they make when you step on them with your bare feet on the way to the head in the middle of the night, or the way they splatter all over your face when you swat one that you mistake for a mosquito that has landed on your nose just as you are falling asleep, or it might even be the guilty and sneaky way they scurry off the left-overs when you flick on the light. I, however, think the real reason we hate and persecute these harmless little insects is a moralistic one; I mean, any creature that can produce 20 to 40 offspring from a single coupling just has to be wicked, amoral, and a poor role model for our children.

Whatever the reasons, all cruisers hate them with a passion bordering on fa-naticism, but the sad, tragic fact is that there is nothing you can do about them. They are a fact of the cruising life just like roily harbors and crooked port captains. You can fumigate the boat with noxious chemicals potent enough to destroy all life (except cockroaches) in a 5-mile radius, you can layer the bottoms of your lockers with boric-acid-balls made from secret recipes (which cruisers pass around the way salespeople pass around dirty jokes), you can buy as many Roach Motels as you'll find in the Miami suburbs, and you can repackage everything you buy into steril-ized plastic containers before you bring it aboard, but the only thing you can hope to accomplish by all this activity is to keep their multitudes in check. Roaches get onto your boat mostly by hiding in your clothing and flying aboard at night, so short of stripping naked every time you come aboard and enclosing the entire craft in mosquito netting, there isn't much you can do. The buggy little buggers have you beat before you start.

While I'm on the subject of cockroaches, there is one more bit of cruising lore that I must dispense with, and that is the balderdash that you must remove all food from cardboard containers before bringing it aboard. The lore-makers say this is necessary because cockroaches like to lay their eggs on cardboard boxes; therefore, removing the food from the containers will somehow prevent the beastly beasts from getting aboard. I have even read that you are supposed to throw away your cardboard egg cartons.

For one thing, the two most common species of cockroach found on boats (the German, which are the little brown ones, and the American, which are the big black ones) both lay their eggs in egg cases that are carried for a while in the ab-domen of the female then dropped. They are loose and never fastened to anything. These egg cases are large enough to be seen with even a cursory inspection and are a lot easier to remove from a box than the contents of the box. For another thing, while you are doing all this work there is probably a big fat cockroach watching the whole process from under your hat brim.

Removing food and other items from cardboard containers is always a good idea when it is convenient and when the container isn't going to be used, but it is a bit silly when it involves boxes of powdered condiments or pancake flour or many other items better left in a box. Unpackaging merchandise on the dock is a routine part of the shopping ritual that most cruisers follow, but it is to get rid of the trash before it comes aboard the boat, not to get rid of cockroaches.

I'm not saying you should learn to like cockroaches, nor would I expect you to ever get used to finding their crunchy little carcasses in your green salad. But of you could develop a slight toleration for them rather than screeching like a stepped-on cat and trying to swat them with the frying pan every time one comes in sight (as does one person I know rather well but who, for the sake of domestic tranquillity, will remain unnamed), you and your shipmates will be much happier.

Eat the local food
Cruisers who strive to eat the same diet they eat at home and don't learn about and sample local foods miss a large part of the joy of cruising, and I put these cruisers in the same category as those who make no effort to learn the language of the lands they visit. They are cruisers in body, not in spirit. Anytime you find yourself in a strange and exotic port, you should make every effort to sample the local food no matter how strange and exotic it might appear at first. There are, of course, some foods that no matter how broad-minded you are, you won't find to your liking, and you will even find some, like trepang (an appalling glop made from sea cucumbers) and Chicken McNuggets (have you ever looked inside a Chicken McNugget?) that are quite revolting. This is particularly true in places like China and California where the cultural differences are the most pronounced and where their normal fare may seem strange to your more sensitive palate.

The point is, of course, that the only way to tell which foods you are going to like and which you are likely to leave in the alley gutter is by trying them all. When I was in Japan as a young man in the early 60s, I horrified my American friends by eating raw fish and slurping raw eggs from the shells. I decided to forgo the raw eggs (yuck), but I developed a passion for sushi and sashimi that is with me to this day.

A few specifics
In Central America you will find delicacies like iguana and *tepesquintal* (a jungle rodent about the size of a large rabbit) on the menus of the better restaurants, along with more normal viands like *caballo* (horse meat) and a large assortment of unidentifiable seafood. Don't leave Mexico without trying the *cabria assado* (grilled goat), and when in the Rio Dulce don't miss *piscados fritadas* (a small local fish), a delicacy that is fried to a crisp on oil-drum skillets by street vendors.

The real joy of eating anywhere in the tropics is the assortment of exotic fruits and vegetables you will encounter. Some, like passion fruit and papaya, you will recognize from the desiccated samples that make it to the North American markets, but many others will be brand-new. Even familiar foods like pineapples and watermelon will take on new dimensions when purchased fresh from the native farmers who grew them. If you think you know what coconuts and bananas are, just wait until you sample the real thing. The little red bananas that some call *dedos de miel* (honey fingers) in South America, and ladies fingers in Australia, are seldom found in markets anywhere and are usually given as a gift by the farmer, and the milk from an unripened coconut is one of the sweetest nectars on earth. I have read that one can live a healthy if somewhat boring life eating nothing but these two foods.

Ironically, one of the things you won't find very often in the tropics is the tough-skinned, rather tasteless banana that we're all used to seeing in our local supermarkets. These are special export bananas that are picked and shipped green, and the natives seldom eat them. Please, however, don't take this as a slam at imported bananas—they are one of the most economical and nutritious foods around, but they aren't nearly as tasty as the real thing.

Some native foods like plantains (they look like a banana but taste more like a wooden potato) and taro (a huge black parsnip with warts and varicose veins) are definitely an acquired taste, but you need to try these tropical staples prepared in several ways in order to give them a chance. I find many of these foods to be tedious but tolerable as long as they are served with other more tasty foods and drenched with hot sauce.

Canned New Zealand butter is available nearly everywhere except in the U.S. and, ironically, New Zealand; it is the best butter you'll find anywhere. Ultrahigh-temperature (UHT) milk is a cruising standard, comes in one-liter boxes, and lasts for six months or more. We buy it by the case. It makes the use of powdered milk unnecessary, but if you do need powdered milk the powdered whole milk available everywhere outside the U.S. is much better than anything you'll find at home. Another New Zealand product available throughout the tropics called Just Juice is a mixture of several fruit juices that also comes in liter boxes that make handy and nutritious drinks for passages, but when you are in port most fruits are so cheap that you can squeeze your own juice.

Some things such as olive oil, anchovies (for the pizza), and basic spices such as oregano, basil, and whole black peppercorns can be scarce or expensive enough to warrant putting in a substantial supply. Unrefrigerated eggs will last for up to a month if they are kept cool and dry (no need to turn them or coat them with Vaseline). Turning the eggs once in a while does help prevent the yolk from sticking to the inside of the shell, but except for your longest passages in the Pacific, there is no reason to keep them long enough so that this becomes necessary.

Properly stored eggs won't spoil for up to a month or more but they do go stale very rapidly. Week-old eggs are nutritious and perfectly safe to eat, as is week-old bread that hasn't gone moldy, but the difference in the taste and texture of a fresh egg over an old egg is so profound that you should never buy more eggs than you will use before your next trip to the market, and it is always worth the effort to find the source of the freshest local eggs when you enter a new harbor. The only time older eggs are superior to fresh is if you are going to boil them. Boiled eggs that are not three or four days old are impossible to peel.

Most of the world outside the U.S. does not refrigerate eggs, and I'm told that in some European countries it is illegal to sell eggs that have been refrigerated or washed. My reading indicates, however, that there is a definite advantage to refrigerating eggs in that they will stay fresh much longer. We don't keep eggs in the refrigerator on *Sultana* (they take up too much room), but if you want to keep your eggs around for a long time, the refrigerator is the place to do it (the idea that refrigerated eggs spoil faster than ones kept at room temperature is yet another cruising myth). Once in the refrigerator, however, leave them there until they are used—they will go bad quite rapidly once removed because the mucous membrane that protects and preserves the egg is very fragile, and exposure to refrigeration or any moisture will destroy it, thereby allowing the egg to spoil.

Fishy fish and foul fowls

In any area you visit, the best source of information on local markets and foods is another cruiser who got there a week or so ahead of you. You'll never go wrong buying local produce from a local market and eating what the natives eat. But watch out for the fish and meat, especially chicken. Much of the developing world outside the major population centers doesn't have adequate refrigeration yet, and many countries (particularly Honduras and Nicaragua) have lengthy power outages. When a power outage causes the meat in the freezer to thaw, most merchants simply refreeze it when the power is restored. A good way to confirm if that's been the case is to check the ice-cream freezer. Ice cream becomes crystalline when re-frozen, so if the ice cream has ice in it, you know that the merchandise has been refrozen after a thaw. (In some countries, ice cream that is free of ice crystals is very hard to find.)

Even though frozen fish, poultry, and meat are available nearly everywhere, it is better to buy fish off the fishing boats (or catch your own), buy live poultry, and avoid beef, pork, horse (popular in Panama and often sold to unsuspecting cruisers as premium beef), and goat altogether unless you know the animal was killed that day. The quality butchers in the rural areas of Central and South America often have no refrigeration at all and will hang the head of the animal in the window as testimony to its freshness.

This problem with frozen food and refrigeration in Third World countries is rapidly becoming less important, especially in the larger cities as more and more merchants invest in portable generators as backups to the municipal power system.

De facto vegetarianism

You will meet many vegetarians among the cruising community, and except for having the general appearance of asparagus stalks, they seem to get along quite well on their meatless diets. Although there are many vegetarians who shun the flesh for moralistic reasons, most vegetarian cruisers don't eat meat for practical reasons. If you can live on a boat without eating meat, you will simplify your life to an enormous extent. Even those cruisers who don't become dedicated vegetarians, including those aboard *Sultana,* find that meat becomes an occasional treat or an ingredient in a sauce or stew rather than the focus of the meal.

Most meat in the U.S. and Canada, especially beef, is hung or aged under moderate refrigeration for about 10 days before it is butchered. This encourages a bacterial process that imparts a lovely flavor and greatly decreases toughness by breaking down natural fibers in the flesh. Aging is not possible in the tropics, how-ever, and most meat in rural areas is eaten or frozen within 24 hours of being slaughtered. Thus, even the best cuts of meat are tough with a strong flavor that most North Americans will find objectionable, and almost all meat, even goat and chicken, is very expensive in most tropical locales, while fresh and wholesome veg-etables and fruits are dirt cheap and readily available.

Another argument for vegetarianism is the tropical weather, which favors a vegetable diet over a meat diet. Your carnivorous author was raised as a bacon-and-egg kind of guy, and even now a slab of fried ham with three sunny-side ups and a side of home fries or grits is my idea of the perfect breakfast. But while cruising, breakfast on *Sultana* is usually a large bowl of fresh papaya, pineapple, and mango with a sliced banana and a big glop of yogurt on top. If Susan isn't looking, I'll cover the whole thing with honey or raw sugar and mix in some corn flakes, wash it down with two or three cups of good Colombian coffee, and after a hearty belch I'm ready for just about anything the day has to offer.

Galley Layout and Hardware

When you bought your new old boat you also bought the galley that was in it and you are pretty much stuck with the basic layout. That doesn't mean, however, that before you start your cruise you can't redo the existing galley to get it just the way you want it, and there are a few things you can do to greatly enhance the utility of this critical area. Except for the very top-of-the-line boats (Morris and Shannons and such), most galleys in newer boats are designed for weekend and coastal cruising in temperate or semitropical climates. The icebox/refrigerator will be hopelessly under-insulated. The stove or range will be appropriate for a camper van. The sink will be a tiny thing that's worthless for any kind of serious kitchen work. Storage will be inadequate. Half of what space you do have will be taken up by the plumbing for that silly little sink, and the rest won't have the baffles and partitions necessary to keep food and utensils from shifting around while sailing.

Older boats are even worse than new boats. They incorporate all the above sins, plus everything will be outdated and worn-out. In addition to being inadequate, the icebox insulation is likely to be saturated with water and the countertops might even be covered with linoleum. Fortunately, a new galley is easy to install and won't kill the kitty if you keep the same basic layout and progress in a logical manner.

The icebox/refrigerator

Unless you are on a strict budget, get over the idea of going cruising in the tropics without a good icebox, and there is no real reason to go without refrigeration. I know Chichester, Slocum, Uncle Freddie, and the rest of the pioneers didn't have refrigerators or even adequate iceboxes but that was only because good refrigeration units and plastic foam insulation weren't available then. If they could've had 'em they would've had 'em.

Modern boat refrigerators are economical and reliable, provided they are installed properly and backed up with an adequate electrical system—yet on many cruising boats they are a constant source of expense and aggravation. Almost all of these troubles with refrigeration units come from installing the compressor in too small an area without adequate ventilation, inadequate insulation in the icebox, or trying to cool a large box with a small compressor. Your compressor/condenser unit is like a mule on a dirt farm: if you overwork it, you're out of business in short order. Take good care of it, however, and it will go on forever. The first thing you should do if your unit isn't working as efficiently as you think it should is to remove the liner of the icebox and install a minimum of 4 inches of urethane foam insulation (the pink stuff sold in lumber yards for insulating the outside of foundations, not Styrofoam). Six inches is better if you have the room for it, especially if you are bound for the tropics. Next, install a blower that delivers fresh air to the condenser unit. A small one that is cheap to buy and efficient to run will do the job. If you have an Adler-Barbour or similar unit you should consider installing the raw-water cooling conversion that they make.

There are several excellent books on marine refrigeration (*Boatowner's Mechanical and Electrical Manual* by Nigel Calder is the best) and although it isn't as critical that you become familiar with refrigeration as with your diesel engine or your electrical system, a working knowledge of the basic principles of refrigeration and an understanding of the idiosyncrasies of your particular unit will prove valuable. I don't know a whole lot about the subject because *Sultana*'s Adler-Barbour Super Cold Machine has done the last four years without a hitch or a glitch and I have never had to fix it. The salt-water cooling pump did give it up in Aitutaki, but it doesn't seem to make much difference in the temperate New Zealand waters so we haven't bothered to replace it yet.

Just one last point: if you happen to be a skilled refrigeration mechanic and have the right tools, you will find no end to the demands for your services among the cruising community and in many of the ports you will visit. Ironically, air-conditioning, which is nothing more than a big refrigerator, is rather unusual in the tropics, and where it does exist it is often broken for want of any local person who knows how to fix it. If you are looking for a trade to support your cruising plans once you get underway, you could do worse than learning all there is to know about refrigeration and air-conditioning.

Ice is nice

In the Caribbean, refrigeration isn't as important as it is in other places because ice is readily available and, unless you buy it at the marina bar, it's cheap. The best source of ice in most tropical areas is the fisherman's wharf where you can usually get more than you can ever use for a few pesos. When we got to Isla Mujeres, the first thing Phillip and I did after clearing in was to head to the fish dock for ice. "¿Grande o pequeño?" asked the ice guy. Since the price was only a few pesos and we needed a lot of ice, I figured I'd better get the big block—whereupon the guy disappeared into the bowels of the icehouse only to reappear pushing a block of ice only slightly smaller than a Volkswagen bus. We chipped off what we needed and I gave the rest to the very amused skipper of a nearby shrimp boat.

Naturally, I felt pretty stupid for making such an obvious blunder, but when I related my tale at a cruisers' potluck supper that night, I discovered that just about everyone I talked to had fallen for the same scam. But what the hell, we got our ice, the skipper of the shrimp boat got a few chuckles at the expense of those crazy cruisers, the ice guy made a few extra pesos, the potluck was delicious, and we learned a bit about conducting business in Latin America. It was a small price to pay for a great day.

A warning though: fish-dock ice is often contaminated with giardia lambia and cryptosporidium (the critters that cause gardiasis, better known as Montezuma's revenge or the cruisers' quickstep) and lots of other unpleasant stuff, so don't use it in drinks. Buy a bag of cubes at the bar to use in your martinis. It's probably contaminated too, so add a little extra gin. It won't kill the germs, but it will make you feel better about drinking them. For some reason, outside the

Caribbean ice is much harder to find, and a refrigerator really pays off. On *Sultana* we always use ice when we can get it and only resort to running the refrigerator when we must because it's easier on the batteries.

The freezer

The refrigeration unit on *Sultana* is capable of making fine ice cubes and keeping a few pounds of meat frozen even in the hottest climates. The problem is that to keep food frozen requires too much battery power and a few ice cubes requires about four hours of engine time. So unless we are motoring for long distances (such as on the Intracoastal Waterway or on days that the wind won't blow), we don't use it. We have met other cruisers, however, with large efficient freezers, and they aren't all rich people either. Some of the older boats designed for the bareboat charter business, such as the CSY 44, come with an excellent cold-plate freezer as standard equipment, and most of the standard marine refrigeration units that are sold today will function as freezers if the box is small enough and the insulation is adequate.

On *Sultana*, which has a large, well-insulated icebox, we use a simple partition cut from sheet Styrofoam to divide the box into two compartments. The compartment with the freezing unit will function as a freezer (if we wanted it to) while the other side stays at normal refrigerator temperatures. This technique is used by many cruisers who use their refrigeration unit as a freezer, and one common procedure is to buy a quantity of meat or prepare a number of one-dish meals (casseroles and such) and have them commercially frozen to a very low temperature before they are placed in the boat freezer. George and Alice on the S/V *Esrac* cruise all over the Caribbean from their base in Florida, and they never leave home without about 20 lovely homemade meat pies in the freezer.

The galley range

A good cruising boat needs a top-of-the-line cook stove with a large oven. In most cases, if you bought a boat that has already been used for cruising, your galley already has an adequate stove, and though it might be a little rusty and worn, if it was a quality unit to begin with it can usually be refurbished. We replaced the burners, knobs, and burner inserts on the 20-year-old Seaward Hiller Range that came with *Sultana* and got a practically new stove out of the deal. After three years of daily use the top of the oven rusted through (our own fault for not cleaning up spills right away), so she'll be getting a new Force 10 for the refit.

Fuel types

In many of the older cruising books and a few of the new ones you'll find a lot of discussion on the best fuel to use for the galley stove. Butane, paraffin or kerosene, alcohol, propane, and compressed natural gas (CNG) all have their advocates, but today propane has emerged as the fuel of choice for 95 percent of all cruising boats, and the other types of fuel aren't really worth bothering with. Propane is now available just about everywhere; it's cheap, clean, and safe if only the most basic safety precautions are taken.

With any other type of fuel you are bound to run into supply problems somewhere in the world. Butane is hard to find in French Polynesia, kerosene is expensive everywhere (and of poor quality in the U.S. and Canada), and CNG is impossible to find outside of big cities. Propane also burns hotter and cooks better than any of the others. Alcohol is a joke everywhere. If you have a good-quality stove of adequate size in your boat when you buy it, stick with it no matter what fuel it burns. If it is CNG, however, and you are headed for foreign waters, you should change the burners and convert it to propane. You will eventually want to replace your stove and when you do, go with propane.

Range size

The ideal range size for your cruising boat is the same size as the one you are used to at home, and although this isn't practical, the larger the stove the happier the cook, and like I said before, the happier the cook, the happier the crew. The more-or-less standard size for cruising ranges is 21 inches wide and 20 inches deep for a full-sized stove (as opposed to 30 by 30 for your home range). Of course, there are a lot of smaller ones made to fit smaller galleys, and it is amazing what wonderful meals a good cook can produce on these tiny ranges.

Most full-sized ranges built for boats crowd four burners onto the cook top in such a way that only two are ever usable. Two burners are usually more than enough, but few two-burner stoves have an adequate oven. Luke makes a two-burner stove that has a good oven, and Force 10 makes a three-burner stove that has a beautiful oven. A broiler is not a necessity but it is real handy for melting the cheese on your French-onion soup and putting an extra crunch in the garlic bread.

Stove safety

Don't buy a stove that doesn't have a good set of fiddles to keep pots and pans from sliding around the cook top. To be effective they should grip the pot at least 2 inches above the stove top. You will also want your propane tanks installed in compliance with the dictates of common sense and the U.S. Coast Guard (even though the two are often at odds), which means they should be enclosed in an isolated locker with an overboard drain and fitted with a remote solenoid shutoff that can be actuated from the galley. The solenoid should be de-energized every time you turn off your stove and should include a large red warning light that indicates when the solenoid is activated. Each installation should include a pressure gauge installed between the tank and the regulator.

The gauge is useless for determining the amount of fuel left in the tank (unless the tank is empty), but it is essential for checking for leaks. Every time a tank is changed or whenever any work is done on the propane system, you should charge the system then shut off the tank and the stove valves, leaving the solenoid and any other in-line valves, such as selector switches, open. Any drop in pressure indicated by the gauge means you have a leak in the line, and all activity must cease until this leak is located and repaired. A little soapy water will usually find the leak in short order, but don't ever be tempted to operate the system until you find it.

Always carry a backup stove on long passages. If you are careful it is unlikely that you will run out of propane, although that does happen, but if you experience an electrical failure your solenoid will be inoperative, and rather than attempt to bypass it to get your stove operating, it makes a lot more sense to do your basic cooking on a backup stove until you get the juice turned back on. The Force 10 Seacook is a very popular emergency unit with cruisers, but at around $200 they are a bit pricey. *Sultana* carries a one-burner stainless camping stove that uses canned butane for fuel. We have only needed it once when we ran out of propane in the Bay of Islands (because New Zealand law forbid the supplier filling our tanks without sending them off for a NZ\$30 inspection sticker), but it has come in handy many other times for camping on the beach and backpack trips inland.

Stove gimbals aren't necessary on many heavy cruising boats that are capable of standing up to a stiff breeze, and they can be a real nuisance and even dangerous. Light boats that heal and bounce around a lot might need them, but do without them if you can. On a stiff boat it often makes more sense to mount the stove athwartship rather than fore and aft if you have a choice (which you probably don't). The porpoising action of many cruising boats around the lateral axis is milder than the rolling action around the longitudinal axis, and an athwartship-mounted stove without gimbals might be more stable than a fore-and-aft mounted stove with gimbals. If you do need gimbals on your stove, make sure a heavy pot placed on the stove top won't tilt the stove enough to cause a spill, and get the kind with which you can lock the stove in place when they aren't in use.

Microwave ovens

A small microwave oven is one of those things that can help to make your boat your home. You don't really need a microwave oven, of course, but they're useful and cheap so if you can spare the space, why not have one? Microwaves are useless for any real cooking but they work fine for a lot of ancillary jobs like melting butter, boiling water, thawing meat, and reheating leftovers. They're also great for putting the steam back in a cup of coffee and can be a lifesaver when you need a quick cup of hot soup on a long cold watch. The smallest one you can buy is plenty big enough for most boats. *Sultana*'s cost \$60 on sale at Sears. They draw a lot of power but only for short spurts, and they work fine on modern inverters. A lot of traditionalists and old-timers sneer at *Sultana*'s microwave; we just sneer back and invite them in for a hot cup of tea: "Be ready in just a second."

The Kitchen Sink

There're a lot of things I don't like about modern production boats and one of the things I don't like the most is the stupid little galley sink that comes in them. I can accept such things as skimpy rigs, undersized fittings, paper-thin hulls, incorrect props, chintzy winches, and engines that are badly mounted in inaccessible places. But those silly little sinks that are too small to wash a teacup in really set me off.

The best way to handle the ship's sink is to rip it out, countertop and all, and chuck it over the side (in an environmentally appropriate manner, of course). Replace the entire countertop with a shallow tray, the same size as the old countertop, made from plastic countertop material such as Corian. Make the sides about 4 inches high and put the drain in a corner instead of in the middle so the plumbing will be out of the way instead of taking up half the under-sink storage space. Now you have a beautiful work surface for preparing food. Use your stainless mixing bowl and your wok to wash and rinse dishes—it's just like the double sink you left at home.

Storage

Storage on any small boat is a problem, and storage of foodstuffs in the galley is particularly vexing, especially if you have been used to large and commodious kitchen cupboards at home (which, if you are a normal sort of person, were also jammed to overflowing, no matter how commodious they were). Neat and orderly storage of food and galley gear is one of the devils with which we on *Sultana* have been wrestling ever since we left Marblehead, and so far the devil is winning. He hasn't quite pinned us to the mat, however, and we are slowly learning how to cope with this problem thanks to a few simple adaptations that I will share with you here.

No vacancies

Don't assume that the builder of your boat spent a lot of time designing the storage lockers in your boat, particularly those in the galley. Plastic boats with molded hull liners are particularly bad in this regard; I have seen a lot of galley lockers with fancy doors and hardware (visible items), and no bottom so that anything placed in the lockers slides right into the bilge. What few shelves there are often won't have fiddles so when you open a starboard locker while you are on the port tack you get a face full of whatever was in there. These ills aren't restricted to newer boats either. We found many places where we were able to gain valuable storage room on *Sultana* with a few minor and inexpensive modifications.

One of the first things you should do is fit every shelf in your boat with a fiddle. Make them from thin (¼-inch thick is fine) strips of an exotic hardwood like mahogany or bubinga cut about 2 inches wide (it's expensive but you don't need much), then give them a shipshape oil finish. Old oak sail battens, from the good old days when battens were made out of oak and yachtsmen were made out of money, make excellent fiddles. Many are already finished so all you have to do is trim them to length and fasten them to the front of your shelves with copper or bronze nails. While you are at it, look for wasted space where additional shelves can be added.

Fit bottoms to any lockers that don't have them. Large lockers can be fitted with false bottoms to give you several layers of storage where before you only had one. The trick here, of course, is to store seldom-used materials in the bottom, less accessible tier, and the more frequently used stuff in the top tier. While this sounds like a commonsense thing to do, it is much harder in practice than in theory. Somehow, the thing you want right now is always in the bottom tier and you have to take everything out of the top tier to get at it. Another trick that can help ease access to large lockers is to fit front-opening ones with a hatch through the top and top-opening ones with a hatch in the front, thus giving you a choice of two ways to go wrong rather than just one when you are searching for some critical item.

I've already discussed the under-sink area that you can open up by getting rid of the sink, but make a careful survey of your boat for any unused space behind bulkheads or under the cabin sole where the addition of a simple hatch or port will provide additional storage. Naturally you will want to make sure there is really nothing behind the bulkhead lest you cut into the nearly full holding tank with your hole saw, but I haven't seen a boat yet where considerable new space couldn't be found with a little looking around.

Yet another possibility is to look under and behind drawers, which are another item that sales-oriented boatbuilders like to provide a lot of, but they invariably make them undersized and put them in illogical places. Drawers that aren't properly constructed waste a huge amount of space—you often can find enough room to store thin flat items under them. Better yet, consider throwing the drawers away, trimming the opening with some of that bubinga left over from the fiddles, and use the entire cavity as a stuff locker.

Be particularly careful about what you store under your floorboards in the bilge. Even a tiny amount of seawater can wreak havoc with anything made out of metal, and if any oil from the engine gets into the seawater, it can make an unbelievable mess of anything stored there. Never store canned food in the bilge and don't put your extra cans of paint in there either. (If you must carry extra paint, put each can in a plastic gallon milk bottle with a cut-off top. That way, when the can rusts through, the milk bottle will contain the mess—somewhat.)

Pots and Pans

You don't need a lot of pots and pans in your galley, but the ones you do need should be the best money can buy. Too many cruisers use worn-out and rejected cookware from home, and while this works just fine for weekend boating, it's a serious mistake when you are living and cruising on your boat full-time. Good cookware is expensive but it will last forever. Cheap cookware is useless.

Except for an 8-inch Ironstone sauté pan for eggs and a Teflon-coated aluminum wok, we on *Sultana* don't buy easy-clean coated pots and pans. The inexpensive ones are too flimsy and even the best lose their coating after a while. Here's a list of the most important items in our galley that has evolved after four years of trial and error:

- Eight-inch and 12-inch titanium-coated aluminum sauté pans, both of which are great for omelets.
- A 16-inch Teflon-coated aluminum wok with a cover for deep frying, stir-frying, and making sauces and stews. It's also just the right size for washing dishes. The coating lasts about a year but the wok woks OK without it, as long as you don't use it for tomato sauces. (Tomato sauce is very acidic and will eat right through aluminum cookware when the coatings wear off. It will ruin your pots but it is not dangerous or unhealthy.)
- A 12-inch *plancha,* which is a handy flat frying pan that is a standard item in Spanish kitchens. You'll probably have to wait until you get to Central America to pick one up. They're made of cast aluminum, are shaped like shallow, flat woks, and are one of the handiest items you can have in your galley. They are good for frying anything and perfect for toasting bread and sandwiches because they require only a tiny amount of butter, oil, or grease. They make wonderful serving dishes and trays, they're the ultimate pizza pan if you like a crisp and crunchy crust, they're lightweight, and they store flat so you could have six of them in the space that an ordinary fry pan would take up. We bought ours for about $2 in Florianis, Guatemala, and when we get back there, I'm going to buy at least three more.
- A 2½-quart stainless covered saucepan for soups and stews and sauces. Ours is Farberware and seems to be indestructible.
- An 8-quart covered stewpot with a steamer rack for cooking pasta, steaming lobsters and shellfish, making stews and goulash, and everything else you need a big pot for. This, too, is Farberware and indestructible.
- A 6-quart stainless mixing bowl that also doubles as a salad bowl and dishpan. Plastic is OK for this sort of thing but it does and will melt when you get it too close to the stove—as is bound to happen in the confines of the largest galley.

- Two stainless bread pans, an assortment of stainless muffin tins, and a popover pan (Susan makes fantastic popovers). These items can be hard to find in stainless steel. We got ours from Williams Sonoma in Boston.
- A 12-inch chef's knife. A good chef's knife is outrageously expensive—our Henckels costs about $100—but you only need one per lifetime, and when you really need a knife you don't need a cheap one or a dull one. A good sharpening steel is also expensive, but get one anyway. A good way to spot a quality knife—besides the price—is to look at how the blade is ground. Cheap knives are usually hollow ground; quality knives are always flat ground. If you don't know the difference between the two grinding methods, don't feel bad, but if you can see a hollow where the knife was sharpened at the factory, it's a cheapo.
- A good paring knife. It won't be as expensive as a chef's knife but it will still cost a few bucks. A good one will make a world of difference in your cooking, however, so spend the money.
- A pepper mill. Nearly all spices and herbs taste much better fresh than pre-ground or dried, but nowhere is the difference more dramatic than with black pepper. The pre-ground stuff is just about tasteless and there is little reason to carry any, but freshly ground pepper makes a world of difference in many dishes. Salt mills are also popular but there is little reason to have one unless you favor sea salt finely ground. Sea salt has a unique flavor reminiscent of Cape Cod in the summer at low tide. It comes in flakes that are fine just the way they are, and I see no reason to grind them up.
- Cookbooks. When we left Marblehead, we had more than 100 cookbooks in our kitchen library; on *Sultana* we have a grand total of four. Susan favors *The Joy of Cooking* by Irma Rombauer and Marion Rombauer Becker because it contains nearly everything a cookbook needs to contain and it gives precise and detailed instructions on hundreds of fantastic recipes. My favorite is *The Fannie Farmer Cookbook* by Marion Cunningham because it is simple and basic and easy for a simple and basic cook like me to understand. The other two are a Mexican cookbook we picked up in Mexico (of all places) and a Chinese cookbook that comes from Australia. Neither is great and we're searching the world for replacements because Chinese and Mexican food are a central part of *Sultana*'s fare.

No-pressure cooking

We do have a pressure cooker on *Sultana,* but in spite of all that is written about the joys of cooking with them, when the refit is finished we will probably sail away without ours. We have found that the utility of the pressure cooker and the slight advantage it may give in cooking time is not worth putting up with a host of disadvantages. For one, you don't really save that much time. Once you finish cooking in the damn things, you must deal with a quantity of boiling water under high pressure. You can release the pressure by removing the little weight from the top, thus filling the boat with steam, which is not what most boats cruising in the tropics really need most of the time, or wait around for the thing to cool off, which takes more time than if you just cooked whatever is in there the normal way.

The big objection I have to cooking in the pressure cooker, however, is the taste of the food that comes out of them. Vegetables cooked under pressure are invariably overcooked, mushy, and tasteless, while 90 percent of the nutrients get thrown out with the water. A simple steamer rack on the bottom of your kettle cooks vegetables better and faster with less water than a pressure cooker. Another favorite use of the pressure cooker is to make soups, stews, and goulashes that can be cooked in about 20 minutes rather that the two hours or so that a real stew needs to simmer. It does save a lot of time but the problem is that the tough meats that make the best stews just get tougher and lose their flavor when cooked quickly over high heat. Stews and soups need to be cooked for a long time over very low heat and the pressure cooker just doesn't make it.

Many cruising books talk about using the pressure cooker as a way to preserve food. The idea is that you cook the food in the pressure cooker then leave the food hermetically sealed in the pressure cooker for a week or so until you are ready to eat it. This looks good in principle, but the problem is that everything is dependent on there being a perfect seal between the lid and the pot, and there is no way of checking the integrity of this seal without breaking it. Thus, you won't know if the food in the pressure cooker has spoiled or not until you go to use it, and you may not even know then because many bacteria, including botulism, don't give off any odor. Who needs to take the chance?

If you really need to preserve food without refrigeration, pack it in salt and hang it in the sun for a week or so the way the Central American Indians do (any one of them can show you how it's done in about 10 minutes). Most foods preserved this way will last longer than a false rumor.

Pressure cookers work just fine in high-altitude places like Denver and Innsbruck and Guatemala City where the reduced atmospheric pressure gives them a definite advantage, but if you plan to do most of your cruising down here at sea level, like most of us, you can do very nicely without a pressure cooker.

Galley Gadgets

There are a lot of other things you'll need in your galley, of course, but try to keep them simple, basic, and stainless, and you can't go too far wrong. Although I have to admit to a weakness for esoteric kitchen tools, avoid collecting gadgets if you can. I fell in love with a tortilla press I bought in Mexico even though it takes up a lot of room and we hardly ever use it. And then there is the coffee filter that we used to have. Before we left Marblehead, I bought a gold-plated guaranteed-for-life coffee filter so we wouldn't have to buy hundreds of those cone-shaped paper coffee filters. It cost a lot of money but I figured, what the hell, at what we were paying for the paper filters we'd break even in less than 20 years. I can still remember the day I threw it overboard with the dishwater. It was beautiful how the gold plating caught the light and reflected the sun and how long it stayed in sight as it drifted away into the depths.

Electric gadgets

With modern inverters and battery systems, if you want electrical gadgets in the galley there is no reason not to have them. Don't waste your money on 12-volt kitchen appliances because they tend to be poorly made, flimsy, and usually cost three or four times what the standard 120-volt household appliances cost. Most of the ones sold in your local department store will work just fine, particularly with the trend away from using metal or casings and other external parts. The plastics revolution is truly a boon to the cruising chef.

Here are a few gadgets you might find handy in your galley:

- A toaster. Toast on a boat is a problem. The little camp gadgets that go over your stovetop burners don't work very well and even the stainless ones rust away in a few months. You can make excellent toast on a *plancha* or in your oven, but *plancha* toast is really fried bread and not very healthy, and making toast in your oven isn't energy efficient. The best bet is a small inexpensive toaster from Sears or Wal-Mart. Like a microwave, they draw a lot of juice but only for short periods. However, make sure your inverter will handle heating elements—many square-wave inverters won't (see chapter 10).
- A coffee grinder. All coffee snobs know that freshly ground coffee is the best, and those handgrinders with the little wooden box on the bottom make great planters for your ivy at home, but they don't grind coffee beans worth . . . well, worth beans. Get a simple 12-volt electric one from a discount department store.
- A blender. Not a Cuisinart or a "food-processing station," but a $20 blender for making bread crumbs, milkshakes, frozen banana daiquiris, and about a zillion other things you can't make any other way.
- A travel iron. Not really a galley gadget, but they're great for those odd occasions when you want a pressed shirt to impress the port captain. Once again, they may not work on square-wave inverters.
- Electric fans. All cruising boats need a few electric fans and the place they need them the most is in the galley. Some excellent 12-volt fans are available at marine chandleries but they will likely cost a lot of money. Try Sears or Wal-Mart or the like—you can get good 120-volt fans that use only a tiny amount of electricity for about $10 each or even less. Look for ones made from plastic with removable guards and blades that can be washed, and always use them on a GFCI-protected circuit (the only kind you should have on your boat).

  The use of such low-current apparatus as fans presupposes a modern efficient inverter that can be left energized for long periods without drawing down the battery. Some of the older inverters use significant battery power just by being turned on and shouldn't be used for such things as fans. If you have one of these older units get a few of the little 100-watt inverters that plug into a cigarette socket and use them for your fans. The West Marine housebrand is the best buy we have found on these handy little gadgets.

Sharing the Chores

Cooking on a boat can either be an ordeal or a creative joy, and there is no reason why it should be anything but the latter other than the attitudes and prejudice of the crew. Anyone can become a passable or even a passionate cook if the task is approached with a positive attitude and a bit of diligence. I recall the first time I cooked for a dinner party at my apartment on Beacon Street in Boston. There were six of us including Susan, whom I had just met and was quite anxious to impress. The menu included roast duck with orange sauce and while the duck was pretty straightforward and came out of the oven in fine shape, the sauce was a disaster. It started out OK and I never did figure where I went wrong, but I ended up with a black goo that resembled road tar—it even smelled like road tar.

With about 10 minutes until my guests were to arrive, I literally ran to the all-night grocery on Newbury Street and bought one bottle of everything I could find that was made from oranges. I bought a quart of orange juice, a jar of orange marmalade, a small jug of Cointreau, and a tiny bottle of grenadine. Back at the apartment with no time to spare, I threw the lot into a saucepan over high heat and stirred up what was to be my very first culinary triumph. Everyone agreed that it was indeed one of the most unusual orange sauces that they had ever tasted, and we're talking serious epicures here. Unfortunately, up until now it has remained my only culinary triumph, but that one experience gave me the confidence to keep trying, and I've come close to triumphing again on several occasions.

Today, Susan and I share the cooking aboard *Sultana,* although I remain in the category of the adventuresome dilettante and her refined and sophisticated cooking skills make my efforts look like those of . . . well, an adventuresome dilettante. Regardless of our relative prowess in the galley, we both enjoy cooking and respect each others tastes and techniques; as a result, the crew of *Sultana* is one of the best fed in the fleet.

A Few Fantastic Recipes from *Sultana's* Galley

I must confess that the hundred or so cookbooks mentioned above (now packed away in a storage bin in Vermont) were purchased by me, not Susan. I am an unrepentant cookbook freak and buy and read them like some people buy and read detective novels. My all-time favorite is *Beard on Bread* by the late James Beard, and my least favorites are any of the many that expend more effort on glossy photography than on refining the recipes, a prejudice that may have come from the years I worked as a slick food photographer. My driving ambition is to someday write my own cookbook to share some of the wonderful recipes I've collected that work well in a cruising galley.

As a preview to this coming opus, I've given in to the clamor of public demand and share below a few samples of what to expect. The following few recipes are selected for their simplicity, versatility, and adaptability to the cruising life. None of these are original, but all have an original element or twist that makes them particularly useful on board *Sultana*. I offer them with the hope that you will find them as useful as we have. All the following recipes are designed to feed four ravenous crew because that's what we have on *Sultana*. Adjust quantities to fit your circumstances.

Pasta

Pasta is one of the most useful and versatile foods to have on a boat. It is nutritious, ridiculously easy to prepare, tasty, and can be prepared in such a variety of ways that you can serve it over and over again without being repetitious or boring (two unforgivable sins of the culinary arts). Pasta is available everywhere, and even in places like Tahiti it is relatively cheap. In the off chance that you can't find any to buy or if you are in the mood for a true gastronomic adventure, you can make your own with the following recipe. This makes about 8 ounces of pasta. If you need more (and you probably will), just double or triple the quantities, then break the dough into small batches for rolling. Unrolled dough also keeps well in the refrigerator, and some even claim this improves the flavor.

BASIC PASTA

1 c. flour (all-purpose works OK, but if you can find any semolina, use that instead—it makes a wonderful light pasta with a chewy texture that is tastier than pasta made with all-purpose flour)
1 large egg
1 tsp. olive oil

1. Place the flour on any flat, nonporous surface and make a well in the middle.
2. Break the egg into the well and stir with your index finger until the egg becomes incorporated into the flour.
3. As the dough becomes too thick to work add the olive oil one drop at a time.
4. When the dough is smooth and about the consistency of heavy modeling clay, roll it out on a heavily floured board, fold it over twice, and roll it out again. Keep folding and rolling until it becomes almost too heavy to roll, then roll it out as thin as you can—1/16 of an inch is about right. It may help if you break the dough into small pieces and roll them out one at a time instead of trying to roll out the entire batch.
5. Cut the rolled-out dough into 1/8-inch-wide strips and drop them right into boiling water for about a minute, or until the pasta tastes just right. Alternatively, you can dry the strips on deck and store them in plastic containers.

This procedure sounds easy and it is easy, but as in many culinary concoctions there is a trick to getting it just right. You may have to experiment with it a few times to get it the way you want it, so don't give up, especially if you can't get the dough thin enough to suit your liking on the first go. The mechanical pasta rollers are a great help in making delicious homemade pasta, but alas, ours was left behind in the storage bin. It is one of the few things we didn't bring that we really miss.

SUSAN'S LINGUINI WITH CLAM SAUCE

I'm forever embarrassing Susan by telling our friends I married her because of this recipe. Susan always blushes and everyone always laughs, but the funny thing is that they all think I'm kidding. This recipe originated in *The Silver Palate Cookbook* by Julee Rosso and Sheila Lukins, but Susan has made a few modifications that make the dish tastier and make preparation on a boat a little easier.

1/4 c. olive oil
1 c. chopped fresh clams, conch, cockles, squid, periwinkles, or any other similar tough-bodied creature you find while snorkeling. Canned baby clams work just fine.

6–12 cloves of garlic, depending on taste, chopped fine but not squished to death in a garlic press. (Chopped garlic retains its flavor better than pressed garlic. Fresh garlic is best, of course, and we seldom encounter any trouble finding a ready supply, but garlic preserved in olive oil will do in a pinch.)

2–3 T. fresh chopped chives (dried chives are a poor but acceptable substitute, and parsley will also work)

1 lb. (approximately) freshly made pasta. (If you don't feel like making pasta, use dried linguini. Pasta is amazing stuff in that spaghetti, lasagna noodles, or any other pasta are all exactly the same thing as linguini, only in different shapes—but the shape makes all the difference.)

1 T. (approximately) ground pepper

Fresh parmesan cheese (or any other hard cheese)

1. Place the oil in a sauté pan and let it get just hot enough so that it doesn't smoke.
2. Add the clams and cook while stirring for two minutes (longer if you are using squid or conch). If you are using canned clams, just heat them through.
3. Add the garlic and the chives and cook just until the garlic starts to turn color—about one minute—but not long enough to cook the flavor out of it. It is perfect if it retains just a hint of raw garlic bite.
4. Pour the sauce over the cooked pasta and add the pepper and cheese. Serve with fresh *plancha* bread (see below), an inquisitive white wine, and a fresh salad. Now sit back and enjoy a trip to heaven.

CAPTAIN GARLIC'S WORLD-FAMOUS SPAGHETTI SAUCE

My friends all know me as a humble man, but when it comes to this sauce I don't mind saying that it's the greatest sauce ever concocted in the history of humanity. I have this habit of inviting large numbers of fellow cruisers aboard for dinner and neglecting to tell Susan that they are coming. This is not one of the best routes to a harmonious cruising relationship, but I can usually smooth things over a bit by doing all the cooking, and the thing I cook the most is my world-famous spaghetti sauce. It takes only about an hour to make, has several uses as leftovers, and rarely fails to make a hit. The following feeds four with some left over, but multiply the recipe to make as much as you can—you're going to need it for some of the recipes that follow.

2 T. olive oil

1 large green onion—the larger and greener the better

2 cans (10-oz.) whole Italian plum tomatoes (or whatever other kinds of tomatoes you might have aboard—fresh are OK, too)

8 oz. tomato paste

1 c. water

½ tsp. salt

1 lb. *carne molieda* (ground beef) or fresh Italian sausage (optional). I prefer hot sausage, but it is best to defer to the taste of your crew and guests, especially if they're wimps.

Garlic, finely chopped (use as many cloves as you think your guests can toler-ate—I seldom use fewer than a dozen cloves)

2–3 large bay leaves

1 tsp. habanero pepper (available in a little spice store in Zona Diez in Guatemala City that is licensed to sell explosives. It is worth every minute of the five-hour bus ride with the pigs and chickens to get some. If you don't have habanero peppers, ahi peppers, fresh hot chilies, or ground red pepper will do just fine.)

½ tsp. salt

2 T. olive oil

1 T. (approximately) freshly ground black pepper (equals about 50 grinds from a pepper mill)

2 T. crushed oregano (use fresh if you can get it)

2 T. crushed basil (ditto on the fresh)

2 T. butter

1 T. sugar

1. Place the olive oil in a large saucepan or small kettle and heat.
2. Chop the onion fine and sauté it in the oil until translucent.
3. Add the tomatoes (undrained) and the tomato paste and stir, breaking the tomatoes into bits. Stir in the water and salt, bring to a boil, and reduce the heat to a simmer.
4. Brown the *carne molieda*, sausage, or any other meat you want to throw in by crumbling it into a hot frying pan; add it to the sauce.
5. Add the garlic, hot pepper, oregano, basil, and the bay leaves and simmer for an hour or so. If the sauce starts spluttering, add some more water until it stops. If you add the garlic at the end of the recipe instead of sautéing it with the onion (as in most inferior recipes), it will retain much more of its flavor.
6. Stir in the butter and sugar and serve over heaps of spaghetti with *plancha* bread or crusty French bread, a fresh garden salad, and lots and lots of cold beer.

Soups and stews

Soups, stews, and casseroles form the basis of many cruising meals and every cruiser you meet will have numerous recipes that they believe are special. One of my favorites is the macaroni and cheese recipe in *The Fannie Farmer Cookbook*, and Susan makes a killer potato scallop from *The Joy of Cooking*. There is little point in repeating these recipes here, but here are two others that are unique.

CAPTAIN GARLIC'S WORLD-FAMOUS CHILI

One way to prepare this zesty dish is to take the leftover spaghetti sauce and add some pinto beans and an extra measure of chili powder. The oregano in the spaghetti sauce won't hurt the chili a bit. Of course, real Texas chili lovers will protest that this isn't real Texas chili but that's because we haven't done much cruising in El Paso. What follows tastes better anyway. If you want to make a from-scratch version that's quick and easy, here's how. Serves six to eight.

Garlic (as much as you think your guests can tolerate—I seldom use fewer than a dozen cloves), finely chopped
1 large green onion
2 T. olive oil
2 cans (10-oz.) whole Italian plum tomatoes (or whatever other kinds of tomatoes you might have aboard—fresh are OK, too)
8 oz. tomato paste
1 c. water
1 can (16-oz. or 450-g) pinto beans, drained
1 lb. *carne molieda* or fresh Italian sausage (optional)
2 T. fresh chili powder (chili powder loses its kick real quick in the tropics, so use a fresh lot whenever you can)
1 tsp. habanero pepper (or ahi peppers, fresh hot chilies, or ground red pepper)
½ tsp. salt
Freshly ground black pepper (about 50 grinds from a pepper mill) and salt to taste
2 T. oregano
1 large Spanish or Bermuda onion, chopped
Grated longhorn or sharp cheddar cheese

1. Chop the garlic and the onion together and sauté in the oil until translucent.
2. Add the tomatoes and the tomato paste with the water and stir, breaking the tomatoes into bits. If you have any fresh tomatoes, peel a few and chuck them in.
3. Add the drained beans.
4. Crumble the meat into a frying pan and brown until it sticks to the pan, then scrape it off and brown some more—you want the meat to be crisp, almost burned—and add it to the pot.
5. Stir in the chili powder and simmer for an hour if you can wait that long.
6. Serve in bowls with the chopped onion and grated cheese sprinkled on top. Make sure there is plenty of crusty bread and butter and cold beer on hand.

Believe it or not, this makes a terrific dish for a hot tropical evening; it will sure take your mind off the heat in a hurry.

CAPTAIN GARLIC'S SPICY BEAN SOUP

OK, so it's just the leftover chili with a little water thrown in to thin it out a bit, but it's simple, easy to prepare, and incredibly delicious. I wonder why no one seems to like it much? Could it be that because by the time we get to the soup, everyone's pretty sick of Captain Garlic's World-Famous Spaghetti Sauce? (Naw, that couldn't be it.)

Onboard bread
Bread is one of the most basic of foods, and the ability to turn out a decent loaf from the ship's oven is one of the easiest and most useful of all the nautical skills. Aboard *Sultana* we make no attempt to bake all of our own bread. To do so would take too

much time away from other more cruiserly activities and would preclude us from sampling breads from the local ovens in the lands we visit. In all our cruising, I can recall only one boat with a crew that claimed to bake all their own bread, and that was an exceedingly thin German couple who appeared to have a limited appetite.

We do bake a lot of bread, however, but usually it is for a special treat, to provide fresh bread on a long passage, or to provide variety when the local fare becomes limited and tedious. My favorite bread recipe is the one on the side of the King Arthur flour bag. In the Caribbean it is known as Cuban bread and it's about as simple a bread recipe as you can find. If you are new to bread making and want a wholesome, nutritious, and easy place to start, this is the first recipe you should try. You will find a version in every cookbook that has bread recipes so I won't repeat it here, but there are some interesting twists that I will tell you about.

ENGLISH MUFFINS

English muffins are a favorite of the entire crew but they are often hard to find and sometimes expensive. You can, though, make delicious English muffins on the galley stove using the basic bread recipe. Roll out the dough to about ½-inch thick and cut out rounds with the floured rim of a large water glass. Set the rounds aside to rise until they are 1-inch high, then cook them in a frying pan or on your *plancha* set over a medium flame. Cook one side until it is browned, then flip the muffin over and cook the other side. Store the muffins in a ventilated container (never wrap or store homemade bread in plastic) until you are ready to use them.

PIZZA A LA *PLANCHA*

The basic bread recipe also makes an excellent pizza dough if you add a tablespoon of olive oil to the mixture, and a *plancha* makes a perfect pizza pan. The trick is to pre-heat the *plancha* and roll the dough out on a floured board. Add your toppings (Captain Garlic's World-Famous Spaghetti Sauce makes an excellent pizza topping— use lots of cheese and don't forget to add the anchovies), then slide the whole works onto the hot *plancha*. The hot pan seals the bottom of the pizza and makes it nice and crusty; if you start with a cold *plancha* the crust will get soggy—it'll be OK but not great. If you don't have a *plancha,* a pizza stone works just as well or even better; a glass pizza pan also works, but remember to get it hot before you slide on the pizza.

SUSAN'S *PLANCHA* BREAD

This is the classic recipe for a delicate Italian bread called foccacia that has been adapted to life on the high seas and cooked on the *plancha* instead of in a brick oven. It was given to Susan by another cruiser to whom we will be forever indebted, but we have completely forgotten who it was. It makes a lovely light bread for sandwiches, makes marvelous toast, and is one of those rare breads that is even better a few days after it is made (though it rarely lasts that long on *Sultana*) than when it is fresh. The secret is in the extra gluten, but if you can't find any, don't worry about it, the bread will taste fine—it just won't be as chewy.

1¼ c. tepid water
2½ tsp. dry yeast
1½ c. all-purpose flour
1 T. sugar
2 tsp. gluten
3 T. olive oil
½ tsp. salt

1. Put the tepid water in a glass measuring cup, add the yeast and sugar, and let it sit until it foams—usually about 10 minutes.
2. Mix the dry ingredients in a large mixing bowl, then add the oil and the yeast mixture a little at a time.
3. Stir into a sticky, wet dough.
4. Turn onto a flowered board and knead for 10 minutes. Try not to incorporate too much flour in the kneading process—you want a thin, light dough.
5. Put the dough back into the bowl and let it rise until it has doubled in bulk, then punch it down.
6. Smear the surface of the *plancha* with vegetable oil and place the dough in the center. It should be thin enough to form itself into a round flat loaf.
7. Let the dough rise once more then place it in a hot (375°F) oven for about 20 minutes.

Genuine foccacia is baked with little holes punched into the top and filled with olive oil; the top is sprinkled with sliced black olives and salt. You can do that if you like or you can cook it in a normal loaf pan or form it into small round rolls. It also makes a dandy pizza crust if you find the basic bread not to your liking or if you just need a change of pace.

A crew that eats well feels well, and a crew that feels well is well. The galley isn't only the most important part of the cruising boat, it's the center of the cruising universe. The trick is to realize that simple, basic, and fresh food is the best food, and to make sure that there is plenty on board at all times.

12

THE ELECTRONICS REVOLUTION

"The difficulty lies, not in the new ideas,

but in escaping from the old ones."

—John Maynard Keynes

Electronic Marvels

Nothing has changed the cruising environment in recent years as much as the electronics revolution. Communications, navigation, and life on a boat today are much easier than they were just a few short years ago and miles ahead of what the cruising pioneers of a few decades ago experienced. But the big news isn't what has happened so far but what is to come. All phases of marine electronics are in the early development stages, and the technology now exists for profound advances that will dwarf the ones we have seen to date.

Imagine an integrated system of electronic charts, onboard transponder, encoding 406 EPIRB, depthfinder, satellite communications link, weather fax, electronic winches, autopilot, radar, and GPS. With such a system you will simply key in your destination and your electronics will do the rest. Your course will be plotted and registered on the Global Central Control computer (located, no doubt, in a hollowed-out mountain not far from Denver), with priority given to weather and other traffic. Steering and sail control will be automatic. You will be informed of traffic in your vicinity down to the type of ship and the names of the crew and their destination. Your course and progress will be automatically relayed to your base station via Global Central.

If you should, God forbid, get into trouble, rescue efforts will be initiated automatically. Your cybernetic danger sensor will activate your EPIRB and Global Central will be notified of your position, your problem, the names and ages of your crew, and their preference for chicken *cordon bleu* or meatloaf. Next, a large mechanical arm will emerge from the lazarette, stuff the crew into survival suits and fling them into the automatically inflated liferaft where they will await the arrival of the satellite-guided rescue helicopter. On the way back to land the crew will enjoy an inflight movie, their specified entrée, and a little packet of stale cookies served by a thin person named Walter.

The fascinating thing about this fanciful scenario is that, with the exception of a few minor bugs in that large mechanical arm, all this technology exists right now, and everything mentioned above is not only possible but very likely. The only obstruction to full implementation at the moment is a rather cumbersome price tag.

Fortunately, it will take a long time for all these advances in cruising technology to filter down to cruisers like you and me, but a significant number of items have already filtered down and are here. Some of them are true boons to the cruising life and others are less so. In chapter 10 we discussed the considerable recent improvements in electronic battery control and charging systems; so let's take a look at a few of the others that are also here now, and we'll worry about what is coming when it gets here.

Over-reliance on electronic marvels

If people tell me that they will not sail without their radar (or GPS or depthfinder), they are telling me that either they have not developed their fundamental navigation skills, or they have not developed confidence in those skills to the point where they can make a major passage safely. Some will say that they can't make a passage safely without a full complement of electronics on board—to that misconception I reply, "Precisely, my dear Watson, and that is the problem."

Not long ago, a well-known British singlehander was feared lost when all attempts to contact him failed about a week after he left New Zealand. Three months later he sailed blithely into Lymington Harbor on the south coast of Britain looking for a berth, a hot bath, and a good meal. He had lost his engine, his radio, and all his electronics while underway, so rather than stop in some remote port where repairs were inefficient and costly, he simply broke out the sextant, hunkered down, and sailed the 9,000 miles to his home port. Now that's what I call a sailor.

No, I don't recommend that any cruiser in such a predicament simply sail home, but I do recommend that all cruisers acquire the skills to do just that before they undertake a serious voyage. How do you acquire these skills? You go cruising. Start with coastal cruising, then try a few overnight passages; when you feel confident enough, try a few two- or three-day passages. Except for your depthsounder and VHF radio, leave your electronics turned off and use them only when you sense danger or when your self-confidence starts to flag and your ego needs a boost. At the end of a year you'll be sailing the way Slocum, Chichester, Robin Lee Graham, and Tania Aebi did it—with your eyeballs, your brain, your sextant, and your good judgment. Then, if your GPS decides to take the day off and you drop your backup handheld unit overboard you can sail on without a care in the world, and the ability to do that will set you head and shoulders above less-skilled cruisers.

Electronic Navigation

I am of two minds about electronic navigation. First, the enormous benefits of the Global Positioning System (GPS), with its array of orbiting satellites broadcasting signals for triangulation to your shipboard receiver, cannot be denied. While at times it took Slocum and Chichester hours to locate themselves within a 10-mile radius of ocean, it now takes a modern cruiser only a few seconds to turn on the GPS and get a location that is exact to within a few meters. Not only that, long-ago cruisers had to wait for clear weather and daylight unless there happened to be a particularly bright moon (star shots really aren't practical on a small boat). Today, the GPS knows exactly where it is regardless of the weather or time of day and it will happily impart that information to anyone with enough smarts to push the right buttons.

But there are problems with over-reliance on GPS. Although your satellite signal may be unerringly accurate, the charts you are using aren't. I know of two cruise ships that went aground while religiously following their GPSs, one off Cape Cod (a large, sandy beach in Massachusetts owned by the Kennedys) and another in the Virgin Islands, and every waterfront pub where cruisers congregate is alive with tales of close calls caused by inaccurate charts. *Sultana* has encountered several instances of reefs, atolls, and even entire islands that are far enough from where they are supposed to be to be a hazard to navigation. Many are in the South Pacific, and the Haí Paí island group in Tonga is full of them. Of course, using a sextant doesn't make charts (even the electronic ones) any more or less accurate than they already are, but when we relied on our sextant as the primary means of offshore navigation, we were aware of the inherent inaccuracy of the instrument and were much more alert and cautious about fixing our position. Today, many of us will accept the GPS readout without question and without regard to external reference (such as looking out the window), which is, of course, potentially dangerous. We need to employ the same caution that we use with the sextant when we use GPS; further, we must realize that the very pinpoint accuracy of GPS can be a hazard when the charts aren't spot on.

In addition, although GPS is one of the most reliable electromechanical contrivances humanity has yet devised—in operational efficiency it is right up there with the space shuttle—we must remember that it is an electromechanical system and as such is subject to failure. Those same waterfront pubs mentioned above are also rife with harrowing tales about GPS receivers that failed to deliver when they were needed the most. Further, the system itself has been known to fail, and it isn't uncommon for entire sections of the system to be taken off-line for maintenance. And then, of course, there is the concept of "selective availability" when, in the case of a major conflict involving our military, the system can be rendered unusable.

So if GPS is such a wonderful thing, what are we to do about that niggling possibility that it might fail just when we need it most? When I first learned navigation, the axiom was that you always fixed your position with three independent observations (which today we call "inputs"). With an increase in vessel traffic and a general decrease in navigation skills, not to mention the number of people sailing around without enough inputs, this rule is even more important today than it was in the past. Every time you take a GPS reading you should reinforce that reading with two other unrelated observations.

Under normal conditions, and using the GPS as your primary navigation tool, how do you get three inputs when you are on the high seas and there is nothing around you but water? Your first input is your GPS position; the second is your dead-reckoning fix; and the third comes from a pair of the most marvelous inputers ever invented, of which most of us have two mounted on the anterior of our skulls somewhat north of our noses. They are called eyeballs. If you are in an area where there is supposed to be an island on the distant horizon, open 'em up and confirm that an island is there. At the same time, scan for traffic.

This sounds sophomoric, I know, but you must develop the habit of keeping your eyes open and using inputs other than electronic readouts. Imagine my embarrassment when, halfway between Panama and Tahiti, in an area of ocean I thought devoid of all humanity, I heard a hail on the VHF and looked up to see a previously unnoticed yacht several hundred yards off our starboard beam. Three days out of Nuka Alofa while sailing on flat seas in light winds on the way to New Zealand, I did a visual scan of the horizon and was startled to see an island where I didn't expect one. It wasn't an uncharted island, it's just that it was printed so small on the chart I was using that I hadn't noticed it. It was only a tiny island, but I have it on good authority that even a smallish island can make a biggish hole in your boat if you hit one.

Yet another problem with the GPS is that on many boats it is always switched on, informing the skipper and crew of their exact position every minute of the day. This may be fine on a tricky coastal passage fraught with natural hazards, but on an ocean passage, particularly a long one with no intervening hazards, knowing right where you are all the time can raise anxiety levels and become a significant psychological drag on your self-confidence and feeling of well-being.

How can this be? The average speed of most cruising sailboats is equivalent to a fast walk or maybe a slow jog for a really fast boat, and when considered on a global scale, as on a world cruise or a long passage, this is almighty slow. So slow that to realize just how slow it is can be psychologically debilitating, especially for new cruisers accustomed to a frantic shoreside life.

For example, when you are halfway between Hawaii and the Marshal Islands and the weather is clear and your boat is sailing well (making a hundred miles a day or so), it is perfectly OK to know you are halfway between Hawaii and the Marshals and let it go at that. But if you regularly check your position and make little X's on your small-scale chart, with even daily fixes those little X's are going to practically touch each other and you are going to get the idea that you aren't going anywhere at all—a depressing feeling in any kind of travel. It is much wiser to use your GPS just as we once used our sextants. Check your position twice a day, once a day, or even (when the conditions are ideal) once every other day, then turn off the GPS and enjoy sailing.

I can hear the armchair traditionalists, including the author of the following statement (taken from a popular boating manual), bellowing in sanctimonious dismay: "A [good sailor] always knows his or her exact position so that in the case of emergency that position can be reported to the appropriate rescuing agency."

This is bunk. It is pure bunk with sugar on top. While sailing on the high seas you are in one of the safest environments on earth; statistically, you are safer in a cruising sailboat that is not in a shipping lane and is clear of land than a baby is in its mother's arms. That's about a thousand times safer than you were in your car driving to work and back when you indulged in such perilous activities. On the odd chance that you do get into trouble out on the open sea there will be plenty of time to get a position from your GPS, and your 406 EPIRB (that most marvelous of all electronic marvels) is going to report your position with unerring accuracy anyway.

In case I haven't made myself clear . . . the problem with GPS is the enthusiasm with which a large segment of the cruising community embraces it as the only means of navigation. We have met several seasoned cruisers who have sold their sextants in the belief that they will never need them again. The new cruiser who devotes the time and energy to becoming a competent navigator with a sextant and timepiece is the rare exception.

Your GPS should be used to fix your position and nothing else. All those other features (waypoints, cross-track error, time to go, miles to go, miles made good, etc.) are great for racing tacticians and computer geeks, but they are useless for a skilled cruising sailor, and for the less experienced skipper they are detriments to acquiring important navigation skills. As soon as a position is fixed on a chart an experienced navigator will automatically, instantly, and often even subconsciously calculate all of these things without referring to any instruments. Overdependence on GPS read-outs will help ensure that you will never develop these important skills.

The only exception to the above is the altitude function that comes as an integral part of the GPS system. When you are sailing somewhere near to nowhere in a favorable wind on gentle seas and you are on watch at the helm reading a Dirk Pitt novel or just basking in the camaraderie of the stars and the sea birds, you will want to refer to the altitude function of your GPS just to make sure you haven't died and gone to heaven.

Celestial navigation calculators
Navigation calculators are little electronic marvels that take all the drudgery out of celestial navigation chores. They contain all the tables in all three HO 229 volumes (I know there are six, but unless you are headed for the Arctic you only need three), the *Air Almanac,* plus at least five years of nautical almanacs. The savings in book-shelf space alone makes the $300 price tag worthwhile (you can spend up to about $1,000 for the professional models). I don't happen to have a spare $300 to spend on one, but I have used these gadgets often enough to know that they really work—and to make me wish that I did (have the money) so I could (buy one).

If you don't have the $300, either, don't worry about not having a navigation calculator. There is no way a calculator can do reductions better than the tables—it just does them faster and without a lot of the clutter that comes with doing reductions manually. If you are a novice navigator still learning to do reductions and are tempted to buy a calculator, go ahead and do so—but leave it in the box until you understand how the tables work and can zip through them without a hitch.

Probably the most popular celestial navigation calculator on the market at present is the Celesticomp V. It performs an amazing range of functions including sight reduction, almanac for all bodies to the year 2100 (that should be adequate for most of us), running fix, dead reckoning, star identification, and many others.

Scientific calculators
If you happen to have a standard programmable scientific calculator on board, it is most likely capable of being programmed to perform LOP calculations. I am presuming that if you have one of these very complicated devices, you know how to use it. I don't, so I can't advise you any further other than to say that I have met several cruisers who use them with very good results and they tell me that the formulae and algorithms needed for navigation functions are often found in the instruction manual. One possibility is the Sharp PC-1270. This is a top-of-the-line programmable scientific calculator that has plug-in modules for celestial navigation. If you need a scientific computer, it might be a good choice. Both the

Celesticomp V and the Sharp PC-1270 cost less than $300 dollars and are available from Starpath Marine.

If you have a big pile of money laying around and would like to get rid of some of it, you might investigate the Tamaya NC-200. It has all the features of the Celesticomp plus it will display LOPs on a screen. It is also easier to use than the other units with simple controls and a larger display. With a price tag of just over $1,200, it is probably of interest only to professional delivery skippers and cruisers with deep pockets. If you are in either category, you can get one from Celestaire, Inc.

Celestial navigation software
Several celestial navigation software packages that you can install in your PC laptop computer are available at only a fraction of the cost (about $100) of a dedicated navigation calculator. They will do just about everything that the expensive units will do, provided, of course, that you have the even more expensive laptop to begin with. I'll talk more about onboard computers below, but for now I'll just say that the problem with all navigation software isn't the software but the computer.

Assuming that your GPS is your primary position-fixing tool, I would not hesitate to embark on a voyage with a navigation calculator without a hard copy of the almanac and tables to back it up. The current models of these devices use dedicated chips from which critical data can't easily be erased. Even a ham-handed, computer-illiterate barnacle buster like me can't mess them up without the help of a hammer.

The calculator, like the GPS, isn't infallible, of course, but the risk is slight and one I would be willing to take. Not so with the laptop/software combination, however. The current models of PCs are sturdy and reliable but they are no match for the marine environment. A single drop of seawater or even a humid day can stop them cold. Computers are also subject to software glitches, viruses, and ignorant operators. They are just not reliable enough to depend on without a hard copy of the tables (or another calculator) to back them up, even when used as a secondary navigation tool.

There are a lot of PC programs that will do celestial sight reductions and LOPs floating around the cruising community. Most of these are pirated versions of commercial programs that have been copied and recopied then passed on. You can use these if you like. Just be sure you have a good antivirus scanner and can handle the guilt associated with pilfering software. If you have access to the Internet, a better way to get an excellent navigation program—one that does everything that the celestial navigation calculators will do—is to download the trial version from Stormy Weather Software (see appendix). If you like it you can send them $45 for the full version which, as far as I can see, is exactly the same thing. If you don't have an Internet connection, no problem—just send them $55 and they will send you a copy on disk. This is a real bargain and everyone who owns both a boat and a computer should have it regardless of what other navigation apparatus you might own.

Electronic charts
Electronic charts are simply marine charts that are rendered digital and stored on a disk rather than rolled up and stored in a tube or in a drawer at your nav sta-

tion. There are presently two general types: one that requires a dedicated electronic device called a chart reader or plotter, and another that can be read on any standard IBM compatible computer that will accept CDs. Many of the charts for the dedicated readers are cartographed or edited by the company that makes the reader, such as the Smartmap cartridges for the Lowrance plotters. Other companies such as Navionics and Chartworks Marine develop and market charts for a number of manufacturers. All these charts vary in quality, but as more and more are coming on the market they are getting better all the time. True worldwide coverage with excellent electronic charts is not far away.

It appears that the dedicated readers are slowly losing ground to the ordinary personal computer, and there are presently more charts available for PCs than for the dedicated readers. Perhaps the market has decided that the greater reliability of the dedicated plotters isn't worth their lack of flexibility and high price. Chartworks Marine, developers of the popular C-MAP dedicated cartridges, now has a good part of the world covered on CD charts, and MapTech/Chart-Kit is producing copies on CD of their collections of existing charts. These are produced under license to NOAA by direct access to their digital files, thus eliminating the laser scan in many cases.

Electronic charts promise to eventually relieve the up-to-date cruiser of one of the most burdensome of cruising burdens—the huge and costly pile of paper charts that even a short cruise requires. But that day is not here yet. Unfortunately, electronic charts are nowhere nearly reliable enough to use without a paper copy handy to back them up (thus negating their primary advantage), and because of the huge areas of ocean most cruisers cover, the electronic charts are still much too expensive to be considered a normal part of the cruising kit. The cost varies a bit between the different types and manufacturers, but it averages between $10 and $15 per chart, which is about the same as the price of a current new paper chart but much more that the $2 or $3 price of the photocopied charts that are so popular among cruisers. MapTech sells a single chart on floppy disk for $15, but in most other cases you must buy an entire CD of charts for a given area, even if you only want one or two. Thus, you could spend several hundred dollars for a disk just to get the few charts you need, which increases the cost of electronic charts over paper charts to ridiculous proportions. Although coverage is now excellent, there are large areas remaining for which electronic charts aren't available. Electronic charts by definition require either a computer or a dedicated chart reader, and I have a particular problem with the charts for the dedicated readers. Many of the older ones leave out certain information that the purveyors of these appliances have deemed unimportant—such as the depth of the water.

C-MAP charts in both dedicated and PC formats are available from Chartwork Inc. For Navionics charts contact Navionics. For a list of retailers of ChartKit and MapTech charts, contact MapTech, Inc. (see the appendix).

Radar

I don't know where it came from, but I seem to have developed the reputation among all my friends for being anti-radar. Both of them tell me that I am constantly putting down radar and advising budding cruisers not to buy one. This is unfair and untrue. Yes, I did remove the perfectly good radar that was installed on *Sultana* when we bought it, but that was because the thing had a masthead unit that weighed more than 80 pounds, a CRT screen that took up half the cabin, and it sucked the juice out of a battery bank the way Democrats suck the money out of a congressional budget.

But on my last trip home I ran into a deal on a radar at my friendly local marine chandlery that I couldn't resist. It has a masthead unit that weighed only 17 pounds, and while it still uses a lot of electricity, it wasn't nearly as greedy as the previous beast. So I bought it and returned to New Zealand with a Furuno 16/21 radar in my luggage.

I have never advised anyone not to buy a radar but I have always preached to all who will listen the same message of caution and restraint that I preach about GPS and all other electronics. Radar is a wonderful device and to deny its many useful functions would be foolish. For tracking shipping in busy channels, for locating major above-the-waterline hazards, for tracking storm cells, and as a navigation tool, radar is unsurpassed for use at night. It is marginally useful in inclement weather and can be a big help in fog. In clear weather and in daylight it is much better to switch your radar off and revert to your Parallel Ocular Rangefinding and Tracking System (PORTS)—a.k.a. your eyeballs—a much more accurate and reliable navigation device.

To use radar as a tool is fine, but to rely on it to the point where you consider it as essential to a safe passage is foolish and dangerous.

Radar no-nos

Like all electronics, radar is a source of information and nothing more. And it is the single most unreliable source of information that you have. Radar will happily tell you that there are massive objects looming right off your bow when there is nothing but clear ocean, and when there is a massive object right off your bow, it can blithely ignore it. Radar can be blanked out by rain or fog or breaking waves or even your own rigging just when you need it the most, and in rough seas or when the boat is heeled at a healthy sailing angle it will be rendered useless. Even the new more efficient sets use a lot of electricity so unless you have a massive reserve of battery power, you will not be able to turn it on except for short periods without running your motor at a fast idle.

Radar technology

My tiny Furuno will squirt out 15,000 watts of pure power at a frequency that approaches 9500 MHz (one MHz is a million cycles a second) at a rate of 500 to several thousand pulses a second. All this energy comes from a magnetron that is just like the one you use to cook frozen tacos in a microwave. When this massive jolt hits an object, a tiny fraction (about a millionth of a watt) is bounced back to the reflector where it is detected in the tiny interval between the outgoing pulses. This information is relayed through the processing unit to the screen where it is displayed as a blip (or a "target" in the jargon of the radar elite—which seems to be an odd thing to call something we most often want to avoid). As technology goes, radar is every bit as remarkable as a transistor or a microchip and it is one of the things that has changed the way cruisers and shoresiders alike live.

The effective use of radar requires extensive training and years of practice in interpreting echoes. It is one thing to look at a blip on a radar screen and announce in an authoritative voice, "We have a target, Captain," and it is another thing to have any inkling of what that target is. Is it a large ship bearing down on us? Is it two or three small fishing boats going away from us? Is it a reflection of our own boat bouncing off a distant sea wall? Is it a small storm cell? Or is it just our radar itself being mischievous and playing little tricks on us? There is no way to tell for sure—not with the tiny yacht-sized radars we are talking about here. If your radar shows a target where there is supposed to be a distant mountain or a close-in buoy, then it is most often a safe assumption that is what it is. But there is no way to tell for sure what a blip on your screen represents. For this reason, radar is never a substitute for a lookout on the bow using those eyeballs we talked about earlier. Radar tells us that there might be something out there. Eyeballs tell us if there is really anything out there and if so, what it is.

Radar efficiency and effectiveness is determined to a large degree by the width of the beam pulse emanating from the magnetron into the parabolic reflector (properly called a radiator) on the top of your mast. That beam width is determined by the length of the radiator. Thus, a really good radar is both large and expensive, just the opposite of what you and I are looking for—a radar that is small and cheap. The most effective big-boat radars use a beam pulse that is one minute of angle (MOA) or less in width, but this requires a radiator that is about half as long as the average boat's main boom—5 feet or so. The radiator on most small radars is less than a foot long and the beam is usually some 1 MOA wide. That is one big fat beam and when that beam gets out there a half mile or so, it is hundreds of feet wide—more than 350 feet wide in fact. Anything that it hits within that football-sized arc is going to show up as a target (if it shows up at all) regardless of its size or shape. It could be a cargo ship or an exposed reef or it might just be a figment of your radar's imagination.

Another result of a short radiator and a wide beam is a phenomenon called Side Lobe Error. Side lobes are caused when some of that energy from the magnetron spills out of the sides of the short radiator. These side lobes are much less powerful than the main beam but if they hit a target it can show a blip just like the main beam. Because the side lobes are directed off to the sides, the blip on the screen will be in a different place than the main blip, and in the worst case where multiple side lobes are bouncing off a single object, your boat can look like it is surrounded by targets when there is really only one. You can get rid of most side-lobe ghosts by detuning the set with the gain control, but in so doing you risk detuning the main target.

Couple the two big problems with small radars, big fat beams and prolific side lobes, with the decidedly inferior display on the new Liquid Crystal Diode (LCD) screens (the Cathode Ray Tube [CRT] display on the old Decca that I gave away was much sharper than any of the new sets) and you have a marginally useful navigating tool. You do not have a device that is essential to a safe or enjoyable cruise nor do you have anything that deserves even a part of the fanatical loyalty that radar seems to engender in a large part of the cruising community. If you can afford one, great, get one. If you can't afford one, that's fine too—go cruising anyway and don't worry about it.

Another less publicized problem with radar is the hypnotic effect using one can have on the operator. Radar is a complicated tool and its use requires that the operator constantly be fiddling with the controls—particularly the gain. To understand the gain control, think of it as the squelch on your VHF radio—it filters out background noise by reducing the sensitivity of the receiver. Newer radar sets have an automatic gain, of course, but it's of limited use because there is never any correct setting for the gain. It is always different depending on the strength of the target, the amount of background noise or scatter, atmospheric conditions, and the range to the target. Close targets require less gain than distant targets. This constant fiddling with the controls takes a lot of concentration and can keep the operator's eyes glued to the set when they would be better employed looking out over the bow.

Blanking the screen with the controls while trying to get rid of ghosts is one of the best ways to sail into disaster as your radar shows a clear screen. In fact, this sort of thing was so common in the early days of radar that the phrase "Radar Assisted Collisions" was coined. Such collisions were common, are still common, and will continue to be so as long as radar operators insist on expecting more from their sets than they can deliver.

There are lots of other ways for the inexperienced operator to go wrong with radar: multiple echoes when a signal is bounced back and forth from a target several times resulting in multiple blips; false targets where there is a strong blip and nothing there; and blind sectors where a target is blanked by a mast or other physical obstruction are just a few. But the biggest failing of radar is in the head of the person using it—the feeling of false security that a blank screen imparts. Radar shows us what is above the water, when it is what lies below that is of primary interest, and it shows us what *might* be out there when it is what is *really* out there that can sink our boat.

Communications

The last time I worked on a book for International Marine, the publisher of this book, *Sultana* was anchored in a tiny jungle backwater off the Rio Dulce in Guatemala. When it came time to mail the manuscript I dinghied into the appropriately named town of Fronteras, then boarded the local bus for an hour-long adventure ride to the slightly larger and inappropriately named town of Morales. The ride through the jungle, jammed in among the Indians and *campenchinoes*—the ladies with their pigs and chickens and baskets of babies and pineapples and the flint-eyed men with their yard-long machetes—was one of those wonderful experiences that we all hope to find while cruising. At the end of the line I walked the several blocks through the market that was jammed with vendors selling anything you ever wanted to buy, until I reached the office where I posted my package. The experience is one I will never forget, but it took an entire day just to mail a few pages of manuscript.

Today, just a few short years hence, *Sultana* is on the hard in Nelson, New Zealand. When I finish the draft of this chapter, I will punch a few buttons on the computer and it will be transmitted intact and instantly via the Internet to Amanda Williams, Kate Mallien, and Nancy Hauswald (my editors), in Rockport, Maine. No dinghy trip, no bus ride through the jungle with the Indian ladies, no walk through the shopping stalls, no fear that *el correodor* will steal the package to get the stamps, and no waiting a week or so to see if it made it. Not a very exciting procedure, true, and one I will forget almost instantly, but there is no way you can argue that it isn't more efficient.

When I wanted to make a phone call from the Rio, I made the same dinghy trip into Fronteras then sat in the telephone office for an hour or so until the operator found an empty line. The call cost about $20 and was often terminated when the line went dead. Today, we communicate with e-mail, and only telephone on special occasions like Mom's birthday or when my brother, Clint, trims his beard.

The Internet

The communications field has recently enjoyed one of the most profound transformations of any technology in a world of changing technology. The ability to call home has changed so quickly that many cruisers I know don't realize that it has changed at all and still look for a phone booth every time they go ashore. But today, a growing number of cruisers are becoming aware of the ease and economies of the Internet for nearly all their communications. Many marinas (perhaps most marinas by the time you read this) have facilities for cruisers to connect their laptops, and if you don't have a laptop some even have computers for their customers to use. As this is written, dedicated e-mail machines are just coming on the market, which means that soon you won't even need a computer. Some of these machines are designed for commercial use in public places and operate off your credit card (soon to become your "smart card" I am told). Good-bye phone booth, hello Smart Card Activated Multifunctional Communications Operations Module—SCAMCOM for short.

The Internet is growing at an amazing pace (the number of subscribers is doubling approximately every hundred days) so that the personal computer will soon rival the telephone as a communication tool regardless of how the telephone companies feel about it. Except for e-mail, as of this writing there is no practical way to gain access to the Internet from a cruising sailboat that is not tied to shore with a land line installed. Even the best satellite service offered today can't maintain the quality of transmission necessary to surf the Web. I understand this is due to limitations in the baud rate (the speed with which data can be transmitted) and that this is scheduled to change once Globstar (one of the new satellite systems) goes on line just before the turn of the century. Even then Internet access will be limited and probably far too expensive for us little guys—at least for the foreseeable future.

Radio telephone service

Most coastal cruisers in the U.S. are familiar with the VHF marine operator—that friendly voice who takes your call and your credit card number anytime you are within range of one of their transmission stations (about 25 miles or so off the U.S. coast or on the Great Lakes). This is a great service available to anyone and it is economical, but it is limited to the coastal waters. Once you are offshore and out of range you are out of luck.

SSB telephone service

Several companies provide telephone service through your SSB radio. The High Seas service offered by my old employer, AT&T, is probably the best known. It offers worldwide coverage (minus a few dead spots in places most of us would never go anyway) and requires no subscription fee or expensive additional equipment. It does require that you pay about $5 per minute for your call, so most cruisers use it only for emergencies.

There are also several companies offering e-mail service through your SSB set, but as far as I know, the only one that is of interest to the small-boat cruiser who doesn't have an extra two grand or so to spend on specialized equipment is SeaMail, an Australian-based service that operates through a worldwide network of high-frequency radio stations. Using SeaMail requires installing a modem that costs about $300, and you need a personal computer, but if you have these things anyway it is an economical service that costs about what you pay for your telephone service ashore.

Marine SSB Internet service works just the same way as your normal shore-side Internet service but with one added step. When an e-mail message is sent to you over the Internet it is routed to your service provider (identified by the bit in your e-mail address after the @) where it is held in file until you call in for it. With marine e-mail, your incoming message goes to a local server where it is held until called for by the marine service provider, who then holds it in file until you call in for it on your SSB radio. While the Internet transmits e-mail with incredible speed, the same message transmitted over the radio is transmitted slowly or very slowly depending on atmospheric conditions. Of course, the transmission is subject to degradation by the same interference that affects your voice transmission, only more so. Thus, the most economical SSB e-mail services, which transmit at a slow 200 to 800 baud, are restricted to short messages that require a clear signal for successful transmission. Some providers, such as SeaMail, will hold all messages until they are successfully transmitted; others will dump them if they are not retrieved within a certain time period, typically three days.

Another possibility for SSB e-mail service while offshore is with the PinOak Digital's PODLink service. This works just like SeaMail but with a much more sophisticated (and costly—about $1,800) modem. The big advantage to PinOak's service is that their modem can interpret signals at a much lower level of propagation than is required with other services. As with all SSB usage, including voice, frequencies are only available during certain times so that while these services offer near worldwide coverage they can't offer true 24-hour coverage. I think that if you are going to spend this kind of money you are better off using the services discussed below because of their greater reliability and versatility.

SeaMail is probably the best bet for cruisers in the Caribbean and the Pacific (expansion plans provide for worldwide coverage soon). To use it you need a PacTOR or GTOR modulated modem (KAM Plus by Kamtronics is a good one), a good SSB radio, and a laptop computer. The size of your document is limited to 5,000 characters (about a page) and you can't transmit or receive attachments. But with a $15 annual subscription fee, about $1 a page for messages (depending on atmospheric conditions), and a $300 to $400 investment for a modem, it is an inexpensive way to communicate, assuming, of course, that you already have a computer and an SSB.

A similar service to PinOaks and SeaMail is offered by Globe Wireless, an established provider of SSB services to the commercial shipping fleet that also offers some services that are attractive to yachts. Their Globetor service and Globe e-mail both require a fairly sophisticated radio (such as the ICOM Model 710 at about $1,900 from HF on Board) that can interface with your computer. They advertise 24-hour, worldwide coverage, but as with all SSB transmissions propagation is always a factor in successful reception and for the money, the satellite services begin to be attractive.

Propagation problems don't exist with satellite e-mail, of course. Once you have the proper antennae and transmission gear, e-mail may be sent and received just as it is from shoreside computers.

Ham radio/telephone service

One of the best reasons for suffering through the ordeal of getting your ham license is the ease with which you can use it to make low-cost telephone calls while far out on the ocean. If you have your general-class ham license (cruisers visiting Mexico can now get a reciprocal license for their no-code novice-class license, which allows full communication privileges), you can make phone-patch calls anywhere in the world at regular land-line rates through your ham radio. All you need do is make contact with a ham on shore who has a modem installed, give the ham the phone number you want to call, and the ham will place a collect call to that number and patch you through. The connection with the shoreside ham is usually made by one of the many marine ham nets that operate all over the world. Most nets have several volunteers standing by just to assist in making such calls. Naturally, all of the normal ham protocol must be observed and the restriction against making business calls over the ham frequencies is strictly enforced. But even so, the calls are easy to make, they're cheap, and they are one of the best and most economical ways to stay in touch.

Ham e-mail

Licensed hams can sometimes get e-mail through a shoreside volunteer station in a manner similar to making a patched phone call and, in a lot of ways, it is even easier than making a phone call. You will need a modem, such as the Kamtronics KAM Plus (at less than $400 with appropriate cables from HF On Board) and a computer. For cruisers on a budget, ham e-mail is a much better option to the commercial stations than it might at first seem, provided you already have your general-class ham license. The shore stations are automated and are using the same technology and equipment as the commercial SSB stations. Because of the restrictions against using the ham network for business, its primary use is for keeping in touch with the folks back home and for emergencies.

Satellite mobile telephone service

With satellite mobile telephone service, anyone who has one of those suddenly ubiquitous and ridiculously tiny cellular telephones (or a device that is nearly identical) can call any other similarly equipped person in the world just as easily as they can call the guy across the street.

Satellite telephone service has been around for a long time now and is most familiar to yachties in the form of the various Inmarsat services (Inmarsat C, M, and 3) offered by Comsat. Up to now these services were available only to the super rich, in part because you needed about 75 feet of waterline length just to carry the bulbous antenna that the service required. But all that is changing dramatically. About a half-dozen companies now spend billions of dollars shooting hundreds of satellites into orbit just to provide you with this service at an economical price. The primary difference between the new services and the old is in the type of satellite used. Inmarsat and several others use geostationary orbiters (a big word that means the satellite stays in one place relative to the earth as it orbits at the same speed as the earth is turning) that require complex gyrostabilized antenna. The new services use a large number of orbiting satellites in Low Earth Orbit (LEO) or Medium Earth Orbit (MEO). Motorola's Iridium satellite system is nearing completion and TRW's Odyssey service isn't far behind; by the time this gets into print, these services will start coming online. The potential is for them to offer integrated fax, voice, and e-mail all on the same service (but no TV or Web surfing). The real difference in these services and the Inmarsat M service we have now will be in the equipment required. All you will have on your boat is a telephone that looks just like a cell phone and a modem for data and e-mail. The antenna and receiving equipment that now take up so much space will no longer be needed.

The decision about which service to use is easy if you are an average cruiser on an average budget. If you have your ham license and an appropriate radio and all you want to do is stay in touch, the ham services, are hard to beat. If you have an SSB, the slight extra cost of a commercial service like SeaMail is in order. Remember, though, that these services are limited to an occasional one-page e-mail message, reliability will vary with location and atmospheric conditions, and you can't use the ham service for anything that even resembles a business transaction. (For example, you can't ask your mom to check prices in the West Marine catalog.) If, however, your communications requirements involve more than an occasional message home, the slow speed and higher transmission fees of the commercial SSB services will quickly negate the savings in equipment over satellite services (Iridium and Inmarsat M). Plus, you have the much higher reliability of the satellite link over the broadcast links. So if you are operating a business while you cruise (there are more than you might think) or if you are a Type-A person who likes to be in touch all the time, the satellite services are the way to go.

On the importance of being licensed

One last thing before we leave the area of cruising communications: make sure all your licenses are in order before you depart on your cruise. At the very least you will need a ship's station license for your VHF, but when you apply for this license you should include your GPS and an SSB radio even if you don't have one yet. These licenses are now good for 10 years and if you want to add equipment that isn't listed on your current license, you must apply for a new one. This can be both expensive and difficult if you are doing it in home waters, and a lot more so if you are trying to do it in a distant port. The important thing to remember is to keep all your licenses current. Using a radio with a lapsed license can be a very expensive mistake.

Speaking of foreign countries, most popular ports will recognize a U.S. radio station license, but you are going to encounter a broad range of VHF radio practices and procedures. (SSB and ham rules are established by international convention and are therefore fairly uniform.) These range from complete anarchy in most South American and Caribbean ports (as well as in many urban ports in the U.S.) to very stiff and formal protocol in Australia and New Zealand (these folks do like to make rules, and they follow them). When you enter a new port, make sure you understand what these procedures are before you go shooting off your mouth and getting into trouble. The best procedure is to monitor Channel 16 as you approach your port, then try to make contact with another cruiser just before you enter. A simple broadcast such as this one should do the trick:

"This is the sailing vessel *Sultana*, Whiskey Zulu Foxtrot 8975 [your radio station license call sign], now approaching the entrance to Aitutaki Harbor. Anybody with information on the entrance channel please come back."

Any cruisers who might be listening will stick their heads out of their hatches to take a look. Then they will wait for someone else to answer your plea. The same thing will happen on your second broadcast. On your third attempt, they will all answer you at once. It never fails. As soon as you make contact, you should ask what the working channels are for cruisers in that area, then switch immediately to one of them. By the time you drop your anchor, not only will you know what radio protocol to follow and all about the clearance procedures but everyone in the harbor will know all about you. What a great way to meet people.

As with any other complex and specialized area of the marine environment, you are well advised to consult a trusted professional before you strike out across the ocean. Unfortunately, most ham radio outfits don't do SSB and vice versa. And the satellite folks don't do either of the others, so it can be difficult to get reliable information on all areas at once. A notable exception is HF Radio on Board in California, a full-service shop run by Don Melcher who is both a communications expert and a cruiser. Don was a big help to me in preparing this section and can be reached at the address and numbers given in the appendix.

Your ham license

The concept of amateur radio dates all the way back to the first radio broadcasts when, if you wanted a radio, you had to build it yourself. Today, ham radio is a vestige of its former self. Its appeal dates to the days when the ability to talk to someone a half a continent away with no wires attached was a miracle, but some ham enthusiasts today don't seem to realize that there have been a few minor improvements in communications technology in the last 75 years or so. They happily pursue their skeds and nets and DXs without a thought for the rest of the world doing the same thing with a few flicks of computer keys. They continue to insist that initiates into the ham world struggle through the laborious process of learning the now functionally useless Morse code to get the general class license that is necessary for international communications. (The last vestige of Morse Code, a regional maritime weather broadcast, was discontinued late in 1998 simply because no one was using it.)

Even though ham radio is yesterday's technology swaddled in arcane rules and hypocritical regulations, it is still a useful, if not critical, tool for the ocean navigator and well worth the effort it takes to get one. You can use ham radio to call home, as stated above, and you will never be out of range of one of the hundreds of maritime ham nets that blanket the globe. These nets are always ready with friendly chat or to lend a hand when medical advice or emergency communications are needed, and they are the best source of information on when to go where and why.

Personal Computers

In the last dozen years or so, I have probably purchased five or six personal computers, every one of which became obsolete as I carried it out of the store. On my last trip back to the U.S., I bought a new moderately priced, moderately fast, Pentium-powered Toshiba Model 220CDS to replace the antiquated and hopelessly inadequate Macintosh Classic I had bought at the beginning of our trip less than four years before when it was state-of-the-art. When I showed my new computer to a New Zealand friend who knows about such things (Kiwis are among the most technologically aware people on earth), he was visibly amused. "Where'd ya get that old dinosaur, mate? Steal it from a museum or something?"

When I took the amazingly compact printer—a Canon BS somthinorother—that I also bought with the computer in for servicing, the person behind the counter gave it a skeptical look. "Oh, you've got one of *them*. Been discontinued, ya know."

"Of course they're discontinued," I answered. "Production stopped the moment I handed the bloke my check."

In spite of an obsolescence half-life that is equivalent to that of a moth approaching a bonfire, and a reliability that is less than that of a politician's campaign promise, there are a few uses for a computer on your cruising boat that might make them worth their considerable cost. Let's drop a few of the more obvious ones into the old toaster and pop them up where we can take a look at them.

Entertainment

If you have children on board, the entertainment value of a computer can't be denied. The kiddies will spend hour after hour blasting space aliens to bits, stomping muscled rivals into mud holes, splattering hostile adversaries with the most incredible variety of weapons imaginable, and generally wallowing in enough gore to make Attila the Hun blanch. All this, we are told, is very healthy for the little dears because it helps prepare them for—get this—"real life."

There are nonviolent computer games, of course, but getting a kid interested in "Carmen San Diego" or "The Math Challenge" when they could be helping Laura (the first ultraviolent cyberhero to break the sex barrier) eviscerate bolrogs and decapitate slime creatures is a challenge worthy of Superparent. Traditional board games—Scrabble, chess, Monopoly, and such—don't translate well into the electronic media, and a computer is no real substitute for the real thing.

Education

Unfortunately, the huge potential of the personal computer as a teaching tool and an education mechanism has never been realized because nearly all the developmental effort has gone into the aforementioned lifestyle games of slaughter and destruction. But the picture is not all grim. There are numerous educational uses for your PC that apply to both children and adults. It is a wonderful tool for onboard reference, and although I am loathe to give up my tattered copy of *Webster's Unabridged Dictionary,* when we leave New Zealand I will leave it behind and sail with the three-disk *Oxford English Dictionary* instead. The encyclopedia that we brought along for the kids' education (and entertainment—it is wonderful to get children out from under the influence of television even if it's only for a little while) will be replaced by a disk version that will save us some 60 pounds of weight and several cubic feet of space.

The other educational advantage of an onboard computer is the computer itself. We are told, by people who claim to know about such things, that it is important that anyone who wants to be functional in our society be "computer literate" and I suppose it's true. I, however, am hopelessly inept when it comes to computers (this computer-generated document stands as a personal monument to determination and perseverance), and Susan and the kids agree that I am equally dysfunctional when it comes to things societal. While I tend to regard this as the triumph of a superior intellect over the plebeian norm, they treat it as just another delusion of advancing age. But most educators agree that a familiarity with computers is an important part modern education, and so be it. We take children cruising to help them understand and cope with society, not to escape from it. Thus, a computer is an important part of any onboard education package.

As a navigation tool

I've discussed this already, of course, so it should be enough to repeat that computers can be quite useful for reducing nav tables when practicing your celestial navigation, and that the charts on CD can be useful, albeit expensive, backups to paper charts. However, computers are not quite reliable enough to replace your paper tables and charts, not yet anyway. Several other programs are also quite useful—some give an up-to-the-minute tide table for the next 200 years, and others have integrated navigation programs that promise to do everything including steer the boat. Many of these whizbang programs are restricted to small areas (such as the East Coast of the U.S.) and are of limited use to the world cruiser. Others (such as The Cap'n) have some of their features (such as seamless charting) localized, while other features (such as plotting) work on a global scale. Most computers, especially those with a PCC slot, will accept a GPS receiver as an attachment that is independent of your main system so that it can serve as a backup. It will also display your exact location on your seamless chart display or you can get a cable for most GPSs that will connect directly to your computer. All of these items might be useful for some and useless for others. It depends on your budget and the kind of cruising you plan to do.

As an onboard organization system

We have met many accomplished cruisers who keep the most amazing sets of records on their personal computers that you can imagine. They know to the penny how much they have spent on fuel, food, charts, entertainment, bubblegum, and taco sauce every day for the past 10 years. They know with scientific precision how many miles they have traveled, how often the oil in the engine has been changed, how much cash is left in the kitty, how much granola is left in the granola bin, and how many times the Jimmy Buffett CDs have been cycled through the CD player. The interesting thing about these folks is that before they had a PC they kept records just as accurately on paper.

If you are a neat and tidy person by nature, your personal computer can elevate your neatness and tidiness to ever loftier plateaus. If, however, you are an unrepentant slob when it comes to records and don't have the slightest inkling of how much you have spent on anything, then the computer is no help at all. In other words, to those fortunate few who don't need help with record keeping, the computer is a tremendous boon, and to those multitudinous masses who are desperate for help, it is of no use at all.

Water, Water, Everywhere

Many cruising books provide a heap of information on water management. Unfortunately, nearly all the information is wrong and focuses on the need for an onboard electromechanical watermaker. The fact is that there is a lot of stuff you don't need on your boat in order to go cruising and one of the things you don't need the most is a watermaker.

If this is true, you might ask, why is there an almost unyielding pressure on boaters in general, but cruisers especially, to buy these functionally useless and very expensive devices? We have all read the articles and product reviews that treat watermakers, radar, and chart plotters as essential gear, and the worst of these give the impression that if we don't have these items on board we are not only uncool and not with it, but quite possibly stupid as well.

The reasons for this incredible hype lie not with the companies that make these devices, nor with the media that tout them, but with the society we live in. We thrive on consumption. If consumption stops or even slows perceptibly, our society will collapse and our people will starve, so in a real sense consumption isn't just essential to our society, it is our society.

I won't bore you with a lot of supporting data on this statement because I have already filleted that particular mackerel and I think you know where I stand on the subject. However, I will repeat for emphasis, if you want to go cruising you must learn to turn your back on consumerism in general and on such things as watermakers in specific.

So what's wrong with watermakers? Although I don't have enough room to do the subject justice, here are a few failings:

- They are expensive to buy. A good one will cost more than your SSB and your 406 EPIRB combined.
- They are expensive to maintain. The monthly bill for pre-filters and biocide can easily equate to a good meal in a first-class restaurant for the whole crew. Plus they will use more electricity than your refrigeration and your radar combined.
- They are complicated. Most cruisers I know have a lot better things to do than work on watermakers. The pickling and maintenance schedule must be followed to the letter or very expensive repairs can result.
- They can't be used in harbors that have less than pristine waters because the filters will clog, thus they are useless about 90 percent of the time.

I won't even mention such things as the space they take up and their lack of reliability, but let's give it a rest after this one last thing. Watermakers aren't necessary. *Sultana* has made it almost halfway around the world and we have yet to run short of water. We catch 90 percent of our water on deck when it rains and the rest we get ashore. We add a bit of bleach to get rid of the germs, then we run our drinking water through a simple filter to get rid of the bleach. We carry 200 liters per person on a long passage. That's a lot, but we use it freely and our total cost for water in five years of cruising won't pay for a single pre-filter. We have, however, encountered several other cruising boats that have run short of water on many occasions. They were all boats that relied on watermakers for their main supply.

There is a good and often-made argument for carrying a hand-operated watermaker in the liferaft or in the abandon-ship bag, and this is excellent advice for those with big piles of spare cash cluttering up their bank balances. The rest of us need to consider the wisdom of spending $500 or $600 (the average price of the smallest watermakers) on a device that you might need once in every 1,000 circumnavigations. Dying of thirst or starvation while floating around in a liferaft is one of those phobic horrors with which advertisers like to terrify us into buying their stuff, but the likelihood of this ever happening is just about the same as being killed by a meteorite. The degree to which you can make your life safer by buying stuff is limited, and if you really need the kind of security that comes from having gadgets like miniature watermakers in your grab bag you might want to consider staying at home with the curtains drawn. Me? I'd rather die of thirst while floating around in a liferaft any day.

Safety at Sea

I have spent a lot of time trashing the consumer society and the profusion of pointless products it foists off on innocent cruisers. Perhaps I can redeem myself in the eyes of manufacturers and advertisers alike by recommending some expensive products that you really should have on board before you depart. Yes, even I will admit that technology has come up with some products that you must have on your boat. GPS is one, of course. A satellite telephone, once they are generally available at a reasonable price, will be another no matter how much curmudgeonly old cruisers bemoan their coming.

There is a huge amount of hypocrisy about safety, and we all like to bandy about such slogans as "One thing you can't compromise on is safety" or "If you can't do it safely, don't do it at all." Of course, if we followed these maxims we would never get out of bed in the morning much less do anything as foolish as crossing the street or going cruising on the ocean in a sailboat. The fact is, many cruisers compromise safety. They do it quite consciously and with the full realization that they could someday get in trouble for it. Many boats are sailing without liferafts aboard because of the amount of space they take up and because they cost so much to purchase and maintain. These people know full well that they would be safer with a liferaft but they have decided that the risk of going without one is worth the savings in space, money, and aggravation.

The same goes for most other expensive gear that is dedicated solely to safety. Most of us carry a good selection of outdated flares; many of us choose not to have a 406 EPIRB on board; few boats carry sea anchors in the low and middle latitudes; and even SSB radio equipment is not found on all cruising boats. Dedicated safety gear is a lot like insurance in that many of us would like to have it, but we are not going to let our inability to get it or pay for it deter us from going cruising.

Sultana carries a four-person Avon liferaft, SSB, 406 EPIRB, and a double complement of updated parachute flares, but this is primarily because we have children on board. The full complement of safety gear helps assuage the considerable guilt associated with exposing children to the slight but undeniable dangers of sailing a small boat on a big ocean. Both kids will be headed off for college at just about the time our liferaft reaches the end of its useful life and we will be faced with the decision to replace it just when our cash situation hits a crisis. I don't know what we will do at that point, but I know we will not stop cruising just because we can't afford a new liferaft.

Much of the resentment against New Zealand's infamous Section 21 (which mandates a liferaft and an EPIRB for all departing cruising boats) is not caused by the expense of the required inspection or by the inconvenience, both of which are minimal, but by the idea of a bunch of lubber bureaucrats telling us how to run our boats and our lives. That being said, let's take an up-close-and-personal look at the two most expensive pieces of safety gear you should have on your boat.

Liferafts

I have no way of knowing just how many of the liferafts carried by cruisers ever get used in an emergency, but I do know the number is very small, no more than one in a thousand, and it is probably much lower than that. I also know that in the past five years of talking to every cruiser who I can corner in conversation, I have yet to meet anyone who has ever had to abandon ship in a situation calling for a liferaft. I know it happens, I've read the liferaft sagas just like everybody, but it doesn't happen often.

The decision to take a liferaft cruising with you is one you must make on your own given your individual needs for security, the size of your boat, and your finances. A liferaft costs a lot of money (between $2,000 and $3,000 is about average), it will take up a huge amount of space on deck or down below, it will be a nuisance to maintain, and worst of all, it will be useful in only a small portion of cruising accidents. Even so, you should most certainly have one along if you can afford it.

Liferafts can and do deteriorate over time even when stored properly and not used. Thus, it is imperative that if you have one you get it inspected at least once every three years—and once a year is not too often. The older the raft, the more frequent the inspections should be. Never attempt to do your own inspection. If you do, I can guarantee you will not be able to get the raft back into the container. Most manufacturers have a list of repair stations authorized to perform inspections, but it can be very costly and a terrible nuisance if you are cruising in the remote areas. Most cruisers who have a liferaft have it inspected whenever they can get it done for a reasonable price, which usually means when in or near a big city, regardless of the schedule. Inspections cost about $300 dollars in the U.S. and can be much higher or lower in other areas. I suspect Europe is the most expensive and South America is the cheapest place to get this work done.

Two general types of liferafts are available to the cruising sailboat: coastal and offshore. The coastal rafts are light-duty, lightly constructed models that usually have a single flotation tube with two chambers, a non-inflating floor, and a manually erected canopy. They are designed for use where there is a high probability of a quick rescue, say within 24 hours. Since the advent of 406 EPIRBs this is a much larger area than it once was, and the cruising boat on a budget can consider the combination of a coastal liferaft and a 406 EPIRB to be adequate in most areas of the world. Offshore liferafts are more robustly made from heavier fabrics. They usually have at least two flotation tubes, an inflatable floor, and an automatic canopy. Naturally, they cost more, but they are heavier and much more durable than the coastal models.

Liferafts are stored either in a canister that is attached to the deck or in a valise that is kept below decks. The deck-stored models are usually the better choice because the valise models are too large and heavy to be easily deployed from below decks. Before you buy a valise liferaft, make sure you realize just how big and cumbersome they are. If you are going to go to the trouble and expense of buying one you will want one that can be deployed almost instantly—15 seconds max.

In many situations, deploying and entering a liferaft is more dangerous than staying on the boat. Storms at sea can be terrifying and there is a natural tendency to draw a false sense of security from the presence of a liferaft—but even a moderate storm can render a liferaft unusable. High winds and steep waves can easily make successful deployment and boarding highly problematical. People have been lost as they attempted to enter a liferaft, only to have the boat recovered later intact and still seaworthy. If you do decide to take a liferaft cruising with you, resolve right now to never attempt to use it unless you must. The raft must be reserved as a last resort and only be used when the boat is on fire or actually sinking. "Always step up into the liferaft" is a tried and true rule.

EPIRBs

Since their inception some 25 years ago, EPIRBs (a cumbersome acronym for Emergency Position Indicating Radio Beacon—even I could have done better than that) have saved the lives of hundreds of people, a significant number of whom have been cruisers. As the name indicates, they are small radio transmitters that, when activated, send out a signal beacon on which rescuers can home in and trace to the victim. EPIRBs were developed for aviation applications and all aircraft have been required to have them aboard ever since the early 70s. There are two basic types most easily identified by the frequencies they use.

The first is a general-purpose EPIRB which, when activated, will broadcast a beacon on 121.5 megahertz (MHz) that can be picked up by passing aircraft, a rescue party with a receiver tuned to this frequency (any radio direction finder will work), or under ideal conditions by a passing SARSAT satellite. They are compact enough to be kept handy at all times, and they are economical enough so that every offshore boat should have one. The drawbacks to these basic units are their low power (less than a tenth of a watt), the fact that satellite reception is incidental (the SARSAT must be right overhead and atmospheric conditions must be perfect), and the high number of false alarms they generate.

The 406 MHz EPIRBs incorporate several improved features over the 121.5 MHz sets, some of which please cruisers, some others that make retailers and manufacturers very happy, and one that is a huge relief to armchair sailors everywhere. We who cruise in offshore sailboats welcome the 406 EPIRBs as the most important advance in marine safety since the life jacket. With a direct satellite link that locates an activated set to within a two-mile radius, worldwide coverage, and a reliability that is nothing but remarkable, a distressed vessel can count on rescue within hours of activating the EPIRB in most areas. Even in the most remote corners of the globe rescue efforts can be organized and executed within a day or so. The reliability of these units is such that you can safely cut back the emergency rations and other supplies packed in your liferaft and in your abandon-ship bag.

Retailers, advertisers, and manufacturers are happy with 406 EPIRBs because they are essential gear (if you don't have one at departure you should work just a few more weeks and get one) and they are, at about $1,000 each, very expensive— a combination that puts them close to consumerist nirvana, making them candidates for the essential-product hall of fame.

And what about the armchair cruisers (that's all of us, isn't it)? We have all read the liferaft sagas about some boat that is sunk by some whale in some remote area of ocean and the crew floats around for several months in a liferaft eating raw seagulls. Now I don't want to sound insensitive here, and my heart goes out to those who have suffered through this ordeal, but after reading two or three of these epics, they get a bit . . . well, tedious, and the very best thing about the advent of the 406 EPIRB is that we will never have to read another one.

The masthead tri-light

Running lights have been used on boats since Phoenician times, of course, but the recent advent of the masthead tri-light is a quantum leap forward in marine safety. These units are far more visible than conventional running lights mounted on the cabintop, are much more visible to crew on the bridge of a large vessel, and they can be seen for a greater distance. When outfitting your boat for departure you should mount one of these units as an adjunct to your regular running lights, not as replacement for them.

Get one with an integral strobe even though it just about doubles the cost (to about $300). Technically, the strobe is to be used only in emergencies when the crew requires rescue, but when craft and crew are in danger it is my personal philosophy to remove them from that danger by whatever means is expedient and to sort out the legality of my actions later. This means turning on the strobe any time there is imminent danger of collision with shipping in any condition of limited visibility. The saddest moment of our entire trip came when the sailboat *Melinda Lee* was run down by a Korean log carrier off the east coast of New Zealand with the loss of three wonderful people. When struck, she was sailing about 300 miles ahead of *Sultana* in thick weather at night, and I can't help but believe that if she had used a masthead strobe in that very dangerous situation, the lost crew would even now be regaling fellow cruisers around the world with the harrowing tale of their near-miss.

So far, I have successfully shattered a few cruising icons, de-mythologized a few cruising myths, and debunked some cruising bunk. I have tracked the dragon of misinformation to its lair and slain it with the golden arrow of truth. Unfortunately, the demise of the dragon will not be met with a universal uproar of praise from the traditionalists. There are those in the cruising community who will continue washing their dishes in nothing but that certain brand of dishwashing detergent. Who will sneer at any boat that does not have softwood plugs wired to all the seacocks, and who will continue to try to wash a 10-inch pot in a 9-inch sink. But, as Gloria Steinem said, "Truth never harms a cause that is just" (or was that Ghandi?), so not only will we stand tall in the shadow of our slain dragon, we will continue the pursuit of false doctrine, and like medieval monks searching heresies, we will smite them as we find them.

However, in the interest of sportsmanship, I will let a few of the small falsehoods get away to become the trophies of tomorrow. For example, it is a long-established axiom that a cruising boat can't have too many anchors. Well, that's what Wyatt Earp said about aces until one day (his last) when he turned up five. *Sultana* left Marblehead with an assortment of eight groundgrabbers aboard, and I will hereby declare that that was too many. We had Bruces, Danforths, CQRs, and Fishermen scattered around the boat like rose petals after a windstorm. They were on bow rollers and on deck chocks, tied to the shrouds and buried in the bilge. They were always in the way and forever breaking their bindings in storms and rattling like the chains of the damned in the middle of the night just when we were about to drop off after a long, wet passage. Too many anchors is too many anchors.

Just one other little thing I'd like to mention. I hereby claim the honor of penning the very first cruising book to not even once quote Kenneth Grahame's *Wind in the Willows*. It's not that I'm not a great fan of Grahame's, mind you—I am—

and *Wind in the Willows* is one of my all-time favorite books, but that particular quote is a tad overcooked and I refuse to perpetuate the travesty.

With that, friends . . . a book, like a long ocean passage, has to come to an end sometime. We have gone far in the last several hundred pages or so, and I hope you have enjoyed the journey as much as I have. If you are still determined to try the cruising life after all that has been said, welcome aboard, Godspeed, and fair winds. And if in your travels you drop the hook in some remote lagoon next to a tattered old ketch with an inordinate number of anchors scattered about the deck, hop in the dinghy and row over. Sit and share a yarn or two and maybe a brew, but no matter what you decide to do with your life just remember: "There is *nothing*—absolutely nothing—half so much worth doing as simply messing about in boats." Oooops . . . damn!

APPENDIX

The following is a list of the addresses and telephone numbers of the businesses and suppliers mentioned in this book.

Celestaire, Inc.
416 S. Pershing
Wichita, KS 67218
Phone 316 686 9785
Fax 316 686 8926
E-mail: info@celestaire.com
www.celestaire.com

Chartwork Inc.
33 Williams Street
Beverly, MA 01915
978 921 4445

HF Radio on Board/Complete Cruising Solutions
Don Melcher
1813 Clement Avenue, Building 24
Alameda Marina
Alameda, CA 94501
510 814 8888

Jamestown Distributors
28 Narragansett Avenue
P.O. Box 348
Jamestown, RI 02835
800 423 0030

KVH Industries, Inc.
50 Enterprise Center
Middletown, RI 02842
401 847 3327

MapTech, Inc.
1 Riverside Drive
Andover, MA 01810
888 839 5551

Navionics
6 Thather Lane
Wareham, MA 02571
800 848 5896

PinOak Digital Corporation
P.O. Box 360
Gladstone, NJ 07934
908 234 2020

SGC, Inc.
P.O. Box 3526
Bellevue, WA 98009
425 745 6410

SeaMail
XAXERO Marine Software Engineering Ltd.
P.O. Box 1
West Park Village, West Harbour
Auckland 1250
New Zealand
64 9 412 7580

Starpath Marine
311 Fulton Street
Seattle, WA 98109-1740
206 284 8328

Stormy Weather Software
Box 125
Picton, ON K0K 2T0
Canada
http://www.stormy.ca
613 476 5779
Fax 613 476 7598

West Marine
P.O. Box 50070
Watsonville, CA 95077-0070
800 262 8464

Worldcruiser Yachts (Westsail)
Bud Taplin
1602 Monrovia Street
Newport Beach, CA 92663
714 549 9331
800 310 WORLD

RECOMMENDED READING

Books

Aebi, Tania, with Bernadette Brennan. *Maiden Voyage.* Reprint, New York: Ballantine Books, 1996.

Benedict, Ruth. *Patterns of Culture.* Reissue, Boston: Houghton Mifflin, 1998.

Bowditch, Nathaniel. *The American Practical Navigator: An Epitome of Navigation.* 1995 edition. Saint Claire Shores, MI: Scholarly Press.

Beard, James. *Beard on Bread.* Reissue, New York: Ballantine Books, 1994.

Bernstein, Peter L. *Against the Gods: The Remarkable Story of Risk.* New York: John Wiley & Sons, 1998.

Bingham, Fred. *Boat Joinery and Cabinetmaking Simplified.* Camden, ME: International Marine, 1993.

Buckley, William F., Jr. *Airborne: A Sentimental Journey.* New York: Collier Books, 1970 (currently out of print).

Calder, Nigel. *Boatowner's Mechanical and Electrical Manual.* 2nd ed. Camden, ME: International Marine, 1996.

Carl, Ann. *The Small World of Long Distance Sailors.* New York: Dodd, Mead & Co., 1985 (currently out of print).

Cornell, Jimmy. *World Cruising Handbook.* Camden, ME: International Marine, 1996.

Cornell, Jimmy. *World Cruising Routes.* Camden, ME: International Marine, 1998.

Cunningham, Marion. *The Fannie Farmer Cookbook.* New York: Bantam Books, 1990.

Dashew, Steve, and Linda Dashew. *Bluewater Handbook: A Guide to Cruising Seamanship.* Tucson: Beowulf Publishing, 1984.

Grahame, Kenneth. *Wind in the Willows.* New York: St. Martin's Press, 1996.

Hays, David, and Daniel Hayes. *My Old Man and the Sea: A Father and Son Sail around Cape Horn.* Reprint, New York: HarperCollins, 1996.

Hill, Annie. *Voyaging on a Small Income.* Dunellen, NJ: Tiller, 1993.

Hiscock, Eric. *Cruising under Sail.* 3d edition. Camden, ME: International Marine, 1989.

Leonard, Beth A. *The Voyager's Handbook: The Essential Guide to Bluewater Cruising.* Camden, ME: International Marine, 1998.

Mahoney, Elbert S., and Charles Frederic Chapman. *Chapman Piloting Seamanship and Small Boat Handling.* 62d ed. New York: Hearst Books, 1996.

Pardey, Lin, and Larry Pardey. *Cruising in* Seraffyn. Revised ed. Dobbs Ferry, NY: Sheridan House, 1992.

Roberts, John, and Susan Roberts. *Why Didn't I Think of That?* Camden, ME: International Marine, 1997.

Rombauer, Irma, and Marion Rombauer Becker. *The Joy of Cooking.* New York: Scribner, 1997.

Rosso, Julee, and Sheila Lukins. *The Silver Palate Cookbook.* New York: Workman Publishing, 1982.

Slocum, Joshua. *Sailing Alone around the World.* Sheridan House, 1985.

Tyson, Eric. *Personal Finance for Dummies.* 2d ed. Indianapolis: IDG Books, 1996.

Periodicals

Cruising World
5 John Clarke Road, Box 3400
Newport, RI 02840-0992
401 847 1588
Fax 401 848 5048
www.cruisingworld.com

Ocean Navigator
P.O. Box 569
Portland, ME 04112-0569
207 772 2466

Seven Seas Cruising Association *Bulletin*
1525 S. Andrews Avenue, Suite 217
Fort Lauderdale, FL 33316
954 463 2431
Fax 954 463 7183
E-mail: office@ssca.org
www.ssca.org/SSCABull.html

Yachting Monthly
Freepost CY1061
P.O. Box 272
Haywards Heath
West Sussex
RH16 3FS
United Kingdom
44 (0)1444 445 599
www.yachtingmonthly.com

WoodenBoat
P.O. Box 78
Brooklin, ME 04616-0078
207 359 4651
Fax 207 359 8920
E-mail: woodenboat@woodenboat.com
www.woodenboat.com

INDEX

Ackerman, Ack, 157
ADRs (American depository receipts), 90
Aebi, Tania, *Maiden Voyage,* 247
Against the Gods (Bernstein), 91, 247
Airborne (Buckley), 29, 247
American Practical Navigator, The (Bowditch), 104, 247
anchors, sea, 193–196
appliances, kitchen
    major, 205–209
    minor, 213–214
arts and crafts skills, income potential of, 128–129
associations, cruising, 77, 100–101, 105–106, 171, 249
automobiles, cheaper models as financing source, 72–74

Bailey, Bill, 96–97
bareboat charters, 96–97
batteries, 181–185
beacons, emergency radio, 242
Beard, James, *Beard on Bread,* 247
Benedict, Ruth, *Patterns of Culture,* 40–41, 247
benefits of cruising, 39–45
Bernstein, Peter L., *Against the Gods,* 91, 247
Bingham, Fred, *Boat Joinery and Cabinetmaking Simplified,* 122, 247
blistering of boats, 153–154, 163
Bluewater Handbook (Dashew), 247
Boat Joinery and Cabinetmaking Simplified (Bingham), 122, 247
boatbuilders, 167–168, 171
Boatowner's Mechanical and Electrical Manual, The (Calder), 120, 206, 247
boats
    as liabilities not assets, 138–139
    batteries, 181–185
    blistering of, 153–154, 163
    building independently, 167–168
    construction and design features, 141–143
    electrical systems, 120–121, 173–181
    engines, 148–151, 186–190
    financing of, 139–140
    galleys, 143, 205–214
    hull designs, 142, 147–148
    insurance, 18, 137, 140–141
    liveaboard, 110–111
    maneuvering, 191–197
    new versus old, 103, 143–144
    price ranges of, 152–155, 159, 161, 163
    repairs, 120–121, 127–128, 170–173, 181
    restoration of, 146
    rigging, 171–173
    selection of, 20–21, 133–135, 144–147, 166–167
    size of, 70, 135–136, 152
    tax laws, 138
    trials of, 190–191
    types of, 21–22, 146, 157–165
boatyards, foreign, 170–171
bonds, investing in, 89, 90. *See also* finances, cruising lifestyle
books about cruising, 247–248
Bowditch, Nathaniel, *The American Practical Navigator,* 104, 247
bread recipes, 219–221
Brennan, Bernadette, *Maiden Voyage,* 247
bribery in foreign ports, 124–125
brokerage firms, all-service discount, 84–85
brownwater cruising, 108
Buckley, William F., Jr., *Airborne,* 29, 247
budget. *See* finances, cruising lifestyle
Bunker, Dick, 185

C-MAP charts, 228
calculators used for navigation, 226–227
Calder, Nigel, *Boatowner's Mechanical and Electrical Manual,* 120, 206, 247
canned food, 199
Caribbean, 107–108
Carl, Ann, *The Small World of Long Distance Sailors,* 105, 247
carpentry skills, 122, 128
cars, cheaper models as financing source, 72–74
CDs (certificates of deposit), 88–89
Celestaire, Inc., 226–227, 245
celestial navigation, 226–227
chainplates, 173
Chapman, Charles Frederic, *Chapman Piloting Seamanship and Small Boat Handling,* 248
charters, bareboat, 96–97
charts
    electronic, 227–228
    required for cruising, 106
Chartwork Inc., 245
children, cruising's effects on, 43
circumnavigation, 107
Coast Guard, U.S. Auxiliary, sailing courses, 99–100
coastal cruising, 109
cockroaches, 200–202
communications technology
    Internet, 232
    telephone services, 232–235
computers
    navigational use of, 227–228
    personal, 237–238
consumerism, cruiser's avoidance of, 69–70
cooking. *See also* diet; food
    learning about, 75
    recipes, 215–221
    with pressure cookers, 212–213
cookware, 211–214
cooling system, 188–189
Cornell, Jimmy
    World Cruising Handbook, 247
    World Cruising Routes, 105
costs. *See* expenses; finances, cruising lifestyle

courses, sailing, 99–100
credit cards, 77–81
crewing, opportunities for learning, 97–99
crews, mixed-sex, 38
crop harvesting for income, 130
cruisers, individuals as
    common traits, 32–34
    types of, 27–31
Cruising in Seraffyn (Pardey), 248
cruising lifestyle
    compared to land living, 32–33
    compared to liveaboards, 110–111
    deciding to go, 56–58
    increasing costs of, 20–21
    minimalism, 69, 70–77
    myths about, 19–21, 45–47, 199–200
    reasons for, 39–45
    sacrifices of, 17–18
Cruising under Sail (Hiscock), 248
Cruising World, 248
CSY 161, 162
Cunningham, Marion, *The Fannie Farmer Cookbook,* 247
currency, exchanging, 63–64

dangers of cruising, 41, 47
Dashew, Steve and Linda, *Bluewater Handbook,* 247
debit cards, 79–80
debt-reduction, 77–81
decision-making process to go cruising, 56–58
deck, cleanliness of, 123
delivery skippers, crewing for, 98–99
design, boat, 141–143
destinations, planning, 105
diesel engines, 150–151, 187, 188
diet, cruiser's, 33–34, 74–75. *See also* cooking; food
dinghy sailing, 97
diplomacy required for foreign ports, 123–125
dishwashing, 19
docking maneuvers, 191
driving maneuvers, 191–197
drogues, 193–195

economics of cruising, 19–22, 45. *See also* finances, cruising lifestyle
education
    cruising's potential for, 42
    use of personal computers, 237–238
electrical system
    rewiring, 174, 177–180
    skills required for repairing, 120–121, 181
    voltage tests, 174–175, 180–181
    wiring kit, 176
electronic charts, 227–228
e-mail, 232–234
Emergency Position Indicating Radio Beacon (EPIRB), 242
engineering skills, income potential of, 129–130
engines, boat, 148–151, 186–190
epiphany, 56–57
EPIRB (Emergency Position Indicating Radio Beacon), 242
exchanger, heat, 190
exchanging currency, 63–64
exercise, 76
exhaust systems, 149
expenses, cruising life. *See also* finances, cruising lifestyle
    clearance fees, 20
    increase in, 20–21
    sacrifices as a result of, 47–48

family cruising, 37, 42–43
Fannie Farmer Cookbook, The (Cunningham), 247
fees, clearance, 20
fiberglass repair, 127–128
filters
    oil, 188
    raw-water, 189
finances, cruising lifestyle
    cruising kitty, definition and types of, 62, 64–67
    debt-reduction plan, 77–81
    growth of through minimalism, 69, 70–77
    investment options, 84–85, 88–93
    jobs as sources of financing, 65–66, 81–83, 126–130

risk management, 85–88
savings goal, 68
size of, 64
fish, buying, 204
food. *See also* cooking; diet
    canned, 199
    eating local, 202–205
    importance of, 198
    myths, 199–200
    overview of cruising, 74–75
    recipes, 215–221
    service work, 129
foreign ports, 123–125, 170–171
freezer, 207
fuel system, 186–188

galleys
    cooking gadgets, 213–214
    layout and hardware, 205–209
    location of, 143
    pots and pans, 211–213
    storage, 209–211
gasoline engines, 150–151
GFCI (ground-fault circuit interrupter), 185–186
GPS (Global Positioning System), 116–117, 118, 223–226
Grahame, Kenneth, *Wind in the Willows,* 243–244, 247
ground-fault circuit interrupter (GFCI), 185–186
Guatemala, 21
guidebooks for cruising, 106–107

ham radios, 234, 236
handcrafting, income potential of, 128–129
Hayes, David and Daniel, *My Old Man and the Sea,* 18, 151, 248
header tank, 188
headsails, 196–197
health benefits of cruising, 33–34
heat exchanger, 190
heaving to, maneuvering technique, 193
heavy weather maneuvering techniques, 192–196
HF Radio on Board/Complete Cruising Solutions, 245

Hill, Annie, *Voyaging on a Small Income,* 20, 102, 248
Hinz, Earl, 116
Hiscock, Eric, *Cruising under Sail,* 70, 248
Hiscock, Susan, 70
homes, owning/renting of, 71–72
housekeeping, 122–123
hulls, construction of, 142, 147–148
hygiene, personal, 123

ice, purchasing, 206–207
income sources while cruising, 126–130
insurance, 18, 137, 140–141
Internet, 232–233
inverter, electrical, 185–186
investing to build cruising finances, 84–85, 88–93

jam cleats, 197
Jamestown Distributors, 245
jobs
    in foreign countries, 65–66
    role of in financing cruising, 81–83, 126–130
Joy of Cooking, The (Rombauer), 248

keels, design of, 142
kitchens. *See* galleys
kitty, cruising. *See* finances, cruising lifestyle
KVH Industries, Inc., 245

languages, foreign, 126
leaks, seacock, 19–20, 189
Lecur, Brian, 24–27
Lecur, Greta, 24–25
Lecur, Sally, 25
Leonard, Beth, *The Voyager's Handbook,* 20, 105, 106, 248
licenses, communication, 235–236
liferafts, 241–242
lights, safety strobe, 243
liveaboards, 110–111
Lukins, Sheila, *The Silver Palate Cookbook,* 248
lying ahull maneuver, 192

magazines about cruising, 248–249
Mahoney, Elbert S., *Chapman Piloting Seamanship and Small Boat Handling,* 248
Maiden Voyage (Aebi and Brennan), 247
maneuvers, boating, 191–197
MapTech, Inc., 245
marriage, cruising's effects on, 48, 57
masts, types of, 143
meat, buying, 204
mechanical skills, 119–120, 127
Melcher, Don, 236
Mexico, 62–63
microwave ovens, 209
minimalism required for cruising, 69, 70–77
money. *See also* finances, cruising lifestyle
    exchanging, 63–64
Moore, Gary, 157
Morgan OutIsland, 158–161
motorsailers, 150
muggings, 125–126
My Old Man and the Sea (Hayes), 18, 151, 248
myths about cruising, 19–21, 45–47, 199–200

navigation
    celestial, 226–227
    electronic, 116–117, 223–228
    personal computers, 238
    radar, 228–231
    sextants, 117–118
    sight, 118–119, 224–225, 229, 230
    software, 227
Navionics, 246
New Zealand, 41, 171, 203
Newporter 40, 156, 157, 159

Ocean Navigator, 248
ocean voyaging. *See* cruising lifestyle
oil system, 188
organizations, cruising, 77, 100–101, 105–106, 171, 249
ovens, microwave, 209

painting skills, 128
Pardey, Lin and Larry, *Cruising in Seraffyn,* 248
pasta recipes, 215–218
Patterns of Culture (Benedict), 40–41, 247
periodicals about cruising, 248–249
Personal Finance for Dummies (Tysen), 84, 248
personality traits of cruisers, 32–34
PinOak Digital Corporation, 246
plan, development of cruising, 105–109
plugs, seacock, 19–20
ports, foreign, 123–125, 170–171
possessions, sale and storage of, 76
pots and pans, 211–213
poultry, buying, 204
Power Squadron, U.S., 99–100
pressure cookers, 212–213
pumps, raw-water, 189–190

radar, 228–231
radio telephone service, 232
radios, ham, 234, 236
rafts, life, 242–242
range, cooking, 207–209
raw-water system, 189–190
recipes for cooking, 215–221
reducing sail, 196–197
refits, boat, 170–171
refrigerator, 205–207
religion, 43–44
repairs, boat, 120–121, 127–128, 170–173, 181
retirees as cruisers, 28–29
rigging, inspection and repair of, 171–173
Rio Dulce, 21
risk management, financial, 85–88
Roberts, John and Susan, *Why Didn't I Think of That?,* 248
Rombauer, Irma and Marion, *The Joy of Cooking,* 248
Rosso, Julee, *The Silver Palate Cookbook,* 248
running before the wind, 193
running lights, 243

safety tools, 240–244
sail, reducing, 196–197
sailing, ways to learn about
bareboat charters, 96
courses, 99–100
crewing opportunities, 97–99
sailing schools, 95
Sailing Alone around the World (Slocum), 18, 248
sailmaking skills, 127
sailors, cruising
common traits, 32–34
types of, 27–31
sails, head, 196–197
satellite mobile telephone services, 234–235
savings accounts, 88
Schwab, Charles, 84–85
sea trials, 190–191
seacocks, 19–20, 189
SeaMail, 232–233, 246
Section 21, 171, 240
seminars about cruising, 100
Seven Seas Cruising Association. *See* SSCA
sewing skills, 127
sextants, 117–118
SGC, Inc., 246
Silver Palate Cookbook, The (Rosso and Lukins), 248
singlehanders
crewing for, 98–99
dangers for, 37
sink, kitchen, 209
skills, cruising
diplomacy, 123–125
foreign language, 126
mechanical/electrical/carpentry, 119–123, 127–128, 181
navigation, 116–118
to sell ashore, 129–130
to sell to other cruisers, 126–129
skippers, delivery, 98–99
Slocum, Joshua, *Sailing Alone around the World,* 18, 248
Small World of Long Distance Sailors, The (Carl), 105, 247
soap, dishwashing, 19

software, celestial navigation, 227
solo cruising, dangers of, 37
soup recipes, 218–219
spirituality, cruising's effects on, 43–44
SSB telephone service, 232–233, 235
SSCA (Seven Seas Cruising
    Association), 77, 100–101, 105–
    106, 171, 249
Starpath Marine, 246
statistics of cruisers, 17
stew recipes, 218–219
stocks, investing in, 89, 90, 91. *See
    also* finances, cruising lifestyle
storage, 209–211
Stormy Weather Software, 227, 246
stove, 207–209
strobe lights, masthead, 243
suppliers, cruising, 245–246
surveyors, boat, 166–167, 190

tank, header, 188
Tartan 37, 163, 165
tax laws effecting boats, 138
teaching skills, income potential of,
    128
technology, types of cruising
    electronic navigation, 116–117,
        223–228
    for communications, 231–236
    radar, 228–231
telephone services, 232–235
television, 75
terminals, electrical, 177–179
test sailing of boats, pre-purchase,
    190–191
thermostat, 188
tourism
    cruising as a means of, 39–40
    guides, 106–107
traits of successful cruisers, 32–34
trials, sea, 190–191
tutoring skills, income potential of, 128

Tyson, Eric, *Personal Finance for
    Dummies*, 84, 248

Valiant 40, 163, 164
varnishing skills, 128
vegetarianism, arguments for, 205–206
Voyager's Handbook, The (Leonard),
    20, 105, 106, 248
Voyaging on a Small Income (Hill), 20,
    102, 248

watchstanding, 118–119
water system, raw, 189–190
watermaker, electromechanical,
    238–240
weather, heavy, 192–196
Welsh, Dick, 51–53
Westsail 32, 158, 159
Why Didn't I Think of That?
    (Roberts), 248
Wind in the Willows (Grahame),
    243–244, 248
wooden boats, 157. *See also* boats
WoodenBoat magazine, 249
woodworking, 122
working
    in foreign countries, 65–66
    skills to sell ashore, 129–130
    skills to sell to other cruisers,
        126–129
    to finance cruising, 81–83
World Cruising Handbook (Cornell),
    247
World Cruising Routes (Cornell), 105
Worldcruiser Yachts (Westsail), 246

Xcalac, 62–63

yacht clubs, crewing for, 97
Yachting Monthly, 249

zincs, 189

ABOUT THE AUTHOR

Jim Trefethen (formerly of Marblehead, Massachusetts) is the author of *Wooden Boat Renovation* (International Marine, 1992) and *Inflatable Boats* (International Marine, 1996). In 1993 he, his wife Susan, and their two children cut the cord and went cruising, Currently they are in New Zealand.